Ideology of Adventure
Volume 1

Theory and History of Literature
Edited by Wlad Godzich and Jochen Schulte-Sasse

For other books in the series, see page 249

Ideology of Adventure

Studies in Modern

Consciousness, 1100-1750

Volume 1

Michael Nerlich

Translation by Ruth Crowley

Foreword by Wlad Godzich

Theory and History of Literature, Volume 42

University of Minnesota Press, Minneapolis

Originally published as *Kritik der Abenteuer-Ideologie: Beitrag zur Erforschung der bürgerlichen Bewußsteinsbildung, 1110-1750,* volume 1, copyright © 1977 by Akademie-Verlag, Berlin.

Published by the University of Minnesota Press
2037 University Avenue Southeast, Minneapolis, MN 55414.
Published simultaneously in Canada
by Fitzhenry & Whiteside Limited, Markham.
Printed in the United States of America.

Library of Congress Cataloging-in-Publication Data

Nerlich, Michael.
   Ideology of adventure.

   (Theory and history of literature; v. 42-43)
   Originally published as: Kritik der Abenteuer-Ideologie.
   Includes bibliographies and index.
     1. Adventure and adventurers—Philosophy.   2. Adventure and adventurers in literature.   I. Title.   II. Series.
G522.N4713   1987   904   86-19354
ISBN 0-8166-1581-0 (set)
ISBN 0-8166-1582-9 (pbk. : set)
ISBN 0-8166-1537-3 (vol. 1)
ISBN 0-8166-1538-1 (pbk. vol. 1)

Contents

Foreword
In-Quest of Modernity
Wlad Godzich

The Ideology of Adventure is a most unusual book. At first sight it appears to be a straightforward narrative explanation of a major question in intellectual history: what accounts for the distinct mode of development of Western civilization, a mode that led it to turn its back upon traditional values and to systematically explore and exploit that which was unknown to it. This question, which is none other than the question of how modernity came to be, receives an original answer in this book: a particular ideological orientation was forged under specific historical circumstances and progressively took on the form of what *Annales* historians have been calling a *mentalité*, a mindset.

Michael Nerlich makes a very persuasive case for the existence of this mindset, which he calls the ideology of adventure. He traces its beginnings in the high Middle Ages and follows its mutations and transformations into the middle of the eighteenth century, that is into the period where most traditional accounts of modernity set the beginning of this stage of development of civilization. Most such accounts do so on the basis of the conjunction of the rise of the industrial revolution with the well-known intellectual achievements of the Enlightenment. They face then the very vexing, and still unresolved, problem of the co-occurrence in time and space of both phenomena. Michael Nerlich's approach avoids this pitfall since it does not seek to account for the occurrence of great individual works—often the staple of intellectual history—the relation of which to anything else that occurs in the same time-frame is most problematical. Instead he pursues doggedly the constitution of the ideological orientation that makes such works possible. As a result, he can turn to major works and offer readings

remarkable for their comprehensiveness and elucidation of major critical co-
nundrums. An extraordinary example of the success of his approach is provided
by the analysis of *The Merchant of Venice*,[1] which, among other things, provides the best discussion to date of the stubborn problem of anti-Semitism in the
play.

To characterize Nerlich's project in this way is to suggest that it is itself a
modern one, for indeed what is more modern than the quest for the origins of
modernity? A number of additional features appear to support such a judgment.
Nerlich embraces the narrative mode of history without any misgivings, in fact
with an enthusiasm all too rare these days; he pursues his inquiry within the
discourse and the analytical framework of Marxist scholarship, again without
any visible discomfort, indeed going so far in his apparent orthodoxy as to ritual-
ly begin his chapters with authoritative quotations from Engels; he evidences an
obvious enthusiasm for his subject matter, indicating repeatedly that it sheds new
light upon what he himself has called "the unknown history of our modernity,"[2] that is that it enlightens us with respect to modernity, thus fulfilling one
of modernity's most abiding concerns.

Modernity has indeed been characterized—not least by Heidegger—as
dominated by the idea that thought progresses from enlightenment to enlightenment in history; it does so by re-examining critically the very ground of its origin
so that this ground becomes ever more secure. As a result, the history of this
thought consists in ever more insistent claims of ground recovery, renewal,
renascence, returns, and the like, all in the name of ever greater forward motion. The key to this conception is the notion of an overcoming of the present
by means of a critical return to the past. In this way, the new is immediately made
valuable, becomes a value in itself, because it is constituted by means of a reap-
propriation of the original ground. This mechanism of modern thought is most
powerful: any critique that is mounted against it will seek to anchor itself in some
ground that it will have to claim to be more originary than the ground of the
thought it criticizes, thereby repeating the very *Denkgestus*—movement of
thought—that it critiques so that, at best, it will take that thought's place but
leave the operating mechanism of modernity intact. The recognition of the power
of such a mechanism has led some—Adorno comes readily to mind—to believe
that there is no overcoming of modernity and that we better hunker down for
the long haul.

Nerlich seems to be oblivious to Adorno's pessimism. For one thing, his conception of *mentalité* does not allow him to imagine a privileged locus into which
one could retreat from the pervasiveness of modernity in order to hibernate until
it is overcome. For another, it is not at all clear that such an overcoming will obtain in time, that is in the very dimension of history that modernity has fostered
upon us. Here, Nerlich's insistence upon the fact that it is the history of our

modernity, unknown or otherwise, that he is concerned with should have tipped us off. The historical mode of modernity would have been satisfied by the phrase "the unknown history of modernity." Such a characterization would have been consonant with the world-historical nature of the construct "modernity" which can then take its place in the development of thought alongside such other periodizing concepts as antiquity and the Middle Ages, all of which function within a distinctly modern conception of history, a conception which is the secular successor to the Christian notion of history as salvation. To insert the modifier "our" in front of history in such a context in order to designate Western European experience is to radically alter the scope and the locus of inscription of the term history, and distance oneself from modernity as well. Modernity is no longer cast as a necessary stage in the progress of thought [or in the *Entwicklung* of the Spirit, as Hegel had it], but as a contingent historical construct in relation to ourselves who are equally contingent. Both of us partake of evenmentiality and we are thus doubly historicized: we in relation to modernity, and modernity in relation to us. Modernity is not something that happens to us; we, such as we are, are constituted by it. But modernity is itself something that we set into motion and have been carrying out as a project, to use Habermas's phrase.

This double historicization and mutual dependency is of considerable theoretical import. The concept of history operative in modernity, and indeed characteristic of the latter inasmuch as historical narrative has been its chief mode of account, was formulated in order to deal with the ever greater production of the new in modernity, and thus to unmoor us from any stable and permanent foundation which could hinder the search for the new, which, as we have seen above, came to be viewed as the supreme value of modernity. At the same time, such an unmooring from stable foundations could not be radical or final, for it would result in the inability to establish any certainty. Modernity's conception of history voids this problem by introducing the concept of development, which permits the foundational ground, be it the subject, the spirit in Hegel's sense, or indeed anything, to evolve in such as way that it provides stability for certainly, and thus defines history as a set of master narratives, in Jean-François Lyotard's formulation.

Nerlich adopts one of these master narratives, the Marxist one, as his framework, but in focusing on ideology he comes upon a foundational ground that is both productive and produced; furthermore, adventure turns out to involve a form of uncertainty, and even of chance, that is not recoverable within any model of development as *Entwicklung*, hence the double historicization that he then effects. This double historicization effectively takes Nerlich outside of modernity, though not through any willful action of his own. On the contrary, he remains far too faithful to the mode of modernity to evince any desire to overcome it. If anything, the features of his mode of arguing and telling the story of modernity through the ideology of adventure are so much in the mold of modernity that they appear to be parodistic of it. Trying to make explicit what is implied in the Marxist analysis of modernity, Nerlich does not seek to be new or to provide something new, and that is how, in spite of the fact that he remains faithful to modernity in every other respect, he is not a modern. He effects a swerve around modernity, a swerve that deserves some examination.

The story of the unknown history of our modernity that he tells remains unfinished as history. In the preface that immediately follows my introductory remarks, Nerlich tells the story of how he came to write this book, why it stops when it does, and that he is presently working on an aesthetics of adventure, both as successor to, and completion of, the present, and more historical, book. It is this movement from the historical to the aesthetic, a movement already adumbrated in *The Ideology of Adventure*, that lies at the heart of Nerlich's swerve.

It is not quite correct to say that Nerlich's history of our modernity remains unfinished as history. To be sure, the story he tells in the pages that follow stops in the middle of the eighteenth century, but this interruption is neither gratuitous nor fortuitous. I would like to suggest that it marks an end, not of our modernity or of its history, but of the historical mode in relation to modernity. The story Nerlich has told until then is that of an emergent and a rising modernity; it is an epic of modernity. Like all epics, it has its heroic figures and high deeds, but like them it is followed by the establishment of an increasingly bureaucratic state that reveres its past heroes only to insure that their example is permanently confined to a safe because irretrievable past. As soon as modernity overcomes opposition residual of older civilizational formations, it changes its relationship to history: no longer *telos*, *eschaton*, or the dimension of emergence and conquest, it is now a structure of legitimation, one that projects the future as the authentic fulfillment of a foundational past. The organization of knowledge in the nineteenth century under the aegis of history is part and parcel of this process. To be sure Marxism and other oppositional movements will continue to seek the mantle of a heroic history for their undertakings, but the battle they wage is successful only when the opponent subscribes to the same conception of heroic history, that is when the opponent is itself an adept of modernity. Such was the case in Russia, in China, and in a number of so-called Third World countries. But as soon as the opponent is modern, such movements falter for they wage their struggle in a dimension that no longer has any genuine existence and therefore cannot sustain their effort.

We have thus two different conceptions of history, both of which pertain to modernity: one which I will continue calling for the sake of convenience heroic history, and which corresponds to the ascendant mode of modernity, and the second, history as the structure of legitimation, once modernity triumphs. Nerlich tells the first kind of history since he is pursuing the constitution and the workings of the ideology that, according to his persuasive account, made our modernity what it has been. But he inevitably has to tell this history in the second mode, the legitimating mode, since neither the telling nor the reading of such a history can be itself heroic, and, in any case, it must be part of modernity's self-accounting. In this respect, Nerlich's "uncovering" of the ideology of adventure as the secret propulsion of modernity qualifies as novel, but its novelty is immediately undercut by the built-in claim that this ideology is the newly established and critically vetted foundational ground of modernity itself. What is new then is the self-consciousness that we as moderns can have of this hitherto unknown ground. So far the movement of Nerlich's work seems to conform to the requirements of what one could call the signifying economy of modernity: both conceptions of history are in play; the position of the new is not only preserved but properly extended from the realm of things to that of consciousness; a new and presumably more stable ground is uncovered and critically vouched for; modernity, once again, will have overcome itself and thus consolidated its hegemony. Nerlich would thus once again appear to be an irretrievable modern, overcoming it by its own rule and thus ultimately not at all able to overcome it and lead us to some putative postmodernity.

Nerlich knows better, however, than to seek to overcome modernity on its own ground. Since his enterprise is inscribed in the dual historical discourse of modernity, any overcoming in the form of a subsequent development he would propose would necessarily turn into one more figure in the phenomenology of modernity—a fate that seems to have befallen quite a few of the recent claims of postmodern status. Instead he focuses on one aspect of the dual historical discourse of modernity: the actual temporal status of history as a structure of legitimation. In the heroic notion of history, temporality is relatively unproblematic since it can be accounted for through the articulation of actions, causes, effects, and catastrophes, however complex this articulation may be in its own right. In history as a structure of legitimation, temporality is far more problematic. The conception of foundational ground that is central to this view of history requires that such a ground be conceived as an originary one, but this requirement does not proceed from the notion of foundational ground itself which is, properly speaking, an ontological notion, but from the fact that this ontological notion is itself inscribed within a historical discourse that is only beginning to disengage itself from the heroic mode of history. In other words, in history as a structure of legitimation the ontological and the temporal are so intertwined as to be subject to confusion. This confusion is precisely what makes possible the claim that a foundational ground that is originary is recovered at some ulterior point in time.³ This is not the place to discuss the whys and wherefores of this confusion. Suffice it to note that Nerlich brings it to bear upon the problem at hand.

The ordinary way in which the ontological and the temporal dimensions of this second conception of history are dealt with in the critical discourse of modernity is to establish the nature and identity of the foundational ground through a critical examination and then to proceed to either claim or establish that this ground is originary in time as well. Nerlich does not follow this procedure; he appears to be oblivious to this order of precedence based upon the unacknowledged yet central dialectic of the ontological and the temporal, or Being and Time as Heidegger had it for short. Such a disregard is far from idiosyncratic to Nerlich; it is part and parcel of the constitutive field of modernity. Because he focuses his analysis of modernity on its constitutive ideology, Nerlich is able to escape the confusion between the ontological and the temporal that is to be found at the core of modernity's ideology, and it is in accordance with the signifying economy of modernity that he is in the process of uncovering, as opposed to its ideology, that he acts as if the originary, or rather the merely earlier in time, had foundational power.

At first this may seem to be an inconsequential move. After all it appears to make precedence in time the rule by which one shall establish right of dominion, and we certainly have enough examples of the prevalence of such a rule, especially in the legal domain, to find it nearly self-evident. But a closer examination reveals its profoundly unsettling nature. To begin with, there is nothing modern about such a rule: it is characteristic of custom-based societies and these take tradition as their supreme value and not the new. If this is a rule of modernity, it is one that robs it of its distinctiveness. This is indeed what happens in Nerlich's analysis.

Nerlich's analysis of the ideology of adventure leads him to place the beginnings of modernity in what is, for most scholars, the high Middle Ages. In fact, in one of his most recent publications, he goes so far as to identify a generally neglected, and certainly misunderstood, text of the Old French writer Chrétien de Troyes, the *Guillaume d'Angleterre* [dated in the last third of the twelfth century], as the locus in which the distinctly modern conception of adventure is first articulated.⁴ The effect of such a placement, the merit of which it would be invidious to discuss in this foreword,⁵ is startling: what is generally known as modernity is not new with respect to what Nerlich identifies as modernity. In and of itself, this should not be surprising given the alteration of the time frames. Yet it is startling all the same because, first of all, the very highest value of modernity, that is the new, is not respected by modernity itself, and, second, because the consequences of such a move produce effects, within what we have traditionally known as modernity, that we have been associating with postmodernity. Again, such an early occurrence of these effects may be explained away by the intimation that they are the result of Nerlich's general move to advance the dates for modernity, but this would beg the issue. If such effects can move at will, they occur independently of their relation to specific temporal markers, and appear instead to be triggered by the playing out of a given sequence; they are then structural rather than historical. Furthermore, what is true of the effects must also obtain for the causes. The category of the historical, as understood within modernity and central to it, begins to dissolve.

This dissolution is not to be confused with the very modern notion of an end of history—whatever form one may give to this end. Nor should it lead us to invoke another very modern distinction: that between history as some sort of objective process in which we are all caught and history as our mode of relating to such a process. This distinction allows modern thinkers to sacrifice the history of consciousness—by definition always partial and unequal to its object—to real or effective history which grows more unknowable, if not mystical, with each such sacrifice. Rather it is meant to bring us to recognize that the very reality that we have fashioned as part of the project of our modernity is characterized by a remarkable degree of immobility, and this in spite, or perhaps because, of the accelerating rate of change and introduction of ever new things and ideas. Lyotard is very much on the mark when he asserts that it is the state that is fond of order—and therefore of history which chronicles the fluctuations of order— and not capitalism, which stands as one of the names by which modernity goes.[6] But capitalism or modernity cannot be studied only through the effects it produces nor through a notion like that of the aesthetics of the sublime, which are but ways of suggesting that modernity or capitalism can only be figured but ultimately is unknowable. It is unknowable only from the perspective of history which, after all, is its very own instrument of legitimation, and as such, cannot be expected to be anything but opaque in relation to modernity. But it has an economy which is both a political and a signifying one, and this economy is cognitively accessible.

When, writing in the historical mode, Nerlich reaches the point where progress becomes routine, he recognizes that this very historical mode becomes obsolete as an analytical tool and can only serve ends of legitimation. Routine is always meant to produce uniformity and to prevent upheavals; it is the very opposite of the new. When the new is routinized, as is the case around us presently, novelty is but an instrument to insure a greater uniformization in the rates of progress, so that ultimately a form of immobilism takes hold under conditions of controlled and uniform forward motion. Progress obtains but it is no longer the progress of the Enlightenment or of the heroic conception of history. It is a form of progress that is a vestige of the very idea of progress. It certainly forecloses the notion of adventure, except as a consumer good [adventure cruises up the Amazon are currently being offered by a travel company].

What is the nature of the immobility we have been speaking about? Can one properly speak of an immobility in an environment given over to change? From a sociological point of view, one could answer by pointing out that the changes in material conditions that are fostered upon us through advertising and other less subtle means do not entail any changes in relations of power or domination, far from it. It may be more useful, however, to address this issue, albeit very briefly, from a philosophical perspective. The apparent paradox of an ever-changing environment and a resultant immobility has been analyzed by Heidegger as the very essence of *tekhne* which, for him, has been the dominant orientation of Western civilization since the post-Socratics. It is the essense of *tekhne* to gain mastery not only over the natural environment by first objecti-fying it to ourselves as knowing subjects, but to put into place an all-encompassing mechanism of mastery that would objectify all of reality, including human beings in order to submit it to its operations. The all-encompassing am-bition of this mechanism Heidegger saw at the root of what for him were the three great totalitarian ventures of the twentieth century: fascism, communism, and Americanism, and there was little doubt that he considered the latter most likely to succeed where the first two had failed, not least because it had gone far further than they had in abandoning any notion of heroic history.

Heidegger sought to characterize the nature of the mastering mechanism. The task proved very arduous since one could never be quite sure that one's very own inquiry was not part and parcel of the mechanism's reach over hitherto free-standing areas. Since this mechanism, which he called the *Ge-stell*, achieved its initial hold over that which it sought to control by turning it into an object of knowledge, by objectifying it, it became progressively clear to Heidegger that any resistance to it would have to work itself through nonobjectifying modes of knowledge, the aesthetic being foremost among these.

The particular intertwining of the logical and the historical discursive modes that we saw earlier inevitably falls into the form of an argumentative narrative in which the developmental logic internal to some entity is forced to vie with com-peting logics, acts of will, or catastrophes. The focus, at all times, is on an ob-ject, either as it is or as it is becoming. The aesthetic mode, by contrast, is an economic one: cognitively, it is far more concerned (if one can speak of concern in this context), with the interaction between all of the constitutive elements of a given happenstance in time and place—what is generally referred to as aesthetic experience. In short, it is far more process oriented than output directed, to speak the language of economics that is adequate to it. The outputs may vary, and in-deed be "new," but the productive mechanism remains remarkably stable even when it "improves" itself. This is as true of the political economy as it is of the signifying one, which is what the aesthetic is concerned with.

In this book Nerlich has studiously avoided aesthetic discussions, for the story he had to tell was still amenable to telling in the mode of history. But as he brings his story to the point where modernity becomes triumphant, it becomes clearer to him that the historical mode will become less and less cognitively rewarding, and that, to maintain the sharpness and the rigor of the analyses he has carried out so far, he needs to take up a different cognitive mode, that of the aesthetic. In this respect he breaks with the discursive mold of modernity that he had faithfully espoused, but he breaks it only because he has pushed it to its limit.

It should be noted, however, that this is a break the fault line of which was already traced in modernity. Nerlich studies the ideology of adventure; his conception of ideology leads to view rather unproblematically the means by which such an ideology was vehicled. These means were stories, plays, novels, and other cultural artefacts. Nothing could be further from an actual adventure, with its dangers, risks, and high feats, than reading about an adventure in the coziness of one's home. To be sure, one can take a psychosocial tack and speak of vicarious enjoyment and ego-building functions; nonetheless, reading, even of adventure stories, is far closer to the older *otium studiosum* than to the new *negotium*. The older *otium studiosum* had as its aim the understanding of what made the world run, the agency that was at work within it, be it God, nature, or human will. *Negotium* has as its aim to be that agency, and for quite a while it was thought that human will, if bold and resolute enough, could indeed be such an agency. But as the human itself came within its purview it became less and less clear that will was enough and a growing suspicion that something like Heidegger's *Ge-stell* was at work began to take hold. The *otium studiosum* of reading has once again regained its right to be. The ideology of adventure may have incited us to become willful agents; the literature of adventure invites us to meditate upon agency, and Michael Nerlich, to reflect upon their articulation.

Notes

1. The success of this analysis must have proven irresistible to Klaus Reichert since he adopts it as his own in his recent book *Fortuna oder die Beständigkeit des Wechsels* (Frankfurt a.M.: Suhrkamp, 1985). There has been an unfortunate tendency on the part of some West German scholars not to acknowledge their debt to publications appearing in East Germany—perhaps in retaliation against similar practices there. Michael Nerlich teaches at the Technical University of West Berlin but the German original of his book on *The Ideology of Adventure* was published in East Berlin.

2. Michael Nerlich, *The Unknown History of our Modernity*, CHS Occasional Papers No. 3 (Minneapolis: University of Minnesota Center for Humanistic Studies, 1986).

3. This confusion leads to a number of aporias that are then elevated to central philosophical problems in modernity, such as the opposition of chance and necessity, where necessity represents the notion of a foundational essence disclosing itself in time, while chance marks the selection for the moments of such disclosure. This opposition then leads to such further philosophemes as the inexorable laws of history, the Hidden Hand, or the idea that human will guided by reason, deter-

mine the course of history. These philosophemes are then sustained by the appropriate master narratives.

4. Michael Nerlich, "Der Kaufmann von Galvaïde, oder die Sünden des Chrestien-Forschung. Ein Essay über die Ursprünge der Moderne-Mentalität in der literarischen Gestaltung," *Lendemains* 45 (1987) 12-39. Once again this is an extraordinarily persuasive essay that proceeds by showing *critically* the shortcomings of traditional scholarship on the subject, and then makes a case for its own reading of the text. Incidentally, *Lendemains*, which Nerlich directs, would profit all those who are concerned with some form of French studies. Its theoretical sophistication, range of historical coverage, and sense of what should command attention single it out among scholarly publications.

5. To dispel any possible misunderstanding, I share Nerlich's view on this matter.

6. Jean-François Lyotard, "Rules and Paradoxes and Svelte Appendix," *Cultural Critique* 5 (Winter 1986-7), p. 215.

Preface
Adventure in a Chance-Determined World

> *The spuriously marvelous was once based on something true,*
> *genuine, just as the monstrous certainly had sufficient cause in real*
> *nature.... At that time, it was called adventure (*aventhura*). Orig-*
> *inally, only the success of a bold enterprise—especially knightly*
> *undertakings, tournaments, and battles...gallant battles...*
> *—was the main idea of the word that runs through so many*
> *writings, poems, romances, and stories of the Middle Ages.... We*
> *would like to see a philosophical history of adventure. What*
> *tendencies and fantasies contributed to adventure at certain times?*
> *How was adventure set in motion? How did adventure erupt as it*
> *did?—How, according to the rules of the imagination and the*
> *circumstances of history, were ideas such as love, religion, virtue,*
> *and chastity able to interweave themselves so as to make adventure,*
> *and how did the proportion of this or that idea change through the*
> *intermixing of peoples and the transformations of time? How did*
> *France, for instance, lose its taste for adventure? Where and why*
> *can remnants still be found in Europe?*

Johann Gottfried Herder

Habent suas adventuras libelli. This book was written more than ten years ago. Although I do not know precisely when I started to work on the idea of adventure, in 1968 I published my first study dealing with adventurous topics: the Spanish picaresque novel. It is a study partially based on the principles of Russian formalism and still profoundly committed to the history of ideas.[1] Nevertheless, in criticizing other scholars' opinions about the meaning and function of picaresque novels, I felt (and expressed) the need to study in depth the concrete social reality of the *Siglo de Oro* in particular, of the time of any art production in general. In order to show the falseness of unhistorical, abstract concepts of genre, I undertook a second study and analyzed twentieth-century novels that had been classified as "modern picaresque novels."[2] And I found so many tremendous aesthetic and political differences among these works that the common denominator "picaresque" not only turned out to be absolutely wrong, but appeared to be a comfortable way of speaking about ignored texts (especially with regard to the *novelas picarescas*).

This work *Kunst, Politik, und Schelmerei* (Art, Politics, and the Picaresque)— whose main concern was a justification of art production as social activity, concluding with an outlook on Walter Benjamin—led me deep into the study of historical dialectical materialism. But the study of historical and dialectical materialism never became an aim in itself for me, and because I was passionately interested in modern art (I studied art and painted and etched in the "tradition" of modern art from the German expressionists to Wols and Giacometti), the Lukácsian concept of Marxist culture and art theory could not appeal to me. In spite of all alleged epistemological qualities of so-called realistic art, I never understood why art or literature had to reflect and by this to reproduce existing reality, and I could not understand what "decadent" meant in the production of art and why artists persecuted by and art burnt and destroyed by (German) fascists should be counterrevolutionary.

In response to my disbelief, I looked for a method that would allow me to prove sociologically and historically the necessity of vanguard art, and as I continued to be fascinated by adventurous thought, I started to analyze the way people think about adventure and put it into practice in economics, politics, philosophy, literature, and art. In 1972, a French journal asked me to write an article on adventurous thought in the twentieth century, and I produced a study of almost two hundred pages, dealing with authors such as Simmel, MacOrlan, and Jankélévitch.

Of course, the journal couldn't publish such a long study, and I was a little perplexed by what had come out of my pen. I submitted the text to many friends in France, Italy, and East and West Germany, seeking their opinions of it. I don't remember whether it was Werner Krauss who recommended publication of the manuscript to Manfred Naumann,[3] or Naumann himself who had the idea of publishing it: in any event, Manfred Naumann suggested publishing the study in the series *Literatur and Gesellschaft* (Literature and Society) of the Akademie-Verlag in Berlin. I might not have accepted the offer if I had known all the negative consequences of publishing in the German Democratic Republic. But at that time, I was excited by the idea of publishing a Brechtian approach to literary history in this socialist country where the official cultural politics are still

Lukácsian despite all condemnation of the Hungarian philosopher, and I accepted the offer.

My book? Well, writing about adventure is to venture in writing. Manfred Naumann and Martin Fontius asked me to write a ten-page introduction to the book, and I jumped at this occasion to revalorize historical thought and to show that essential feature of adventure-thought, adventure-practice, and adventure-mentality in the twentieth century find their origins in the so-called Middle Ages. To understand the importance of this approach, it may be useful to know that East German research in literary criticism is strongly oriented toward certain Western currents that East German scholars believe to be the most advanced and that they try to fashion into Marxist shapes. This is especially the case with the theory of reception represented above all by Hans Robert Jauss who—though a brilliant medievalist—has elaborated the theory of "alterity" of the Middle Ages. Without discussing how those ideas about "alterity" influenced the attitude of East German scholars toward former times, especially the Middle Ages, we must realize that their infatuation with West German currents of literary criticism concurs with the manifest tendency of the official Marxist ideology of German Democratic Republic to present modern captialism as having been generated at the earliest in the eighteenth century. Frequently in East German publications, definitions that Marx and Engels had drawn from capitalist development in the thirteenth or fourteenth century are used to characterize capitalism in the eighteenth and even nineteenth centuries (perhaps by cutting off the real history of the phenomenon, East German Marxists give capitalism a rather ephemeral character and provide revolutionary optimism for overcoming it soon).

Disappointed by the East German researcher's sacrifice of the study of the Middle Ages, disbelieving the validity of Jauss's "alterity" philosophy, and convinced by the dialectical continuity, I started to write the introduction. I intended to show this dialectical continuity of adventurous thought, thought that I believed to be the most important in modern society. But I underestimated the task. When I finished two years later, I had written *Ideolody of Adventure: Studies in Modern Consciousness, 1100-1750.*

Unexpectedly, this "introduction" entirely changed my ideas about my study's point of departure: adventurous thought in the twentieth century. Consequently the initial study has never been published and never will be published, for it appeared finally to be a preparatory study for the present book. *Ideology of Adventure* excited an extremely animated, controversial reception, oscillating from accusations of my being a "paid useful idiot"[4] (German expression for a naïve intellectual abused by communists) to comparisons of my study to the works of Groethuysen, Borkenau, Elias, and Max Weber.[5] A most interesting critique was published by Hermann Ley in *Deutsche Zeitschrift für Philosophie*

(1981, no. 6: 715-20), the official philosophical journal of the German Democratic Republic. Ley claimed that I was a radical bourgeois leftist, an identity revealed by the emphasis I put on *movement* (anarchy) as opposed to (bourgeois) order.

Of course, I could have replied that a book on adventure logically has to deal more with movement than with immobility, more with anarchy than with order. But Hermann Ley may have seen more than I personally did when the book was first published. Because, looking back on the text after more than ten years (a time that has been dedicated to a great extent to further reflection on adventure), not only do I measure the distance between my ideas exposed in the book and the ideas I am formulating now in what will perhaps be my last word on adventure (*A Philosophical History of the Adventure: Prolegomena to Another Aesthetics*), but I see, too, what frightened Hermann Ley: apparently this book still follows an almost classical (or orthodox) path in presenting development from good (revolutionary, antifeudal) adventure-thought in the past (since the taking over of knightly thought by the *borjois* in the Middle Ages) to bad (counterrevolutionary, antiemancipative) adventure-thought in modern times.

But suddenly a doubt arises. Manifest already in this text. Is the mad (counterrevolutionary, antiemancipative) adventure-thought necessarily the result of the good one? and—more important still—does the formation of the bad adventure-thought mean the end of the good?

Despite all its criticism of bourgeois adventure-ideology, *Ideology of Adventure* denies *de facto* the end of good adventure-thought, and that is what kept me from rewriting my initial study. I can't give a precise summary of my work-in-progress, the *Philosophical History of the Adventure*,[6] but some essential points may be present. In *Ideology of Adventure* I disregarded an essential concept: in the passage from the twelfth to the thirteenth century, knight and *borjois* brought forth what I called the ideology of adventure,[7] that is, the systematic glorification of the (knightly, then bourgeois) adventurer as the most developed and most important human being, and by this they defined the inalienable fundamental condition of human existence.

The fact that *li borjois*, the plebeian traders, assimilated chivalric ideology to denote their own precapitalist or capitalist practice, constitutes without any doubt one of the most decisive moments of human history. They combined one of the strongest bio-psychological desires of human beings, transformed it into the ideology of a social group, and brought forth the most dynamic adventuresome activity (capitalistic commerce and. . .capitalistic production in general).

However, we cannot reduce adventure-desires, adventure-mentality, and adventure-ideology to products of capitalist society just on this basis. Adventure-deisre, adventure-mentality, adventure-thoughts, and adventure-practice are, and have been from the very beginning, values, qualities, desires, and activities that transgress the boundaries between social groups and classes.

Integration of chivalric adventure-ideology into bourgeois consciousness and its use in denoting capitalist activity meant an extension of adventure-desire, adventure-thought, and adventure-mentality ultimately to all domains of social practice. This gives us a starting point for rewriting the history of humankind, that is, for rewriting the history of our modernity. Adventure-ideology and adventure-mentality as well as adventure-practice meant and still mean:

1) Acceptance of economic, social, cultural, and mental changes and revolutions. Disorder is conceived of as a mode of producing a new order; order itself is conceived of as change.

2) Acceptance of the unknown as a positive value; the deliberate leaving of the known for the unknown; desire for the new.

3) Acceptance of blindness with regard to the unknown; acceptance of economic, social, and cultural risks.

4) Acceptance of chance. Chance, constitutive of any adventure, becomes an essential value of adventure-ideology and -mentality. Translated into the philosophical terminology of so-called scholastic philosophy, this means that *accidens* becomes *essentia*. Here we are confronted with the birth of the individual and the beginning of questioning the divine sense of life.

5) Recognition of the other (other races, other languages, other manners, other societies, other necessities, other desires, etc.). Integration of the other into one's own, whether by peaceful means or not; transformation of the other into a business partner, destruction of the other.

6) Elaboration of "search systems," calculation of chances, minimizing of risks, elaboration of insurances, and so on.[8]

As Marx says succinctly, Prehistory ends here—and to make reversible what has been started in this mental revolution constitutes nothing less than the destruction of the modern individual, a destruction born out of social practice. And this is precisely what (with the morally best intentions of the world) has been tried and still continues to be tried in the socialist countries where the adventurous individual is—morally, politically—invited (and obliged) to yield in favor of collectives. But the invitation, the obligation is unaccepted and unacceptable because it is against social and natural reality: the individual collapses, is destroyed, develops strategies of resistance, or rebels. That this destruction of individual adventure-mentality is against (social) nature, nothing can prove better than mathematics and natural sciences because they only can exist and develop by taking into account *chance*. Not to take into account chance is the end of mathematics and of natural sciences.

But if the most precise, the most calculable regions of human understanding are chance-determined, what about life in general? Without any doubt, life, the social practice of individuals, is indefinitely more determined by chance than are mathematics and natural sciences. Does this mean that I am pleading for anarchy and chaos? Not at all. I plead for the recognition of chaos, anarchy, movement, disorder as an inalienable quality of reality. Not to accept this is irrational. To be sure, human beings need order and system, not only to live better, but even to survive. But human beings can't produce better orders and systems if they are not conscious of the fact that chances determine their lives, if they are not allowed to face this reality, to calculate the chances, to work with them, to bring them into new orders and systems that are always mobile, transitory orders and systems. Innovative capacity of collectives results from the dialectical play of the adventurous qualities of individuals. If individuals can't develop their adventurous qualities, the collective will be sterile.

Social practice in the socialist states, based on planning, is permanently challenged by chance-determined reality, especially by the necessity of dealing with technological progress, by mathematics and natural sciences. In 1980 responding to this challenge, East German philosopher Herbert Hörz tried to resolve the impossible. In a book called *Zufall—Eine philosophische Untersuchung*, (Chance: A Philosophical Investigation), Hörz admits the existence of objective chance and the need for mathematics and natural sciences to take chance into account. He even adits that chance exists and is important outside of mathematics and natural sciences. But in order to diminish the importance of this explosive statement, Hörz introduces a hierarchy of the (social) importance of chance divided in four categories. The fourth is defined as follows: "Until now we spoke about essential chances. But there are nonessential chances, too, that we can ignore."[9]

The rest of the book deals with important chances, that is, with chances in mathematics and natural sciences, and we may deduce from this that the chances we may ignore are the chances in the daily social practice of human beings. Such a conclusion fits perfectly with Hörz's idea of the need to reduce chances in the socialist society: "The conscious organization of social development, made possible on the basis of material social conditions in socialist society, whose aim is an always improving satisfaction of the material and cultural needs of the whole people, leads to social liberty through organization of the overall will according to an overall plan. But even then there is no automatic accomplishment of the intended aims. Even if the spontaneity of the social manifestation of the relation between law and chance is reduced, it is not eliminated. Chance continues to exist, and it is to be taken into account. Chances as manifestations of necessity can be better controlled and organized, but not eliminated."[10]

To be sure, chance will always subsist. Hörz admits it. But the ideal of social practice is—in his eyes—the reduction of chance to the impossibility of its becoming active. In other words: complete freedom would result from the total elimination (or at least paralyzing) of chance. Frightening as this ideal may be, for Hörz freedom doesn't consist in the setting free of human activity in an ever increasing volume of law-chance dialectics, but in the reduction and ultimately the destruction of this volume. Freedom would hold the world at a standstill.

It is not surprising that under these circumstances Hörz doesn't take into account the great chance-philosophers Nietzsche and Peirce or, more recently, Ilya Prigogine, nor can it surprise us that even the concept of entropy doesn't plan any significant role in *Zufall* (whose merits after all shall not be denied). Nevertheless, the exclusion of the irreversible, thermodynamic multiplication and diversification of systems as defined by Isabelle Stengers and Ilya Prigogine[11] is not at all insignificant because it simply means the exclusion of the real world (and this is surprising in a book that pretends to be a Marxist study). But, Hörz's description of what effectively happens in socialist practice (the reduction of chance to the strictest minimum) corresponds perfectly to the reduction of historical and dialectical materialism to an isolated, a priori system in which otherness and movement are suppressed. In other words: historical and dialectical materialism, derived from (adventurous) non- (systematically) historical and dialectical thought, cuts off its productive basis, its *conditio sine qua non* of existence, by establishing itself as the only (exclusive) system of thought (epistemology, and so on). This, naturally, is absurd because to be productive, to be able to overcome systemic sclerosis, to integrate newness, to be innovative, historical and dialectical materialism needs the otherness, needs all other forms of thought. Historical and dialectical materialism commits suicide by establishing itself as the absolute truth.

From the historical critique of adventure-thought, adventure-mentality, and adventure-practice in *Ideology of Adventure*, we may deduce three things. *First*, insight into the adventurous condition of human beings means rational insight into reality, and consequently adventure-mentality, -thought, and -practice mean rational mentality, thought, and practice. *Second*, the glorification of adventure as noninterested, antisocial activity in the capitalistic world doesn't have anything to do with real adventure. Whatever adventure's purpose may be, its essence is irrationalism (suicide, destruction, non-sense, and at best play, gambling). *Third*, excluding adventure-mentality, -thought, and -practice from socialist social practice, prohibiting to the individual's adventure-mentality, -thought, and -practice, is as irrational as eliminating (reducing) chance in social planning instead of exploiting chance in this very planning.

I do not want to immobilize this discussion in conclusions, but it seems as if a critique of capitalistic social and economic politics as well as of socialist social, economic, and cultural politics has to emerge from insight into rational adventure-behavior in the chance-determined reality of the universe, society, and practice. And critiques that could not be accomplished on the basis of a priori (ethical, political, economic, cultural) systems will finally be produced by the material necessity of insight into the laws of rational adventure-behavior in the chance-determined, moving, changing reality. That this rationalism will be of another quality than the rationalism of classical science seems evident: "We know that societies are immensely complex systems involving a potentially enormous number of bifurcations exemplified by the variety of cultures that have evolved in the relatively short span of human history," write Isabelle Stengers and Ilya Prigogine, and they continue, "We know that such systems are highly sensitive to fluctuations. This leads both to hope and a threat: hope, since even small fluctuations may grow and change the overall structure. As a result, individual activity is not doomed to insignificance. On the other hand, this is also a threat, since in our universe the security of stable, permanent rules seem gone forever. We are living in a dangerous and uncertain world that inspires no blind confidence."[12] Yes, but without adventuring in this uncertain world we could not have even cultivated our garden.

[English by Michael Nerlich]

Ideology of Adventure
Volume 1

Chapter 1
The Adventure of the *Chevalier*

From Fate to Adventure

The word adventure derives from (old) French *aventure*, and this in turn is derived from the reconstructed colloquial Latin *adventura*. The asterisk in front of the word means that it is not attested or that its etymology is not known. Since we know of no written occurrence of *adventura*, we cannot say for certain what meaning the word had, though the meaning could be reconstructed from *advenire*, that which happens to a person, and assumed as the probable meaning for *ad-ventura*. Let us also assume for the moment that adventure, according to general understanding, is a special event that takes one by surprise ("événement, fait inopiné, fortuit, surprenant. . . . Entreprise hasardeuse ou événement extraordinaire," says the *Petit Larousse*, France's most popular dictionary) ["event, unexpected, accidental, surprising act. . . . Bold undertaking or extraordinary event"]; we can then state that adventures in this sense have always happened everywhere. But this is not our concern. Our concern is the glorification of adventure, of the quest for adventure, of the adventurer (that is, of the person who goes out to seek adventure), and this glorification has by no means always existed everywhere.

Classical antiquity certainly knew and gave literary form to the person who, like Odysseus, experienced and endured adventures in the reconstructed sense of *ad-ventura* or in the "modern" sense of an extraordinary event, but in antiquity the (voluntary) quest for adventure was not elevated to the meaning of life, nor was the (voluntary) adventurer or seeker after adventure considered an exemplar, a model human being. The adventures of Odysseus, who wants

3

to reach home, are blows of fate dealt him at the decision of the gods (in the eighteenth century, by the way, Montesquieu thought they were reported in order to frighten off competitors of the Greeks in sea travel or trade).[1] The same holds for Jason and his companions the Argonauts even though later times have wanted to see in them the symbol of the modern adventurer's existence. And when Hercules sets out to kill the Hydra, he does so not because he sees the meaning of his existence in daring, in risk, and in adventure, but because the gods have decreed that he is to serve the king of Mycenae.

As Mikhail Bakhtin has convincingly shown,[2] this enduring of adventures, this passive or at most reactive attitude toward adventure in the sense mentioned earlier, holds even for the late Hellenistic and Latin novels of adventure (and hence for all of classical antiquity). For this period Bakhtin distinguishes two types of adventure novels:[3] the "adventure novel of ordeal," in which the gods decree that individuals (usually a pair of lovers) encounter unanticipated and surprising events that drive them into foreign lands and that are visited on them as trials that must be withstood (primarily so the lovers, who are usually separated by the events, can be happily reunited). The individuals themselves are not changed by the events that happen to them, by their adventures—nor are social conditions. The characters of the individuals are invariable and prove their constancy in enduring the ordeal visited on them.[4]

The second type of adventure novel (Bakhtin has in mind particularly *The Golden Ass* by Apuleius and the *Satiricon* by Petronius) differs from the first in that the events that happen to the protagonists do not lead them abroad but instead force them to a close observation of daily life (from a socially subordinate perspective; in the case of *The Golden Ass* from the perspective of an animal).[5] The people who have these adventures are purified by them; they are not the same afterward; they have changed.[6] What concerns us in connection with our topic is Bakhtin's correct observation that all figures of the Greek and Latin novels of adventure are "involuntary" adventurers: "It goes without saying that in this type of time, an individual can be nothing other than completely *passive*, completely *unchanging*. As we have said earlier, to such an individual things can merely *happen*. He himself is deprived of any initiative. He is merely the physical subject of the action."[7]

What Bakhtin overlooks, strangely enough, is the fact that the passive, suffering, unchanging human being to whom things happen is the absolute opposite of the modern view of adventure or of the adventurer. While we must concur wholeheartedly with Bakhtin's analysis of the adventure novels of classical antiquity and their protagonists, his attempts to apply his findings to modern (that is, postclassical, vernacular) literature of adventure belong to the realm of pure intellectual history and are just as problematic as that genre.

The adventure novels of classical antiquity, with their protagonists who are not adventurers in the modern sense, owe their existence to certain social conditions that did not exist either in the Middle Ages or in the Renaissance. But at this later time a new conception of the adventurer arose, one fundamentally different from that of classical antiquity. The essential hallmark that distinguishes it from the classical conception is that adventures are undertaken on a *voluntary* basis, they are *sought out* (*la quête de l'aventure*, "the quest for adventure"), and this quest and hence the adventurer himself are glorified. Of course, the classical adventure novel played an important role in the formation of the "modern" conception of adventure (not in its basic attitudes toward the theme of adventure, but rather in the eventful nature of the stories, the material that, in adaptation, as for instance of Heliodorus's *Aithiopika*, served medieval and modern authors as a vehicle for their own worldviews). We shall not pursue the influence of classical adventure novels on the modern literature of adventure, however, since our main attempt is to ascertain and name the essential social causes for the formation of the conceptions of adventure. These conceptions are absolutely not unitary, are subject to the historical change in social conditions, and are often self-contradictory and incoherent. It remains for a future investigation to clarify the extent to which literary and philosophical conceptions of the past or of non-European literatures have contributed to shaping these views, where research has not determined that in individual cases.

The first more or less systematic ideology of adventure, which demands and celebrates voluntary daring, the quest for extraordinary events, i.e., adventures, with (more or less) unpredictable risk, the "enduring of danger-filled adventures" as the highest ethical achievement, as "honor" (*êre*) and "knighthood" (*rîterschaft*),[8] is the courtly-knightly ideology. This ideology developed around the end of the twelfth century in France in the courtly romance, especially in the verse romances of Chrestien de Troyes (ca. 1150-90) about King Arthur and his Round Table, Yvain, and Lancelot. When we speak of "adventure" in the courtly-knightly ideology, we must be precise: we mean the (old French) *aventure*, and as Elena Ebenwein writes, "only in medieval expression can we search for what this word contains of the world and reality of those times."[9] *Aventure*, which in its literary occurrences before the courtly romance means fate, chance, has become, in the knightly-courtly system of relations, an event that the knight must seek out and endure, although this event does continue to be unpredictable, a surprise of fate.[10] The decisive factor, however, is that the surprising event, the *aventure*, is *sought*, and within the framework of this intentionality it is planned for and hence predicted. A change has taken place from *aventure* as fate to *aventure* as "adventure";[11] we shall not discuss whether this concept from the very beginning had the connotation of *advenio/adventus* [to come to/an arrival] or *evenio/eventus* [to come out/a result][12] (which seems problematic to say the least, given the unattested and hence undefinable meaning of **ad-ventura*).

The knight sets out to experience *aventure*; indeed, it is only in experiencing *aventure* that the (knightly) human being realizes himself in his true "essence":

> Setting out at random into the uncertain has lost all its terror,
> although of course the aventure has not lost its indispensable element
> of danger: aventure is always also, and often exclusively, "danger."
> The danger of the life the knight errant leads becomes a characteristic
> that confers meaning, becomes the highest virtue of the class itself. On
> that basis, in a significant passage of *Yvain*,[13] aventure becomes the
> mark of the abysmal distance between the knightly human being and
> the rest of society.[14]

Knight, King, and *Vilains*

The quest for adventure, *la queste de l'aventure*, is thus a distinctive hallmark of a class: among other things, it distinguishes the knight from the *vilains*, the "man who does not belong to the nobility," and especially from the *borjois*, the "city dweller," for whom the knight in principle has nothing but contempt and hatred, as the words for the *borjois* show: *vilenaille, chien enragié, pute servaille*[15] (roughly, "bourgeois rabble, rabid dog, servile whoresons"). The *chevalier*, the "knight," distinguishes himself from the king as well as from the *borjois*. The king should have all the other knightly virtues (especially *largesse*, generosity), but even in literature he never or very seldom goes out on a quest for *aventure*:

> As the first among a number of select knights, Arthur must be a glow-
> ing representative of the exemplary humanity represented by his circle.
> This same quality of being first, being king, condemns him at the same
> time, however, to being a weakling who would be helpless in the face
> of insults by suddenly appearing enemies except that his hand-picked
> group of model knights wage a constant battle to guarantee the power
> and honor of his court.[16]

A certain social class thus has an exclusive right to adventure and its glorification. This class gives itself the honorific "knight" or *chevalier* and points out to the *vilains* that he is to occupy a subordinate position and to the king or prince that he is dependent on the *chevalier* for his own protection. Only with the clergy is there no overt behavior of demarcation and competition, in part because the clergy could not assume the function of the knights, in part because the knight depended on both the philosophical (religious) agreement of the church and the intellectual help of the (literate) clergy in developing his courtly ideology,[17] the main basis for which was, incidentally, mediated by the clergy via the ideal of the Christian soldier, *miles christianus*.[18] According to this ideology, the meaning of the knightly existence is the fulfillment of ethical principles in the experience of *aventures* and the demonstration of all knightly virtues like bravery and loyalty to a revered lady, to the prince or king, and—to God, whereby, as Erich Köhler correctly writes, "adventure [appears] as a self-testing with no specific task, with no office, with no concrete historical or political context,"[19] as a general ethical duty.

Aventure Unmasked

Erich Köhler, who has thoroughly demonstrated the social relativity of the ideology of *aventure*, places the development of that ideology in conjunction with the "impoverishment" of the (petty) nobility:

> The quest for adventure does not justify itself on its own terms, since in actuality it disrupts rather than maintains the social order, and as a mere warlike action without a moral meaning it stands in opposition to the medieval respect for *ordo* ["order"—R.C.]. The Middle Ages understands a positive social condition like the ordering of everything that exists as a ranking in the sense of a more or less perfect existence, of a greater or lesser closeness to God.[20]

For that reason, he continues, the search for adventure had to be moralized:

> The loss of a concrete political function throws the knight back on his own resources, and only the claim of belonging to the highest class gives aventure, raised to the level of a very personal trial, a place in the community, that is, in the noble class and hence under the law of feudal ethics.[21]

More recent research, however, has consistently pointed out that the origin of the knightly ideology cannot be traced to the process of the impoverishment of the (petty) nobility alone (in the beginning, knights were not drawn exclusively from the nobility).[22] Rather, the (partial) impoverishment of the nobility, the rise of the *milites*, the military caste, feudalist centralization, and the emergence of the bourgeoisie form a dialectical unity to which the knightly ideology, including *aventure*, owes its dialectical character. For that reason the assertion that the quest for adventure "disrupts rather than maintains the social order" is as problematic as the undifferentiated opposition between *aventure* and *ordo*: any statement about when the *queste de l'aventure* was or became disruptive can be made only under consideration of the actual social conditions. At the time of the origin and development of the courtly ideology (that is, at the time of the romances of Chrestien de Troyes), that was by no means the case. At that time *aventure* for the *chevalerie* (knighthood) itself was chiefly a rude material necessity and thus also a decisive factor for order (albeit still within a very disrupted feudal structure). One could even claim that the entire economic and political structure would have been destroyed if the *chevaliers* had not set out on adventures. Georges Duby determines that the great princely houses (the "grandes maisons seigneuriales") were threatened primarily by two factors: the long life expectancy of the established great nobility, which was much higher than for the lower classes because of their superior and privileged conditions and their related high birth rate.[23] The established great nobility were supported by their land, which had to be shared between father and first-born son and with the (often numerous) succeeding children as well. The eldest son thus had to wait out the time until his father retired: "The rules of managing the aristocratic patrimony thus encouraged the eldest son to set forth in quest of adventure, but he had of course brothers, sometimes many brothers."[24] Necessity soon became law: the first-born son became the chief or sole heir, starting in the great princely houses, with counts, princes, and especially kings. But toward the end of the twelfth century, at the time of the development of the courtly ideology, the right of primogeniture became the rule with the petty nobility too.[25] The younger sons had to be provided for:

> Two or three of them could expect lucrative positions within the church. The others sometimes received a small part of the inheritance, usually from some recent acquisition or from possessions coming from their mother's side. But possession in such cases was precarious, and fragments such as these bred discord between brothers, encouraged cupidity and sharpened the temptation of other brothers or nephews to seize whatever they could by force. When deprived of any hope of certain inheritance, younger brothers had often no other prospect but adventure.[26]

And it must not be forgotten that it was for exactly this reason that the knightly orders that were gradually developing took on the function of caring for the deserving Christian knight adventurer.[27]

How Adventurous Was *Aventure*?

If we disregard for the moment the other purposes of *aventure*, one of the most important goals of the *queste* was a good match, a rich marriage. And it should help our understanding of the *roman courtois* (courtly romance) to remember that all unmarried "adventuring" knights, as well as married knights without children, were called *juvenes* (*jeunes*, "youths"), sometimes without regard for their actual age.[28] They remained *jeunes* until they made an adequate marriage. As Georges Duby writes:

> All *juvenes* were on the lookout for an heiress. If they came across one, they tried to reserve her before she was nubile. . . . The search for a rich girl with a fine establishment was . . . not always doomed to disappointment. But certain obvious hazards and obstacles of the hunt

were inherent in the uncertain supply of suitable quarry, that is by the frequent eclipse of noble families which resulted in the entire inheritance devolving upon an heiress. Indeed, the whole phenomenon is intimately bound up with the existence of the class of "youths," with their peculiar circumstances, their adventurous life, and the dangers they ran which so reduced their ranks.[29]

The *queste de l'aventure* was thus, at least at the time of Chrestien de Troyes, the great ideologue of *chevalerie*, the only form of guaranteeing a living, a certain way of earning their livelihood, for a large part of the itinerant knighthood. The risk associated with this way of earning a living was relatively small. The word *aventure* still had, and rightly so, the connotation "dare," but—and this is the other side of the coin—if the knight did not embark on an adventure, he was certain to perish. That means first of all that the risk was greater for him if he did not set out on *aventures*. He was not alone in being subject to this pressure, however;[30] famines and epidemics drove thousands of *vilains*, the utterly impoverished populace, who became itinerant in part for the same reasons that the knights did (for example, the land of the small farmer could not support his children[31]) and were driven to wandering in part as a result of wars, battles between feudal lords, or natural catastrophes. Faced with the choice of certain starvation where they lived or a chance of survival in a different, more favorable place (for instance, along the pilgrimage route), the *vilains* did as the knights had done: they set out after *aventure*, without, however, idealizing it (or being able to idealize it). Crowds of knights also traveled along in this army of the wandering populace, and probably—in anticipation of the later robber barons—had many small occasional *aventures* or picked up some booty under way. They occupied a thoroughly privileged position: apart from the fact that they were armed and on horseback, they were accompanied by a retinue of young vassals' sons, whose departure also alleviated the burden on the courtly economy. They protected the knights and thus reduced the risk. To be sure, risk was still present, but compared to the fate of the impoverished population forced to wander the countryside, it was hardly as great as the authors of courtly novels would have us believe.

From the Uncourtly Knight to the Knightly Courtier

We should not overlook the fact that the courtly ideology of knightly adventure was articulated at a relatively late date; it is by no means contemporaneous with the birth of knighthood. As Arno Borst writes, "The birth of knighthood occurred in the late ninth century, a period in which the Carolingian, greater Frankish state was disintegrating."[32] The only (anarchic) principle of order within the general anarchy was the right of the stronger, the striking force of the larger or smaller feudal lords, who had to protect their territory and the peasants and craftsmen living there not only against Normans, Saracens, Hungarians, but also against their (noble) neighbors. In this discussion it should be borne in mind that the relationship between noble or knightly protectors and non-noble protégés was one of division of labor, that is, a mutual one. The knight was the specialist in defense or war, who needed material support from the peasants or craftsmen for his weapons and for training in the use of weapons, just as the peasants and the craftsmen needed his protection.[33]

We should also recall that until the late twelfth century many knights were not much more than a highly uncultured "gang of unscrupulous fellows"[34] who would accept even non-nobles. "It was up to the nobles themselves whether to promote bondsmen and peasants into the nobility by knighting them and vouching for them; they were not stingy with this privilege."[35] But these knights were still far removed from the courtly style of life or a courtly ideology (of *aventure*). Only in the course of the twelfth century did this change (along with the social composition of the professional knightly estate in France), when the princes on the one hand and the kings on the other began to consolidate their political and economic power. The knights at that time gained a multifold new importance. Just as the princes needed vassals for their policy of consolidation, in order to maintain themselves or to prevail against other princes and against the king, the king needed vassals against the princes, in order to enforce his claims.

> The king and the great princes had long been competing to develop their territories into institutionalized landed states, but the most effective means to accomplish that were still military power and the right of investiture. If the king wanted to destroy the influence of the princes and win for himself the small vassals in their independently built castles, then he had to woo them with royal fiefs or beseige them. . . . The great lords could find military help in mercenaries, who were above the awkward and undependable offer of a fief, but politically they needed the small dominions of the lower nobility if the concentration of the state was to encompass wider areas.[36]

This was the hour of the knights; princes and kings needed them. On the one hand, that gave them an increasing military and political importance, but on the other, their deficient education and their exclusive emphasis on the arts of war meant they were fit for little else than making war. Hence, a general and a political education was a social necessity to allow the members of this group to qualify for higher tasks, and that is the political importance of courtly literature and the ideology of knighthood. To the extent that this literature was directed at the (young) knights themselves, it was literature of education and (ideological) indoctrination;[37] to the extent it was directed at the king, it was the combat literature of a social class that was now, typically, refusing to accept elements from the non-noble classes. Thus it is also propaganda literature against competing social groups, and this function increased as the princes and then especially the king succeeded in asserting themselves. The prerequisites for courtly literature were first, the existence of the knightly class itself with its simultaneous metamorphosis into the military; second, the politics of the church, of the clergy;[38] third, and especially important, the development of the cities,[39] the emergence of a self-aware bourgeoisie. The princes played the bourgeoisie off against the vassals; the king used it against the princes.[40] And in the course of the twelfth century the knights were already increasingly being forced to take a position against the bourgeoisie (in league with the clergy, with whom the knights by and large could—and had to—make common cause) to prevent that class from pushing them back into the relative insignificance of an existence as soldier knights.

Only from this perspective can we completely understand the development of the ideology of the noble knight. On the one hand, martial activity itself had to be designated the highest ethical value, by means of *aventure* (the rising bourgeoisie—at first, in any case—could not compete in this area). On the other hand, under pressure from the clergy, this martial activity had to have a Christian motivation, and under pressure from the bourgeoisie, it had to be glorified as a class-specific noble activity. This explains the nobility's readiness on principle to adopt the knightly ideology altogether and (partially) to fuse itself with the knightly class (not necessarily identical with it originally).[41] It also explains the permanent polemics against *li vilains* and *li borjois*[42] that begin at this point and the constant warning to princes or to the king to make only nobles their advisers.

> The consolidation of the knightly class to an institution based on noble birth and consecrated by the ritual of dubbing, with its religious trappings, comes about under the distressing pressure of the strength of the bourgeoisie, which comes to economic and political prominence in the twelfth century and whose further development is incalculable.[43]

The glorification of *aventure* as the highest meaning of human existence was motivated by nobility of birth and by religion. It is thus the political platform of one class in its attempt to reach an arrangement with other classes: with princes and kings, in order to ally itself with them, even to make itself indispensable to them; with the clergy, in order to come to terms with it ideologically; with the bourgeoisie, in order to oppose it. The courtly ideology was supposed to secure the social position of the petty or knightly nobility: an *aventure* can only be an *aventure* if it can be concluded, that is, if the person who set out on the *aventure* can come back after he has been through it. Indeed, he has to come back, since setting out on *aventures* became or was declared a principle of order that held sway at the point of departure and return, the court.[44] In this sense, the order which is defended and realized in the *aventure* is maintained:

While aventure is being elevated to an ideal characteristic of the *entire* class, the petty nobility is reintegrating itself into a select community which, according to literary and courtly fiction, was indifferent to possessions. . . . The constantly threatening existence of impoverished knights places aventure in the midst of a tense existence in which the petty nobility finds itself again with the feudal nobility, although the opponents are only partly the same. If the ideal of aventure is unimaginable with respect to the powerful feudal nobility, at least the courtly romance, especially in its beginnings, is under the sign of the low knighthood. . . . If the elevation of aventure from a necessity to a virtue can be adequately explained by the tension between life style and the demand for recognition in the petty nobility, still the apparently unconditional consensus on the part of the feudal upper nobility needs a thorough historical substantiation. The tensions within the knightly class were considerable and were intensified by the rapid development of municipalities and the money economy. The uniformity of the class was so endangered that the discrediting of poor adventure-seeking knights as a result of their rapid increase, which was usual within the class itself, finally was turned against the class as a whole. But the decisive factor was probably the common threat to all levels of nobility posed by the economic revolution of the twelfth century. . . and by the emerging antifeudal alliance between monarchy and bourgeoisie.[45]

Aventure and *Mervoille*

If the quest for *aventure* and the survival of *aventure* was ideologized, idealized, and elevated to the essential purpose of existence, to the criterion of "true" humanity, then it is obvious that this *aventure* could no longer be just any, however dangerous, event, say a passage of arms; it most certainly could not be a special line of business. *Aventure* itself had to become qualitatively different, had to become a special event, had to be "ennobled." Quite early on the concept of *aventure* was so closely joined with that of the *mervoille,* the "miraculous," that they were sometimes used interchangeably.[46] All (fictive) means were employed in order to "ennoble" *aventure* in the context of courtly ideology: giants, magicians, fairies, enchanted forests—the entire fairy-tale repertoire is already established in the early courtly romances on which the author of *Amadís* and its epigones will draw. The *aventure* has disguised itself as a courtly celebration.

We find the clearest expression of the way *aventure* is ennobled by transposing it into fairy-tale fictionality in the courtly verse romances based on the *matière de Bretagne* that were written by Chrestien de Troyes. In 1178-81 he wrote the romance about Yvain, *Le Chevalier au lion* (The Lion Knight), in which we encounter a knight named Calogrenant who tells Arthur's Round Table about his adventure at a magic fountain. As Erich Auerbach summarizes it:

> [The magic fountain—R. C.] flows under a beautiful tree. A golden vessel hangs nearby, and when water from the spring is poured from the vessel over an emerald tablet which lies beside it, such a terrible storm arises in the forest that no one has ever lived through it. Calogrenant attempts the adventure. He withstands the storm and then enjoys the sunny calm which follows, enlivened by the song of many birds. . . . Calogrenant's story makes a great impression on the knights at Arthur's court. The King decides to ride to the magic spring himself, with a large following. However, one of the knights, Calogrenant's cousin Yvain, gets there before him, defeats and kills the knight of the spring, and, by means which are partly miraculous and partly very natural, wins the love of his widow.[47]

The passage chosen by Auerbach is in fact especially typical. Nature mysticism and the fairy world join forces—by means of a fairy-tale *aventure*—in courtly adoration of the lady, in courtly love:

> The landscape is the enchanted landscape of fairy tale; we are surrounded by mystery, by secret murmurings and whispers. . . . It is from Breton folklore that the courtly romance took its elements of mystery, of something sprung from the soil, concealing its roots, and inaccessible to rational explanation; it incorporated them and made use of them in its elaboration of the knightly ideal; the *matière de Bretagne* apparently proved to be the most suitable medium for the cultivation of that ideal.[48]

Auerbach does not fully recognize the function of the fairy-tale-like fictionalizing of real *aventure* in the adoption of the Breton folk tale, the *matière de Bretagne*. Starting with the assumption that the individual *aventure* lacks any real historical foundation, Auerbach takes the fairy-tale adventure to be a screen separating noble society from its relations with the social reality surrounding it, in order to elevate to an end in itself the impervious "self-portrayal of feudal knighthood with its mores and ideals."[49] Still, he is fully correct in observing that even where the real world shines through in the courtly novel, as in the description of the working conditions of weavers in *Chevalier au lion*, this reality appears "as though sprung from the ground"—from the ground of fairy-tale, that is.[50]

> The world of knightly proving is a world of adventure. It not only contains a practically uninterrupted series of adventures; more specifically, it contains nothing but the requisites of adventure.

Nothing is found in it which is not either accessory or preparatory to an adventure. It is a world specifically created and designed to give the knight opportunity to prove himself.[51]

As a result, the courtly ideology of *aventure* could exercise only a very limited effect on *aventure* itself.

From the Ideology of *Aventure* to the Ideology of the *Courtisan*

Even knights could not fail to see that the real world was not set up for courtly *aventure*. The courtly ideology of *aventure* already heralds its own end. It could have arisen only in the historical situation we have described: increasing centralization of the feudal state, with the knights on the one hand contributing to the success of centralization with their real martial activity, but on the other hand being drawn into the wake of this centralization and forced to give up existing or earning a living through adventure. The princes or kings needed the knights in order to defeat their competitors, the great feudal lords, but they no longer needed the knights as small troops or as individuals. Instead, they needed them as warriors in ever larger armies of knights. Before long there were not enough knights to guarantee the necessary army size, and non-nobles were also pressed into armed service. In the fourteenth century at the latest, the knightly form of battle began to be obsolete. At this time of transition, anyone who did not make the leap to becoming a courtier or a member of the military nobility (which largely amounted to the same thing) perished, fell back into the class of the non-nobles, or came down in the world to become a robber baron (and was sooner or later strung up "from the closest tree").[52] The individual *aventure* now actually became an anarchic, disruptive factor in the centralized and increasingly peaceful feudal state, which had to have an effect on the ideology of *aventure*. *Aventure* did not simply become useless; it developed further, and its least relevant aspect, the *aventure mervoille*, was pushed further and further into the background until it finally disappeared altogether. The decisive factor for the further development of courtly reality and courtly ideology was the knightly ethic that remained after the fairy-tale *aventure* had fallen away (it continued to be tolerated as a literary vehicle as long as it did not hinder the development toward courtly life under an absolute monarchy, as long as it did not interfere with the serious business of living). Directly or indirectly, therefore, *aventure* had to be eliminated from courtly ideology in order for it to function as the courtiers' ideology. A milestone in this development is the treatise *De Amore*, written around 1185 by Andreas Capellanus, the chaplain of the French king. This work attempts to unite the courtly love ethos with a new noble ethic based on moral and spiritual values. This is an early harbinger of the *courtisan*, the "courtier," for whom more than three hundred years later Baldassare Castiglione was to write the manual. The *courtisan* is unimaginable without Lancelot or Yvain, without the inheritance of the courtly ideology of *aventure*. But it would have been unthinkable for the *courtisan* to set out in quest of fairy-tale *aventures*. The knightly praxis of adventure follows the general assimilation of the knighthood into the realms of the regular military and the life of the court, which included the tournament (from as early as the twelfth century).[53] In times of war, the two realms were reunited chiefly in the person of the military noble, who constituted the nobility of the sword, fighting in the army of knights or commanding the army composed of knights and commoners.

The War of Plunder

The army of knights of course existed in the time *before* the origin of the courtly ideology of *aventure*, but here, as everywhere in history, the decisive question is: When does a quantitative difference became qualitative? (a question that also applies to the internal composition of the knightly army). By the end of the twelfth century in France, the age of the knight-errant and his *aventure*-filled existence is fundamentally over. Now when he leaves the court of the prince, where he keeps fit by participating in tournaments, it is no longer to embark on an individual adventure but to be integrated into a larger army, even though this group might consist mainly of knights, in which he exercises command functions, among other things.

The transitional time with which we are concerned, however, is largely a time of social catastrophes for knights. To understand this process, we must once more go back in time. Knights were being forced to integrate themselves into the nobility at court, but were often not able to do so (there were too many knights for the courts to accept them all; many knights did not have the money to live at court). This position contributed substantially to the élan with which masses of knights plunged headlong into the Crusades. The Crusades offered the knights the chance of continuing to earn their living by means of adventure and to acquire property and status through looting, as Guibert von Nogent ascertained as early as 1108 in the *Gesta Dei per Francos*.[54] The despair with which tens of thousands of impoverished knights and peasants threw themselves upon this hope is almost inconceivable. Their hope must have seemed even more firmly based when the Pope himself proclaimed the "ideology of the holy war" against the "infidels" who had allegedly desecrated Christ's grave. Before the first crusade could even form, masses of impoverished peasants and knights rushed to the south:

A popular crusade of peasants and poor people with no military
organization set out first. It was a true swarm of people that broke in
two waves. One group consisted mostly of Germans under the leader-

ship of Walter Ohne Habe, the other primarily of Frenchmen, led by Petrus von Amiens through the Byzantine empire; they plundered and killed the Jews along their way. In Asia Minor in November 1096 they were killed by the Turks or sold off as slaves.[55]

Later crusaders were better organized and managed to bring Jerusalem largely under Christian control in the twelfth century, although the process was so barbaric that even contemporaries were outraged:[56] the "infidels" were butchered en masse, and women and children were not spared. It is a moot question whether we should attribute the pessimism of the last Arthurian novels, in which the Grail could be symbolic of the Holy Sepulchre,[57] to disappointment that in spite of everything, the Holy Land could not be held in the long run (still, the loss of Jerusalem at the end of the twelfth century did not mean the end of the Crusades). But it is clear that this truly collective adventure of the twelfth century, during which the courtly ideology of adventure was developed, had nothing in common with the courtly *aventure* existence, even though barons, princes, and kings (like Louis IX of France, in the thirteenth century) took part in it. Instead, it was a series of expeditions to plunder and loot that often resembled a violent train of colonists.[58] The knights who participated in it might have felt themselves to be complete knights, but it was not the desire for *aventure* that drove them on; rather, it was the indissoluble union of religious fanaticism and the striving for economic and political power (which was able to silence the religious motive completely, as many arrangements made with the Islamic enemy testify).[59]

An impressive testimony for the above is the report on the Fourth Crusade by Geoffroy de Villehardouin, who was one of its leaders. Villehardouin is familiar with the concept of *aventure* and uses it as well, but never in any sense corresponding to the courtly ideology of *aventure*, although that ideology was fully developed by the time of the Fourth Crusade (1199-1207). *Aventure* is quite simply the event, the incident: "les aventures avienent ensi con Dieu plaist," "events happen as God wills."[60] Such an *aventure* can be the natural death of a baron as well as the winning of great plunder. Plunder is, indeed, quite clearly central. Large armies consisting of princes, knights, and mercenaries did proceed to the Holy Land with many pious speeches, for the purpose of liberating the Holy Land; but from the very beginning there was discord over the investments by various parties. The disagreement became overt when the Venetians' passage to Asia Minor had to be paid. "The passage was to have been paid by taking up a collection in the army. But there were many who said that they could not pay their passage."[61]

The dispute about money and booty is a leitmotif. Pious thought, knightly behavior are pushed into the background, as Villehardouin states. Only the division of the land that was conquered with every atrocity imaginable seemed to move spirits. Before Constantinople was conquered in 1204, the division of the spoils was decided on: "He who is elected ruler is to receive one quarter of the entire conquest, and the other three quarters should be divided in half and one half given to the Venetians and one half to the [French—M. N.] army."[62] The city was put to the torch during the conquest. "Then you could have seen how the Greeks were butchered and horses and steeds, donkeys and asses and other plunder taken. And there were so many dead and wounded that there was no counting them and no end to them."[63] Anyone plundering on his own account was punished, to be sure; even a knight was hanged for independent plundering.[64] The booty was collected and divided as agreed. Afterward, the countryside was conquered. "Then people began to divide the land. The Venetians received their share, and the army of pilgrims theirs. And as each of them heard what land was apportioned him, he was seized by earthly greed, which had already caused so much damage: everyone began to do wrong in his land, some more, some less, so that the Greeks began to hate them."[65]

From Knight to Mercenary

What was a fact and a necessity from the very beginning of the Crusades increasingly determined the conduct of war among the European princes and kings. Fundamentally, the military nobility had the power of command, but the mass of fighters increasingly came from the non-noble populace, especially from the peasantry. This development began at the end of the twelfth century under Philippe II of France, who brought mercenaries into military service,[66] but the system did not actually prevail until a hundred years later. As Engels wrote:

Fighting the feudal economy with a feudal army, in which soldiers were more closely bound to their immediate feudal lord than to the royal commander of the army, would obviously mean moving in a vicious circle and getting nowhere. From the beginning of the fourteenth century on the kings strove to emancipate themselves from this feudal army, to create an army of their own. From this time on we find an increasing portion of hired or rented troops in the royal armies. . . . In the beginnings they are mostly foot soldiers, Lombards, Genovese, Germans, Belgians, etc., used for occupying cities and for seiges, but scarcely fit for open battle in the field. But as early as the end of the Middle Ages we also find knights who rent themselves and their motley assemblage of followers to foreign princes and thus herald the irreversible collapse of the feudal system of war. At the same time the basic condition for a foot soldiery capable of waging war arose in the cities and among the free peasants. Up until then knights with their mounted followers had been not just the heart of the army, but actually the army itself; the train of serfs who followed along on foot as servants did not count; in the field they seemed to be good for nothing but deserting and plundering. As long as feudalism was in full sway, until the end of the thirteenth century, those on horseback fought and decided all battles. From that time on things changed.[67]

Things changed definitively after the battle near Coutrai in 1302, when the French army of knights suffered an annihilating defeat at the hands of Flemish burgher militias.[68] The defeat of the French knightly army by English non-noble archers near Crécy years later, during the Hundred Years' War, and again, nine years later, near Poitiers, had an even more horrifying effect.

The new, serious defeat plunged the French state into a deep crisis. The hatred of the people for the nobility which had failed so obviously in the exercise of its martial duties intensified far beyond the normal measure. The chronicler Jean de Venette reported that the Parisians, "since they placed little trust in the nobility," fortified their city and prepared to defend it.[69]

But it was not only the burghers who drew a lesson from these incidents. Toward the end of the Hundred Years' War, from 1445 to 1448, Charles VII drew his own conclusion from the internal threat to France represented by unreliable feudal lords and the external threat by the competing English king. Charles equipped a standing army, consisting of fifteen companies of one hundred armed and mounted men each accompanied by five men with light arms, and of infantry companies (of archers). This army could be supported only through special taxes that the King, after resistance from the *Etats Généraux*, soon began to collect directly, over their heads.[70] While some complained about this arrangement, chiefly the infantry, the so-called *Francs-Archers*, recruited from non-nobles and called "free" because they were exempt from taxation (not much later we meet them in *Tirant lo Blanc*, where they are presented with no value judgment),[71] others like Jean de Bueil welcomed the military innovation in his *Le Jouvencel* (1463-66). Jean de Bueil immediately tried to grasp this innovation theoretically and didactically, and it is obvious that the last reminiscence of courtly *aventure* has disappeared. "As to battle on foot," he writes, "it is quite the opposite of mounted battle, for foot soldiers may never pursue the enemy but must always remain standing, save their strength, and try with all the means at their disposal to make the enemy march on them."[72]

Even though the Free Archer Corps were dissolved in 1479, the establishment of a standing army and the combination of standing and mobile troops is a crucial event in the history of warfare (and the decline of knightly warfare). A new type of warrior has arisen: the mercenary, who will determine the course of wars until well into the eighteenth century and who in the fifteenth century is given a name by which the *chevaliers* had not called themselves: adventurer or *aventurier*. In

1534, Rabelais's *Gargantua* describes a military vanguard. It consisted of "sixteen thousand and fourteen harquebussiers or firelocks, together with thirty thousand and eleven volunteer adventurers"[73]—burlesque numbers, to be sure, but the matter of the *aventuriers*, the mercenaries, the infantry, was serious. According to Engels:

> A class of men had been formed who lived upon war and by war; and though tactics might have gained thereby, the character of the men, the material composing armies as well as their *morale*, had certainly suffered. Central Europe was overrun by *condottieri* of all kinds, who took religious and political quarrels for their pretext to plunder and devastate the whole country. The character degradation which went on increasing until the French revolution finally swept away this system of mercenary service.[74]

The licentiousness of the mass of mercenaries, which also became a security risk for their military leaders,[75] may well be the reason that the concept of *aventurier* quickly became suspect as a military term or dropped out of use. Already in the sixteenth century the terms *chevetain, souldoyer*, and *avanturier* remind Henri Estienne (1531-98) of the *vielle guerre*, the old warfare. In *Contes et Discours d'Eutrapel* by Noël Du Fail (1585), someone who thinks he sees *pietons* and *avanturiers* is told that that is the *brave fanterie*, the "brave infantry." And Etienne Pasquier declared in his *Recherches de la France* (1560): We would not be soldiers [*guerriers*] if we did not call the old pietons and avanturiers the infantry.[76] But apart from military usage, the term *aventurier* survived as a pejorative or mildly disparaging word to designate mercenaries until well into the eighteenth century. In this sense it was made known by lexicographers even in England, where the term was not current. In 1611 Randle Cotgrave, in his *A Dictionary of the French and English Tongues* (reprint Hildesheim and New York, 1970), explains the French concept *aventurier* as follows: "An aduenturer, one that freely and without compulsion, or charge goes to the warres; also, a freebooter, or boot-haler." The last two meanings are not mentioned by Jacob le Duchat (1658-1735), Rabelais's editor and Bayle's collaborator, although—as we will see—*aventurier* was commonly used at least for free-booter: "Avanturiers... a sort of old French troops," as we read in his work. Then he cites examples from Rabelais and concludes: "That they were called avanturiers I attribute to the fact that they served without pay, in hopes of making their fortune in avantures like the knights-errant who used to visit inns without paying and who gradually, from being the poor unknown men they almost always were, became great lords."[77]

Chapter 2
The Adventure of the *Hidalgo*

The Knight in Reality

All of knighthood and of knightly ideology was summed up between 1450 and 1455, at the time when Charles VII was developing the standing army in France, by the Catalan Joannot Martorell, in his novel *Tirant lo Blanc*. It remained unfinished; Martí Joan de Galba wrote an ending for it and had it published in 1490.[1] To fully understand the importance of this book, which has been underappreciated by literary scholars,[2] we must first review the situation of knighthood in Spain, which was of great importance for the ideology of adventure as a whole. As we determined, the high point of real knighthood lay before and during the time when centralized feudal power or the centralized monarchy was formed (that is, from the ninth to the thirteenth centuries); Spain constitutes an exception with respect to France and to all other European countries, and this alone explains why the second wave of courtly ideology in the fifteenth and sixteenth centuries comes out of Spain.

While all other European countries emerged from the confrontation among princes or kings, petty feudal nobility, and the rising bourgeoisie with modern national constitutions for centralized or city-state governments, up to 1492 Spain was in a situation very similar to that of France from the ninth to the thirteenth centuries. Just as the high point and end of the fighting and wandering knights in France converge with the development of the knightly ideology of *aventure* in the twelfth century, so too in Spain three centuries later, with the development of the ideology of *aventura* in the *libro de caballeria*, the "Spanish knightly romance."

The reason is as follows. Not until 1492 did Spain succeed in finishing the *Reconquista*, the reconquest of Spain from the Moors, who had occupied the Iberian peninsula in 711. The *Reconquista* began seven years later, in 718, but as Pierre Vilar wrote: "Spain—and especially Castile—was a society in constant battle from 711 to 1492. 'The fighting class' of course won first place in this society. More than anywhere else, the great nobility became powerful and the petty nobility proliferated."[3] For more than seven centuries this nobility, especially the petty nobility (the knights), was forced to do battle in every known form, from great battles to small skirmishes with Moorish neighbors at home. The daily encounter with real danger, with the real enemy who shared the land under dispute, did not allow a fairy-tale-like *aventure* ideology to develop—and this is the source of the realism in Spanish literature, which as everywhere else was chiefly the literature of the leading class, of the nobility. In fact, the *matière de Bretagne* in the form of courtly novels, which was well known, as various witnesses attest,[4] seems to have been almost as irrelevant as fairy tales for everything that had to do with *aventure*. The proof of this assertion is that the *matière de Bretagne* did not find an echo in Spain, did not inspire any significant Spanish product, until well into the fifteenth century. The reasons are obvious. They have absolutely nothing to do with a specially ("racially" determined!) Spanish "national character," as has often been claimed.[5] The major obstacle to an unlimited assimilation or adaptation of the *matière de Bretagne* must be seen in its fairy-tale-like fictionalization of knightly *aventure,* which could not withstand comparison with the knightly life of battle the Spanish nobles lived. It was simply unacceptable. But what was acceptable was the knightly ethic, with the exclusion of the fairy-tale-like *queste de l'aventure.*

When French knighthood began to find its literary articulation, its high point already lay to some extent in the past, and it was already in the midst of the transition to courtly nobility. When knighthood in Spain first found literary expression, it was still involved in its heroic battles and was still three centuries removed from the development of central royal power and hence from courtly nobility. The image of the knight was thus chiefly determined by his real historical manifestation and his real martial activity. In other words, the Spanish knight did not need to invent fairy tales to make himself important; he was needed *as a knight* until 1492. The first knight we encounter immediately became a national hero: Rodrigo Diaz from Vivar, who bore the Arabic honorific *Cid*, meaning "Lord." The *Cantar de Mio Cid, a cantar de gesta* (heroic epic), presents the noble Rodrigo Diaz, exiled by King Alfonso VI of Castile (1072-1109) ostensibly because he embezzled tribute money. The Cid sets out in search of *aventura*; that is, he goes on a war of plunder against the Moors, conquers Valencia, and gradually pacifies the king with gifts from the booty he has taken. In contrast to French *chansons de geste* like the *Song of Roland*, the *Cantar de Mio Cid* (probably written around

1140) deals with a recent historical occurrence and is distinguished by its realistic presentation, including details of geography and daily life. Given the circumstances, only a nonrealistic portrayal would be surprising. Villehardouin's description of the Fourth Crusade only sixty years later is no less realistic.

Caballero—Hidalgo

The everyday reality of knightly war experience determines the other *cantares de gesta,*[6] the chronicles, and the remaining literary genres as well. But that does not mean that French courtly literature had no influence. On the contrary, when we recall that until well into the fifteenth century Spanish knights came not exclusively from the nobility but always from other classes as well, especially from the peasantry, it becomes clear that the king must have welcomed the knightly-courtly system of virtues, developed in France primarily in the courtly novel, as a means of disciplining those "rough fellows." Thus, in the legal texts of the *Siete Partidas*, written under Alfonso the Wise (1221-84), we find at Titulo XXI [the twenty-first law—R. C.] an extensive code of honor and behavior for the knightly class which would have been unthinkable without the French model but which is completely free of any unrealistic or fairy-tale-like elements (if one discounts the speculation about the etymology of the Latin word for knight, *miles*).

It must be remembered that the knight, the *caballero*, was not necessarily a nobleman, an idea we can follow all the way up to *Tirant lo Blanc*. To be sure, in the normal case a knight was of "good background," and that included being well endowed with property (*fijo de algo*, "son of someone or something," which later became *hijodealgo* or *hidalgo*). That is, the *caballero* normally came from the nobility. But it was also possible to become a knight on the basis of certain mental or physical (martial) qualities. Anyone who rose into the knightly class, the *caballería*, received a special noble status as well as the *hidalguía*, the material advantage of exemption from taxes. The *Siete Partidas* does not say who was able to rise to the rank of knight, but it does specify who was not able to: clergymen, madmen, minors, paupers (ostensibly because knights were not permitted to beg), cripples, traders, traitors, criminals, and murderers (unless they had been exonerated and the charge against them withdrawn). Nor can the rank of *caballero* be purchased, because nobility cannot be purchased.[7]

Although the legal text is not clear in all details, it does emerge that acceptance into the *caballería* was understood to be acceptance into the *hidalguía*, the nobility, so that despite all distinctions between *hidalgo* and *caballero*, we can assume a fundamental convergence of the two categories (a *hidalgo* is *hidalgo* and *caballero* by heritage, a *caballero* is *caballero* and *hidalgo* through merit and service; in principle, the *hidalgo* is also a *caballero* and vice versa).

The Courtly Education of the *Caballero*

Whether noble or not, as we have already indicated, we must imagine the *caballeros* engaged in the *Reconquista* as a wild bunch of warriors, far removed from the ideal of the courtly knight on the French model. This made an intensive ideological indoctrination all the more necessary, in order to inculcate in the knights certain principles of military virtue and courtly loyalty to the feudal lord. Already in the *Siete Partidas*, in the twentieth law,[8] we read that a knight must be made familiar with the appropriate literature whenever he is not waging war. All reading other than the *cantares de gesta* and other war stories was forbidden.

Toward the end of the thirteenth or the beginning of the fourteenth century, a famous contemporary of Alfonso's, Ramón Llull, wrote what is perhaps the most important treatise on knighthood, the *Libro del Orde de Cavallería* (Book of the Knightly Order), which a few years later inspired Don Juan Manuel to write his *Libro del Caballero y del Escudero* (The Book of the Knight and the Squire).[9] Llull's work, widely read even in translation, is a treatise on the duties and virtues of a knight that in part expands on and develops laws from the *Siete Partidas*. An old hermit who was a brave knight in his youth recites the knightly rules. An *escuyer*, a young knight or more precisely a "squire," comes to him on his way to a great tournament and receives instruction. The most important element of this instruction is the definition of the social function of the knight as the king's tool for police and military purposes. From this function follow his specific tasks: protection of the Church, of the king, and of lay society. As in the *matière de Bretagne*, the king is presented as being weak on his own[10] (even the king, by the way, has to earn the rank of knight, which he receives from a knightly order), and the knight is charged with the duty of defending the royal power as well as the rights of non-nobles and of the poor.[11] The knight is thus also an "escut" (a shield) between the "Rey et son poble" (the king and his people).[12]

If there is any trace of the courtly *aventure* ideal, it is in the exhortation that the knight must participate in tournaments in order to practice using weapons and to train himself in martial virtues.[13] The actual individual adventure, however, has clearly been relegated to the category of illegal robbery and ambush:[14] the most general and encompassing duty of the knight is to serve the general welfare. The knight must be "amador de be comu," must love the general welfare (for the reward of exemption from taxes).[15]

The *Hildalgo* and the Development of the Spanish Nation

In the fourteenth century the *Reconquista* became almost exclusively the affair of the inland state, Castile, since in that century both Portugal and Aragon/Catalonia were attending to the increasing development of their urban bourgeoisie and of sea trade. Especially Aragon/Catalonia, with its trade center, Barcelona, experienced a powerful economic and political advance: it conquered Tunis, established the dominion of the kings of Aragon over Sicily, occupied parts of Greece, set up trading posts in Asia Minor, and contended with the trade rivals in Pisa and Genoa. In Barcelona the trading bourgeoisie founded the *Counsell de Cent*[16] (the Council of a Hundred), and the *Corts* (the Estates General), but political and economic crises at the beginning of the fifteenth century forced Aragon/Catalonia to accept the rule of Castile despite bitter resistance on the part of the burghers, especially in Barcelona. This rule began with Juan II (1406–54) and was continued under Enrique IV (1454–74) despite considerable internal political difficulties. The accession to power of Enrique's sister Isabel, who was married to Fernando, king of Aragon, brought about the final political union of Spain.

Spanish unification and the development of the absolute monarchy occasioned significant economic progress in the second half of the century (merchant voyages, exportation of wool).[17] In this period, too, the *Reconquista* was concluded with the conquest of Granada in 1492. During this time the number of *hidalgos* or *caballeros* needed for military service had increased considerably. After the *Reconquista* was concluded, the absolute monarchy established, and the land restored to peace, the *hidalgos* were plunged into the same sort of crisis that knights in France had already largely weathered in the thirteenth century. Juan II had already elevated large numbers of peasants and craftsmen into the knightly class "so that the Cortes of Zamora in 1432 presented to the king the heavy burden on the tax-paying part of the population, if so many people were newly elevated into knighthood and thus received the privilege of tax exemption."[18] But Juan II needed the new knights in his battle with the rebellious feudal lords, and Enrique IV and Isabel and Fernando, *los Reyes Católicos* (the Catholic majesties), continued this policy, which was bound to lead the *hidalgos* into a great social dilemma. The kings (especially Isabel and Fernando who had themselves named Grand Master of the three knightly orders in Spain, thus winning direct command over Spanish knighthood) played the rising bourgeoisie of the cities and the knights off against the great nobles, but at the same time they used the *hermandades,*[19] the privileged burgher militia supported by the "Catholic majesties" to combat the knights in 1486 and 1488.

Tirant lo Blanc

During this period when non-nobles considerably swelled the ranks of knights and power was centralized at the royal court as a result, the question inevitably arose for the *hidalgos* as to their social function: either as soldiers in the army (of knights), which was made up in part of newly created *hidalgos*, or as courtiers. (It was no coincidence that among the writings of Don Enrique de Villena from the 1440s is his *The Art of Cutting with a Knife*, a treatise on courtly behavior.)

The attempt to influence or even halt the decline of the warrior knight that was beginning to become apparent and to create a new social position for the knight as a combination of individual warrior, soldier, military leader, and courtier is evident in the novel *Tirant lo Blanc*, written just at the turn of the century. This novel contains all the realism of the battle literature of the Castilian nobility, the *cantares de gesta*, as well as illustrating the standard of noble and courtly behavior for knights promulgated by Ramón Llull, whose treatise Martorell includes in the novel. It was a stroke of brilliance to transform the *Libre del Orde de Cavalleria* into the parent element of a novel that was designed to demonstrate the importance of the knight to the *republica*, to the "common good."[20] But—and this gives the novel quite tragic dimensions—it actually only demonstrates his fall. (It is not by chance that Cervantes admired this novel,[21] or that the protagonist, Tirant lo Blanc, dies an unknightly death at the end of the novel.)

Martorell extends the episode Llull created, the meeting between the old hermit and the young knight, into the past and the future: the hermit's life story is told up to the time he meets the young squire, and the squire's, that is Tirant lo Blanc's, story is then told up to his death. The book is designed as a summation and as a test: the idea of knighthood that the hermit presents (in the transcription of the *Libre del Orde de Cavalleria*) is the result of the knighthood in his story, and the life of the young knight Tirant lo Blanc is the attempt to realize the (ethical and social) accomplishments of knighthood in contemporary reality, to test them against reality. A fairy-tale-like fictionalization would thus have been diametrically opposed to the author's intention. He does, to be sure, know the *matière de Bretagne* and mentions for instance "les aventures de Lançalot,"[22] but he eschews all fairy-tale scenes in favor of the impressive realism that so pleased Cervantes.

Since *Tirant lo Blanc* is undoubtedly a political novel, its realism is more than understandable: one could hardly influence the fifteenth-century reality of war in Castile and Catalonia with stories of fairies and sorcerers. Martorell therefore constructs his novel from elements of contemporary Catalonian history, going up to the battle for Rhodes in 1444, to a point, that is, almost contemporary with the origin of the novel itself. The most important part of the structure—the theme of the conquest of Constantinople by Tirant lo Blanc, of the battles in Asia Minor and Africa that constitute the major part of the novel and thus of Tirant lo Blanc's life story—comes from the chronicle of Ramón Muntaner, who in 1302 was a member of the Catalonian army of adventurers that set forth under the leadership of Roger de Flor against their trading rival Genoa and against the Turks. The peace of Caltabellota, concluded in 1302, left this army without an occupation, "without the possibility of earning good pay or providing itself with rich booty that the war had given it."[23] Roger de Flor, a member of the Knights Templar, was therefore given permission by the king of Aragon to mount a pillaging expedition against the Turks that resembled in many respects the expedition of the Fourth Crusade described by Villehardouin. Martorell took Roger de Flor as the model for his Tirant lo Blanc and was perfectly aware of the army's materialistic motives as well as of the fact that that army was a wild bunch of soldiers rather than knights, who staged massacres and pillaged throughout Asia Minor. He tried to bring the reality into harmony with the ideal of courtly civilization. He used a variety of methods to accomplish this, but his basic idea is quite clear.[24]

Martorell is trying to justify the change from knighthood to a military soldiery by imputing to the old knights "modern" methods of battle: the old hermit not only had been a knight, but also had become a specialist in the ruses of war in his battles with the "infidels" (even though he had of course been forced into this by the baseness of the enemy). In one episode he takes over the leadership of his country (in Martorell's work, England) and its army of knights and attacks the (Islamic) aggressor with tricks, explosives, and mantraps (and atrocities at every turn). Martorell leads us from these "modern" martial tactics to a scene of "primitive" knighthood: a duel between the hermit/king/commander and the Islamic commander/king decides the war. After his victory in the duel the hermit returns to his solitude to serve God as his piety dictates and to study the ideal of knighthood. He then passes his knowledge on to Tirant lo Blanc. Tirant in turn, familiar with (Llull's) doctrine of knighthood, goes first to court, where he survives tournaments and duels, and then leaves England as the captain of a ship bound to liberate Rhodes. More and more knights join this voyage, including great lords like the son of the king of France and, somewhat later, even the king of Sicily. The story is of no further concern to us, but it is important that the knight-errant Tirant (a knight of the tournaments) becomes the leader of a mass army, conquers and exploits colonial possessions, and ends up as the Caesar of his empire ("Princip i Cèsar de l'Imperi grec"). The knight thus ceases to exist. That is also expressed in the fact that Tirant's love for Princess Carmesina remains unfulfilled and that Tirant dies of an illness in an unknightly way like a non-noble, a burgher, or—a king.

From *Hidalgo* to Soldier

Tirant lo Blanc is the last, desperate attempt "to assimilate the traditional knightly way of battle to the modern strategic way, but also to reconcile the claims of the ideal and the 'demands of life' and the new with the traditional."[25] But the realism of the presentation triumphs (as later in Balzac) over the probable intention of the author (whose partially ironic tone probably arises from the discrepancy between reality and the ideal, which he wants to bridge). The true reasons for contemporary waging of war could no longer be concealed: possession of land, exploitation, (sea) trade were the actual motives for wars that had nothing knightly about them in the sense of ideals and that had become mass battles fought by mercenaries. *Tirant lo Blanc* does not obscure these motives, and Martorell describes the battles in all their ferocity.

For the army of knights in the Spanish interior, for the mass of the *hidalgos* (in some areas half the population was *hidalgos*),[26] the novels of Martorell and Galba no longer offered any useful perspective.[27] The pillaging adventure,[28] once commonly practiced as a means of livelihood, was becoming less and less feasible with the increasing centralization and pacification of the country. Apart from that, the reconquest of Constantinople by the Turks, the development of competitive trade in other nations, and the resultant (albeit precarious) international balance all meant that pillaging expeditions like Roger de Flor's were also impossible. Instead of the plundering by motley armies of adventurers made up of all nationalities, there was now a power struggle among nation-states that necessitated another way of making war and an available mass army. Gonçalvo de Córdoba (1443–1515), called "El Gran Capitán," who conquered Naples in 1504 for the Spanish crown, laid the foundations for such an army in Spain. A large part of the unemployed knights was absorbed into this army.

What to Do with the *Hidalgos*?

"The hidalguía as an honor and a privilege of a warrior class had thus lost its meaning.... The craft of arms had become a mere means of making a living and was no longer compatible with the nobility's concept of honor and the ideas of the traditional social order."[29] Hence, it is not surprising that many *hidalgos* did not choose to become soldiers. Nor did many take advantage of the opportunity to give up the *hidalguía* and to start over as burghers.[30] In giving up the *hidalguía* the poor *hidalgo* would have been relinquishing his only privilege, exemption from taxes, without getting anything in return, because even within the bourgeoisie one could not rise without capital, nor could the social structure have absorbed the masses of knights. The existence of impoverished, unemployed masses of *hidalgos* thus became one of the most aggravating social problems of Spain in the late fifteenth, sixteenth, and seventeenth centuries. Even the creation of more and more civil service positions reserved for the *hidalguía* did not provide significant relief.

A *hidalgo* who prized his *hidalguía* had the possibility either of rising at court as a *cortesano*, a "courtier," or of the honorable but unbearable role of the nobleman without occupation who occasionally starved (of which the literature of the sixteenth and seventeenth century shows many examples). There was, of course, an enormous rush to the court, and with it (that is, with the development of the absolute monarchy), there arose the new Spanish ideal of the courtier, as propagated for instance by Antonio de Guevara (1480–1545) in his mirror for the prince, *Libro áureo del Emperador Marco Aurel* (The Golden Book of the

Emperor Marcus Aurelius).[31] But Guevara also saw the social problems that were emerging from centralization for the mass of the *hidalgos*, and hence for society at large. He dedicated an extensive commentary to them in which he united suggestions for a "practical" solution to the problem with the propagation of a new "noble" ideology: the *Menosprecio de Corte y Alabanza de Aldea* (Disparagement of the Court and Praise of the Village, 1539). The courtier Guevara embedded his advice in numerous moral observations. He discussed, for instance, the advantages of an active life over the disadvantages of a passive one, which necessarily led to melancholy[32]—a theme that will be very important for the whole era of the development of modern capitalism.[33] Against the background of general praise for the active life in the country, which has the advantage of being peaceful and healthy, Guevara's political intentions stand out clearly: "It is the advantage of the village that the hidalgo or the rich man who lives there is the best or one of the best among the good, which cannot be the case at court or in the large cities, because many others live there who are superior to him in wealth."[34] While life at court is expensive, he continues, life in the country offers economic advantages, because household costs and personal expenses, for instance, are less.[35] There is no need for a (courtly) servant or a squire,[36] and even with poor clothes the *hidalgo* would be more respected in the village than a noble in furs at court.[37] "I ask the readers of this work to take this to heart rather than laughing at it, because it is reasonable advice for the poor hidalgo to look for food mounted on an ass instead of for hunger on a horse."[38]

Who Does Not Cross the Sea Has No Adventures

Guevara's advice was not created from whole cloth. For one thing, as he was writing his treatise, sheep raising and hence the wool trade was flourishing; for another, not only numerous nobles but also numerous city dwellers were moving to the country;[39] but for either group, a minimum of capital was necessary, and even that was no longer enough when the great crisis of 1550 began in Spain. Thus, his advice was not capable of mitigating the situation in any major way, provided it was even followed.

Nor did the discovery and conquest of America bring much easing of the *hidalgo* problem. To be sure, along with shepherds and mercenaries, *hidalgos* "who had been ruined by large property-owners"[40] did go to America. They held the relatively few command posts there, or they tried to continue their existence as *caballero* adventurers without settling down and thus ensured the continuity abroad of the medieval Spanish knightly ideology.[41] But after 1560 at the latest this possibility was largely exhausted,[42] and the adventurer existence came to an end in this respect too, so that the Spanish proverb *Quien no se aventura, no pasa la mar* (Who dares nothing does not cross the sea—it probably arose at the time of the *Conquista*) could have been turned around to read Who does not cross the sea has no adventures, since apart from the few scant possibilities mentioned above, the only recourse in Spain was to enter a monastery or become a priest. That is not the least of the reasons for the enormous number of priests after 1570, who became a regular (equally unproductive) plague in the land, as writers like Quevedo point out.

The Waning of Knighthood and The Romance of Chivalry

The time of the development of the absolute monarchy, with all its consequences for knights (transformation into the military, development into *cortesanos*, the impoverishment of the *hidalguía*, emigration, becoming civil servants, becoming priests) is, in Spain as everywhere else, the time of the waning of knighthood, of the decline of the *caballero*. The *hidalgos* who were unable to adapt to the new circumstances were legion. It is exactly at this time (not surprisingly) that the *matière de Bretagne* was taken up and adapted in Spain; moreover, there was suddenly an enormous production of unrealistic, fairy-tale-like romances of chivalry, characterized by dragons and sorcerers, giants and fairies.[43] The loss of the real meaning of knighthood corresponds to the mass propagation of the fairy-tale-like ideal of the adventurer knight.[44] Garcí Ordoñes de Montalvo's famous *Amadís de Gaula* (1492) was both the first work in this genre and the most significant. It was followed by a flood of more or less important imitations, which are of no concern to us. They are all condemned in *Don Quijote*, in contrast to *Tirant lo Blanc* and to *Amadís* itself.

The fate of the protagonist, Amadís, is determined by the evil sorcerer Arcalaus and the good fairy Urganda, who stands by Amadís during his *aventuras*. Thus Amadís, whose birth was accompanied by unusual events, becomes largely the plaything of forces that dominate him and against which he cannot protect himself (a typical example of this is the chapter in which Amadís, put under a spell by Arcalaus and pronounced dead, is released from the spell, because a man like Amadís must not die in such a way; God would prefer that his "hand bring death to others who deserve it"). To quote the short and incisive analysis of Hans-Jörg Neuschäfer:

> In this way the hero . . . becomes so dependent on the magic of the good fairy that his aventure becomes a fairy tale; it also remains without a function, because of its lack of a goal, and seems largely to be only a game for the game's sake. The adventure is also without a function in the sense that it is no longer a mission on behalf of and for the glory of a feudal society that is firmly delineated and fixed in one spot, Arthur's court; instead, it is undertaken, as it were, on one's own account.
> Amadís thus no longer has a fixed "position" from which he leaves and

to which he could return at the end; he is only a knight-errant, always wandering in the world.[45]

If we recall that the year of America's discovery also signals the end of Spanish knighthood and hence of knighthood in general, the translation of the knightly adventure into the irrationality of the fictional literary fairy tale is an adequate and brilliant expression of a historical situation, which may have saved *Amadís*—and not only from the condemnation Cervantes reserves for its epigones. Even more interesting than the romances of chivalry themselves, however, is their echo; they spread in huge numbers throughout all European countries.

Chapter 3
The Counterrevolutionary Ideology of Knightly Adventure

The Spanish Knightly Romance

In his essay "The Peasant War in Germany," Friedrich Engels described with admirable clarity the fractionating of the various classes at the end of the fifteenth and the beginning of the sixteenth century. Although he was discussing specifically German conditions, the basic structure of the conditions he analyzed is representative for Europe in general (though always in their specific national form, which could vary significantly from the German, as the Italian and English forms did):

> The middle nobility of the medieval feudal hierarchy had almost entirely disappeared; it had either risen to acquire the independence of petty princes, or sunk into the ranks of the lesser nobility. The *lesser nobility*, or *knighthood*, was fast moving towards extinction. Much of it was already totally impoverished.... The development of military science, the growing importance of the infantry, and the improvement of fire-arms dwarfed the knighthood's military merits as heavy cavalry, and also put an end to the invincibility of its castles.... The knights' need for money considerably hastened their ruin. The luxury of their palaces, rivalry in the magnificence of tournaments and feasts, the price of armaments and horses—all increased with the development of society, while the sources of income increased but little, if at all. As time went on, feuds with their attendant plunder and extortion, highway robbery and similar noble occupations became too dangerous.... To satisfy their growing requirements, the gracious

knights had to resort to the same means as the princes. The peasantry was plundered by the nobility with a dexterity that increased every year. The serfs were sucked dry. . . . Justice was denied or sold for money, and when the knight could not get at the peasant's money in any other way, he threw him into the tower without further ado and forced him to pay a ransom.[1]

Even with the other estates, the princes, the clergy, and the cities,

the lesser nobility. . . [was] anything but friendly. . . . The knight. . . was continually at loggerheads with the towns, he was always in debt to them, he made his living by plundering their territory, robbing their merchants, and by holding for ransom prisoners captured in the feuds. And the knights' struggle with all these became the more violent the more the money question became to them as well a question of life.[2]

We have already seen that what Engels determines about the petty German nobility was all the more true of the *hidalguía* in Spain. It produced its corresponding polemical literature, which spread across all Europe like wildfire. For when we ask whose interests are represented by the literature of knightly adventure in the wake of *Amadís*, we can answer the question at least in the negative with some sort of precision. It is quite certain that this literature, which glorified the adventuring knights-errant (the *chevaliers errants*) and thus necessarily also the social behavior of the knighthood described by Engels, did *not* represent the interests of the peasants and the lower burghers. But even the urban burghers had trouble recognizing themselves in the knightly adventurer, and it must have been the same with the prince or the king.[3] Still, the attitude of the prince or king, as well as that of the clergy and of the bourgeois factions that were allied with the prince and the clergy, toward the modern ideology of knighthood must have been ambivalent, because the prince and the higher clergy were primarily concerned with playing the enemy classes off against each other or keeping the class oppositions in the most favorable balance possible:

As the state arose from the need to hold class antagonisms in check, but as it arose, at the same time, in the midst of the conflict of these classes, it is, as a rule, the state of the most powerful, economically dominant class, which, through the medium of the state, becomes also the politically dominant class, and thus acquires new means of holding down and exploiting the oppressed class.[4]

Of course, there were divergent, warring factions within the various classes; there were also alliances between factions of different classes. This was also true for the ideological expression of these diverging or converging class interests, even with respect to the ideology of the declining petty nobility, which created a vehicle for itself in the knightly adventure romance, among other things. Many scholars have become accustomed to viewing these knightly romances as remote from class struggles and class interests, considering them from an abstract, modern point of view as largely class-unspecific entertainment literature for an equally abstract (mass) public. But the same holds for the sixteenth-century ideology of knightly adventure as what Engels determined about the religious disputes:

> Even the so-called religious wars of the sixteenth century mainly con-
> cerned very positive material class interests; those wars were class
> wars, too, just as the later internal collisions in England and France.
> Although the class struggles of those days were clothed in religious
> shibboleths, and though the interests, requirements, and demands of
> the various classes were concealed behind a religious screen, this
> changed nothing at all and is easily explained by the conditions of the
> times.[5]

Although the theological differences between supporters of the Reformation and of the Counter-Reformation, between Protestants and Catholics, had completely different dimensions from the discussion about the knightly romances, still this discussion is by no means insignificant, since the fairy-tale-like shibboleth of knightly adventure cannot be separated from the religious disputes; rather, the battle about the knightly romances reached far into the internal church disputes. But as "German ideology" saw "nothing except violent theological bickering in the struggles that brought the Middle Ages to an end,"[6] scholarship up to the present (with notable exceptions) has seen the dispute about the knightly romance as nothing more than a controversy of taste involving humanists, neo-Aristotelians, visionaries, and moralists, or as an internal problem of literary genre.

Werner Krauss, in his "Die Kritik des Siglo de oro am Ritter- und Schäfer-roman,"[7] attempted a differentiated analysis of the reception of the knightly romance. We will not elaborate on this, but will merely try to place the reaction Krauss analyzes to the knightly (and pastoral) romance in relation to the fundamental class relations of that time. Spanish criticism will serve as a paradigm,[8] and we will have to abstract from the differences in ideological detail.

First: "It is understandable that the new worldly literature was first described without distinction as a Christian vexation," Krauss writes,[9] and one can supplement this idea with a quote from Engels.

> The *clergy*, that bearer of the medieval feudal ideology, felt the in-
> fluence of historic change just as acutely. Book-printing and the claims
> of growing commerce robbed it of its monopoly not only in reading
> and writing, but also in higher education.[10]

In the case of the knightly ideology of the sixteenth century, an additional factor was the fact that the alliance between the clergy and the knighthood, the two pillars of medieval feudal power, had weakened, and the petty or knightly nobility was now forced to look for worldly justification. That means the repression of the Christian ethic in favor of more worldly virtues, especially in favor of the (physical and spiritual) love between man and woman. To this extent, even the knightly romance had a progressive element, which was relativized, however, by the fairy-tale-like fictionalization. On the other hand, the clergy could not afford to break entirely with the petty or knightly nobility, since the factions it represented and especially its ideology reached all the way up to the courtly or great nobility. The church was clever in roundly condemning the knightly romance but never putting it on the Index;[11] instead, it even produced and disseminated clerical propaganda literature in the guise of knightly adventure.[12]

Second: While the Church condemned but did not ban the knightly romance, in 1531 King Charles V of Spain did forbid the export of knightly romances to America and their printing there, and in 1555 the *Cortes* (Estates General) called for a general ban in Spain as well. The romances already printed were to be recalled and burned.[13] In fact, though, the knightly romances were left completely unmolested. And that is quite comprehensible: while the knightly romances did not represent the interests of the absolute monarchy, the monarchy was interested in a compromise with, or the appeasement of, the petty nobility (which is of course especially true of Spain), particularly since civil servants were recruited from that class, and the knightly ideology had an effect on the ideology of the court nobles as well. From this perspective it is comprehensible that the knightly ideology found entrée into the courtly behavior and thought of the absolute monarchy (especially in Spain, but in France and elsewhere as well): in 1549, for instance, a knightly romance was presented before Charles V.[14]

Third: The judgment of the humanists, the learned representatives of the bourgeoisie, on the knightly romance was nearly unanimously negative; they did not ban the romance, however, because they were unable to. Their criteria for condemning it were primarily that reading knightly romances distracted one from active life in reality and led to a senseless waste of time and to untrammeled daydreaming and that the knightly romance violated the neo-Aristotelian principle of verisimilitude. The attitude that is here justified in terms of literary theory has its origin in class struggle: the bourgeoisie and the changes it had realized in the real world were barred from the knightly adventure romances. These romances were instead propaganda in the interest of another class and its allies; they produced a distorted, unrealistic image of the world, an image that was moreover shaped in such a way as to influence the masses and that was available to the masses through printing. It is obvious that this literature had an especially decisive political effect in Spain, where the bourgeoisie did not make the transition to modern industrial capitalism and suffered a serious crisis after 1550 from which it was very slow to recover.

Knight, Courtier, Hero

The flood of knightly adventure romances pouring over Europe called forth an equally massive resistance to them, nourished by various sources. Again, we will describe only a few stages of this development, which varies from country to country but is essentially determined by two poles: the bourgeoisie and the absolute monarchy, to which the ideology of knightly adventure was wholly or partially unacceptable. It is significant that the origin and high point of the modern ideology of knightly adventure occurs in the transitional period from feudal disruption to absolutist nation-states, to the beginning of the absolute monarchy. How virulent the petty nobility still was at this time is shown not least by the revolt of the nobles in Germany in 1522[15] and by the religious wars in France.

In Spain, however, things developed differently from the rest of Europe, on the basis of the defeat of the bourgeoisie in the second half of the sixteenth century. We have shown that the court of Charles V partially assimilated the knightly ideology; in this process the goal of appeasing and including the petty nobility in the bureaucracy of the absolute monarchy played a decisive role. Translated into Spanish in 1534 by Juan Boscán, the *Cortegiano* (*Book of the Courtier*) of Baldassare Castiglione (1528) played an important ideological mediating function here, blending the glorification of the (knightly) craft of arms with modern courtly views of life and love (with obvious influence by *Amadís*).[16] The *Cortegiano* is no longer a treatise on the courtly ideology of adventure;[17] rather, it is the draft of an ideal courtier whose dimensions, however, are determined by the Italian circumstances in which he exists. The reception of this work in other countries furnishes the courtier in each case with a specific, different function. Nonetheless, even in Spain it provides points of departure for an ideology of the knightly petty nobility as well as for the ideology of the absolute monarchy.

The ideal of humanity is no longer the knight-errant. Rather, this new ideal is based on the heroic warrior, the hero (who is then given attributes of the knightly as well as the humanist ideals). The model for this hero is no longer Lancelot or even Amadís, but is now Alexander or Achilles. To be sure, this hero is accepted only when he is of noble descent and, besides being skilled at arms, is at home in literature, music, and art, so that he can behave in a courtly fashion, for instance in the company of a noble lady.

There is no doubt that the *Cortegiano* provided an important ideological orientation in the formation of the (Spanish) court ritual, which could not continue to be shaped by the ideology of knightly adventure. The formation of the absolute monarchy necessitated a special genre, and not only in Spain, because the absolute monarch could no longer be glorified as King Arthur or as one of his knights-errant, or as an Amadís. The appropriate model came from neo-Aristotelian literary theory, although as a result of the social conditions in Spain, which lacked a strong bourgeoisie and so retained some of the stiff feudal class structure of the Middle Ages, this theory was not accepted everywhere and certainly not in the pure form one finds in France. (This model—interpretation in terms of Aristotelian-Horatian poetics—was also determined by social necessity.) The epic, on the pattern of Homer and especially of Virgil, seemed the only adequate genre for expressing the dignity and importance of the royal or even imperial head of state. A *Carolea* appeared two years after the death of Charles V, and six years later Luis Zapata wrote an epic clearly opposed to the knightly romance, *Carlos famoso* (The Famous Charles). The production of epics was to continue in Spain until far into the nineteenth century (!) and to inflame primarily literary theorists.[18] But until well into the seventeenth century, the epic and the knightly romance existed side by side, the one as an attempt to contribute to the glorification and stabilization of the Spanish monarchy (with much better results, incidentally, than for example in France), the other as the dream of a class which, condemned to end, cannot disappear because there was no decisive, revolutionary bourgeoisie to give it the death blow. Instead, the bourgeoisie became infected with the nostalgia of the *hidalguía* and dreamed lethargically of fairy-tale adventures.

The Tragic Adventure

The discovery of America temporarily alleviated Spain's social misery a little. But with the great crisis after 1550, the bourgeoisie lost its historical perspective. It began to imitate the nobility, bought land, and withdrew onto its holdings, out of the *vita activa* (active life), out of trade.[19] The glorification of adventure, whether it was a colonial adventure in America or—even a knightly adventure— in Spain, could now evoke only bitterness or irony. Along with the experience of the émigrés, the *Brevísima relación de la destrucción de las Indias* (*A Briefe Narration of the Destruction of the Indies by the Spaniards*, written 1542) by Las Casas had contributed substantially to this disillusionment, with its description of the atrocities that the Spaniards had committed against the Indians. Twelve years later, a short, anonymous novel, *La vida de Lazarillo de Tormes y de sus fortunas y adversidades* (The Life of Lazarillo Tormes and His Good and Bad Luck), appeared; literary histories still class it, quite incorrectly, as an adventure novel.[20] It is actually a dedicated antiadventure novel, because the adventures described in this novel in autobiographical form were not sought out voluntarily by an adventurer. They are blows of fate suffered by a beggar boy, by which he is pushed and pulled around: deceived, half starved, almost crippled by beatings. If they have any relationship to adventure, then only in the context of the reconstructed meaning of *ad-venture, that which simply befalls a passive person. Given the gap between the (good) intentions of Lazarillo the protagonist, who is the beggar boy and guide for the blind, and the (evil) adventures that befall him in the form of social injustice and inhuman treatment by his contemporaries, which force him into evil actions or to resignation, we can even say that Lazarillo's "adventures" belong more to what Kurt von Fritz has described as the "tragic"[21] than to any of the historical variants of adventure we have discussed.

Lazarillo, little Lazarus, is introduced as a representative of the lumpen-proletariat, one of the hundreds of thousands in the sixteenth century who were vegetating throughout Europe, but especially in Spain, and for whom there was no hope of liberation from their social misery before their transition into the proletariat. The "solutions" offered in the Spanish literature of this time are actually nothing of the kind. For the poorest of the poor, only inhuman possibilities are open: life as a beggar or a criminal (with the almost certain finish on the gallows), a hopeless emigration into the unknown (if at all), or—still the best solution by far—a lackey's existence in religious hypocrisy and moral shabbiness. Lazarillo at least gets that far. The anonymous author narrates as autobiography the fate of this person who, as a child in Salamanca, was given to a blind man as a servant or guide by his mother. The blind man has nothing better to do than to brutalize Lazarillo and to torture his human feelings out of him, treatment that he is made to suffer by all the other masters whose servant he becomes (especially by a priest, who beats him nearly to death).

The episode of greatest interest to us is his service with Escudero, an insignificant knight who belongs to the *hidalguía* and demands to be treated and respected as a *hidalgo*. This *hidalgo* is completely impoverished, so that Lazarillo has to become one of his beggars. Nothing shows the decline of the *hidalguía* better than the fact that, as in this doubtless not very unusual example, it has to rely on lumpenproletariat beggars to support it. Of course, a *hidalgo* cannot himself beg, since that would violate his honor, his *honra*.

This little novel takes place in a precisely pinpointed and named world; it contains nothing of the fairy tale; it precisely describes misery, hunger, and humiliation. Yet with astonishing stubbornness, scholars (among them prominent ones like Marcel Bataillon) have claimed over and over, and continue to claim, that it is not realistic, that it contains no sort of social commentary, that it is nothing other than a lighthearted literary work of art.[22] Anyone who calls this book lighthearted, as Marcel Bataillon does, "un livre pour rire" (a book to make you laugh),[23] must also find it lighthearted when, to name one of many similar episodes, the blind beggar hits Lazarillo in the face with a jug: "The blow was so hard that I lost consciousness, and the impact was so great that the shards of the jug which were forced into my face ripped it open in several places and broke off my teeth, which have been missing since."[24] He must find not only this and other attacks on a child lighthearted, but also murder, uninterrupted hunger, and constant humiliation. He must also find the end of the little novel lighthearted for Lazarillo becomes someone who announces the wines at meals and is allowed to marry the maid of a priest who sleeps with her: "That was my great time," the anonymous author has Lazarillo say, "and I had arrived at the peak of my happiness."[25]

It is surprising that Marcel Bataillon (in agreement with some critics, but in contrast to others) denies that *Lazarillo* is a critique of the prevailing conditions, because he knows the facts that clearly speak against this thesis. He knows that the country was in a deep economic and political crisis and that massive segments of the population were forced into beggary. He also knows that the unemployed, poor *hidalgos* were a social problem of the first order. His thesis that this is exclusively "a book to make you laugh" is based above all on the fact that the anonymous author of *Lazarillo* makes use of elements of the so-called popular farce, which prestructure certain eipsodes of the novel (but he never asks why these farces were produced and distributed).[26] This undeniable fact is, however, relatively unrevealing, because the anonymous author completely altered the farcical elements by placing them in a particular functional relation, turning them into an autobiographical report, and putting them in an exact context of time and place. The action takes place in Salamanca and Toledo, and the mentions of contemporary events point clearly to the reign of Charles V. The novel must have been taken as a political pamphlet when it was published, and the ban of 1559[27] shows that this was indeed the case. Bataillon's reaction here is again surprising. He dismisses this ban as immaterial, along with the fact that all subsequent editions of *Lazarillo* in Spain (but also in Catholic, as opposed to Protestant, Germany) were allowed to be published only in "expurgated" form.

To evaluate properly the political significance of the novel, we must ask who wrote it. Many suppositions about the author have been voiced; the thesis that he could have been a reform cleric, influenced by Erasmus or Protestantism, a thesis also held by Bataillon,[28] is thoroughly plausible. We will proceed here by negation: the author is not identical with the narrating protagonist Lazarillo because the lumpenproletariat is illiterate and the author is a highly educated man. Moreover, the author does not represent the *hidalguía* or the degenerate clergy of his time (even if he might belong to one or the other group, sociologically speaking, he does not represent their interests). On the other hand, it is hardly conceivable that the author seriously meant to represent the interests of the lumpenproletariat. The figure of Lazarillo is put forward by the author and his misery is used in order to articulate the interests of the only class that could overthrow or alter these corrupt conditions. Using the figure of Lazarillo, he succeeds in denouncing and unmasking certain classes and their morality, classes that stand in the way of social progress: the upper nobility as well as the commercial bourgeoisie are spared his criticism. Except for the blind beggar, the lords whom Lazarillo serves are all representatives of the lower clergy, the lowest lawcourt officials, and the *hidalguía*. Still, it is a fact of enormous importance that in the figure of Lazarillo at the same time the lowest of all classes, the forerunner of the proletariat, makes its literary entrance into world history. In this

parody of the knightly romance of adventure and the critique of its hero the
hidalgo by a representative of the lumpenproletariat, it becomes apparent for
the first time that for these precursors of the modern proletariat (just as later
for the modern working class), adventure and the ideology of (knightly) adventure are not weapons that can be used in the class struggle, in the struggle for
freedom. On the contrary, adventure and the ideology of (knightly) adventure
are exclusively inimical to those deprived of rights. Lazarillo's attempt is to escape
the adventures imposed by an inhuman society. But neither he nor his
anonymous creator can see how that is possible in his time.

The Optimistic Death of Don Quijote

The world in which Lazarillo is beaten, in which he suffers hunger, and in which
he searches for a place where he can manage even a minimally bearable life is
a world without perspective and optimism because the only class that could partially remove the poverty and revolutionize conditions, could spreach optimism
and the hope of liberation from misery—the bourgeoisie—is languishing. The
bourgeoisie is capable only of conformity with the Counter-Reformation's ideas,
as is already documented in the first "successor" to *Lazarillo, Guzmán de
Alfarache* by Mateo Aleman (1599-1604). The only options are the affirmation
of prevailing conditions or a utopian-reactionary critique of them in the glorification of times gone by, which were better, more knightly, and whose ethical and
social norms are portrayed as still valid. Or there are the options of resignation
and cynicism, as in Carlos García's *La desordenada codicia de los bienes ajenos*
(Slovenly Lust for the Possessions of Others, 1619)[29], or Quevedo's *Historia de
la vida del Buscón* (The Life of Buscón, written 1603-4, published 1626), or finally
of melancholy, as in the *Ingenioso Hidalgo Don Quijote de la Mancha* by Miguel
Cervantes Saavedra, 1600-15.

In *Buscón*, a representative of the poorest stratum of the population fails in
his attempt to rise to prosperity and social respectability in an honorable way,
is pushed by his opponents from higher classes into a criminal existence, and
finally emigrates to America in the company of a prostitute, without hope for
a better life. Don Quijote, on the other hand, Alonso Quijana from La Mancha, a representative of the impoverished *hidalguía*, undertakes unrealizable
adventures in Spain, batters himself bloody against social reality, and finally dies
of it. The melancholy of Alonso Quijana, who has to dream up a second existence
as Don Quijote because he can no longer bear his "wretched existence" (Werner
Krauss), is the melancholy of the Spanish people, condemned to inactivity, who
had buried their last hopes for great (naval) adventures with the defeat of the
Armada in 1588; it is actually the melancholy of the *hidalguía* and its
ideologues, but it is also—since Don Quijote's melancholy is of course also the
melancholy of Cervantes—the melancholy of the Spanish bourgeoisie.[30] As

Werner Krauss writes, "Next to the actual middle class, which was formed by the hidalgos, the Spanish bourgeoisie played no important role. With the closing of the Spanish manufactories, the economic power of the bourgeoisie was ended."[31]

Lazarillo survives in humiliation and in feigned agreement with his society, Buscón emigrates and knows that that will change nothing, but Don Quijote dies and begs the people, represented by Sancho Panza, for forgiveness because he, the *hidalgo*, has led them astray: "Forgive me, friend, for giving you cause to seem as crazy as I, when I let you commit the same error I did, that of believing that there were knights errant in this world."[32] On his deathbed Don Quijote reveals what he in truth has been: the ideologue of knightly adventure, the counterrevolutionary ideologue who—although in good faith—seduced the people. His death is the only gleam of hope in a melancholy world.[33] With his death also ends an epoch of useless dreaming, of social stagnation (or at least it was supposed to end). What remains when the dream is finally over, after Don Quijote has died, except the illusion-free affirmation of the real world, of active life?

The Hero in No-Man's-Land

When Baltasar Gracián was writing his novel *El Criticón* in 1661-67, Spain's economic and political decline was sealed with the fall of Portugal, the rebellion of Catalonia, and the independence of the Netherlands settled in the Peace of Münster in 1648. Like Cervantes, Gracián introduces a traveling pair of friends (but for good reason, Gracián has dropped the master-servant relationship; it would never have occurred to him to make the people the protagonist of one of his works). Critilo and Andrenio travel through Spain, Italy, France, and Germany, and Gracián uses the basic pattern and the narrative strategy of the Greek-Byzantine or picaresque novel to portray their journey. To be sure, the correspondences with the Greek novel are only formal and external: in reality this is an antiadventure novel, whose goal is clear before the journey begins: "Critilo and Andrenio," as Karl Borinski writes, "are ... theoretical spirits, that is, neither Eulenspiegels nor 'problematic natures.'... They do not travel on for the sake of adventure, but they are simply traveling through the world, through life."[34] To be precise, it is a journey through the soul of a human being, and thus it is not a journey at all (although the adherence to concrete historical data like the voyages of discovery of overseas trade run counter to this abstraction), but rather an attempt at a complete unmasking of a human being, the laying bare of all human weakness and baseness. It combines praise of the past with condemnation of the present; the present is like a jungle in which the human being has to struggle against his fellows for his life, "because everyone is a wolf to his fellows."[35] "Believe me," Critilo says to his friend and protégé Andrenio, "There is no wolf, no lion, no tiger, no basilisk, who is as bad as man: he surpasses them in savagery."[36]

All human vices are allegorized or brought as exempla by Gracián in his *Criticón*. All wickedness, all crimes, all social injustices are derived from this endless catalogue of vices, from the spiritual defects of the human being. This gives the novel a sterile, abstract character, despite its detailed inventory of human vices and their effects on human social life. It is not the position of the concrete human being in society, not the real economic and political (class) struggle, that decides the moral and social qualities of the human being and the position Gracián or his protagonists take on them. Instead, abstract moral ideas provide the foundation for judging and condemning an equally abstract human being, unspecified as to class and fundamentally depraved.

Gracián's worldview can be explained only by the economic and political situation of Spain, or more precisely, by the lack of a political power on which to base optimism. The hopes he placed in the Spanish monarchy, in Felipe IV, in his early writings had vanished in the face of Spain's crises and defeats. The only power that could have halted Spain's fall, the rising bourgeoisie, was as good as nonexistent in Spain. Gracián treats the bourgeoisie only from the point of view of their regrettable mercenary spirit, their greed, and their soul-deadening wealth. He was by no means indifferent to the unequal distribution of property, the growing wealth of the rich at the expense of the poor—on the contrary;[37] but from the perspective of eternity, of religion, of the human soul, he is not too concerned about this: Fortuna, who can see,[38] has the function of divine providence, the poor man will be rewarded in the afterworld (only the attitude of the pitiless rich is outrageous), and the true Christian in any case puts little value on material possession. Indeed, only in poverty, especially when it results from the loss of prior wealth (as in the case of Critilo himself), can the human being change from an animal ruled by vicious drives to a human being, a *persona*.[39] "The blessings of poverty made up for the bad luck that wealth brought me," says Critilo to Andrenio. "I can truly say that, because in poverty I found wisdom, which I had never before known. . . . I began to read, I began to know, and to be a human being [*persona*], because up to that time I had led not a reasonable life [*vida racional*], but a bestial one."[40]

Gracián's condemnation of the striving for possession is categorical: in money, in wealth and luxury he sees the basic evils of his time. He goes beyond the abstract condemnation of wealth itself that is found in the Bible and in Christian teachings in general and sees the striving for possession in the perspective of the history of nation-states, although he does not penetrate to the actual economic laws governing Spain's decline. Or rather, because he does not penetrate to these economic laws, he can come to this special condemnation of wealth and the striving for possession. For on the surface, historical events seem to prove him right. He sees that Spain arrived at its unity and greatness before wealth, before gold and silver from America were brought to Spain and began to determine its policies. With the politics of power based on gold and silver, however, Spain's decline also began (just as Critilo's moral decline occurs as a result of his colonial possessions in America). This also explains the fact that Gracián transferred his hatred of the powerful man perverted by greed for wealth to the huge mass of the poor, the *populacho* or *vulgo*, as he says.[41] For is it not precisely the poor who strive to better their material situation instead of bearing their poverty with equanimity and spiritual virtue (as did the moral apostle Gracián, who still had enough, however, to live on)? Thus, their souls are already stained with greed and spoiled, which is all the more dangerous since they are just the ones ready to take risks, because they have nothing to lose.

Gracián does not look to Sancho Panza; his hope does not rest in the people, whom he fears.[42] Instead, his glance does not go beyond the swamp of the metropolis of the Spanish monarchy, dominated by the life at court. He describes it subtly and devastatingly (including the *hidalgos* who have come down in the world, the "Gentilhombres o Escuderos").[43] The positive ideal of humanity which he opposes to the (abstract) human being of his time, a wolf among wolves, is gleaned from an idealized past. *Gigantes*, "giants," and *pigmeos*, "pygmies," are categories that come up again and again: the modern human being (in Spain at that time and in Gracián's view) is sometimes a giant in outward appearance, but a pygmy in the realm of the spiritual—or the other way around;[44] the harmony between body and soul, external appearance and inner disposition, even the harmony between practice and Christian worldview, has been lost. The actual giants disappeared with the heroic age in which kings themselves still fought with the sword instead of leaving it to deputies, "for it makes a great difference whether the master fights or the servant."[45] At that time society, according to Gracián, was still masculine. But now, "men are weak and effeminate,"[46] "the generals of today" go about "dressed in taffeta" and disperse "sword-blows made of silk."[47] "How short-lived was bravery in this world," Andrenio cries out, and learns that one reason for this was a poison, a powder: gunpowder.[48]

Compared to the heroes of the past (especially in Spain), El Cid, King Jaime, Fernando the Catholic, Charles V (the "non plus ultra of all emperors"),[49] or even compared to a Cortés,[50] the illustrious men of the present seem to be mere shadows[51] who allow Spain to bleed to death (especially to the advantage of France).[52] As a clear criticism of the conditions of the time of Felipe IV, Critilo stands before the wheel of time and waits for "those famous Fifths" to appear again

who were praised and admired throughout the whole world: a Don Fernando V, a Charles V, a Pius V. I hope this happens and a Don Felipe V appears in Spain. And if he is born, what a great king he will have to be, uniting in himself all the bravery and wisdom of his predecessors. But unfortunately it is certain that all the evils come around before improvement.[53]

For Gracián, true heroism, based on wisdom, justice, and bravery, has vanished from the world, has even become contemptible. When Critilo and Andrenio enter immortality at the end of their life's journey, they see the true heroes of the past like Roland and El Cid, who hold their eyes shut.[54] Critilo and Andrenio, however, had followed the path of "outstanding virtue, heroic bravery," and had come to true "glory, to the throne of respect and to the center of immortality."[55]

But who were or are Critilo and Andrenio? This is the real problem of Gracián's teachings on virtue: Critilo, the purified social human being, and Andrenio, the natural human being who is aware of the baseness of the world (*desengañado*), form a unity: the heroic wise man, the—if one were to translate it into the language of our time— incorruptible intellectual, the *ingenio agigantado*.[56] The ideal of the abstract human being Gracián creates by negation is not a heroic ideal that can be realized by the ruler or the nobility, and least of all by the bourgeoisie (quite apart from its specific situation in Spain). It is the stoic-Christian ideal of virtue of the intellectuals of his time, of the *culto varon* (the enlightened man) who sees through the world, does not close his eyes to its corruption and its dangers but instead, masculine and brave, defying the dangers among the wolf-men, travels the path to his own integration, to his *perfección*,[57] with military cleverness. The writings of Gracián are a strategic guide for this hero's struggle in the modern world, which for him is fundamentally without perspective except for himself. Werner Krauss has correctly pointed out that it would be a mistake to dismiss Gracián simply as a reactionary (and thereby to atone for the sins of his exegetes in the nineteenth century).[58] As a gifted critic of his time, he is part of the militant forefront of humanism, mobilizing and militarizing the spirit against the corruption of a decaying feudal absolutist system.[59] If he shifts the perspective on the struggle to the interior of the heroically wise human being and draws the measure of this human being from the idealized past, that is because Spanish reality allowed, or seemed to allow, no other perspective. Gracián's pessimism corresponds to the general lack of orientation in Spain. His ideal for humanity, remote from life and unviable, is at home in the no-man's-land of the class struggle (he is not a petty-bourgeois ideologue—there was no petty bourgeoisie in Spain at that time—although the petty-bourgeois ideologues of the nineteenth century were to use his ideologemes, from masculinity right up to the praise of being without possessions, for their own purposes). And this ideal is serviceable neither for the reactionary powers of the feudal absolutist monarchy nor for the rising bourgeoisie (to say nothing of the people, the peasants, the craftsmen, the manufactory workers). "The people get in his way as a destructive force, incomprehensible in their stupidity," Werner Krauss writes. "Thus the exemplary nature of the heroic human being has lost its roots in the original power of existence from the very beginning. It needs some kind of transcendence, an irradiation by otherworldly powers, in order to assert itself at this remove from the people."[60] As early as 1637, in his treatise *El Héroe*, Gracián had given an unmistakable indication that this ideal could not be realized: "To be a hero of the earthly world is little or nothing; but a hero of heaven is a great deal."[61]

If Gracián's ideal was without respect to the real powers of his people in Spain, it was completely unserviceable anywhere (as in France or England) that the bourgeoisie was opening the perspective on revolutionary changes (as it was also for the representatives of the feudal absolutist monarchy, which explains Gracián's relatively minor importance for the ideological debates of the seventeenth and eighteenth centuries[62] or his complete condemnation by the forces of the Enlightenment). The bourgeoisie first had to overcome the nobility and produce the industrial proletariat before liberated petty-bourgeois ideologues, from their own new lack of perspective, could mistakenly glimpse in Gracián a kindred spirit and precursor. Instead of his good Christian conscience, his heroic despair, and his angry criticism, we now have the shabby apologetics of an oppressed class that used the refashioned ideologemes of Gracián to decorate itself as pseudohistoric adventurers.

Chapter 4
The Adventurous Prince

The Birth of the *Condottiere*

For a wide variety of reasons, Italy contributed relatively little to the formation of an original, specifically Italian variant of the *knightly* ideology of adventure: from the *Reali di Francia* to Boiardo's *Orlando innamorato* and Ariosto's *Orlando Furioso* to Torquato Tasso's *Gerusalemme liberata* or his *Goffredo,* everything produced in Italy is an Italian adaptation of French heroic epics or knightly romances. The basic development of Italian literature is carried on by bourgeois-humanist forces, which quite early had developed, as the novellas of Boccaccio show, a literary means for creating a realistic presentation of the world and of themselves.[1] The human being is beginning to separate himself from the hierarchical medieval structure of *ordo* and to design his own, individual life: "Such a possibility of choice was present neither for the cat in the exemplum nor for Alexius (both automatically follow their destiny), nor even for the courtly knight," as Hans-Jörg Neuschäfer writes. "Thus in Boccaccio's novellas, the human being receives an unprecedented degree of moral freedom, but also has to assert himself in this freedom and answer for himself."[2] The precondition for this development, as well as for Italy's contribution to the formation of the modern ideology of adventure, is the development of the Italian cities and Italian commercial capitalism. Because of its special situation, which we cannot describe in detail here (such as the investiture battle between the Pope and the Emperor and the political splintering of Italy), as early as the thirteenth century a group of city-states, including Genoa and Venice, Milan and Florence, had formed in Italy. What kept Italy, however, from following a path like England's to modern capitalism was the lack of a central (royal) power, the formation of the nation at the end of the Middle Ages.

> To be sure, during the entire Middle Ages there was a great discrepancy between linguistic boundaries and national boundaries; but with the partial exception of Italy, each nationality was represented by its own large state in Europe, and the tendency to establish nation-states, which emerges ever more clearly and consciously, forms one of the most essential levers for progress of the Middle Ages.

Thus writes Engels, analyzing the role of the central state power in forming the modern world. He continues:

> In each of these medieval states, the king alone was at the peak of the entire feudal hierarchy, a peak which the vassals were unable to do without and against which they were also in a state of permanent rebellion. . . . That is the reason for this century-long alternation of the vassals' attraction to the royal center, as the only force that can protect them from external threats and from each other, and their repulsion from the center, which that attraction constantly and inescapably becomes; that is the reason for the constant struggle between throne and vassals, whose tedious din drowns out everything else for that whole long time when plundering was the only source of income worthy of a free man; that is the reason for that endless, ever regenerating series of betrayal, assassination, poisoning, treachery, and every conceivable vileness that hides behind the poetic name of knighthood and speaks incessantly of honor and loyalty. It is obvious that in this general chaos, the throne was the progressive element. It represented order in the midst of disorder, the emerging nations over against the disintegration into rebellious vassal states. Every revolutionary element that developed beneath the surface of feudalism was just as dependent on the throne as the throne was on it.[3]

As one can assume from Engels's indication that Italy is an exception, things did not come to such a pass there. The cities were at war with the princes and with each other and were competing against each other, and in this battling the power of commercial capitalism, which had developed early, constituted a crucial basis for the general anarchy. There was on the one hand competition for markets, on the other the uncertainty of trade routes, and the bourgeoisie, which determined the rise of the cities, tried to secure markets and trade routes. At first they themselves, armed and surrounded by armed men, accompanied the goods transports on land and on water, but soon they transferred the military function of guarding the goods to their agents. Yves Renouard writes:

> Repeated armed encounters disturb the trading companies: . . . In the fourteenth century the businessmen stop wearing swords and enroll-

ing... in the city militia. They decide to wage wars, they finance wars, but they do not engage in them any longer in person. Even those among them who are of noble birth have lost the taste for using arms.... Is it not more reasonable and economical ... to finance mercenaries, who fight while the merchants are active in their offices, earning the money to pay them? This is the system of *condotta:* the businessman ... created the condottiere: these two opposite and complementary human types characterize Italian society of the sixteenth century.[4]

But soon these *condottiere* become a regular plague on the land, as leaders of the mercenary armies which were sometimes brought over the Alps to Italy:

The mere existence of the [mercenary] companies constituted a constant incitement to war and devastation, because they wanted to make a living and even to accumulate riches and treasures, and when they were not able to do that in the service of a particular master, then they would do it on their own.... Other countries, to be sure,... saw the beginnings of the same phenomena, but the power of the state was still so strong there that they could not develop properly.[5]

We will not pursue this in detail; but it is certain that the *condottieri* did not simply remain the leaders of gangs or mercenaries, but rather—and this is a particularly Italian phenomenon, which was able to develop only because of Italy's political splintering—they seized power in some city-states and were able to become dukes (like Francesco Sforza in Milan in 1450).

The *Condottiere* as Prince

Niccolò Machiavelli, in his famous work *Il Principe* (The Prince; first edition 1513), analyzes and bemoans this state of affairs:

Before Charles, King of France, passed into Italy, this province was under the imperium of the Pope, the Venetians, the King of Naples, the Duke of Milan, and the Florentines. These potentates had to have two principal cares: one, that no one among themselves seize more states. Those of whom they had to take the most care were the Pope and the Venetians. And to restrain the Venetians, all the others had to unite, as occurred in the defense of Ferrara. The Roman barons served to keep the Pope down, and since they were divided into two factions, the Orsini and Colonnas, there was always a cause of disruptions between them. But standing with arms in hand before the eyes of the pontiff, they kept the pontificate weak and infirm.[6]

One cause of this divisiveness in Italy, which made it possible for foreign powers (Charles VIII, Fernando the Catholic, and others)[7] to attack Italy and in part to subjugate it, was, in Machiavelli's justified opinion, the mercenary system:

> I should not have to work very hard to persuade anyone of this point, for the ruin of Italy today is caused by nothing other than her reliance for many years upon mercenary arms.... I wish to demonstrate better the infelicity of these arms. Mercenary captains are either men excellent in arms or they are not. If they are, then you cannot trust them, because they will always aspire to their own greatness, by either oppressing you, their patron, or by oppressing others quite contrary to your intentions; but if the captain is not virtuous, you are ordinarily ruined.[8]

The only proven means of avoiding this dilemma is, according to Machiavelli, that

> a prince ought in person to take the office of captain; a republic has to send her citizens—and when it sends one who does not prove a worthy man, it ought to replace him, and when he is worthy, keep him within the laws so he does not overstep the mark.[9]

In Italian reality, however, the mercenary captain, the *condottiere,* is kept in bounds neither by a strong prince or king nor by a strong city republic. Machiavelli cites example upon example, among which especially Francesco Sforza and Cesare Borgia occupy a prominent place.

Machiavelli did not, however, leave things at a diagnosis and a lament. What Marx calls his "penetrating Italian genius" proved itself in the fact that his method was dialectical or at least constantly tended toward real dialectics.[10] Machiavelli's negative assessment of Italian conditions is not simply a negation. On the contrary, in a dialectical sublation of certain qualities present in Italian conditions and of the general political constitution of Italy and its *condottiere* system, as well as of other political constitutions (for instance, the absolute monarchy in France or Spain) and their system of organization and worldview, Machiavelli drafts a conception of political sovereignty whose advantages and disadvantages lie in its realism. He takes from the *condottieri* system the fundamental political qualities of the ruler who would be able to guarantee the unification of Italy Machiavelli himself desired and hence would also guarantee the rise of the bourgeoisie to the modern forms of its existence. But Machiavelli's basic error is that while he sometimes recognizes and states that the historical development is characterized by class struggle,[11] he does not consider class struggle to be the actual motor of that development but instead sees the course of history as dependent on the will of the (great) individual.

The ideal of the ruler, the *principe,* that he develops does, therefore, certainly contain the traits of the "great adventurer" that a modern follower of Burckhardt saw in him.[12] But it also contains traits of the great prince or the absolute monarch; more, it contains traits of the settled urban burgher and even of the knight. This is all quite appropriate given the internal condition of Italy, but it makes this mirror of the prince relatively unsuited for use outside Italy (and we should remember that even in Italy, Machiavelli's work had no practical application). Machiavelli's public spirit, which is directed toward knowledge of the real world and toward praxis, comes through again and again, "omitting, then, the things about an imagined prince, and discussing those which are true."[13] Among the things which are true for him is this knowledge, which an ideologue of the system of knighthood, of feudal nobility, or of the absolute monarchy would never have formulated in this way: "For one sees in the things that conduct them to the end that each has before him, that is to say, glory and riches, that men proceed there variously."[14]

The prince to whom Machiavelli gives his general and concrete sympathy is the ruler who has risen from the ranks of the bourgeoisie, who has seized his power: his work is dedicated to Lorenzo di Medici, who began his rule in Florence in 1513. His family had begun its rise as a rich merchant family in the thirteenth century. But more important than the individual origin of one of its rulers was the general political constitution of Italy: the fusion of bourgeoisie and princely aristocracy seemed to Machiavelli to offer especially favorable preconditions for the establishment of a modern, centralized Italy (and this is the most important reason why his treatise was not useful outside Italy).

The individual qualities of the prince that Machiavelli draws up are determined by the striving for glory and riches that he imputes to every human being and by the real governing practice of the Italian potentates; since Machiavelli lets himself be guided by the fact that the *condottiere* are fighting men, he sees the most important quality as the individual ability of the prince himself to conduct war or battles. But this is another reason why his treatise could not be used in the development of the modern state: the absolute monarch can no longer wield a sword himself, let along personally study battle and field technology, as Machiavelli recommends (the ruler should do everything, even "choose encampments, lead armies, prepare the order of battle").[15] In this case, where he allows himself to be influenced by the system of knighthood (or by the fact that the *condottiere* are fighting men), Machiavelli is clearly facing backwards, which shows not least in his demand that the king, in contrast to the burgher, should train himself athletically (for instance by hunting).

In contrast to these useless suggestions (useless with respect to the power politics of an absolute monarch and the formation of a nation-state) is Machiavelli's farsightedness about the standing army, which he considers a necessary prerequisite for executing the policies of the prince. It is noteworthy that he correctly considers Charles VII of France as the founder of modern army policy and believes that it was foolish to abolish the infantry (of *Francs-Archers*) again. *The Prince* is thus riddled with contradictions: on the one hand, Machiavelli polemicizes against the fact that the mercenaries are unreliable adventurers, but he makes the adventuring spirit of the mercenary captain an integral part of the prince's praxis in conquest and governing. He tries to stabilize this anarchic element by attempting to integrate decisive characteristics of the absolute monarchy into his ideal government, which shows especially in the propagation of the standing army and of the power politics of the nation-state. As a consequence of these fundamental contradictions, he includes further heterogeneous elements from the bourgeois and knightly forms of existence in the ideal construction of his prince, of whom one can say that he is supposed to unite the function of an absolute monarch with those of a *condottiere* adventurer, a profit-mad commerical burgher, and a knight proficient in tournaments and hunting. It is in the nature of things and also in the nature of the real power relations in Italy that the ethical systems originating in and corresponding to various social realms have little relevance for this contradictory figure. Machiavelli is so realistic here that in this respect as well his treatise was useless for his contemporaries in England, France, and Spain. Machiavelli's radical thought must have been as unacceptable to the absolute ruler as to the bourgeoisie, which needed the absolute ruler in order to develop in this epoch:

> You ought to know, then, that there are two kinds of fighting: one
> with the laws, the other with force. The first one is proper to man; the
> second to the beasts; but because the first proves many times to be
> insufficient, one needs must resort to the second. Therefore it is
> necessary for a prince to know well how to use the beast and the
> man.[16]

This idea, which Machiavelli intended as a (dialectical) reflection on the role of force in history, will not be seen as valid until the epoch of imperialism, when it is accepted as an (undialectical) "philosophical-anthropological" principle. It then receives a validity that Machiavelli neither could nor wanted to give it: Mussolini, the *Duce,* tried to legitimate his rule by deriving it from the pseudo-Machiavellian *condottiere* prince.

Chapter 5
The Business of the Adventurer

The Economic Adventure

Scholarship has ignored the fact that the *chevalier* of the courtly romance who goes out to look for *aventure* does not hit on the idea of calling himself *aventurier*, "adventurer."[1] This is of course not surprising because, as we have established, the glorification of *aventure* in the courtly romances of the twelfth and thirteenth centuries was only a pretext. What was really sought after was the opposite, a secure society, peace, and order—basically the bureaucratization of the court (hence the constant appeals to the *largesse*, the generosity, of the king).

Let us return once more to the concept of *aventure*. Elena Eberwein says, with respect to her own definition of the concept of *aventure* in the *Lais* of Marie de France: "Not only did I have to make a selection among the purely lexicographical choices: for instance, purely legal meanings were not considered, because they would in part have led too far afield, or in part they contributed nothing new."[2] Whether these are her actual reasons (and their dubiousness becomes obvious when one considers that she, like the other interpreters of the courtly ideology of *aventure*, did not even test whether the "legal" meaning was sometimes joined with the non-"legal"), or whether she did not simply leave out other meanings of *aventure* so as not to threaten the balance of her own interpretation, her repeated and furious attacks on Frédéric Godefroy[3] call her motives into question. Godefroy's selection of examples of *aventure* in his *Dictionnaire de l'ancienne langue française* is, to be sure, one-sided, but it is of particular interest to us because his examples are almost exclusively of legal or economic meanings, with the first examples going all the way back to the late thirteenth century. Alongside the meaning of "output, earnings, income"

("Tous les droiz, *aventures,* emolumenz, seignouries," 1305; "Et tous les profiz, esploiz, *aventures,* et esmolumanz du dit cenz ou rente," 1345), the word *aventure* also occurs with the meaning of "catch, booty, or harvest," which is to be expected (Godefroy circumscribes this meaning himself, somewhat inexactly, with "produit éventuel"): "Aulcuns pescheurs avoient jectet en mer leurs roits, ung illec present acheta l'*aventure* de ce cop" [Some fishers had cast their nets in the sea; one of them who was present bought the (expected) catch]. Or: "Dont acheta l'*aventure* future des oliviers" [(he) bought the expected olive harvest].[4]

Of course, we must guard against overhasty conclusions, but we may still determine that it is unlikely that at this time, when the ideology of the knight adventurer was still in the very center of courtly thinking and courtly production of romances, that is, when it was still weighted down with all the ideological ballast of meaning, the term should suddenly be used in a sense which seems to contain nothing at all of the courtly ideology (and which in fact contains nothing of it), unless it had already long been used in this sense. That *aventure* is first attested in a literary text (and hence also in a literary context) that has nothing to do with legal or economic terminology is simply a result of the fact that legal texts were written in Latin until the year 1200. Only after that were legal or "economic" texts composed in the vulgate as well. Thus it seems probable that *aventure* in this sense was already in use in colloquial language. Despite all theories about *eventus,* etc., I believe that this is the original meaning, since it is difficult to see why an **ad-ventura* would have had to be invented when *eventus* already covered the meaning. This conviction is strengthened by the fact that *aventure* in the sense of "yield, profit, or booty" not only coincides completely with the way the knight adventurers earned their living, but also could throw some light on many obscure examples of *aventure* in courtly literature.[5] It cannot be denied that *aventure* could have this meaning at least in the literature of the Crusades; we saw this in the case of Villehardouin.

Li borjois chevalier

It is probable that the existence of *aventure* in a legal and economic sense (or in the sense of booty, catch) and the simultaneous idealization of *aventure* in the courtly sense delayed the origin of the concept *aventurier* or at least impeded the acceptance of this term in courtly literature; but there is not currently enough documentary evidence to decide the question. It is, however, noteworthy that the first attestations all come from the fifteenth century, when the term crops up not only in French, but also in German (*ofenthürer* and similar words), in Spanish and Italian (*aventurero, avventuriero*), and in English as well ("adventurer"). The term never refers to a knight, but instead (in a pejorative sense) to a bandit and (in a positive sense) to a soldier or—and this will be our main focus of interest—a merchant.

Compared with England, where the concept "adventurer" indicates a new epoch of humanity, the use of the concept *aventurier* for merchant is relatively infrequent in France; this must be seen as a result of social conditions. Let us return again to the time of the courtly ideology of adventure and remind ourselves how aggressive the courtly ideologues were against *li vilains* or *li borjois*; we explained this aggression on the basis of class oppositions. This hostility vis-à-vis the bourgeoisie began at the moment when they began to pass the petty nobility in economic and partly also in political importance, at the moment when the (petty or knightly) nobility had, except for its knightly military abilities, nothing more to throw in the balance than its courtly ideology. It began the battle for a worldview against the bourgeoisie, which to be sure had many facets and was certainly not present in all (literary) documents.

The epic *Le Moniage Guillaume* (William's Monkhood), for instance, part of the William cycle—the *chansons de geste* about William of Aquitaine (d. 812) who fought the Arabs in the south of France and in Spain among other things—was written in 1180, at the same time as the courtly romances of Chrestien de Troyes. It contains important scenes which blatantly contradict the courtly antibourgeois passion. In the fish market, a free burgher ("un frans bourjois") spots William, disguised (and derided) as a monk, and invites him to eat with him at home. If William accepts the invitation, the burgher says, he would feel greatly honored ("jou meisme en serai honorés"). William and his servant (Famulus) go along ("voluntiers et de gré"—"with greatest pleasure"), are shown lavish hospitality, and want to pay after the meal, which greatly angers their host ("mout en est aires"). He had recognized William despite his monk's habit and explains that he himself had received many blessings from William and is now happy to be able to help William in turn. William then calls him "brave and wise" and makes himself fully known. When he leaves, he thanks his host for the honor ("ounor") he has done him with the invitation. The burgher offers to accompany him to protect him from bandits: "G'irai o vous, se vous le comandés" (I will go with you, if you order it), but William does not allow this.[6] This scene shows a different relation to the bourgeoisie, which also corresponds to historical reality: the good relation between prince or king and the rich urban bourgeoisie. The *frans borjois* is the burgher whom the king plays off against the refractory feudal nobility and who managed to prevail despite attempts by the nobles to contain him. There is another scene as important as the one between William and the free urban burgher, one in which Landris, William's cousin, poses as a merchant shipper and probably functions as one as well. To the heathen king Synagon, who has captured his ship, he explains:

> Lord, I will not lie to you. We are traveling over the sea to Sicily and
> live from our wares, from the silk cloth and materials from Almería.
> We often sell alum, Brazil wood, and wax, . . . cinnamon, incense, and
> licorice, pepper and caraway and other good spices. We are
> merchants.[7]

Although Ernst Robert Curtius goes too far in claiming that Landris *is* a merchant,[8] he did recognize the importance of this scene, which together with the one mentioned above proves that there was also a noble probourgeois ideology opposed to the courtly antibourgeois ideology: Landris has absolutely no moral scruples about passing himself off as a sea trader and acting as one. This would not occur to a "conservative" courtly knight.

These two scenes characterize the two essential poles of the positive relations between king / great nobility and bourgeoisie: while the king at first enters into a relation of positive interest with the urban bourgeoisie,[9] the Crusade nobility forms an alliance with the sea traders, which is exactly what happened in historical reality. From the early Middle Ages, the Mediterranean was aswarm with merchant voyagers and trading companies,[10] on which the Crusaders were dependent from the very beginning for transport and nourishment. Very soon the crusading knights and the shippers joined together or the knights themselves took over the function of the shippers, turned into ship captains and merchants—a process that we can read most impressively in the texts of Villehardouin and Martorell, which we have excerpted earlier: "If the Crusaders are the great losers in the Christian expansion of the twelfth century," writes Le Goff, "then the great winners in the end are the traders, who ventured ever further from their western point of departure."[11] Nobles had a share in this (especially the urban aristocracy of Italy, but also that of Catalonia); and many burghers rose via the shipping trade into the ranks of the nobility.[12]

The position of the front is by no means as clear as Italo Siciliano claimed in 1968.[13] In judging the relations between the bourgeoisie and the nobility, the various factions must be carefully distinguished and judged in a differentiated way. The greatest hostility was doubtless found where the king played off the urban bourgeoisie against the feudal nobility in order to establish the royal power. In this process the king also elevated burghers (especially in France) to the aristocracy or granted them privileges that put them on equal footing with the aristocracy and contributed in an essential way to the formation of the group of urban patricians.[14] This fact also explains the success that courtly culture and courtly literature enjoyed among the *frans borjois* of France: it continued until the time of Molière's *Bourgeois gentilhomme* and beyond.[15]

The *Chevaliers du Commerce*

Merchants in France had of course always had to endure *aventures* in in the sense of troubles that befell them, on water and on land. For that reason they soon banded together in *compaignies,* "defensive alliances" or "guilds": as early as the ninth century, a *confrérie des marchands de l'eau* (brotherhood of marine merchants) was in existence.[16] The formation of cities, of *communes* with their commitments to mutual assistance which the *borjois* exchanged, contributed significantly to the formation of such organizations.[17] Thus as early as from 1072 to 1083, guilds or Hansas of *marchands* were formed in Paris that gave each other mutual protection on water and on land with their transport of goods; their armaments were prescribed in great detail, and violation of these ordinances was a punishable offense.[18] These defensive alliances changed at the latest in the thirteenth century, in the process of the development of the cities and of the cooperation between king and the bourgeoisie that was rising into the nobility or to the noblelike patriciate. "The guilds now become aristocratic alliances and isolate themselves [from the artisans and other cooperatives—M. N.]."[19] The economic stagnation of the fourteenth and fifteenth centuries, the time of great famines and plague epidemics as well as of the Hundred Years' War, intensified this development: "The great burghers, grown rich, from now on live from revenues or else buy feudal properties and imitate the feudal lords."[20]

E. Coornaert gives an impression of this process:

> In the north, the guild members relatively early became patricians: in Valenciennes and in Tournai (the citizens of these cities were noble) the cloth merchants formed a chevalerie. Arras had a "prince of the wine-trade" around 1430, and in Reims the great merchants were called the "knights of the nation of Reims." The merchant-"knights" of Languedoc, who were registered in the "military militia of the Order of Traded Goods," had the clear right to regard themselves as members of an aristocracy. The Six Corporations of Paris had constituted such an aristocracy since the fifteenth century—had not the goldsmiths among them received from Philippe de Valois the right to have coats of arms? . . . Soon the members of "commerce" were commonly called "nobles" ["nobles hommes"].[21]

This more or less intensive assimilation of the commercial bourgeoisie into the nobility (together with the striving for the *noblesse de robe,* the "nobility of magistrates") was to remain a decisive characteristic of the development of the bourgeoisie in France.

Hallowed Risk

The decisive turning point in the history of the ideology of adventure was initiated in England. In France, the rising bourgeoisie was assimilated to the (upper) nobility or to the nobility of magistrates (in either case, it imitated the noble way of life and largely adopted the courtly ideology); in England, the bourgeoisie began to follow its path to world-historical significance, to the success of its economic system, to capitalism, in opposition to the upper nobility and the clergy but in alliance with the petty nobility. One of its weapons was adventure. As early as the fourteenth century, Chaucer wrote in the *Canterbury Tales:*

> Us moste putte oure good in aventure.
> A marchaunt, truly, may not ay endure,

> Truste me wel, in his prosperitye,
> Some tyme his good is drowned in the see,
> And some tyme cometh it sauf unto the londe.[22]

We have to run risks with our wares. Believe me: a merchant doesn't necessarily keep his possessions. Sometimes his wares sink in the sea and sometimes they come safe to land.

There is a clear echo of Thomas Aquinas in these lines: "Sicut navis undis marinis jactatur in altum nunc, & nunc in profundis; sic homo per fortunam nunc in prosperitate levatur, nunc in adversitate dejicitur."[23] [As a ship is sometimes carried high by the waves of the sea and sometimes plunged downward, thus the human being is sometimes raised to riches by Fortuna and sometimes plunged into misery.] This is all the more understandable, since *fortuna* as a concept (fate, luck) and as allegory (Dame Fortune) was used quite early as a synonym for *aventure,* as the example in Watriquet de Couvin's *Li miroir as Dames* (Mirror of the Ladies) shows. Fortuna here introduces herself: "Brothers, call me Aventure, / God put me to work on earth."[24] In the English version of the Alexius song from around 1400, there is talk of "dame auenture," and in a glossary from 1440 we read: "Awntyr... or happe: Fortuna fortuitis."[25]

Chaucer does not depart from this context of meaning in the passage above when he talks about the risks a merchant runs.[26] A merchant runs risks, and he can do so with pride; not only did Jesus himself "adventure" (by risking his life), as William Langland wrote also in the fourteenth century,[27] but the church as well had emphatically sanctified the risk involved in financial operations or commerce. That may sound paradoxical, but it is comprehensible.[28] The church had banned usury, moneylending against interest, quite early. But it by no means put a ban on changing money from one currency into another.[29] The original bankers (in northern Italy) were thus at first primarily (officially) moneychangers. "In the Middle Ages, fare il banco [to bank] and fare il cambio [to change money] were synonyms.[30] The theologians, like Thomas Aquinas, legitimized these exchange operations: they allowed bankers to invest their money so as to earn a profit as long as this involved a risk, namely the exchange from one currency into another, so that there were no grounds for the charge of usury against the moneychangers.[31]

Money was changed by the merchants, the "marcheants" of whom *Le Moniage Guillaume* speaks and who quite early on were engaging in long-distance trade on water and land. When the exchange system developed in the eleventh and twelfth centuries, the "ambulatory" character of trade had already been given an international organizational framework with the traveling merchants and their guilds and Hansas. Various currencies therefore had to be used in trade, which gave the bankers the opportunity for hidden loan or usury operations.[32] To be sure, such operations (*mutuum in fraudem usurarum,* "exchange for usurious purposes") were officially forbidden by the church, but it was very difficult to trace them (should that even have been desirable).

The cover for this usury was the officially permitted exchange of money: *Cambium non est mutuum* (exchange of money is not usury), the church had decided, because the *cambium* in contrast to *mutuum* contained an (actual) risk for the moneychanger. Moneychanging was understood as moving currency from one place to another.[33] In principle, that usually meant that a trader had a certain sum of money paid out at a certain place in the currency valid there. This sum was to be paid back at a predetermined place in the currency valid there, with a profit for the moneychanger (the banker), because he had undergone the risk of losing his money (the trade routes were unsafe, the distances sometimes huge, so that it could be quite a long time before the banker got his money back).

It was in fact possible to cloak this process in Christian love of neighbor. For instance, a traveler in a foreign land could be in need, so that it was only Christian charity to help him out of his need by giving him money so he could return home; he then would repay the money lent him. And this was in fact how it was done, with the fine, crucial distinction that the borrower was normally no traveler in need but rather a merchant who used the borrowed money to buy goods abroad, loaded them on his wagon or ship, traveled with them to a predetermined place, sold his goods there for a profit, and financed his expenses and his living (or increased his wealth) and also paid the banker's profit (the hidden interest) from the realized profit. As primitive or complicated as these financial transactions were—and they corresponded to the complicated nature of commercial transactions in general at that time—they were not only the beginning of the modern financial transactions of commercial capitalism, they also gave a fitting name to a certain type of trade: *aventure* trade, which lasted in a rudimentary way until into the nineteenth century.[34]

The Merchant Adventurers

In France, the courtly ideology of adventure, supported by both the nobility and often by the rising or arrived bourgeoisie, seems to have if not prevented, then at least severely limited, the positive use of *aventurier* (instead of *chevalier*) for trader, merchant. In Germany, however, the term *aventure,* in its different dialect variants, was part of the common terminology of trade. Its widest spread was in the sense of risk (which was also called *angst*):[35] as early as 1300 it occurred in this sense in Braunschweig,[36] and in the Hanseatic trade contracts it is quite common: "Trade contracts are drawn up in Lübeck between two partners *up user twiger aventhure* (the adventure of the two of us), in Königsberg among three partners *up user 3 eventuer.*"[37] But "adventure" can also be the profit itself, as Erich Maschke proves with documents from the Ravensburg Society: "In 1479 the Valencia branch expected good *abentyr* in the sugar business, and *auben-*

türiger saffra is profitable saffron.''[38] Goods themselves can be called "adventure," and the merchant finally applies the title of adventurer to himself: "In this context, traveling merchants and especially jewel dealers are called adventurers, with no negative connotations," as Werner Welzig writes. "Rather, it is a regular professional title. Thus the Strassburg municipal council decreed in 1482 an 'Ordnung der Goltschmiede und Ofentürer' [Order of Goldsmiths and Adventurers].''[39] And in fact, it would have been more than strange if the concept "adventurer" as the designation for a merchant had had "negative connotations," given the courtly ideology of adventure and the church's sanctification of risk. If even "jewel dealers," as Welzig says, or goldsmiths called themselves adventurers from time to time, that was based on the fact that they are also, and primarily, moneychangers or moneylenders (in England, the term "goldsmith" was synonymous with banker well into the eighteenth century) and were involved in the *aventure* trade (that is, underwent risks) through this activity. Thus it was not "especially jewel dealers" who called themselves adventurers, but the long-distance merchants. As Bruno Kuske writes:

> The narrowing of the concept "adventure" to the economic context and in that context to capital risk was of importance from the Middle Ages on. A distinction was made between *aventiure* trade and the sale to known customers. *Aventiure* trade covered those cases in which the merchant set off with his goods without knowing exactly what market he would find for them or in which he sent them off to representatives or agents. Quite a variety of practices developed in these cases— especially in the agreements of trading companies or of contracting parties. "Aventiure" was reserved for certain amounts of common sales, for limited stretches of the trade routes. . . . On an order, say, from the Lower Rhine to Venice, merchants retained the right to carry only half of the *eventure* and to assign the other half to a partner. . . . The long-distance trader who was also able and had enough capital to undertake the risk of getting his goods to their destination therefore self-confidently called himself an "adventurer" by profession in the Middle Ages.[40]

The term gains world-historical importance in England, where it was the proud professional designation for "that corporation of English merchants whose long-distance trade was especially risky."[41] The first occurrences of merchants calling themselves adventurers are from 1443/44 ("Adventurers of the Mercery"; for the sake of comparison, in France the stay-at-home traders called themselves *chevaliers de la mercerie*). Already toward the end of the fifteenth century, adventurers, as merchant adventurers, figure in the London *City Book*.[42] The awareness of undertaking risks played an important role in this self-designation. The Guild of St. George in Hull admitted as members only those who had no other means of support than "by grete aventoure." That meant primarily the risk of sea trade, as an occurrence in the year 1439 shows: "Maistres and Mariners of certein Schippes and Vesseles . . . aswell of aventure of Wynde and of the See, as by rekelesnesse . . . have hert and brused other Schippes and Vesseles."[43] [Owners and sailors of certain ships and boats have, both for reason of dangers of wind and sea and out of carelessness, rammed and destroyed other ships.]

The formation of the merchant adventurer associations was connected with the increasing importance of the English wool and cloth manufacture and the related shipping trade in the fifteenth century, although the beginnings were at first quite modest; until well into the sixteenth century the lion's share of the sea trade with English wool and cloth was carried on by the Hanseatic League, which had its headquarters in London in the famous Steelyard. "The increasing volume of overseas trade handled by English men of affairs was reflected in the growing importance in English society of merchants specializing in foreign commerce, particularly in the marketing of cloth," writes E. M. Carus-Wilson.[44] The cloth merchants, the merchant adventurers, were to be distinguished from the wool traders, the merchant staplers, who belonged to the Company of Staple and were allowed only to transport their raw material, wool, as far as Calais.

As shippers of cloth they were bound to no one company and to no one port, nor were they assured of a sale for their wares. Despatching them north, south, east and west, wherever they could find an opening, they strove to capture from foreign manufacturers markets which at any moment might be closed against them by war or diplomacy; hazarding their goods, and sometimes their persons, on voyages to alien and not always welcoming lands. Venturers in fact, they became venturers in name. As "venturers" or "adventurers" they became individually distinguished both from the Merchant Staplers and from the stay-at-home traders.[45]

To assert their interests, the merchant adventurers were soon forced to form organizations, since otherwise the predominance of the other domestic and foreign sea traders who were organized into fellowships (the so-called nations) would have been too great. As " 'fellowships of adventurers,' drawn together by common interests, they associated into groups both at home and abroad,"[46] although the principle of association actually seems to run counter to the commitment to risk-filled adventure. The fellowship was supposed to remove adventure as far as possible from any incalculable risk (an internal contradiction to which we will return later).

The development of the adventurer associations was a decisive event for all of English sea trade. In 1457 the "felyship adventurers" already had permission to collect duty on every cloth shipment brought to England on certain ships.[47] To the dismay of other traders, a special jurisdiction was formed, administered by the Court of Adventurers,[48] which led to tensions (and sometimes to murder) between the mercer adventurers and other "divers felyshippes aventerers."[49] In 1489 we find an exact list of these other "Fellowship Adventurers" of the City (London), organized in the "Courte of the felishippes aventerers": drapers, grocers, skinners, and others "as well as oure Compeny of the Mercery."[50] But haberdashers, fish dealers, or tailors could also belong, though they seldom did.[51]

The greatest association of adventurers was doubtless the "Company of Merchant Adventurers of England, trading to Holland, Zealand, Brabant, Hainault and Flanders," later called simply the "Merchant Adventurers of England." It is telling that Holland was named first because in the fifteenth century the sea trade between England and Holland was of prime importance. The headquarters of the "Merchant Adventurers of England" was in Bruges or in Antwerp, while that of the Hanseatic League was in London. The shipping trade was not yet a national affair, but it was drawn into the wake of the formation of the nation-states or of the absolute monarchies. Thus the merchant adventurers began to owe duty to the King of England in exchange for trade charters. With the death of Edward IV at the latest this had become such a burden to the fellowships that they began to resist it and demanded among other things greater privileges for their money.[52] The pressure of competition and shared interests (especially over against the Hanseatic League and hence against all *foreign* competitors) soon led to the consolidation of all adventurer fellowships. This organization became so important to the English economy that the adventurers were forced, and were able, to ask the king for military assistance in their undertakings; this was the impetus for the establishment of a "royal navy."[53] In 1492 adventure ships sailed out under the protection of the navy; this became the rule under Henry VII and Henry VIII.[54] At about the same time the adventurers began to take the offensive against the Hanseatic League, their greatest rivals apart from the staplers.[55] The king soon lent them support in this struggle because he began to see the significance of the policy of a national merchant marine. In the process of forming his mercantile policy, he also increasingly protected his own sea trade to the disadvantage of foreign sea trade, especially of the Hanseatic League, whose privileges Elizabeth I then significantly reduced in the second half of the sixteenth century.

The Rise of the Burgher in Literature

In looking for the reason why the (long-distance) merchant called himself an adventurer, we must not lose sight of the courtly ideology of adventure. The commitment to risk, as an affirmation of the real bourgeois (commercial) adventure, certainly stood in defiant opposition to the courtly ideology of adventure, but on the other hand it was also, whenever possible, cloaked in the forms of courtly ideology itself. What scholars call the "bourgeois tendency of courtly literature" is a dialectical process. The bourgeoisie, in assimilating courtly culture and ideology, not only won for itself the social privileges of the nobility, it not only changed courtly culture and ideology in its own direction in this assimilation (that is, in the direction of bourgeois interest and the expression of this interest), it also changed itself in this assimilation,[56] became more of a competitor—and that means that it used the cultural and ideological weapons of the nobility (in part unconsciously) in the class struggle against that very nobility.[57]

To be sure, this tactic can be effective in the class struggle only as long as mimicry does not become assimilation to the nobility or identification with it (as happened for instance especially in France, but also in Italy and other places). This danger was not so great in England, because of the economic and political development there,[58] that is, because of the different situation of the class struggle: there never was an English system of knighthood as there was in France or even in Germany or Spain.[59] As early as the fourteenth century there was an economic and political union between the rich urban bourgeoisie and the gentry, who, as the House of Commons, opposed the upper nobility and the upper clergy, as the House of Lords, in Parliament. An unconditional propagation of the courtly ideology that disavowed non-nobles (which the bourgeoisie in France during its rise sometimes fell prey to or even propagated) can have had little appeal to the English bourgeoisie, and in fact the courtly ideology of adventure played a much smaller role in England than in France, whence it was imported. Until well into the fourteenth century French was the language of the English aristocracy and hence the official language of state. The courtly ideology was thus brought to England in the original language of its French products; this circumstance severely limited its reception (especially since at that time texts were only handwritten or circulated orally). There never was a real English knightly romance.[60] When people in England began to write English novels, the time of knighthood was already past, and there was already a need for another kind of literature which was no longer exclusively that of knighthood. Quite the contrary: the exclusively courtly-knightly literature written after the beginning of the fourteenth century exhibited thoroughly "counterrevolutionary" traits in the forms of the time.

Nonetheless, we may not see the historical development in England as a disconnected sequence of different classes and their (far from unified, in fact highly contradictory) ideological systems, and this is also true for the relation of the medieval English bourgeoisie to courtly literature. This bourgeoisie (of which the merchant adventurers were merely an avant-garde), like that of France, Germany, or elsewhere, did not at first erect a world view radically opposed to courtly ideology. Instead, it gradually "re-functioned" courtly ideology before going on the offensive against it (with weapons in part won in the refunctioning, that is, from the assimilated and altered culture). That occurred on various levels. The bourgeoisie made courtly literature or ideology bourgeois in a linguistic, formal, and ideological sense—whether courtly literature was parodied, whether the bourgeois world was introduced as background, whether active characters appeared as representatives of the bourgeoisie, the boundaries and transitions were fluid and corresponded to the changing, contradictory, or convergent interests of the different classes.

This dialectical process of making courtly literature or ideology bourgeois and making the rising bourgeoisie courtly began relatively early in England. To be precise, it began as soon as English won out as the official language of state and thereby also became acceptable as a vehicle for literature at court. Chaucer's *Canterbury Tales* presents a representative selection of figures from the different classes of society. To be sure, hierarchy is strictly observed, but the "parfit gentil knight"[61] who introduces the series of characters can already be distinguished by his social position from the model knight of the French courtly romance. The background for his *aventures* is no fairy-tale world, but instead the precisely detailed topography from Russia to the Mediterranean. But still more important: he is on a pilgrimage in the company of quite uncourtly people, a group of pilgrims whose feeling of community Chaucer emphasizes,[62] and a merchant also belongs to this group of pilgrims; he is presented in detail and with sympathy. But the pilgrim is not the only merchant we meet. In the story told by the mariner, another member of the community of pilgrims, we encounter another (cuckolded and deceived, but thoroughly honorable) merchant as a protagonist. It is interesting for our investigation to note that Chaucer tried to give his readers some understanding of the contemporary system of loans and usury within the framework of this story.

The dialectical process of making courtly literature bourgeois took place with differing intensity in the various countries. We cannot discuss it here in detail but will instead only point out a few central points in the development that are of particular importance for the formation of the ideology of adventure. In general, we can state that besides the courtly literature that was being made bourgeois, a literature was growing up that was an ever more open expression of the rising class, with national differences in development (although it was characterized everywhere by an increasing realism).[63] We see a change in the valuation of the nobility and knightly *aventure* as early as 1275, when Jean de Meun, in his continuation of the *Roman de la Rose,* converts Andreas Capellanus's rules for making a knight courtly into implicit censure of the nobility and an upward revaluation of non-nobles. In imitations of sources from antiquity, he has the allegorical figure of Nature give information about the natural (moral) equality of human beings and determines that no one is a *gentilhomme* except on the basis of the appropriate virtues, and no one is a *vilain* except through lack of these virtues. "Noblesse," he writes, "comes from having the right courage, because nobility of descent alone is nobility worth nothing, unless a great heart [that is, bravery—M. N.] is joined to it." To learn bravery, the *gentilhomme* should remember the heroic deeds of his predecessors, in which task the *clercs,* that is basically the intellectuals, can be helpful; the *clercs,* who themselves should be noble or noble by virtue of their mental and moral superiority, can as literati transmit the deeds of the ancients. The *clerc,* Jean de Meun writes, "reads in the old stories / the vilenies [shameful deeds—M. N.] of all vilains / and the heroic deeds of the dead heroes: / truly a rich source of courtoisie." Jean de Meun by no means questions the importance and function of the aristocracy or knights, but we cannot overlook his indication that a man who earns his living by working with his hands is not for that reason a *vilain*; nor can we ignore his indication that many heroes of ancient times were of lowly birth. Still more important: he proclaims the principle of the *vita activa,* the "active life." *Paresse,* "laziness," and *noblesse* are incompatible. To be sure, his main concern with respect to the nobility or knights is military activity. However, the truly noble man must emulate Duke Robert d'Artois, the brother of Louis IX, Saint Louis, who was killed during the Seventh Crusade. He must never be idle, must be educated, and must actively practice "largece [*largesse*—M. N.], eneur [honor—M. N.], chevalerie."[64] With this affirmation of the *vita activa,* a polemic directed against the idle aristocracy, the ideological ground is prepared for a critique of the fairy-tale-like, irrational knightly *aventure*; on this ground will grow parodies, such as *Dit d'aventures* (the first parody of the knightly romance, as Mikhail Bakhtin has determined),[65] written as early as the thirteenth century. In this work, literary and bourgeois self-awareness is expressed in implicit and explicit criticism of the courtly ideology of *aventure* from the *Roman de Renart,* in its different variations, all the way down to *Ulenspiegel* (ca. 1478) and *Reinke de Vos* (1498).[66]

If we are kept waiting a rather long time for a positive model of the bourgeois ideal of humanity, that can be attributed to the development of the class struggle, which led to the previously described forms of appropriation of courtly culture. Then too, no group within the bourgeoisie had yet asserted itself as an avant-garde of the rising class or had been recognized by the bourgeoisie as its own avant-garde. The fact that the shipping merchant and the shipping trade played a relatively subordinate role in general can only be attributed to the fractionating of the bourgeoisie in the Middle Ages, to which Armando Sapori correctly calls attention. Sapori distinguishes (in the case of Italy) between the world of the artisans and their apprentices and the world of the avant-garde, as he calls it, the world of the great or long-distance merchants and their trade organizations.[67] If the ideologues of the medieval bourgeoisie viewed the great merchants and their trade organizations with some reservation, that was because they were not yet able to see in them the major representatives of their own interests, because long-distance trade was in fact not yet the power that was to revolutionize all social relations; moreover, the world of large-scale trade (chiefly in Italy, but also in France) touched the world of the nobles, was allied with it, was in part even identical with it, which brought still other ideological factors into play (characterized by distrust).[68] Not until the great nobility or the princes and kings and the bourgeoisie began to face each other as antagonistic but mutually dependent classes in the battle against the petty nobility and the small feudal lords did the position of the merchant or the long-distance merchant gradually change in the bourgeois consciousness or in the literary articulation of that consciousness.

It is characteristic that the common weal, the good of the country (that is, of the gradually developing nation-states) is in the foreground from the very beginning. Thus we read at the beginning of the fourteenth century, in Gilles de Muisit's *C'est les marchands* (On Merchants):

> No country can hold its own by its own strength;
> For that reason the merchants struggle and strive
> To bring what is lacking in the lands to all lands;
> For that reason one must never drive them out without cause.
> The merchants travel over the sea and back,
> In order to provide for the lands and to be loved by their own
>   kind.
> And good merchants do nothing one could blame them for,
> But rather act so that one loves them and considers them
>   loyal and good.
> They cause care and love to bloom in all lands,
> And for that reason one should rejoice when they become rich.[69]

And we read in *Dit des marchands*

> that one must honor merchants
> More than all other people,
> Because they travel over land and sea
> And into many foreign countries
> To buy gray and many-colored wool
>
> . . . .
> May God protect all merchants from harm
>
> . . . .
> The Holy Church was first founded by merchants,
> And know, that knights are to protect the merchants[70]

because merchants guarantee the necessary luxuries.

Fortunatus

It is relevant that bourgeois self-awareness showed an especially strong development where social relations had made the most revolutionary turn toward commercial capitalism, that is, in Italy; bourgeois self-awareness there had developed by delimiting itself from the knightly nobility and its ideology as well as by adapting knightly-courtly thinking or by conserving or imitating noble ways of life (especially where the nobility itself was the carrier of commerical capitalism). It was a self-contradictory mix of ideologemes, as we saw in the case of Machiavelli; that is explained by the anarchic conditions in Italy. We will not go into detail about the Italian development here, because it contributed less to the formation of the modern bourgeois worldview(s) and hence had less effect on the formation of the modern bourgeois ideology of adventure than intellectual history would have had us believe up to now. Its contribution is largely indirect.

To avoid misunderstandings: it is of course impossible to place too high a value on Italy's contribution, and the contribution of the Italian Renaissance from Dante on, to the formation of modern European philosophy, literature, and art, but this contribution lost its preeminence at the latest by the end of the sixteenth or the beginning of the seventeenth century. This is a process that began as early as the early sixteenth century, with the formation of the absolutist-bourgeois national cultures or literatures in England and France, but also with the later interrupted development in Germany as well as in Portugal and Spain. The reasons for this are not to be found in philosophy, in art, or in literature. The movement of the superstructure, its development, is dependent on the development of the ensemble of social relations, and that means on the development of the human being, and in the "final" (or first) analysis, that is determined by economic development, the development of the forces of production and of the relations of production or social relations that are changed or revolutionized thereby. But toward the end of the fifteenth century at the latest, from the time of the discovery of the New World and of the European-East Indian trade route around the Cape of Good Hope, the center of the capitalist means of production shifted from Italy and the Mediterranean to Portugal, Spain, England, the Netherlands, and France (the development in Germany was also decisively affected by this historical event). That means that in areas which were somewhat backwards compared to Italy, the development of the forces of production was continued beyond the Italian relations of production; in other words, it was in these areas, and not in Italy, that the foundations of modern capitalism were laid (after the decline of Portugal and Spain in the second half of the sixteenth and first half of the seventeenth ceutury, this occurred especially in England, the Netherlands, and France). The development of the forces of production and the revolution in the relations of production it entailed in these countries called for norms and methods of intellectual discussion, of knowledge, of orientation, which could not develop in Italy or could develop only in rudiments because of the lack of a corresponding material development and hence of the necessity for dealing with it intellectually. The (very dynamic) relationship of the revolutionary class, the bourgeoisie, in the countries where modern capitalism prevailed was therefore that of a beneficiary vis-à-vis Italy and its culture. That is, the economic and political development of Italy until the sixteenth century was more advanced, had gone further in the direction of capitalism and the breaking of feudal bonds than all other European countries, and had therefore produced a correspondingly progressive superstructure. But as soon as this development was not only overtaken by the other countries but also began to stagnate, these other countries were able to become the cultural, ideological, political heirs of Italy (and that means of the Italian Renaissance). Of course the intellectual development of Italy (like its economic development) did not come crashing to a halt, but from the end of the seventeenth century on Italy has been one of the economic-political, as well as intellectual, provinces of Europe. Italy's contribution to the formation of the modern worldview from the middle or end of the seventeenth century on is relatively insignificant (this changes somewhat only in the twentieth century); its important share lies in the Renaissance, whose accomplishments were passed on into the modern age by the bourgeoisie in the developed capitalist states before the working class began to appropriate and preserve them for itself (as has been shown by Gramsci, for instance).

The beginning of this (world-historical) shift of the center of European economic and intellectual development from the Mediterranean area to the west and northwest of Europe is reflected in a small novel that has only recently started to receive more attention but whose overall importance still has not, I believe, been properly appreciated. This novel is the anonymous *Fortunatus*, published in 1509 in Augsburg and doubtless written immediately before;[71] its title already expresses the changed consciousness of the modern European bourgeoisie as compared to the (commercial) bourgeois thought of the Italian Renaissance.

In order to illuminate the dimensions of this change in consciousness, we shall use Leon Battista Alberti's treatise *Della Famiglia* (1434) as an example. Alberti's work is informed by his zeal to deliver proof of the social and moral importance of his family. According to his presentation, this family has every imaginable quality and virtue, is decent, diligent, socially minded, and conscious of its duty to the nation. The ideal burgher whom Alberti draws in *Della Famiglia* is the exact counterpart of Machiavelli's ideal prince: knightly virtues (the affirmation of physical preparation for battle as part of the education of children and youths by means of such activities as archery and riding) are joined with nonknightly ideals (thrift, endurance, diligence, and bookkeeping). The remarks of Gianozzo Alberti are characteristic of this ambivalent attitude toward these spheres of ideal social virtues that basically reflect class antagonisms. In the dialogue he answers with a genealogical enumeration the question whether all the Albertis were knights by birth (or whether they were simply called knights because of their merits): "But enough of this genealogy which has nothing to do with our discussion of good management."[72]

Alberti's efforts to prove the value and importance of his family are augmented by the fear that it could lose that importance, could disappear from history like so many famous families before it. According to Alberti, the fault for this would then lie exclusively with bad luck, fate, accident—in short, with fickle Fortuna. In fact, in the concept of Fortuna is concentrated the whole self-understanding of the (commercial) burgher of the Italian Renaissance with respect to this world and the next and to social relations, especially to the historical class antagonisms in Italy.[73] From the viewpoint of the (commercial) burgher of the Italian Renaissance, the human being (that is, himself, the burgher) is subject to the will of blind Fortuna, the planetary constellations, accident (of unstable relations), the will of God (or that of the relevant prince).[74] The burgher is still fundamentally passive over against Fortuna (that is, he does not yet fully dominate society). Alfred Doren is correct in stating that Alberti's *Della Famiglia* is an

> attempt to protect himself and others from the seductive demons who again and again enticed one onto the dangerous paths of the world, of the incalculable, of adventure, and in this attempt he seemed, at least in literature, to confine the endangered ego to a stuffy, closed room, protected from any kind of draft, which was broken open over and over by the lively, active human being.[75]

This does not, to be sure, exhaust all of Alberti, because in *Della Famiglia* he also gives instructions on how to subjugate Fortuna (which also give a clear indication of his fear of her), and in other writings he expresses himself in a still more aggressive and derogatory way about her (he even speaks of her weakness when one confronts her decisively).[76] Other documents of the time doubtlessly also show a more decisive, daring attitude toward Fortuna,[77] in accordance with which the "new entrepreneur [is] at once a world conqueror and a carefully alert, cautiously pondering paterfamilias, trusting to Fortuna's favor, who fills his sails with wind as he, a virtuoso of life, his hand firmly on the tiller, guides the little boat of his fate and his business enterprises through stormy waves."[78] But this new orientation, present at first only in its bare beginnings, comes too late, from a world-historical point of view. It is not the Italian bourgeoisie but that of other countries that will conquer the world and thus subjugate Fortuna, a process the anonymous author of *Fortunatus* portrays in a fairy tale (which seems naïve to its interpreters of the nineteenth and twentieth centuries).

As we have mentioned, the changed consciousness of the bourgeoisie active in large-scale European trade, its consciousness of being definitively superior to the petty nobility, the knights, of interacting as near equals with the representatives of the upper nobility, of if not dominating the king, at least manipulating him, is expressed by the name of the protagonist and in the novel's title: Fortunatus, "Fortuna's chosen." Fortuna in (allegorical) person plays only a relatively modest role in the novel. She shows herself once for a short time to the active, daring man who earns her favor, since she needs to reveal herself and give herself only once to the bourgeois(ie), because her appearance (in the novel or in the history of the class struggle) is no longer necessary. The burgher has control of her, rules her in his activity, knows how he can constantly "exploit" her anew: she is present in all his actions, and where she evades him, this is not because of some obscure, impenetrable error of blind Fortuna but because of demonstrable practical errors made by the burgher or the bourgeoisie.

But let us proceed systematically: Fortunatus—the son of bourgeois, rather well-to-do parents who have lost their fortune through the carelessness of the father, who wanted to live too high in knightly fashion—sees no future for himself in his hometown, Famagusta on Cyprus. He sets out for distant lands, after many adventures arrives in London, is exiled from that country, arrives in France, gets lost in a deep wood in Brittany, there meets Fortuna who gives him a "little moneybag"; he wanders throughout Europe, settles again in Famagusta, and starts a family. After a while he sets out again, leaving his wife and his two sons, Ampedo and Andolosia, behind, heading for Greece, Asia Minor, and India. He returns after having stolen a "wishing cap" from King Soldan of Alexandria, which lets him wish himself to anyplace he wants. Fortunatus dies; contrary to his will, which stated that moneybag and wishing cap should never be separated, his sons fight about the inheritance. The outcome is that Ampedo stays in Famagusta with the cap and Andolosia, who wants to travel, sets off on adventures with the moneybag. He promises to return after six years and then give his brother the magic purse for the same amount of time. Andolosia arrives in London on his travels, where the royal princess Agrippina steals his bag. Andolosia returns to Cyprus, steals the wishing cap, and wishes himself back to London. There he at first loses the wishing cap to Agrippina as well, but then with trickery and magic he regains the magic cap and the magic purse and becomes so indispensable to the King of England that he himself arranges the marriage of Agrippina to the "young king of Cyprus." After the wedding, however, he is captured by two counts and murdered. But the magic of the moneybag is tied to Fortunatus or his biological heirs. Thus, the magic purse loses its power because in the meantime Andolosia's brother has died of chagrin; before his death he destroyed the wishing cap. The king orders the two counts, who have betrayed themselves, executed and buries Andolosia with full ceremony in Famagusta.

We will not examine all the details of this work, which was among the most widely read novels from the sixteenth into the eighteenth century,[79] but some aspects of it are very significant for our theme. *Fortunatus*, as recent scholarship (non-Marxist as well) unanimously agrees, has "torn away from the family its sentimental veil and has reduced the family relation" and all other human feelings and ties "to a mere money relation."[80] The "nexus between man and man" is nothing other than "naked self-interest, than callous 'cash payment,'"[81] about which both Fortunatus and Andolosia speak.[82] Where there is no money, "all love is gone."[83]

In this undisguised equation of human relationships and "cash payment" relations in *Fortunatus*, we see the relative helplessness on the part of the anonymous author, who does not really understand the actual monetary and exchange economy of his epoch and merely diagnoses its magical effect. Moneychanging is mentioned in only two places, once in a polemical way: a young Florentine merchant deceives his father with the uncanny means of exchange,[84] and once in a mystifying, fairy-tale way: the moneybag has been stolen from Fortunatus, and in looking for it, he says, "I care more about the bag than about the money I've lost. There is a little letter of exchange in it that no one can get a pennyworth of use from."[85] Even the "place where the moneychangers and purchasers were"[86] serves only as background for a new draw of money from the inexhaustible magic purse. From this perspective we can understand why the anonymous author had recourse to the fairy tale of the magic bag, although at the same time one must assume (the "wishing cap" theme suggests this too, as we will see) that he is consciously using mystification, since the author is obviously not in a position to cloak and to justify what he verifies as the importance and effect of early capitalist monetarism with an adequate bourgeois ethic.

The Pimp as Financial Expert

If we start by observing only the path of Fortunatus's life, we will see that the decisive events of his life have to do with shipping and take place in harbor towns,[87] from his birth in the harbor town of Famagusta to London, Venice, Alexandria, back to Famagusta, where he dies. But the development of social relations that the anonymous author tries to present begins before the birth of Fortunatus. His father, Theodorus, is a well-to-do burgher who lives from land rents. We are not told how his ancestors acquired property, but Theodorus, who leads a life of leisure, imitates the life style of the nobility, with "jousting, tilting, many squires, expensive horses," which leads to the sale of his inheritance and hence to his ruin. Fortunatus tries to evade poverty and goes to sea: "a ship was just in port, a ship from Venice that was carrying pilgrims to Jerusalem."[88]

The importance of the Crusades for the development of trade has already been mentioned; the beginning of the (individual) rise of Fortunatus is logically embedded in this historical context of the origin of long-distance trade. It is important for our purposes that it is not a vague desire to see distant lands that drives Fortunatus into the world, but instead the wish for a better life: "I am young, strong, and healthy, I want to go to foreign lands and serve. There is still much fortune in this world, I hope to God, I will get my share of it."[89] His course leads

him to London, "where merchants from all over the world are now located, ply-
ing their trade."[90] There Fortunatus enters the service of a Florentine merchant,
who hires him immediately. "He was to load goods into the ships and when ships
came, to unload them."[91]

Fortunatus is then exiled from the land because of a murder in which he is
indirectly involved, through his connection to a business friend of his master.
He has already learned the essential thing: that it is not so much a matter of
possession, not even the possession of money, but of the increase of this possession. Every time he earns money, he spends it and is ruined, so that the pimp
of the prostitute with whom Fortunatus ran through his money gives him this
lesson: "What kind of fool are you, who had five hundred kroner and didn't
invest them in another merchant treasure, but instead spent them on the stupid
woman."[92]

The Magic Purse of Fortunatus

We can sum up as follows: to the anonymous author of *Fortunatus* two things
are clear, though of course not in this terminology nor with this sharp focus.
First, "Greed as such is impossible without money; all other kinds of accumulation and mania for accumulation appear as primitive, restricted by needs on the
one hand and by the restricted nature of products on the other."[93] This restricted
nature is what caused the downfall of the nobility, as well as that of Fortunatus's
father, who imitated the nobility. Second, the exclusive accumulation of gold
and silver, of money, while it puts one in the position to be able to spend, "is
the first historic appearance of the gathering-together of capital and the first great
means thereto,"[94] but the wealth so gathered together always tends to decrease
unless it is constantly increased (at least by the amount of expenditures). "For
that, the reentry of what has been accumulated into circulation would itself have
to be posited as the moment and the means of accumulation."[95]

This is precisely the lesson that the pimp gave Fortunatus. Fortunatus
understands that money must breed money, and since he is the product of his
author, we can conclude that the author knows that money as commercial capital
breeds money. He even knows with what means one must operate in buying and
selling goods in order to receive the highest profits. He seems not to know or
not to want to know only one thing: how it is possible at the time of writing *Fortunatus* to earn more money than one needs to live, in order to invest it. The conversion of money as a means of exchange into money as capital is a mystery to
the author. He sends Fortunatus to the fairy-tale Breton wood, where he meets
the "lady of luck," Fortuna, who gives him the magic purse: "Take this little
bag and whenever you reach into it (in whatever country you are or travel to,
whatever currency is used in that country), you will find ten pieces of gold in the
currency of that same country."[96]

From the Mad Capitalist to the Rational Miser

The anonymous author of *Fortunatus* killed two flies with one blow by reaching into the chest of fairy tales: first, the magic purse obviates the difficult explanation of economic interconnections; second, it allows him to use a fairy-tale justification for the (bourgeois) wealth of a few and thus—since it is a gift of fate, of Fortuna—the poverty of many. The wealth of the burgher Fortunatus is explained by a fairy tale: he travels throughout Europe with an adviser named Lüpoldus and a train of servants, visiting especially trading and harbor cities. If we ask ourselves what burghers of that time actually traveled in this manner and with this kind of accompaniment through Europe, we will find that it was the merchants who did so and that Fortunatus therefore represents the medieval merchant, who was still running risks in person and enduring adventures.[97]

As corresponds to the general development of the rising (continental) bourgeoisie in the early Middle Ages, Fortunatus sees social equality with the upper nobility as a worthwhile goal. While his father wasted his property in competition with the petty or knightly nobility, Fortunatus employs his (inexhaustible) fortune to build magnificent spiritual and temporal edifices in his home town, Famagusta, to which he had returned.[98] He decides to marry, and here too we see the historical sense of the anonymous author: the rising bourgeoisie is of greatest importance for the country's prince or king, who gives it privileges which are in no way inferior to those of the nobility or who elevates it into the nobility. The King of Cyprus insists that Fortunatus marry into the nobility and mediates the marriage with Cassandra, daughter of an impoverished count. The marriage meets considerable resistance in the count's family, which distrusts the modern sign of wealth, money.[99] In recounting this resistance, the count gives voice to economic reason (of the past): "He has neither land nor retinue," the count says to the King of Cyprus, "whether he had or has much money, you see that he has spent a great deal on buildings that do no good, so he might lose what he has and become poor, as his father did, for it happens very quickly that a large amount of money disappears."[100] That is correct in principle, but the means of prevention that especially the countess, the mother-in-law, demands,[101] is not very clever: Fortunatus is to buy "land and retinue," that is, he is to become a feudal lord. In reality, however, "land and retinue" at that time (with regional variations in development) had become a millstone around the neck of the nobility, pulling it down in its competition with the bourgeoisie. The proof—apart from the poverty of the countess herself—is evident in Fortunatus's buying the property of the Count of Ligorno because the Count "is in need and has to have money."[102]

Thus it is by no means "highly illogical," as Dieter Kartschoke believes,[103] that Fortunatus lets his money "work," that is, invests it in traded goods, although he has an inexhaustible magic moneybag; on the contrary, it could be called "illogical" that the anonymous author uses the help of a fairy-tale construct despite his precise observations and knowledge. To be sure, this construct allows him to lead the bourgeoisie (Fortunatus) not only into the (educational) blind alley, but also to lead it out again. The blind alley is that of the merging of the bourgeoisie with the nobility and with the function of the large feudal landowner. The stagnation of the bourgeoisie inherent in this merging can be overcome only if the bourgeoisie (Fortunatus) breaks the bonds of imitating the nobility. That in turn is possible only if the bourgeoisie (Fortunatus) again engages in trade, becomes active. Since Fortunatus has a magic moneybag and therefore cannot be ruined by imitating the nobility (in contrast to his father), he has the necessary capital to invest in commerce again and to become instead of the "miser" Fortunatus, "the mad capitalist," the modern capitalist, the "rational miser": "The ceaseless augmentation of value, which the miser seeks to attain by saving his money from circulation, is achieved by the more acute capitalist by means of throwing his money again and again into circulation." [104]

Fortunatus, whose boredom is not alleviated by "entertainment" and taking rides, therefore leaves Famagusta again, this time with a wealth of experience that he (the bourgeoisie) has collected: "I have seen half the world, he says, meaning Europe, now I want to see the other half." [105] He leaves for India. But he no longer travels as a single adventurer with a train of servants, he travels—as a merchant adventurer, who finances the adventure and lets others carry it out: [106] "Fortunatus quickly had a good ship built, with all advantages. While the ship was being built, he hired merchants and sent them out to buy merchant treasure with all kinds of goods, which he was then well able to use among the heathen." [107]

From the outside, Fortunatus is already traveling as a tourist because his employees are taking care of his business. When he arrives in Alexandria, he sends his ship, under the command of a navigator ("patron"), on a trading voyage, "and Fortunatus set another patron in his own place, ordered him to sail the ship and the other merchants and all the goods in the name of God to Catalonia, Portugal, Spain, England, Flanders, and to voyage from one country to the next and increase their profits." [108] Fortunatus travels on alone to India and commands the "patron" to pick him up two years later in Alexandria. After two years, on Fortunatus's return from India, the ship does arrive in Alexandria, "and although Fortunatus had not been with them, they had still made such profits and brought the ships so well laden with goods and costly merchant treasure that it was three times better than what Fortunatus had sent them out with." [109]

The Ubiquitous Capitalist

Fortunatus brings back from India something besides profit from his adventure trade: the magic cap that he steals from King Soldan of Alexandria. Whoever puts it on and wishes himself somewhere finds himself immediately in that place. While the interpreters of *Fortunatus* have given the magic purse much thought, the magic cap has been largely ignored, although the one (fairy-tale) motif is related to the other and the two cannot be separated. On the journey that takes Fortunatus to India, he seems to be merely an interested private traveler, but in truth he is investigating trade possibilities and the supply of goods (he brings sample goods back with him).[110] The trade route to India leads through Alexandria, and there the Turks do their intermediate trading and raise the import price of goods from India, that is, they decrease the profit for the importers in Europe.[111] Their European trading partners are Venice, Genoa, Florence, and Catalonia, all of which are somewhat dismayed for this reason at the unexpected competition from Famagusta.[112] After Fortunatus has returned to Famagusta with the magic cap from Soldan of Alexandria, Soldan sends a negotiator to Fortunatus who asks him to return the magic cap. This negotiator is, characteristically, a Venetian merchant.

The explanation of this episode seems to be as important as it is simple and clear: in 1498, six years after the discovery of America, the Portuguese discovered the sea trade route to India around the Cape of Good Hope. The importance of this discovery for the European shipping trade is difficult to estimate today.[113] For Alexandria, however, the opening of the sea trade route around the Cape of Good Hope meant a nearly instantaneous decline, and Venetian trade was also substantially damaged (as it was by the discovery of America). These discoveries could, however, not be undone. Fortunatus can therefore not return his magic cap, which symbolizes the possibility for the European sea trader, who now can conduct trade (reach into his magic purse) anywhere in the world. For that reason he answers calmly, "Fortunatus . . . does not ask whether he has angered King Soldan, since he never intends to visit his land again"[114] because the route around the Cape of Good Hope is now open. Only in such a way can we explain the situation at the death of Fortunatus: he no longer travels (in person), although he has just stolen the magic cap; instead, he stays at home, is immeasurably wealthy, and can reach out to anywhere in the world (without moving!). The capitalist trading principle has prevailed throughout the world.

New Dimension of the Class Struggle

The conversion of money into capital (the magic purse) and the conquest of the entire world as a staging place for trade (the magic cap) are the two pillars of bourgeois prosperity and bourgeois power. Where the one is neglected in favor of the other (to the extent that this is possible), wealth must dry up. Therefore Fortunatus orders his sons to share the moneybag and the cap and to keep them together always, an order they fail to follow. And that is their ruin. Ampedo providently withdrew money from the magic purse before Andolosia left. While he fails to let his money "work," Andolosia travels through the world, imitating the upper nobility, competing with it in courtly games and amours, and spending his money senselessly. This reflects a change in the political situation or the class situation.

While the King of Cyprus played Fortunatus, as the rising bourgeoisie, off against the nobility and needed and promoted Fortunatus to shore up his own royal power, the King of England now (after the ruin of the petty nobility) sees the bourgeoisie (Andolosia) as a direct class opponent and competitor (although he still needs it, but he has yet to learn that: it was never understood in Spain). In the figure of his daughter Agrippina, the King of England seizes first the magic purse and then the magic cap. But since he cannot use the magic cap (Agrippina throws it carelessly under the bed, where Andolosia finds it again)[115] because the absolute monarch of course cannot "adventure" like a trader,[116] in a dogged battle with Agrippina (the monarchy), Andolosia succeeds in winning both attributes back and in convincing the king that he is indispensable and useful.

He saves the king or the monarchy (by saving Agrippina and thus ensuring the succession) and becomes the adviser and producer of prosperity: the commercial capitalist bourgeoisie triumphs over all other classes, which necessarily arouses the envy of these others. After the wedding of Agrippina and the King of Cyprus, which Andolosia had recommended, a great tournament is held.

> And on one day the king and the dukes jousted, on the next day the counts, barons, and knights, on the third day the nobles and the prince and lords, squires, and servants. . . . Now Andolosia jousted among them and when the counts, barons, and knights jousted, he appeared on the field more expensively and better outfitted than anyone else; the only one he did not outdo was the king; and he was best in all the knightly games they played, and often won the prize.[117]

The real victor is Andolosia (the bourgeoisie). There is now only the king (and the dukes as well) above him. For the sake of the order of the classes ("for reasons of honor"), that is, for political reasons, the prize is however given to Count Theodoro of England, a member of the (lesser) upper nobility that has actually already been conquered by the bourgeoisie, so that the prize "in fairness" should go to Andolosia. The (lesser and impoverished) upper nobility is angry, for obvious reasons, about Andolosia's wealth and his political successes (as adviser and financier of the king), robs him of his magic purse and murders him, whereby the magic purse loses its effect (because the upper nobility does not understand how to conduct trade). The king sentences Andolosia's murderers, thus avenging the bourgeoisie or putting the upper nobility in its place, and seals a world-historical alliance by taking the part of the bourgeoisie against the nobility.[118] As Engels writes:

It is the epoch which had its rise in the latter half of the fifteenth century. Royalty, with the support of the burghers of the towns, broke the power of the feudal nobility and established the great monarchies, based essentially on nationality, within which the modern European nations and modern bourgeois society came to development. And while the burghers and nobles were still fighting one another, the German Peasant War pointed prophetically to future class struggles, by bringing onto the stage not only the peasants in revolt . . . but behind them the beginnings of the modern proletariat, with the red flag in their hands and the demand for common ownership of goods on their lips.[119]

Chapter 6
The Times That Bred Giants

The Guildsman Adventurer

In the "Supplement and Addendum to Volume 3 of *Capital*," Engels writes: "The merchant was the revolutionary element in this society, in which everything else was stable as if by heredity."[1] He is referring here to the feudal society of the Middle Ages and is thinking, not of the merchant's political-revolutionary consciousness, but of his social activity: "Into this world now steps the merchant, and he is the starting-point of its transformation. Not, however, as a conscious revolutionary; on the contrary, as its own flesh and blood. The medieval merchant was no individualist, he was essentially a guildsman like all his contemporaries."[2]

What Engels has to say about the medieval merchant in general is true of the merchant adventurers in particular; as paradoxical as it might appear at first, the concept of the adventurer is connected for us with that of the individualist (on the basis of the ideological spadework by bourgeois ideologues) and by no means with that of members of corporate or cooperative organizations. Nonetheless, the adventurers' right to this self-appellation derives from just this necessity of cooperative association. We have already mentioned the uncertainty of the trade routes and the risks of transporting goods on water and land. As an additional factor, there was no international trade law, so the merchant was subject to the (princely or municipal) whim of whatever domestic or foreign trading point he might visit. As discussed, this led on the one hand to guildlike trade organizations, and on the other hand presupposed within these organizations a common intercession for shared interests that was different from or opposed to other, competing trade organizations (guilds, Hansas). That was especially true at foreign points of trade, where the merchants were at pains to found cooperative settlements for their organization ("nation").

> At these marketplaces as well, it was necessary for foreign merchants to share counsel and to present a harmonious front. The society of one's countrymen, which had to be cultivated all the more by the merchants because the much lower level of international communication made national differences stand out the more strongly, and the circumstance that privileges were usually granted to the members of a given empire for economic and political reasons, led to the expansion of these ties not only to the members of individual cities but to those of whole nations. The effort that characterized the entire Middle Ages, of allowing disputes abroad to be adjudicated by countrymen of the participants and sentence to be passed in accordance with their native laws, led to the same result. This custom...entailed the necessity of setting up one of the eldest of the "nation" as judges, who were then charged with representing the common interests to the authorities, with surveillance over the houses and chapels of the nation, and with collecting the dues owed by the countrymen.[3]

Engels exposes the essential core of these organizations:

> The focal point of the entire organization was the equal participation of each associate in the rights and customs enjoyed by the group as a whole.... Nor is this less true of the merchant companies that brought overseas trade into being. The Venetians and Genoans in the ports of Alexandria and Constantinople, each "nation" in its own *"fondaco"*—a dwelling house, inn, warehouse, exhibition and sales room as well as a central office—formed complete trading partnerships closed off against competitors and customers, which sold at prices agreed among themselves, with commodities of a definite quality, guaranteed by official inspection and often hall-marked, and combined together to decide the prices the local people should pay for their products, etc. The Hanse proceeded in the same way on the German "bridge" (*Tydske Bryggen*) at Bergen in Norway, and so did their Dutch and English competitors. Woe to anyone who sold below price, or bought above it! The boycott he encountered meant unmitigated ruin, leaving aside the direct penalties the society would impose on the guilty party.[4]

The merchant adventurers were bound by the stint of trade, a rule according to which the individual adventurer was allowed to sell only a certain quantity of goods per year,[5] and certain ordinances forbade poor conduct, brawling, cursing, gambling,[6] and marriage with foreigners,[7] but primarily they prohibited the adventurer from taking away the customers of another.[8] In other words, free competition among merchant adventurers was strictly prohibited by the guilds. The fellowship of adventurers, which later organized itself into so-called mysteries (from Latin *ministerium*), had the character of a monopoly that was based on privileges and cooperative shares and that had as a precondition undeveloped feudalistic production, as we shall see. Engels tells us that

> the efforts of the merchants are in fact deliberately and consciously bent towards equalizing this profit rate for all parties involved. With both the Venetians in the Levant and the Hanse league in the North, each merchant paid the same prices for his product as did his neighbour, they cost him the same in transport, he received the same prices for them, and similarly bought return cargo at the same price as every other merchant in his "nation." The rate of profit was therefore the same for each. With the big trading companies, the distribution of profit in proportion to the share of capital put in is ... automatic.... The equal rate of profit, which is one of the end results of capitalist production in its full development, thus emerges in this case in its most simple form as one of the points from which capital has historically proceeded, in fact as a direct offshoot of the mark community, which is in turn a direct offshoot of primitive communism. This original rate of profit was necessarily very high. Business was very risky, not just on account of the widespread practice of piracy, but also because the competing nations often indulged in all kinds of violent action when the opportunity presented itself; finally, the market outlet and conditions depended on privileges granted by foreign rulers, which were frequently enough broken or revoked. Profit had therefore to include a high insurance premium. On top of this, the turnover was slow, the conclusion of deals tedious, though in the best periods, which seldom lasted very long, commerce was a monopoly trade with monopoly profit. The high level of the average rate of profit is also shown by the equally high levels of interest that prevailed, which still had always to be less on the whole than the customary percentage profit on trade.[9]

The riskiness of trade, which Engels correctly stresses, the internal and external risks of doing business, furnish the justification for the title "adventurer," since the merchant at this time still normally ran risks of a physical kind in person, on board his ships. For just as the undeveloped, medieval-cooperative trade of (not only) the adventurers fundamentally excluded individual large-scale trading or the large-scale commercial capitalist (with individual exceptions and regional variations), so the limitation of the individual merchant's activity to the framework of the fellowship, guild, or Hansa necessitated on principle the individual activity of the merchant. That means, as Brakel explains in his investigation of the merchant adventurers, that in the Middle Ages the person of the merchant was the bearer of his enterprise and his personal competence was actually the moving force of trade. Capital was important only in a secondary sense; it was as if annexed to the merchant.... Even the idea that a person in some circumstances functioned as an agent of a firm or the organ of a business had to be strange to the Middle Ages. For even when the merchant did not accompany his goods himself but turned their sale over to a servant or factor, the latter probably had to present himself independently to the foreigners. The distance and the lack of a postal system made communication with home extremely difficult.[10]

Dismantling the Myth of the Beast of Prey

That the capitalist and his managers must be "enterprising," "decisive," "daring," "willing to take risks," and show "leadership qualities," is one of the standard pieces of wisdom with which apologists for the capitalist system still influence public opinion even today; we will look at this more closely later.[11] The thesis behind these words is often tacit but more often boldly expressed: not everyone has these qualities, certainly not the working class (an argument that comes up again and again in the discussion about participatory management). One must be born to them.

One of the major propagandists of this sort of ideologeme was Werner Sombart, whose importance cannot be overestimated in view of the fact that such ideologemes have meantime become common coin (also via the massive spread of trashy imperialistic literature and films). In his book *The Quintessence of Capitalism*, among other places, Sombart purported to derive the "spirit of enterprise" from racial, biological qualities. We will investigate here only one aspect of the work of this apologist for the "capitalist spirit," who later converted entirely to Fascism, whose methods of plundering and distorting Marx's works were precisely characterized by Lenin,[12] and who called himself a believer in the "power of blood" as early as 1913.[13] This is an aspect that haunts the works of bourgeois ideologues even today, in countless variations.

Sombart divides the world into "heroic" and "trading peoples," and of course, during the flowering of German imperialism, subsumes the German people under the "heroic peoples" (through Teutons and Frisians). But since this "heroic people" also conducted trade quite well, some way had to be found of uniting and justifying heroism and profit. Sombart uses biology to accomplish this: the "capitalist spirit" that must be justified originates, as he pretends to think,[14] where hero (the entrepreneur) and trader (the bourgeois) cross-breed (ignoring other circumstances):

We have thus observed how the capitalist spirit thrives in bourgeois natures (these being a hybrid between undertaking and middle-class natures). In other words, we have realized that there are people in the world who are so constituted mentally that they are able to develop the capitalist spirit more rapidly than others; who incline in a more marked degree than those others themselves to become capitalist undertakers [i.e., entrepreneurs—R. C.] who cultivate the middle-class virtues much more easily; who possess the qualities needful for success in economic life in a larger measure.[15]

What interests us about these theorems is the "heroic" element. The (original) hero, who developed his qualities in the "precapitalist" era, is half a warrior and half a freebooter, a pirate, a robber, resembling a beast of prey. According to Sombart, piracy plays a decisive role here: "Piracy as an institution already existed in the Italian seaports in the Middle Ages. Amalfi, Genoa, Pisa, Venice, all alike were centres of organized sea-robbery . . . and their piratical expeditions were the first forms of capitalist undertaking."[16] We will ignore what, according to Sombart, happened after that (he leads us a merry chase through time and space). Let us retain only the fact that the warriorlike, rapacious character of the bourgeois (the capitalist) is formed via sea trade and is inherited: "One . . . difference is to be noted, that between inland and oversea trade. The latter continues for a long time to have a dash of adventurous freebooting about it. Oversea trade therefore produced the dare-devil merchants who will take risks."[17] Here too we will pass over the irrationalism with which Sombart purportedly functions as a historian: the modern capitalist, the super-entrepreneur [*Überunternehmer*], as Sombart puts it, in an echo of Nietzsche's superman [*Übermensch*], takes his place in this (blood)line of heirs of the "dare-devil merchant": "His [the super-entrepreneur's] great characteristic is that he unites within himself several independent types. He may be freebooter, unscrupulous calculator, landlord, and speculator all in one. Any [American—M. N.] trust-magnate will serve as an illustration.[18]

What we encounter here is an important variant of the apologetics of capitalism by means of the ideology of adventure, and we will now examine it briefly, before analyzing it in the context of German imperialism of the nineteenth and twentieth centuries, because it makes sea trade, as derived from piracy, from freebooting, one of its most effective axioms. The pseudoargument supporting this view always proceeds in the same direction: capitalism arises from the innate drive for profit and adventure (Sombart calls it an "instinct"); this drive is the privilege of the few and—of course—at the same time the justification for oppressing and exploiting the masses. That among a confusion of other "intellectual"-historical facts the merchant adventurers were also called into play is almost a matter of course.[19] Let us therefore draw attention to several false imputations used manipulatively in this argument. As we saw, the concept of *aventure* or adventure was used in the course of its historical development by various social forces or classes to designate different things and activities. Originally the concept *adventura* probably (or definitely, in the first legal examples of its occurrence) referred to a more or less certain increase in fortune, a yield, a harvest, a catch. Because the nature of the yield was not absolutely certain, the concept moved into the semantic area of reference to risk and was used to designate a form of life or earning a living, when those who lived or earned their livings in this way needed an ideological justification of the changing situation of the class struggle. This ideological justification signals the end of that very form of life or earning a living: the glorification of the knightly *aventure* has as its primary purpose stabilizing a social situation or, concretely, guaranteeing the privileged position of the petty nobility in the framework of the developing princely or kingly courts. The thinking about *aventure* thus serves as the exact opposite of the life of *aventure*; it serves to protect against social risks, to guarantee social privileges, and to oppress or combat the rising revolutionary class, the bourgeoisie.

We will have to analyze a similar dialectical process of the formation and use of the ideology of adventure from the side of the bourgeoisie: from its function as an emancipatory ideology of the rising bourgeoisie within the feudal system, aimed at first unconsciously and then consciously against the feudal system (where the bourgeois self-designation as *aventurier*, "adventurer," is only a preliminary form) to its use as an ideology of exploitation and oppression, where its dialectical character is reflected in other respects as well. The bourgeois ideology of adventure as emancipatory is aimed against the nobility; as exploitative, it is aimed against the proletariat or against the restless petty bourgeoisie. And *from its beginnings*, it contains the dialectic of expansion, of the extension of power, of the increase of profit and security. The way in which this dialectic comes to the fore or takes effect depends on the actual historical process, on the development of the class struggle.

The (commerical) bourgeoisie, as had the knights, used the ideological concept of adventure, pilfered from their class opponents, to designate a long-existing form of life or of earning a living, the reasons for whose origin lie in the relations of production and not in an intellectual or biological-intellectual approach to the world. The (commercial) burgher calls his undertaking "adventure" because it is dangerous and not because he is looking for danger. On the contrary, from the *beginning* he makes every effort to reduce the risks of his form of life or making a living, as is reflected among others in the founding of the guilds and Hansas.[20] But by no means does he seek out risk for the sake of risk or because he is a born adventurer, a beast of prey, a man of violence. The speculations about a birth of capitalism from the spirit of adventure or rapine, derived from the ideologizing of capitalist phenomena, are completely untenable. In essence, Engels already said what needs to be said in his refutation of Eugen

Dühring who, like Sombart, tried to define modern (capitalist) property relations as "property founded on force." That is, by the assertion that capitalist property relations rest on property taken by force (for example, pillage), Dühring claims that capitalism is "that form of domination *at the root of which lies* not merely the exclusion of fellow-men from the use of the natural means of subsistence, but also, what is far more important, the subjugation of man to make him do servile work."[21] Engels is right in saying that Dühring

is making the whole relationship stand on its head. The subjugation of a man to make him do servile work, in all its forms, presupposes that the subjugator has at his disposal the instruments of labour with the help of which alone he is able to employ the person placed in bondage, and in the case of slavery, in addition, the means of subsistence which enable him to keep his slave alive. In all cases, therefore, it presupposes the possession of a certain amount of property, in excess of the average. How did this property come into existence? In any case it is clear that it may in fact have been robbed, and therefore may be based on *force*, but that this is by no means necessary. It may have been got by labour. . . . In fact, it must have been obtained by labour before there was any possibility of its being robbed. Private property by no means makes its appearance in history as the result of robbery or force. On the contrary. It already existed, though limited to certain objects, in the ancient primitive communes of all civilized peoples. It developed into the form of commodities within these communes, at first through barter with foreigners. The more the products of the commune assumed the commodity form, that is, the less they were produced for their producers' own use and the more for the purpose of exchange, and the more the original natural division of labour was extruded by exchange also within the commune, the more did inequality develop in the property owned by the individual members of the commune, the more deeply was the ancient common ownership of the land undermined, and the more rapidly did the commune develop towards its dissolution and transformation into a village of smallholding peasants. . . . Even the formation of a primitive aristocracy . . . took place on the basis of common ownership of the land, and at first was not based in any way on force, but on voluntariness and custom. Wherever private property evolved it was the result of altered relations of production and exchange, in the interest of increased production and in furtherance of intercourse—hence as a result of economic causes. Force plays no part in this at all. Indeed, it is clear that the institution of private property must already be in existence for a robber to be able to *appropriate* another person's property, and that therefore force may be able to change the possession of, but cannot create, private property as such.[22]

Petty Cooperative Robbery

Robbery and piracy, as practiced by the bourgeoisie, are of course linked with the precapitalist practice of trade, but they are relatively unimportant in view of the power relations in the feudal Middle Ages and compared with the violence that, on the one hand, is reflected in feudal exploitation or in the policy of wars of plunder and, on the other, was to arise from the prevalence of capitalism in trade and production and from its innate principle of free competition—although robbery and piracy by burghers did occur with greater frequency during the times of the feudal wars of plunder (for instance, during the Crusades). In other words, the violent appropriation practiced by commercial capital in the Middle Ages corresponded to the undeveloped economic relations or the undeveloped economic and political power of the commercial bourgeoisie itself. The commercial bourgeoisie as a fundamentally oppressed class could engage in robbery and piracy only within the framework of what was possible for it (although in Italy the situation was actually somewhat different). It could not hold up ships of the nobility, let alone of princes or kings; at best it had to make do with the ships of competitors from other "nations" or with pirates. In this undertaking, the cooperative organizations put reins on the commercial bourgeoisie, and the relative smallness of the booty (the ships had only a small loading capacity) made robbery and piracy necessarily a sideline, which it was also from an economic point of view (though in individual cases and measured against the general yardsticks of the time, it was lucrative). Plunder and robbery appear as derived forms of commercial capital in the "stages that preceded capitalist society,"[23] where it represents "simply the mediating movement between extremes it does not dominate and preconditions it does not create."[24] Commercial capital functions as a mediator between "exchanging producers"[25] or "spheres of production which in their internal structure are still oriented principally to the production of use-values."[26] The "extremes," the "exchanging producers," "remain separate from the circulation process," that is, they produce not for exchange, but for use; they therefore produce use-values and not goods. Merchants, however, take over the exchange of use-values from their producers:

> Here the product becomes a commodity through trade. It is trade that shapes the products into commodities; not the produced commodities whose movement constitutes trade. Capital as capital, therefore, appears first of all in the circulation process. In this circulation process, money develops into capital. It is in circulation that the product first develops as an exchange-value, as commodity and money. Capital can be formed in the circulation process, and must be formed there, before it learns to master its extremes, the various spheres of production between which circulation mediates.[27]

To be sure, trade, with its conversion of products into goods, had a loosening effect on the old relations of production; but until trade contributed to breaking down these old relations, they placed restrictions on it. As long as production is largely oriented to use-value, only a limited movement of goods can take place in circulation, even if this movement contains both the tendency to translate products into goods, that is, to break down the feudal relations of production, and the tendency to an unrestrained competitive battle, hence also to robbery and plunder. When the two "extremes," seller and buyer of products, are fundamentally opposed to each other as producers of use-values, when product is the equivalent of product, then the interposed trade must make its profit from the rate above the product equivalent.[28] As Marx writes:

> When commercial capital exchanges the products of undeveloped communities, commercial profit not only appears as defrauding and cheating but to a large extent does derive precisely from this. Apart from the fact that it exploits the difference between production prices in various countries (and in this connection it acts to equalize and establish commodity values), these modes of production enable commercial capital to appropriate for itself a preponderant part of the surplus product: partly by acting as middleman between communities whose production is still basically oriented to use-value, so that the sale of that part of their product that in some way or other steps into circulation, and thus the sale of products at their value in general, is of subordinate importance for their economic organization; and partly because in those earlier modes of production the principal proprietors of the surplus product whom the merchant trades with, i.e. the slave-owner, the feudal lord and the state . . . represent the consumption wealth which the merchant sets out to trap.[29]

There were still limitations set on determining the value of goods by the fact of having to defraud the "principal proprietors of the surplus product." The limitations arose also from the organization of trade into associations that set rates of profit by discussion within the "nations" and by profit shares, as Engels analyzed it. The rate of profit was not yet determined by free competition, as it would be in the epoch of fully developed commercial (and industrial) capitalism; instead, competition took place among the various "nations":

> But the high if equal level of the profit rate associated with this form of cooperation, a rate that was the same for all parties, held good only within the company, i.e. in this case the "nation." Venetians Genoans, Hanseatics, Dutch, each nation had a particular rate of profit, and one that was also to begin with more or less specific to each individual market area. The equalization of these various company rates of profit was brought about in the opposite way, by competition. First

of all, equalization between the profit rates in different markets for one and the same nation. If Alexandria offered higher profit for Venetian goods than did Cyprus, Constantinople or Trebizond, then the Venetians directed more capital to Alexandria and withdrew this from their trade with the other markets. Next came the gradual equalization of profit rates between the individual nations exporting the same or similar commodities to the same markets, which very often meant that certain of these nations were displaced and vanished from the scene. This process was constantly interrupted, however, by political events.[30]

or determined by those events, since the competitive behavior among the nations arranged itself according to political events; according to political relations, competition could take the form of privateering, of plunder, of warlike clashes between the members of enemy "nations" or between the latter and privateers or interlopers (trading ships belonging to no "nation").

The Dawn of the Era of Capitalist Production

"There can be no doubt," Marx declares,

—and this very fact has led to false conceptions—that the great revolutions that took place in trade in the sixteenth and seventeenth centuries, along with the geographical discoveries of that epoch, and which rapidly advanced the development of commercial capital, were a major moment in promoting the transition from the feudal to the capitalist mode of production. The sudden expansion of the world market, the multiplication of commodities in circulation, the competition among the European nations for the seizure of Asiatic products and American treasures, the colonial system, all made a fundamental contribution towards shattering the feudal barriers to production. And yet the modern mode of production in its first period, that of manufacture, developed only where the conditions for it had been created in the Middle Ages. Compare Holland with Portugal, for example.[31]

In fact it would be a cardinal error to derive the development of (commercial) capitalism from the discovery of new trade routes, of the New World and its exploitation. Instead, relations of production had already developed to such a point by the time of the discovery of the trade route around the Cape of Good Hope and of America that the expansion of trade and the discovery of new (shorter, hence faster) trade routes had become absolutely necessary. It is by no means an inconsiderable fact that Columbus did not set out to discover a new world but instead was looking for a faster and more comfortable route to India. It is equally noteworthy, as Engels points out, that trade to India and America was carried on "as before, predominantly by trading companies."[32] That means, on the one hand, that the trading companies had risen so high that they needed to expand their markets and, on the other hand, that in this transitional phase they were in the position to undertake this expansion.

The basis and point of departure for the entire development was primitive accumulation,[33] which played a significant role in trade:

> In themselves, money and commodities are no more capital than the means of production and subsistence are. They need to be transformed into capital. But this transformation can itself only take place under particular circumstances, which meet together at this point: the confrontation of, and the contact between, two very different kinds of commodity owners; on the one hand, the owners of money, means of production, means of subsistence, who are eager to valorize the sum of values they have appropriated by buying the labour-power of others; on the other hand, free workers, the sellers of their own labour-power, and therefore the sellers of labour. Free workers, in the double sense that they neither form part of the means of production themselves, as would be the case with slaves, serfs, etc., nor do they own the means of production, as would be the case with self-employed peasant proprietors. The free workers are therefore free from, unencumbered by, any means of production of their own. With the polarization of the commodity-market into these two classes, the fundamental conditions of capitalist production are present. The capital-relation presupposes a complete separation between the workers and the ownership of the conditions for the realization of their labour. . . . So-called primitive accumulation, therefore, is nothing else than the historical process of divorcing the producer from the means of production.[34]

We will not describe in detail the process of primitive accumulation, which Marx analyzes using England as an example: it has its "basis" in the "expropriation of the agricultural producer, of the peasant, from the soil"[35] by the bloodiest and most brutal methods (and its basis is thus in the agricultural revolution, in the genesis of the large capitalist farmer and in the repercussions for industry, from the "emancipation" of the banished peasant to his transformation into a wage laborer or proletarian). Instead—assuming this process as necessary for the development of commercial capital—we will sketch the repercussions of commercial capitalism for the formation of modern (industrial) capitalism, using Marx and Engels. "Trade naturally reacts back to a greater or lesser extent on the communities between which it is pursued," Marx determines; "it subjects production more and more to exchange-value, by making consumption and existence more dependent on sale than on the direct use of the product. In this way it dissolves the old relationships. . . . This solvent effect, however, depends very much on the nature of the community of producers."[36]

History proves that in countries like England and Holland, where the process of primitive accumulation was already far advanced, the repercussions of trade on this process were more serious than in less developed countries like Portugal and Spain. Fundamentally, however, there as elsewhere the "development of trade and commercial capital always gives production a growing orientation towards exchange-value," that is, from use- to exchange-value and hence to the dissolution of the original production.

> But how far it leads to the dissolution of the old mode of production depends first and foremost on the solidity and inner articulation of this mode of production itself. And what comes out of this process of dissolution, i.e. what new mode of production arises in place of the old, does not depend on trade, but rather on the character of the old mode of production itself. . . . In the modern world [as opposed to the ancient, slave-holding world—M. N.]. . . its outcome is the capitalist mode of production. It follows that this result is itself conditioned by quite other circumstances than the development of commercial capital.[37]

One of these other circumstances was the separation of "urban industry from agriculture,"[38] that is, the development of the cities. A further factor, however, was the breaking through geographical limits by means of the discovery of new trade routes or the New World, as we mentioned earlier.[39] But this process, too, is dialectical from the outset: the relations of production gave impetus to geographical expansion and the acceleration of trade; trade had a retroactive effect on the relations of production:

> Whereas in the sixteenth century, and partly still in the seventeenth, the sudden expansion of trade and the creation of a new world market had an overwhelming influence on the defeat of the old mode of production and the rise of the capitalist mode, this happened in reverse on the basis of the capitalist mode of production, once it had been created. The world market itself forms the basis for this mode of production. On the other hand, the immanent need that this has to produce on an ever greater scale drives it to the constant expansion of the world market, so that now it is not trade that revolutionizes industry, but rather industry that constantly revolutionizes trade.[40]

Engels shows that there were still other factors of decisive importance in this process; he points to the political influence of each different national development. In other words, the situation of the class struggle played a decisive role in this development (but this too was of course always the result of the process of economic development, which has been described in its main features). Where the party of the nobles, which was on the side of the absolute monarchy, showed itself ready, together with the prince or king, to enter an (economically and politically necessary) alliance with the commercial bourgeoisie (as for instance in England), where "in the sixteenth and seventeenth centuries, when modern bourgeois society was in its infancy, nations and princes were driven by a general desire for money to embark on crusades to distant lands in quest of the golden grail,"[41] this development was considerably accelerated. To be sure, it was the trading companies at first that carried on trade with the exploited lands overseas, as Engels states.

> But firstly, greater nations stood behind these trading companies. In place of the Catalonians who traded with the Levant, it was the whole of a vast and united Spain[42] that traded with America; next to it two countries as important as England and France; even Holland and Portugal, the smallest, were at least as big and powerful as Venice, the largest and strongest trading nation of the previous period. This gave the travelling merchant, the "merchant adventurer" of the sixteenth and seventeenth centuries, a backing that made the company which offered its members armed protection more and more superfluous, thereby making its expenses directly burdensome. Then, too, wealth in individual hands was now developing far more rapidly, so that soon individual merchants could deploy the same funds on an undertaking as a whole company could before. The trading companies, where they still continued to exist, were mostly transformed into armed corporations which conquered entire newly discovered countries, under the protection and ultimate sovereignty of the mother country, and exploited them monopolistically. But the more that colonies in the new zones were founded principally for the sake of the state, the more company trade retreated in the face of the individual merchant, so that the equalization of the rate of profit became ever more the exclusive result of competition.[43]

Let us pass over the details of the mechanism by which competition regulates rate of profit[44] (and also the problem of the distorted reflection of economic relations in competition)[45] and proceed to the (Marxian) formula: competition is the "most furious combat" "between the capitalists for their individual share in the market," which they attempt to expand by "cheapness of the product."[46] On the one hand, that affects the degree of exploitation of the work force (the worker) for the increase of the rate of profit, which then can be lowered through competition; on the other hand, it also affects the methods of blocking competitors from the sources of raw materials or from the market, where nation-state power politics are thoroughly united with the individual interest of the company or the single capitalist (at least in the "early stages of modern bourgeois society").

Competition (along with credit) is the "most powerful lever" for annihilating the competing capitalist (or for the centralization of dispersed capital). In contrast to the cooperative capitalist, the emancipated modern capitalist no longer recognizes his fellows and can no longer recognize them, on the basis of the inescapable "immanent laws" of capitalist production: "One capitalist always strikes down many others."[47] In the epoch that interests us here, however, first of all, the capitalist allies himself with his prince or king and the party of nobles supporting the sovereign and strikes down, in addition to the political opponents of the king (and hence also of the bourgeoisie), the feudal opposition party of nobles; later, in addition to the competitors from his own class, he strikes down the natives of distant lands. Or he enslaves them by turning them into goods (as goods in the slave trade) or into wage slaves (especially for the stolen or conquered mines). Just after Marx's statement that commercial capital derives from "defrauding and cheating" when it "exchanges the products of undeveloped communities," he writes that "commercial capital, when it holds a dominant position, is thus in all cases a system of plunder, just as its development in the trading peoples of both ancient and modern times is directly bound up with violent plunder, piracy, the taking of slaves and subjugation of colonies."[48] And in volume 1 of *Capital* he specifies:

The discovery of gold and silver in America, the extirpation, enslavement and entombment in mines of the indigenous population of that continent, the beginnings of the conquest and plunder of India, and the conversion of Africa into a preserve for the commercial hunting of blackskins, are all things which characterize the dawn of the era of capitalist production. These idyllic proceedings are the chief moments of primitive accumulation. Hard on their heels follows the commerical war of the European nations, which has the globe as its battlefield.[49]

Usury Restricts the Spirit of Enterprise

The anarchy of the process of revolutionizing the relations of production, whose protagonist was the commercial or manufacturing bourgeoisie, can hardly be imagined: violent expropriation of small peasants accompanied peasant uprisings, revolts by the nobility, wars of religion, wars of plunder, slave trade, and genocide. The political framework in which this anarchic upheaval took place was that of the developing absolute monarchy. The monarchy depended on the bourgeoisie as much as on the latter's immediate class opponent, the feudal nobility, who resisted the formation of the absolute monarchy and therefore stood in opposition to the king as well as to his henchmen, the bourgeoisie. In the course of this struggle, both the king (and with him the absolutist party of the nobles) and the reactionary feudal nobility became dependent on the bourgeoisie, whose best weapon was money. As the bourgeoisie lent money to one or the other party, it made that party its debtor, with varying results. The king and the absolutist party of the nobility used the borrowed money (remember the spectacular example of the Fuggers!) to buy the means to power in order to subjugate the recalcitrant feudal nobility and to ensure political dominance (over the feudal nobility *and* the bourgeoisie), to unite the country, and to pursue a policy of foreign conquest. But the bourgeois moneylenders bled the antiabsolutist nobility or the petty nobility dry (through usurious interest). As Engels tells us:

> The nobles were no longer able to do without [money—M. N.] and because they had little or nothing left to sell, and because plundering was no longer so easy, they had to decide to borrow from bourgeois usurers. Long before the knightly castles had been breached by the new guns, they were undermined by money.... Money was the great political leveler of the bourgeoisie. Wherever a personal relation was displaced by a money relation, a natural achievement by an achievement of money, there a bourgeois relation displaced a feudal one. To be sure, the old brutal natural economy in most cases continued to exist in the country; but there were already whole districts where lords and subjects had already taken the first decisive step toward the transition to landowners and tenants, that is, where even in the country the political arrangements of feudalism were losing their social basis.[50]

They would not have lost it if in the meantime the previously described process of primitive accumulation had not taken place at the same time as the formation of commercial capital or of increasing production of goods. For usury by itself cannot revolutionize social relations:

> Two of the forms in which usurer's capital exists in phases prior to the capitalist mode of production are particularly characteristic.... These two forms are, *firstly*, usury by lending money to extravagant magnates, essentially to landed proprietors; *secondly*, usury by lending money to small producers who possess their own conditions of labour, including artisans, but particularly and especially peasants.... Both of these things, the ruining of rich landed proprietors by usury and the impoverishment of the small producers, lead to the formation and concentration of large money capitals. But the extent to which this process abolishes the old mode of production, as was the case in modern Europe, and whether it establishes the capitalist mode of production in its place, depends entirely on the historical level of development and the conditions that this provides.[51]

The precapitalist form of usury is basically consumer credit:[52] the money loaned—to simplify—is completely expended by the borrowers, and thus does not breed new money. Repayment under usurious conditions (interest rates of over 200 percent were not uncommon,[53] although the amount of interest was less crucial than the fact that the money was not "working") had to be made from the "surplus labour" of the "victim":[54] from what the serf or small producer produced beyond what was needed for his own use or for the feudal lord. Even when the usurer's demands go further than this "surplus labour of his victim" and he "gradually obtains the ownership title to his [the victim's—R. C.] conditions of labour themselves—land, house, etc.—and consistently sets out to expropriate him in this way"[55] (which Luther, for instance, fully recognizes and condemns),[56] that still does not cause a change in the mode of production.

> Where the means of production are fragmented, usury centralizes monetary wealth. It does not change the mode of production, but clings on to it like a parasite and impoverishes it. It sucks it dry, emasculates it and forces reproduction to proceed under ever more pitiable conditions. Hence the popular hatred of usury.... Usury has a revolutionary effect on precapitalist modes of production only in so far as it destroys and dissolves the forms of ownership which provide a firm basis for the articulation of political life and whose constant reproduction in the same form is a necessity for that life.[57]

In the case of Luther, for instance, this "popular hatred" is linked with religious zeal and theological polemics (especially against the Catholic conception of usury),[58] which makes him impervious to any modern form of usury as well. His verdict is categorical: he distrusts usury in every form.[59] To be sure, usury at just that time was undergoing a crucial metamorphosis that was determining the public discussion and that would be incomprehensible without the process of the formation of capitalist production we have sketched out. On the one hand, usurer's capital was finding use in commercial capitalism, from which it developed, to the degree that trade was expanding: usurer's capital transformed itself into the capital of financial transactions.[60] On the other hand, usurer's capital was changed by the very process of primitive accumulation, which also allowed trade to grow increasingly. Marx writes:

> The Middle Ages had handed down two distinct forms of capital . . . usurer's capital and merchant's capital. . . . The money capital formed by means of usury and commerce was prevented from turning into industrial capital by the feudal organization of the countryside and the guild organization of the towns. These fetters vanished with the dissolution of the feudal bands of retainers, and the expropriation and partial eviction of the rural population. The new manufactures were established at sea-ports, or at points in the countryside which were beyond the control of the old municipalities and their guilds.[61]

Usurer's capital, in connection with this development, was a brake on capitalist production in its beginnings: money as commercial capital (but also as capital for manufacturing)[62] was increasingly more necessary, but the high rate of usurious interest and the slow circulation of money capital within feudal production made it difficult to raise money (to purchase goods). The merchant (as a merchant—often he was a usurer as well) began to polemicize ever more strongly against usury in its medieval form (and not as a matter of principle, like Luther).[63] Then too, increasing capitalist production entailed an ever greater expansion of markets and distances, so that even the usurer's capital wrung from feudal production together with the commercial capital resulting from feudal production and trade could no longer manage the movement of goods.[64] Marx draws the conclusion that "credit is thus indispensable here," credit that could only be drawn from the surplus value earned in capitalist production:

> a credit that grows in volume with the growing value of production and grows in duration with the increasing distance of the markets. A reciprocal effect takes place here. The development of the production process expands credit, while credit in turn leads to an expansion of industrial and commerical operations.[65]

Here, too, let us pass over the details of this development from medieval usury to modern credit as a special manifestation of (industrial) capital "that exists in a certain phase of the reproduction process."[66] "In its early phase capitalist production, having gained strength, seeks to subordinate interest-bearing capital [usurer's capital—M. N.] to industrial [or commercial—M. N.] capital by force,"[67] by combating and polemicizing against high interest rates and the means of collection of usurer's capital (that is, there is a fundamental recognition of the necessity of money trade = usury and a protest against its manifestations and "against the amount of interest").[68] This is reflected among other things in the demand for the enforced setting of a (low) rate of interest. For "interest-bearing capital proves itself as such only insofar as the money lent really is transformed into capital and produces a surplus, of which interest is one part."[69] That was, however, not to be achieved by usurer's capital.

As surprising as it might at first seem, the polemics against usurer's capital or usurious interest contribute to the formation of the modern ideology of adventure (and form—in part up to the present[70]—an integral element of this ideology). Marx referred to this in passing, in speaking of the transformation of credit from (usurer's) consumer credit to interest-bearing capital credit:

> What distinguishes interest-bearing capital . . . from usurer's capital is in no way the nature or character of this capital itself. It is simply the changed conditions under which it functions, and hence also the totally transformed figure of the borrower who confronts the money-lender. Even where a man without means obtains credit as an industrialist or merchant, it is given in the expectation that he will function as a capitalist, will use the capital borrowed to appropriate unpaid labour. He is given credit as a potential capitalist. And this fact so very much admired by the economic apologists, that a man without wealth but with energy, determination, ability and business acumen

can transform himself into a capitalist in this way—just as the commercial value of each person is always assessed more or less correctly in the capitalist mode of production—much as it constantly drives an unwelcome series of new soldiers of fortune onto the field alongside and against the various individual capitalists already present, actually reinforces the rule of capital itself, widens its basis and enables it to recruit ever new forces from the lower strata of society.[71]

It is a matter of course that this state of affairs analyzed by Marx became an increasingly rare exception (in view of the centralization of capital funds). In the early phase, however, there were very real possibilities here, which find their ideological expression in the glorification—of enterprising, daring youth (a phenomenon that must have been quite foreign to the hierarchically ordered feudal Middle Ages). Usury in its traditional form appeared as the old, the outmoded; credit, on the other hand, as the new, the lively: "The credit system originally is a *polemical form* directed against the old-fashioned usurers (goldsmiths in England, Jews, Lombards, and others). The seventeenth-century writings in which its first mysteries are discussed are all produced in this polemical form."[72]

This polemical attitude toward old-fashioned usury is expressed in Thomas Wilson's *Discourse upon Usury* of 1572, although the author rejects usury altogether. In this treatise, written as a dialogue, he has a lawyer give arguments for modern forms of usury, and it is noteworthy that he needs a new word for (commercial) credit in order to distinguish this from medieval usury. He asks why, if, for instance, four people banded together, two of whom contributed capital and the other two their labor and efforts, those who risk their money (who adventure) should not participate in the profits from the common enterprise, even if they sit at home idle. The lawyer says to his conversation partner: "But you wil saye, perhappes: this is no usury. I cannot tell what you call usurye."[73]

A year before the appearance of this treatise, a memorandum circulated in the government determined: "Usury and trewe interest be things as contrary as falshed is to trewth. For usury contayneth in itself inequalitie and unnaturall dealige and trewe interest observeth equitie and naturall dealinge."[74] Usury, it continued, destroys the prosperity of the society; true interest on the other hand is an accomplishment for human society. The lawyer in *Discourse upon Usury* argues in a very similar way (and in part also the learned doctor, who cites Calvin as a witness for churchly or theological tolerance of moderate interest):[75] he asks what one can gain from letting earned money lie fallow instead of placing it at the disposal of another merchant for his use.[76] Forbidding moneylending could even be a sign of hardheartedness.[77] None of these parties (except the merchant, who sees it as a restriction) questions the (medieval) view of the justified exchange of money (*cambium*) and of trade in general, to the extent that risk (adventure) is present or work is done. They reject financial and other business dealings where both things are absent.[78]

Only the merchant, parodistically named Gromelgayner, opposes this view; his position is exaggerated by Wilson so that it can be demolished better and more simply. Gromelgayner is against any kind of limitation of trade and of financial transactions as well as against setting rates of interest[79] (while the lawyer, for instance, suggests setting the rate of interest):[80] anyone who forbids (unlimited) profit, says Gromelgayner, destroys trade, because where there is nothing to be gained, no one will venture anything.[81] Quite apart from that, one cannot forbid moneylending, because both state and nobility are dependent on borrowing from the merchants: "We lend not for usurie, but for interest, and by exchange,"[82] he determines. His apprentice (actually an employee), however, states what Marx calls the dream of the capitalist, pure and simple (the direct conversion of M into M_1): wherever possible, the capitalist would realize profits without risking his capital in "Adventure . . . in merchaundizes beyonde the seas," without exposing himself to loss through shipwreck, pirates, or unreliable employees.[83] The merchant's arguments are so radical and hence so unusable that they also impinge on the effect of the lawyer's arguments, and as Wilson wanted, the final victor is the clergyman with his (medieval) point of view; the merchant indicates that he is repentant.

But—and this is not insignificant—the modern radical and moderate views on usury and credit are also presented. In fact, this is already an indication of what R. H. Tawney calls the fundamental tendency of the further development: "the secularisation of the whole discussion,"[84] a process that is already substantially concluded with Francis Bacon. In Bacon we find confirmation for what Marx says about the seventeenth-century writings on the usury question: with a basic recognition of the necessity of money trade (of credit), Francis Bacon polemicizes against the "old-fashioned usurers." This by no means leads him to blindness about credit. In the third edition of his *Essays* of 1625, he says in the chapter "Of Usury," which is significantly placed between the chapters "Of Fortune" and "Of Youth and Age": "Many have made witty invectives against usury."[85] He would prefer, however, to weigh the disadvantages and advantages of money trade against each other. His fundamental result with respect to the disadvantages is that usury in its traditional form takes money out of circulation and inhibits trade, thus damaging the state, which collects fewer taxes, and so forth.

> On the other side, the commodities of usury are, first, that howsoever usury in some respect hindereth merchandizing, yet in some other it advanceth it, for it is certain that the greatest part of trade is driven by young merchants upon borrowing at interest; so as if the usurer either call in or keep back his money, there will ensue presently a great stand in trade. . . . Therefore to speak of the abolishing of usury is idle.[86]

Bacon's suggestions are aimed at alleviating the disadvantages while keeping the advantages. To accomplish this, two things must be united:

> The one, that the tooth of usury be grinded, that it bite not too much; the other, that there be left open a means to invite monied men to lend to the merchants for the continuing and quickening of trade. This cannot be done except you introduce two several sorts of usury, a less and a greater. For if you reduce usury to one low rate, it will ease the common borrower, but the merchant will be to seek for money. And it is to be noted that the trade of merchandize, being the most lucrative, may bear usury at a good rate; other contracts not so. To serve both intentions, the way would be briefly thus. That there be two rates of usury; the one free and general for all, the other under licence only to certain persons and in certain places of merchandizing.[87]

As the lower rate of interest, Bacon suggests 5 percent. That should be the general base. Authorized usurers should lend to well-known merchants at a higher rate. That means not only that less-known merchants, especially young merchants, should be allowed to borrow at the lower rate, but also that larger merchants should not be bled too hard:

> Secondly, let there be certain persons licensed to lend to known merchants upon usury at a higher rate, and let it be with the cautions following. Let the rate be, even with the merchant himself, somewhat more easy than he used formerly to pay, for by that means all borrowers shall have some ease by this reformation, be he merchant or whosoever.[88]

The compromise Bacon here proposes extends into his considerations about youth and age, where the emphasis is on the combination of youthful spirit of enterprise and the expertise of age:

> Young men in the conduct and manage of actions embrace more than they can hold; stir more than they can quiet; fly to the end, without consideration of the means and degrees; pursue some few principles which they have chanced upon absurdly; care not to innovate, which draws unknown inconveniences.... Men of age object too much, consult too long, adventure too little, repent too soon, ... content themselves with a mediocrity of success. Certainly it is good to compound employments of both, for that will be good for the present.[89]

Thirty-nine years after Bacon's *Essays*, the treatise by Thomas Mun, *England's Treasure by Forraign Trade*, appeared. (Mun lived from 1571 to 1641, and from 1615 on was a member of the board of directors of the East India Company.) This treatise once again underlines the usefulness of financial transactions for "younger and poorer Merchants" (without further specification of the rate of interest): "How many Merchants, and Shop-keepers have begun with little or nothing of their own, and yet are grown very rich by trading with other men's money?"[90] Five years later, in 1669, Josiah Child (1630-99, from 1674 on also a member of the board of directors of the East India Company) wrote his major work, *A Discourse of Trade*, in which he—one of the most determined opponents of a high rate of interest—polemicized sharply against old-fashioned usury. Marx excerpted from a French translation what interests us here. These excerpts contain arguments that we will encounter over and over in eighteenth-century France, as an integral part of the basic argument against the feudal-governmental limitation of trade and hence also against feudal oppression in general: the affirmation of risk (of courage), the polemics against laziness, and the implicit conclusion that daring and diligence, realized in trade and manufacturing, are useful for the state. Josiah Child reproaches an opponent (Thomas Manley) in the discussion about interest rates: "As the champion of the timid and trembling band of usurers he erects his main batteries at that point which I have declared to be the weakest a high interest rate . . . I am the defender of industry and my opponent defends laziness and sloth. The patriotic conclusion is that if it is commerce that enriches a country, and if a lowering of interest increases commerce, then a lowering of interest or a restriction of usury is doubtless a fruitful primary cause of the wealth of a nation."[91]

On the Little Thief and the Big Thief; or, The Fear of Anarchy

Let us return to the violent, anarchic upheaval of social relations at the beginning of the sixteenth century: it naturally brought with it fear and horror. An example of this is Luther, who by the way had a much sharper eye than later apologists of the capitalist system (like Sombart, for instance) for the fact that it was not the hierarchic, guildsman merchant of the Middle Ages but the modern commercial capitalist (in keeping with the greater scope of his activities) who developed the qualities of a "beast of prey." "Now the merchants make great complaint about the nobles or robbers,—saying that they have to transact business at great risk and are imprisoned and beaten and taxed and robbed,"[92] Luther writes in his treatise "On Trading and Usury" (1524). The merchants under discussion here can only be the small, hierarchically ordered, guildsman traders that the Middle Ages produced and of which, as we will see, Luther basically approves. Nonetheless he makes fun of them in this passage, not because he wants to defend highwaymen and robber barons (he would like to see the barons punished by the prince or king), but because he wants to mount a polemic against the large-scale merchants, the modern commercial capitalists, and also against the large trading companies, on whom he calls down the wrath of God. For these merchants whom he detests are of course beyond the reach of highwaymen and robber barons (recall again the Fuggers), are subject to no dangers of that sort, unless something were to happen to one of their goods transports on land or sea. But even that would not significantly reduce their wealth, and that is what outrages Luther, who sees in the large-scale merchants, or more precisely in the alliance of the commercial bourgeoisie and the prince or king, a threat to the hierarchic feudal order, because it is a divine order. He correctly recognizes that money is to blame for this threat, that money is from the devil:

> How could it ever be right and according to God's will that a man should in a short time grow so rich that he could buy out kings and emperors? But they have brought things to such a pass that the whole world must do business at a risk and at a loss, winning this year and losing next year, while they always win, making up their losses by increased profits, and so it is no wonder that they quickly seize upon the wealth of all the world, for a *pfennig* that is permanent and sure is better than a *gulden* that is temporary and uncertain. But these companies trade with permanent and sure *gulden*, and we with temporary and uncertain *pfennigs*. No wonder they become kings and we beggars![93]

Actually, Luther believes, kings and princes ought to put a stop to this disruption of order, to the accumulation of money and the concomitant increase in power:

> But I hear that they have an interest in them, and the saying of Isaiah is fulfilled, "Thy princes have become companions of thieves." They hang thieves who have stolen a *gulden* or half a *gulden* and trade with those who rob the whole world and steal more than all the rest, so that the proverb may hold true: Big thieves hang the little ones.[94]

Luther prophesies a global conflagration if an end is not put to the large-scale merchants or the trading companies.[95] But since no one is doing that at the moment, God is punishing the large-scale merchants in the small ones, by sending highwaymen and robber barons after them:

> To be sure, it may happen that one of them suffers some wrong before God, in that he has to suffer for another in whose company he is found and pay for another man's sins; but because of the great wrong that is done and the unchristian thievery and robbery that is practiced by the merchants themselves all over the world, even against one another, what wonder is it if God causes this great wealth, wrongfully acquired, to be lost or taken by robbers, and the merchants themselves to be beaten over the head or imprisoned besides?[96]

To be sure, Luther, in talking about "all over the world," does not mean possible injustice to the plundered natives of distant lands (for these are not Christians); he means the new forms of commercial capital that have an effect primarily in competition, which he calls "thievery and robbery. . . against one another," profiteering by means of trade monopolies and especially lending money to the upper nobility, which creates a dependence of the nobility on commercial and usurer's capital. Martin Luther warns against the impending overthrow of social relations, out of which merchants could emerge as "kings." "All over the world" means the Christian world in its feudal version.

Utopia; or, The Attempt to Tame Anarchy

The implicit warning to princes and kings to see to the divine order—that is, to restore the old order by depriving the bourgeoisie of power—at first sounded without echo; the reaction of the absolutist nobility occurred only later. But it was not only the great Protestant theologian who felt anxiety about the anarchy developing in the relations of production or the social order; anxiety also shapes the work of Thomas More, his *Utopia* (1516), incorrectly labeled by scholarship "the first great English romance" of nautical literature;[97] sea travel, after all, plays a very ambiguous role in this novel. Supported by a self-aware bourgeoisie diametrically opposed to Luther, *Utopia* represents the attempt to direct the unleashed (productive) forces on the right path in the interest of the bourgeoisie, to convert the internal and external anarchy of excess or of adventurous distant travel into a rational, surveyable (insular) order. It is clear that this cannot take place without internal contradictions. Censure of the nobles and princes, which bears impressive witness to the self-consciousness of the English bourgeoisie, is joined with praise of the *vita activa*, moderated by the bourgeois code of virtue, religious tolerance, and wisdom in national politics, to form a political treatise that cannot be understood as utopian, or not in the sense in which we use that term today.[98] *Utopia* does not contain a vision of the future with desirable or undesirable social relations (or technical developments); instead it presents the negation of concrete social relations in England. The draft of another, in More's view better, social order arrived at through this negation contains retrograde, as well as progressive, elements of an ideology that must be understood as an attempt at orienting a moderate bourgeoisie toward trade (as contemporaries like Guillaume Budé did understand it).[99] Nevertheless, while it is quite true "that More with his *Utopia* tries to give an answer to the problems of his time, an answer to the question as to how the individual, liberated by the economic development, can be integrated in a new way into a humane and just social order,"[100] because he does not penetrate the economic laws governing this development, his plan for a solution must remain unrealizable. The novel can be called "utopian" only in the very narrow sense of "not practically realizable": in contrast to most of his imitators, More did not shift his social counterimage to the English state of his time into a dream realm beyond this world or into a dreamed-up future but places it in the quite possible reality of the *as yet undiscovered world*. His novel appeared only twenty-four years after the discovery of America, when the new continent was still hardly explored and the discovery of previously unknown peoples and social orders was absolutely not impossible (just ten years after the appearance of *Utopia*, Pizarro discovered, conquered, and destroyed the Inca nation, which by the way had startling similarities to the state drafted by More).

More himself anchors his novel firmly in the historical context of his time, in the "agricultural revolution" of England on the one hand, in which the peasants were driven off so that the arable land could be converted into grazing land (for wool production), a time when "[sheep] are becoming so greedy and wild that they devour men themselves, as I hear. They devastate and pillage fields, houses, and towns."[101] On the other hand, More sets his work in the context of the voyages of discovery and conquest at the turn of the century. The Portuguese adventurer Raphael Hythlodeus appears as a critic of English conditions and the reporter about the nation Utopia; he sailed with Amerigo Vespucci (1451-1512). And that constitutes one of the basic contradictions in More's work: he pleads in favor of voyages of discovery, for the geographic decoding of the world, while at the same time polemicizing against the unlimited large-scale trade and the developing link between commercial and industrial capital. More designed a "communist" society in which no one works more than six hours a day, in which production is collectively planned to cover the needs of the society, to make possible exportation of the surplus and to limit imports to very few, necessary wares, "not only such goods as they lack at home (in fact, the one important thing they lack is iron) but immense quantities of silver and gold."[102] His economic idea in fact presents a remarkable mixture of "communist" and mercantilist thinking but is basically, in respect of the inner organization of production, oriented toward the medieval, hierarchic production of use-values.[103] With his economic idea, however, Thomas More removes in theory the causes of its origin.

His plea for a substantial enclosure of the land from the rest of the world (Utopia is an island like England; in fact, it was forcibly and pointedly separated from the mainland by the Utopians, by means of a huge canal)[104] necessarily leads to numerous absurdities. It is characteristic that travel, one of the most important social activities in the age of beginning capitalism,[105] constitutes a particular problem for More. He imputes to the Utopians a certain indifference to travel in general (when they travel at all, then only as a sort of touring business travelers).[106] Because they dislike travel and are an island people relatively isolated from the rest of the world, the Utopians are unable on their own to gain any geographical knowledge or information about other people and their trade; at the same time, they are also dependent on this information. They must therefore get their information from foreigners: "Any sightseer coming to their land who has some special intellectual gift, or who has traveled widely and seen many countries, is sure of a special welcome, for they love to hear what is happening throughout the world."[107] The Utopians are thus interested in the information that they cannot or will not gather themselves. But they are quite happy to have others instruct them; therefore there must be some value in it for them. In fact, did not a sailor tell the English island people, to their advantage, the history of Utopia after he had first told the Utopians about Europe? What Thomas More denies to the island population of Utopia and hence also to England, long sea voyages, adventure voyages, he affirms in the person of Raphael Hythlodeus, whom he respectfully calls a new "Ulysses," even a "Plato," and who is a passionate adventurer, arrived at Utopia "in this way... altogether agreeable to him, as he was more anxious to pursue his travels than afraid of death."[108]

But the Utopians are dependent on the chance that brings such an adventurer to them, for "few merchants, however, go there to trade. What could they bring except iron—or else gold and silver, which everyone would rather bring home than send abroad?"[109] Bring home from where? More here touches a central nerve of the economic prosperity of the late fifteenth and early sixteenth century: What would England be without the shipping trade? what would Utopia be? Once again he involves himself in contradictions. The Utopians are cut off from the world on the one hand; since they do not travel, they need information from foreigners who come to them because of love of travel; on the other hand, they do engage in sea trade, even more *intelligently* than the English themselves: "As for their export trade, the Utopians prefer to do their own transportation, rather than invite strangers to do it. By carrying their own cargoes they are able to learn more about their neighbors and keep up their skill in navigation."[110]

What More here imputes to his Utopians as the maxim of their trading is one of the most important battle cries of the English commercial bourgeoisie of this time, when the merchant adventurers' increasingly importunate appeals to the king were piling up. Sea trade should no longer be left to foreigners; specifically, the cloth and wool export from England should no longer be left to the Hanseatic League, which had a much greater share of it than the merchant adventurers,[111] or the foreigners should no longer be granted corresponding privileges; instead, these privileges should be given to the "kynges subiettes marchauntes."[112] Paradoxically, with his demand that the Utopians be emulated (also in their trade practices), More, the advocate of insular isolation, thus finds himself in complete agreement with the demands of the mobile, traveling, sailing, expanding avant-garde of his class, whose self-awareness prevails in just this inner contradiction in More's design of a state.

That is true also of his polemics against the useless classes:

Now isn't this an unjust and ungrateful commonwealth? It lavishes rich rewards on so-called gentry, bankers, and goldsmiths [usurers— M. N.] and the rest of that crew, who don't work at all, are mere parasites, or purveyors of empty pleasures. And yet it makes no provision whatever for the welfare of farmers and colliers, laborers, carters, and carpenters, without whom the commonwealth would simply cease to exist.[113]

To be sure, his censure of the nobility is more than justified, and he even correctly censures the terrible consequences of the large feudal landowners' driving off the peasants. But as in the case of his polemics against long-distance sea travel or the preeminence of gold or money (with his simultaneous affirmation of an economy of exchange and credit run by the state,[114] or of a mercantile policy of national treasure), More does not (and probably could not) see that what he attacks furnishes the basis that enables him, as representative of a rational bourgeoisie, to announce through the mouth of Raphael Hythlodeus "that men choose a king for their own sake, not for his. . . . This is why, I would say, it is the king's duty to take more care of his people's welfare than of his own."[115] Nor does More penetrate the dynamic process of class struggle in the (temporary) historical alliance between the bourgeoisie and the king along with the absolutist-oriented party of the nobles. The political design of his state is thus also useless for a society whose relations of production, and hence also the relations of the class struggle, are being revolutionized.

Once a year, every group of thirty households elects an official, formerly called the syphogrant, but now called the phylarch. Over every group of ten syphogrants with their households there is another official, once called the tranibor, but now known as the head phylarch. All the syphogrants, two hundred in number, are brought together to elect the prince. They take an oath to choose the man they think best qualified; and then by secret ballot they elect the prince from among four men nominated by the people of the four sections of the city. The prince holds office for life, unless he is suspect of aiming at a tyranny.[116]

Laughter; or, The Fundamental Affirmation of Anarchy

A group of 9,876,543,210 Utopians (excluding of course women and children), "artificers of all trades, and professors of all sciences," found a colony in Dipsody in order "to people, cultivate, and improve that country."[117] The novel in which this is narrated appeared in 1546: *Le Tiers Livre des Faicts et Dicts Héroiques du Bon Pantagruel* (The Third Book of the Heroic Deeds and Tales of the Good Pantagruel) by François Rabelais. Pantagruel, son of the giant

Gargantua, King of Utopia, liberated his country from the enemy and conquered the land of his opponents, Dipsody. Now he is settling it. What makes more sense than to bring in good, diligent Utopians, since Rabelais himself had settled the race of giants, the Grandgousier, Gargantua and Pantagruel, in this Utopia? To be sure, it resembles Thomas More's Utopia not at all, which does not mean that Rabelais and More have nothing in common. They share the abhorrence of the senseless wars of conquest of their times (if Pantagruel himself conquers a land, it is because his own was first attacked and occupied and because he liberates the land of the enemy from a tyrant); they share the bourgeois self-confidence before the thrones of princes; they share the affirmation of the practical sciences; and they share the tolerance in religious matters.

But otherwise, what a difference between More, concerned with measure and discipline, rules and industry, and Rabelais, immoderate in every respect, whose books about Gargantua and Pantagruel, despite or because of their excessiveness, are much more realistic than the novel by More, who by the way is as humorless as the life of the Utopians he imagined, with their syphogrants: "The chief and almost the only business of the syphogrants is to manage matters so that no one sits around in idleness, and assure that everyone works hard at his trade."[118] This idea of permanent supervision of every individual must have been unbearable to Rabelais. His ideal is that of the human being responsible for himself, educated to (individual and social) freedom in intellectual and physical harmony, as produced by the (élite) school the Abbey of Thélème, which Pantagruel's father had Frère Jean des Entommeurs build, equip, and administer. "Do what thou wilt" is the motto of this university of the art of living, "because men that are free, well-born, well-bred, and conversant in honest companies, have naturally an instinct and spur that prompteth them unto virtuous actions, and withdraws them from vice, which is called honor."[119]

This honor is only distantly related to the knightly-courtly concept of honor. What is represented in the Abbey of Thélème is the principle of Epicurean, Renaissance-enlightened affirmation of life, behind which, however, there still lurks a remnant of skepticism, for it must not be forgotten that everything— hence also everything Rabelais affirms—is decisively relativized by the grotesque, by the laughter with which Rabelais presents it. There can certainly be some doubt whether Rabelais completely affirms the revolution of his time, the escape of the (bourgeois) human being from his (medieval) prison, but he was fully aware of its contradictions and atrocities. Where Pantagruel sees the key to social harmony in the creation of a new order, specifically in the new form of government of absolute monarchy (symbolized by the counseling of the gigantic prince Pantagruel by his non-noble advisers), his friend and companion Panurge finds the key to human happiness in an anarchic principle that continually overturns social relations and impels them forward: the credit system. Pantagruel has installed Panurge as administrator of a lairdship, but Panurge administers "so providently well and prudently, that in less than fourteen days he wasted and dilapidated all the certain and uncertain revenue of his lairdship for three whole years."[120] Pantagruel (quite in the spirit of Thomas More) reproaches him and stresses the necessity for ensuring prosperity. If Panurge wants to become rich, he must first of all save.[121] But Panurge expresses little respect for this kind of wealth. In his opinion, real wealth rests on debt, that is, on the assumption of credit: if I have not all my life-time held debt to be as an union or conjunction of the heavens with the earth, and the whole cement whereby the race of mankind is kept together.[122]

It is idle to speculate whether Rabelais was as naïve about the system of trade and money of his time as this and other passages in his novel make it appear, but even in the vagueness of the episode described above, the antagonism of the two principles of the rational miser (Panurge) and the irrational capitalist (Pantagruel) shows through. This antagonism is not completely worked out or acted upon, but is cloaked in burlesque and sealed with a shrug by Pantagruel, who does not believe Panurge; it is the same antagonism that determines the action in *Fortunatus* with greater precision, but also with greater sobriety and dryness. And yet, what Fortunatus or the anonymous author of the Augsburg novel knows is also known to Rabelais and is all the more sharply profiled as a skeptical sediment within the burlesque. Just as Fortunatus recognizes that love is over without capital or money, so Panurge recognizes that money alone, in its modern form, determines human behavior: "It will be but lost labour to expect aid or succour from any, or to cry fire, water, murder, for none will put to their helping hand. Why? He lent no money, there is nothing due to him. . . . In short, Faith, Hope, and Charity would be quite banished from such a world"[123]—unless further loans be assumed, more financial transactions be set in motion. And already a burlesque irony shows through: if there were no more financial transactions, then "Faith, Hope, and Charity" would vanish from the world: "for men are born to relieve and assist one another."[124] Thus credit and mercy have become one. When Pantagruel, despite his opposite opinion to Panurge's, passes over this with a shrug, that is because the wealth of the world seems inexhaustible:[125] compared to that, what is the prodigality of Panurge, whose rational core he cannot or will not accept? The huge numbers Rabelais juggles are not without function. They signal the inexhaustible nature of earthly wealth, the excess of this (bloody) escape from the old, unfree, feudal relations that Rabelais commemorates with his laughter. If the reader (still, and especially, today) feels horror at this laughter, that is fully justified by the historical reality. Rabelais's optimism is boundless, embraces all lands and continents. It is directed at the future, toward which one must wade through a sea of blood: only unworldly scholars or cynics can take as a mere literary game the numbers of those who die by impaling, by the spear, by burning, by quartering, by beheading in his novels in view of the numbers who died by impalement, by the spear, by burning, by quartering, by beheading in the real world. The people who banned Rabelais's books and persecuted Rabelais certainly did not take it as a game (although their reasons were probably only partly to be found in the realism of the atrocities he describes: they were too much an everyday occurrence). The optimism of the bourgeoisie has its price partly in the mad paroxysms of this time, and laughter alone makes them bearable and makes the price seem not too high.[126]

Scholarship has repeatedly stressed that in Rabelais's novels, among other things, one can find a parody of the knightly romance of adventure. That is basically true, but the function of this parody must be clarified. The Spanish picaresque novels, the *novelas picarescas*, also represent, as we have seen, parodies of the knightly romance of adventure, but they are an expression of hopelessness, as are the knightly romances themselves (although the class-specific causes are different). Neither the knightly romance nor the Spanish picaresque novel can be given closure or were given closure by their authors: if in the knightly romance the search for adventure goes off into the infinite fairy-tale world or into a fairy-tale-like infinity, the passive adventures of most of the protagonists of the Spanish picaresque novels have no end. The protagonists set off on their way without having or reaching a real goal.

In Rabelais, things are different: there is a goal. It is the "dive bouteille," the "divine bottle." It is not improbable that this can be considered a parody of the grail which King Arthur's knights sought. Their quest was for an unattainable goal beyond the real world; that of Pantagruel, Panurge, Frère Jean des Entommeurs, Epistemon, has a pointedly earthly goal: wine, which of course has a symbolic function (and is simultaneously real wine). "Good people, most illustrious drinkers,"[127] Rabelais addresses his readers and invites them to drink from his cask to their hearts' content because this cask is "inexhaustible," and at its bottom, which is unreachable, there is hope, "non désespoir," "not despair."[128]

The cask is Rabelais's book; the wine that can be drunk from it and that is inexhaustible and full of hope is the infinite plenitude of life. Everything is in motion toward this plenitude; it is the goal of another endless journey, not because there is no goal to the journey but because the goal is inexhaustible. The journey therefore can never end, and yet ceaselessly takes place within the goal itself. The goal is constantly being reached in the activity of living: the journey through life to life takes place in human praxis, and when Rabelais speaks of a journey, he means the journey as symbol and as real journey on land and sea. Like the anonymous author of *Fortunatus* or Thomas More before him, Rabelais anchors his grotesque, gigantic, symbolic journeys firmly in the historical context of his times. Jacques Cartier (1494-?) set off toward the west in 1534 and a year later discovered Canada. Pantagruel follows Cartier's path with his ships and his companions,[129] and the choice of this travel route is a conscious rejection of the travel route to the East Indies, which the Portuguese follow and which is too long, "through the torrid zone, and Cape Bona Speranze."[130]

We will not explore the details of the geography of Pantagruel's journey with his companions. They are less important than the fundamental acceptance of ship travel (for trade), to which Rabelais in his way gives a gigantic form: "Do with my treasures what unto yourself shall seem most expedient.... Take... whatsoever equipage, furniture, or provision you please, together with such pilots, mariners, and truchmen, as you have a mind to, and with the first fair and favorable wind set sail and make out to sea, in the name of God our Savior."[131]

Pantagruel and Panurge

If we ask, quite prosaically, about the two protagonists of the novel cycle (apart from *Gargantua*), we can determine the following (while ignoring for a moment the fact that both are more than this, as burlesque and simultaneously serious symbolic figures): Pantagruel is a prince, and Panurge is an adventurer who accompanies and advises the prince. We have here, along with other constellations of characters, as one of the most important elements of the novel a partnership of prince and non-noble, which we encountered in *Fortunatus* as well as in *Utopia*, where Thomas More advises the king to take the counsel of scholars (among the advisers of François I were burghers at the beginning of his reign, and for the rest he had a special staff of advisers, the *Conseil des Affaires*, who advised him just as Pantagruel's companions advised him).[132] This partnership is neither so prosaic nor so fairy-tale-like as in *Utopia* or *Fortunatus*; it oversteps historical reality just as it oversteps the pragmatism of Thomas More or the outmoded fairy-tale nature of *Fortunatus*.

As Erich Auerbach correctly observes, the individual figures in Rabelais's novels—in contradiction to the neo-Aristotelian theory of literature, which Rabelais must have known—represent remarkable types, but by no means "unified characters":

> Rabelais has created very strongly marked and unmistakable characters, but he is not always inclined to keep them unmistakable; they begin to change, and suddenly another personage peers out of them, as the situation or the author's whim demands. What a change in Pantagruel and Panurge during the course of the work! And even at the given moment, Rabelais is not much concerned with the unity of a character, when he mingles complacent cunning, wit, and humanism, with an elementally pitiless cruelty which is perpetually flickering in the background.[133]

It is therefore senseless to play one figure off against another in order to present them as especially typical for their time or, least of all, as "Renaissance men" following Burckhardt's example.[134] The image that Rabelais draws of the human being of his time is, in its negation of the present, partially the image of the physically and intellectually liberated human being of the future. With a certain validity, one can say of this image of the human being that it is exemplary for the time we call the Renaissance (though we must not forget that More's Utopians, Fortunatus, and also the *cortegiano* and his companions belong to the image of the human being of that time). It is the image derived from the totality of the new human qualities assembled in all the figures of the Pantagruel novels. As inappropriate as it is to see all these qualities collected into one figure, it is just as inappropriate to isolate one figure and to see in it one certain quality, abstracted from the whole context:

> This rise of man to wholeness in the natural world, this triumph of the animal and the creatural, offers us the opportunity to remark in more detail how ambiguous and therefore subject to misconstruction is the word individualism, which is often, and certainly not unjustifiably, used in connection with the Renaissance. There is no doubt that, in Rabelais' view of the world, in which all possibilities are open, which plays with every aspect, man is freer in his thinking, in realizing his instincts and his wishes, than he was earlier. But is he therefore more individualistic? It is not easy to say. At least he is less closely confined to his own idiosyncrasy, he is more protean, more inclined to slip into someone else's shoes; and his general, super-individual traits, especially his animal and instinctive traits, are greatly emphasized.[135]

With this as a premise, let us pay special attention to the education of Pantagruel and the function of Panurge. Pantagruel is not only particularly gifted by nature, both physically and intellectually, but also was raised according to the most progressive pedagogical views. His father, Gargantua, sends him to Paris, where after a certain time he receives the letter that has become famous as a document of the humanist thought of that time, in which Gargantua challenges him to perfect himself "In virtue, honesty, and valour, as in all liberal knowledge and civility."[136] Gargantua delivers a critique of the past, of the decline of the sciences (in the Middle Ages) that prevented him from being educated in the way now possible for his son. The study of old languages (Greek, Latin, Hebrew, Chaldean) has come into new flower, and the possibility of applying oneself to it is greater than ever before (in fact, François I had given impetus to the reform in this area): "I see robbers, hangmen, free-booters, tapsters, ostlers, and such like, of the very rubbish of the people, more learned now than the doctors and preachers were in my time."[137] Even women and girls have now fallen prey to the hunger for learning (Rabelais dedicates *Le Tiers Livre* to the spirit of Marguerite de Navarre); but Pantagruel should learn languages above all and in addition school himself in the *artes liberales* like geometry, arithmetic, and music (but should leave astrology strictly alone). Great weight should be placed on geography and natural science ("faictz de nature") as well as on the study of medicine and finally on the Holy Scripture. Pantagruel is to have studied all of this by the time of his return, because then will begin his schooling in "chevalerie et les armes," in the arts of war, so that he will be able to protect and govern the land.

Immediately after receiving this letter, Pantagruel encounters a young, poorly dressed man who will complement him and his knowledge in a meaningful way, whom he immediately accepts and loves, and who will never leave him:

> Do you see that man . . . ? By my faith, he is only poor in fortune; for
> I may assure you, that by his physiognomy it appeareth, that nature
> hath extracted him from some rich and noble race, and that too much
> curiosity hath thrown him upon adventures, which possibly have
> reduced him to this indigence, want, and penury.[138]

It is Panurge, whom Pantagruel addresses and who answers him in fourteen languages (among them Hebrew, Greek, Latin, Italian, Spanish, German, English, and Dutch).

Much has been written about the figure of Panurge, with a stress among other things on his relationship to the ancient god Hermes.[139] This is correct, but we could also draw up the account differently. Hermes is, among other his functions, the god of travelers and of merchants. But just as the figure of Panurge in its function as Hermes is embedded with all realism in the contemporary present (the first information about Panurge's life refers to his participation in a historical expedition against the Turks in 1502),[140] so also the figure, as a friend and adviser of Pantagruel, actively participating in the (burlesque) events, is more than a mere mythological reminiscence or a citation from humanistic education: the prince Pantagruel allies himself with the god of trade and thereby with the commercial bourgeoisie itself. Panurge represents therefore not only the god Hermes, but also the merchant, the avant-garde of the bourgeoisie, which explains not only his views on the credit system but also his ability to get money in exactly thirty-six different ways, as well as his practical accomplishments and his knowledge (but also his lack of heroism and his preference for trickery, which is also appropriate to him as Hermes). The episode in which his talent for trade, his function as a merchant most clearly links him with the ram-bearing Hermes is the one in which he buys the best wether from a merchant and thereby ruins this merchant (his competitor).[141]

Chapter 7
The Merchant Adventurer Leaves the Ship

The Threefold Birth of the Capitalist

Pantagruel and Panurge—who, if not they, embodies in literature the dimensions of that time about which Engels writes:

> It was the greatest progressive revolution that mankind has so far experienced, a time which called for giants and produced giants—giants in power of thought, passion and character, in universality and learning. The men who founded the modern rule of the bourgeoisie had anything but bourgeois limitations. On the contrary, the adventurous character of the times inspired them to a greater or lesser degree. There was hardly any man of importance then living who had not travelled extensively, who did not speak four or five languages, who did not shine in a number of fields.... The heroes of that time were not yet in thrall to the division of labour, the restricting effect of which, with its production of one-sidedness, we so often notice in their successors. But what is especially characteristic of them is that they almost all live and pursue their activities in the midst of the contemporary movements, in the practical struggles; they take sides and join in the fight, one by speaking and writing, another with the sword, many with both. Hence the fullness and force of character that makes them complete men. Men of the study are the exception—either persons of second or third rank or cautious philistines who do not want to burn their fingers.[1]

Engels names a few representative heroes of that time: Leonardo da Vinci,

Dürer, Machiavelli, Luther. But what was called for was the man who no longer wanted to burn his fingers, who paid and still pays for others to do his dirty work, make his profits, who was no longer one of the adventurers, the giants, but who, faceless, manipulated the strings from which they all more or less hung, which made the adventurers jump until they had been corrupted into managers, agents, hirelings, or advertising specialists: the capitalist. He was born in this time of the "dominant position" of commercial capital, a transitional time in which—as is already clear from the very formulation—along with the "dominant" mode of production, other modes of production continued to exist or new modes were arising. On the one hand, the feudal mode of production of course continued (with extreme regional variations); on the other, the caste-based guild trade also continued until around the end of the seventeenth century (in England):

> But with the extension of the production of commodities, and
> especially with the introduction of the capitalist mode of production,
> the laws of commodity-production, hitherto latent, came into action
> more openly and with greater force. The old bonds were loosened, the
> old exclusive limits broken through, the producers were more and
> more turned into independent, isolated producers of commodities. The
> anarchy of social production became apparent and grew to greater and
> greater height.[2]

The protagonist of this process was the *homo novus*, the "New Man," the capitalist, who appeared in a threefold form on the stage of world history—in order to disappear from it in his individuality:

> First, the merchant becomes an industrialist directly; this is the case
> with crafts that are founded on trade, such as those in the luxury in-
> dustries, where the merchants import both raw materials and workers
> from abroad, as they were imported into Italy from Constantinople in
> the fifteenth century. Second, the merchant makes the small masters
> into his middlemen, or even buys directly from the independent pro-
> ducer; he leaves him nominally independent and leaves his mode of
> production unchanged. Third, the industrialist becomes a merchant
> and produces directly on a large scale for the market.[3]

Without further exploring the qualitative difference here ("The producer may become a merchant and capitalist. . . . This is the really revolutionary way," as Marx says elsewhere),[4] all three types of capitalist have in common the appropriation of the means of production (although in varying forms, which is quite relevant for us). The previous owner of the means of production who had used them to produce independently is thereby transformed into a paid worker who, instead of selling his product as he had done, now sells his labor. The transformation into a wage laborer, however, also transforms the purchaser of the labor, the capitalist:

Concentration of large masses of the means of production in the hands of individual capitalists is a material condition for the co-operation of wage-labourers, and the extent of co-operation, or the scale of production, depends on the extent of this concentration. We saw in a former chapter that a certain minimum amount of capital was necessary in order that the number of workers simultaneously employed, and consequently the amount of surplus-value produced, might suffice to liberate the employer the [future capitalist—M. N.] himself from manual labour, to convert him from a small master into a capitalist, and thus formally to establish the capital-relation.[5]

"To liberate the employer himself from manual labour"—that means first of all that the capitalist (in his revolutionary form, as an industrialist who will become merchant and capitalist) is no longer active in the material process of production. This, along with other premises, is also of course true of the capitalist who takes charge of the means of production as a merchant: not only is he himself not active in the material process of production, but he no longer needs to be personally involved in trade, carrying goods to sell himself, carrying out transports, and so forth. One can even say that this process of retreat from the material execution of the process of production begins in the age of the "dominant position" of commercial capital: the larger the commercial capitalist becomes (and at the same time the more he thereby gives impetus to the development of modern capitalism), the less he needs to intervene himself in the difficulties and dangers of transporting goods.[6] But that means merely that the capitalist (in whichever of his three forms) in person and by means of his own person, with its physical qualities and manifestations, has become irrelevant to the process of production and circulation, a development we already saw in *Fortunatus*, where the author presented us with two stages of the development of commercial capital. The first stage is determined by Fortunatus, active himself as a merchant adventurer; the second, by Fortunatus as a commercial capitalist, who turns over the execution of his business to agents, employees, captains, "patrons."

It is a matter of total indifference to capitalist production how the individual who functions as a capitalist looks. Whether he is short or tall, handsome or ugly, strong or weak, brilliant or uneducated, all that has no effect whatsoever on the process of production or circulation, even if he guides that process himself, at least in the early stages, and sometimes even today.[7]

As the conscious bearer [*Träger*] of this movement [of capital—M. N.] the possessor of money becomes a capitalist. His person, or rather his pocket, is the point from which the money starts, and to which it returns. The objective content of the circulation we have been discussing— the valorization of value—is his subjective purpose, and it is only in so far as the appropriation of ever more wealth in the abstract is the sole driving force behind his operations that he functions as a capitalist, i.e. as capital personified and endowed with consciousness and a will.[8]

The function of the capitalist is "as capital personified and endowed with consciousness and a will," but his individuality is completely irrelevant for the process of production. In other words, his individual manifestation (young or old; handsome or ugly; brave or cowardly) can no longer give information about his *social function* or reveal it. This fact creates considerable difficulties for the apologists for capital (but also for those who—as opponents of capital—give literary or artistic form to the capitalist):

> Except as capital personified, the capitalist has no historical value, and no right to that historical existence which, to use Lichnowsky's amusing expression, "ain't got no date." It is only to this extent that the necessity of the capitalist's own transitory existence is implied in the transitory necessity of the capitalist mode of production. But, in so far as he is capital personified, his motivating force is not the acquisition and enjoyment of use-values, but the acquisition and augmentation of exchange-values. He is fanatically intent on the valorization of value; consequently he ruthlessly forces the human race to produce for production's sake.... Only as a personification of capital is the capitalist respectable. As such, he shares with the miser an absolute drive towards self-enrichment. But what appears in the miser as the mania of an individual is in the capitalist the effect of a social mechanism in which he is merely a cog. Moreover, the development of capitalist production makes it necessary constantly to increase the amount of capital laid out in a given industrial undertaking, and competition subordinates every individual capitalist to the immanent laws of capitalist production, as external and coercive laws.[9]

We cannot ignore the fact that as it develops, there will be a change in the relation of the capitalist's attitude to accumulated capital; he will cease to be "merely the incarnation of capital,"[10] that is, he will continue to be the incarnation of capital *as well* as acquiring new qualities, which will be reflected especially in the relation of the capitalist to the social public sphere ("Luxury enters into capital's expenses of representation").[11] But that does not affect the state of affairs: the capitalist as capitalist in his self-presentation or as presented by his apologists places less and less value on being portrayed as an adventurer (where this does occur, as for instance in Spengler, among others, it corresponds to the historical situation of the class struggle, a development we will have to analyze). The man who consciously presented himself as an adventurer, as a bold, risk-seeking entrepreneur who defies every risk, is gradually becoming, in the presentation of his apologists, an entrepreneur who is subjected to adventures, is exposed to risks, is concerned about the common weal, is at pains to create order (this is also the current presentation). This shift in the (self-)presentation of the capitalist from adventurer to order-loving entrepreneur who maintains the state and is endangered, even persecuted, is only possible because his individual appearance does not reveal that he is the one who sets all adventures and all adventurers in motion, who pays (in order to make a profit), that he is the one who supports "the anarchic system of competition,"[12] "the anarchy and proneness to catastrophe of capitalist production," and hence the anarchy of the capitalist system in general. "As capital personified and endowed with consciousness and a will," he functions as competition "subordinates" him to "the immanent laws of the capitalist mode of production" "as external and coercive laws," but he, invisible in his individuality, no longer gets his hands dirty.

The Other Side of Capitalist Anarchy

Two factors enable the capitalist to appear as a guarantor of order, among other things: the fact that one cannot tell by looking at the capitalist individual that he, as personified capital, is the financier and organizer of the "anarchy and proneness to catastrophe of capitalist production"[13] and hence of social anarchy in general; and his function as financier and supervisor of the greatest machinery of subjugation in world history, within which the strictest hierarchical order reigns: capitalist production. As Marx says,

> at first, the subjection of labour to capital was only a formal result of the fact that the worker, instead of working for himself, works for, and consequently under, the capitalist. Through the co-operation of numerous wage-labourers, the command of capital develops into a requirement for carrying on the labour process itself, into a real condition of production. That a capitalist should command in the field of production is now as indispensable as that a general should command on the field of battle. All directly social or communal labour on a large scale requires, to a greater or lesser degree, a directing authority.... The work of directing, superintending and adjusting becomes one of the functions of capital, from the moment that the labour under capital's control becomes co-operative. As a specific function of capital, the directing function acquires its own special characteristics.[14]

The greater the mass of workers subject to exploitation, the greater becomes the antagonism "between the exploiter and the raw material of his exploitation,"[15] the workers:

> The co-operation of wage-labourers is . . . brought about by the capital that employs them. Their unification into one single productive body, and the establishment of a connection between their individual func-

tions, lies outside their competence. These things are not their own act, but the act of the capital that brings them together and maintains them in that situation. Hence the interconnection between their various labours confronts them, in the realm of ideas, as a plan drawn up by the capitalist, and, in practice, as his authority, as the powerful will of a being outside them, who subjects their activity to his purpose.[16]

That means that the capitalist mode of production produces, in addition to the *homo novus* or the capitalist, his "shadow" (Engels) the wage laborer or the proletarian—and the "shadows" increase in number as production grows. This army of workers is forced into the "despotic form" of capitalist production. The proletarian appears on the stage of world history from the very beginning as subject to this "despotism," as someone pigeonholed, subordinated, commanded, exploited: as the *antitype* to the adventurer and—in his figure as a revolutionary element, as a class called upon to remove or sublate the social anarchy of the capitalist mode of production, whose material producer he at the same time is—as *antiadventurer*. His activity is prescribed for him, every motion is decreed, his time is subject to an exact schedule, even his life is for the most part transformed into strictly regulated work time. He lacks everything that makes the adventurer an adventurer: the possibility of setting out and returning of his own volition, of seeking out hazardous enterprises in distant lands. His radius of action is the route from his dwelling to the factory and from the factory to his dwelling (later he will have to fight for any increase of his radius of action as a member of an organized working class: more freedom, then vacation, and even the right to travel at all). His only freedom consists in selling his labor, to the extent he finds a buyer for it. If (for economic and political reasons) the capitalist as capitalist is no longer *allowed* to present himself as an adventurer (and if he does no longer do so), the worker as worker *cannot* be an adventurer (or he would cease to exist as a worker). If he tries, voluntarily or through coercion, to be an adventurer, he joins the lumpenproletariat, becomes a thief or is treated as such (as in England, by forced expropriation).[17] His existence as a wage laborer of capital extends from the Scylla of proletarian existence to the Charybdis of unemployment. The worker as worker cannot break out of this vicious social circle, cannot liberate himself from this "despotism" that dominates him, by an (impossible or fantasized) transformation into an adventurer. That can happen only elsewhere than in the realm of adventure, though at this time he cannot yet realize that. "It is the compelling force of anarchy in the production of society at large that more and more completely turns the great majority of men into proletarians; and it is the masses of the proletariat again who will finally put an end to anarchy in production."[18]

For the critique of the modern ideology of adventure (especially in the nineteenth and twentieth centuries), the precondition is the state of affairs noted in relation to the capitalist and the proletarian; this is also true for particularly cynical variants in which, for instance, unemployment is spoken of as a particularly favorable precondition for the wage laborer's breaking through the limitations of his existence in his search for adventure. At this time, to be sure, the mass army of the proletariat exists only in its very rudimentary stages. It coexists with the great mass of feudal serfs and the very small producers of handicrafts before capitalist production forces them all into the enslavement of material production in the "social anarchy of production":

> chief means by aid of which the capitalist mode of production intensified this anarchy of socialized production was the exact opposite of anarchy. It was the increasing organization of production, upon a social basis, in every individual productive establishment. By this, the old, peaceful, stable condition of things was ended. Wherever this organization of production was introduced into a branch of industry, it brooked no other method of production by its side. . . . The field of labour became a battle-ground. The great geographical discoveries, and the colonization following upon them, multiplied markets and quickened the transformation of handicraft into manufacture. The war did not simply break out between the individual producers of particular localities. The local struggles begat in their turn national conflicts, the commercial wars of the seventeenth and eighteenth centuries. . . . The contradiction between socialized production and capitalistic appropriation now presents itself as *an antagonism between the organization of production in the individual workshop and the anarchy of production in society generally.*[19]

The dialectics of this process contain the key to the fact that the capitalist can strip off his adventurer's skin and can transfer to his agents, his employees, his anarchic function as personified, faceless capital, something he is also forced to do by the mode of production. We must here take a historical change into account that corresponds to the development of capitalist production and the resultant division of labor. In the initial phase of adventure trade, the execution of business, the supervision of the persons working on it, the transport, and the concluding of business were all in the hands of a "patron" who often called himself an adventurer, a captain, for instance, who functioned as a manager, overseer, and agent with a proxy. Gradually this function was divided up and spread over various persons, corresponding to the development of production that made necessary an increasingly specialized division of labor. The curve extends from the manager to the salesman who goes from house to house offering the goods of a company (by the way, the advertising for this occupation uses every conceivable cliché from the ideology of adventure). The original adventurer employee gradually becomes the more specialized "commercial wage laborer," who by the way assumes a very special heritage: the external manifestations of the former guildsman adventurer and of the small feudal merchant, divided by work function. The manager with proxy must be "decisive" and "willing to take risks" (although he will of course be fired if he is too decisive or too willing to risk); the traveling salesman must be good-looking, young (it is the rule to fire these salespeople for reasons of age, with forty often being the limit); he, like the office employee or the (good-looking) secretary, must know foreign languages.[20] They must all be well dressed, well behaved, must carry out their orders without complaint; the commercial wage laborer assumes all these qualities, divided up by work function, as an inheritance from the codes of behavior and appearance of the feudal guildsman merchants, as we encounter them in the most various handbooks of the epoch or in the rules of the guilds. All these qualities, which are a duty for the commercial wage laborer or a precondition for his even finding work, are fundamentally inessential for the personification of capital, the capitalist. These qualities too, present or not present or inessential, correspond to the dialectics of external anarchy and internal hierarchical order described by Engels:

> Although on the basis of capitalist production the social character of their production confronts the mass of immediate producers in the form of a strict governing authority, and the social mechanism of the labour process has received here a completely hierarchical articulation— though this authority accrues to its bearers only as the personification of the conditions of labour vis-à-vis labour itself, not to them as political or theocratic rulers as in earlier forms of production—the most complete anarchy reigns among the bearers of this authority, the capitalists themselves, who confront one another simply as owners of commodities, and within this anarchy the social interconnection of production prevails over individual caprice only as an overwhelming natural law.[21]

On Cut-Throats

But the development is still far from that stage; true adventurers still exist side by side with commercial capitalists who hire adventurers to work for them; risk is still present for large-scale merchants, who give up their risky activities only gradually, in order to function as the faceless personification of capital, and also for manufacturers. Risk is still not socialized in the same measure as profit is privitized, via insurance companies, banking and credit systems, and currency profiteering. The early industrialists still even call themselves adventurers[22] because their business is uncertain and they could disappear again tomorrow in the general anarchic revolution, swallowed up by a stronger competitor or annihilated or driven off by a class enemy, the absolutist nobility and its monarch (for even given the alliance between the absolutist nobility and the bourgeoisie, we must not forget that it is an alliance between bourgeoisie and one faction of their class antagonists, the nobility, against another faction of the nobility, and that as the other faction is removed or eliminated, the class antagonism again becomes acute, sometimes leading to the naked oppression of the bourgeoisie). There is still an oppressor class over the true adventurers, over the artisans in feudal caste-based guilds, but also over the early capitalist in his threefold form. The time of revolutionizing the relations of production was also a time of extremely bitter class struggles, and if this time called for giants, then giants were also called for in the battle against the oppressive nobility. The time needed giants and engendered them, and the glorification of entrepreneurship, of activity, of travel, of trade, of—adventure, was determined by this situation of class struggle: "But this mighty revolution in the conditions of the economic life of society was, however, not followed by any immediate corresponding change in its political structure. The political order remained feudal, while society became more and more bourgeois."[23] And in the battle against this order, the bourgeois glorification of adventure was also effective. It was the bourgeois glorification of adventure and not the counterrevolutionary knightly ideology of adventure that was effective; the knightly ideology—especially as an import from Spain— was quite virulent.

> Where economic relations required freedom and equality of rights, the political system opposed them at every step with guild restrictions and special privileges. Local privileges, differential duties, exceptional laws of all kinds affected in trade not only foreigners and people living in the colonies, but often enough also whole categories of the nationals of the country concerned; everywhere and ever anew the privileges of the guilds barred the development of manufacture. Nowhere was the road clear and the chances equal for the bourgeois competitors—and yet that this be so was the prime and ever more pressing demand.[24]

And this was the first demand also within the bourgeois glorification of adventure, with which the bourgeoisie implicitly and explicitly pleaded against existing limitations and for a striking out for new, distant horizons. The bourgeois glorification of adventure was still a vehicle for the fundamental postulates of freedom and hence a weapon in the battle for the liberation of the human being (or it would become such a weapon once it was formulated):

> The demand for liberation from feudal fetters and the establishment of equality of rights by the abolition of feudal inequalities was bound soon to assume wider dimensions, once the economic advance of society had placed it on the order of the day. If it was raised in the interests of industry and trade, it was also necessary to demand the same equality of rights for the great mass of the peasantry who, in every degree of bondage, from total serfdom onwards, were compelled to give the greater part of their labour-time to their gracious feudal lord

without compensation and in addition to render innumerable other dues to him and to the state.[25]

The transformation of production from use- to exchange-values, the gradual replacement of the feudal by the capitalist mode of production, still provided— and, except in England, basically continued to provide until the French Revolution of 1789—the basis for the free development of the individual (with the simultaneous creation of the unliberated working class, subjugated after the victory of the bourgeoisie). As Marx writes in the *Grundrisse*:

> Universally developed individuals, whose social relations, as their own communal relations, are hence also subordinated to their own communal control, are no product of nature, but of history. The degree and the universality of the development of wealth where *this* individuality becomes possible supposes production on the basis of exchange values as a prior condition, whose universality produces not only the alienation of the individual from himself and from others, but also the universality and the comprehensiveness of his relations and capacities.[26]

The link between "production on the basis of exchange values" and the creation of the "universally developed" individual was already obvious in *Fortunatus*: the knowledge and skills Fortunatus acquires all serve his purpose of becoming rich (as a commercial capitalist), just as wealth then serves to satisfy his curiosity about getting to know the people and the country. The expansion of trade drives Fortunatus into the world because he wants to become rich, and his activity in the world (of trade) entails the necessity of learning foreign languages and geography, acquiring information about the customs and mores of various nations (which then is immediately reflected in individual inclination, individual interest). About half a century before the appearance of the first German (trade) route handbook, the *Raissbüchlin* by Jörg Gail (which, significantly, appeared in Augsburg in 1563), Fortunatus writes down everything that strikes him as noteworthy on his travels through Europe and he organizes it in a primitive kind of card catalog,

> since he traveled through all the countries and kingdoms, noted and saw their customs and mores and their beliefs with exactitude, even made himself a little book where he wrote down all the kings and dukes, counts, barons, and also the princes of the Church, bishops, abbots, prelates, and land and people he had traveled among and had seen, and what each of them was capable of.[27]

Marco Polo's description of his travels to China made the late thirteenth century aware of the connection between travel description and the collection of geographic and social information that was useful for trade. The famous treatise by Giovanni Pegolotti, *Practica della mercatura* (Handbook of Trade, 1342), made the fourteenth century aware of this connection; this work was followed in the fifteenth century by Alberti's *Della Famiglia* as well as by the writings of Giovanni da Uzzano and Bennedetto Cotrugli.[28] These works, however, do not as yet show a view of the unboundedness of the world and the individual that characterizes Fortunatus or the novel by the same name. Of course the "universally developed" individual manifests himself in the fairy-tale-like figure of Fortunatus, but also in the figure of Raphael Hythlodeus and even in faint outline in the figures of the companions of Pantagruel. But *Fortunatus* already contains a sketch of the course of development that leads to figures like Francis Bacon, who in his foundation of modern natural science, the *Novum Organum*, London, 1620, wrote with pride about the universal nature of his activities, from scientist to statesman ("me videant, hominem inter homines aetatis meae civilibus negotiis occupatissimum"—"look at me, the most involved of all human beings of my time in the business of state").[29] What links Fortunatus with Bacon and with the "universally developed" individual discussed by Marx is curiosity, the thirst for learning, for physical and intellectual mobility, the desire for practically useful knowledge, for the connection between knowledge and activity in society. The age was in fact full of such individuals; Engels calls them "giants" who speak "four or five languages" and have "travelled extensively," who "shine in a number of fields."

And nevertheless, as we have mentioned, this is also the age in which that type of human being was born (and did not go unnoticed by his contemporaries) who distanced himself personally from the "movement of the times," who absented himself from the "practical struggle" or let others conduct it, who did not want to burn his fingers, who moved into faceless anonymity, to the same degree that the activity he himself first carried out, then directed and organized, assured his social rise.[30] Not surprisingly, it is Luther who smells a rat wherever the talk is of large-scale merchants:

> Again it is called "living off the street" [i.e., on someone else's money—R. C.] if a merchant has a purseful of money and wishes no longer to subject his goods to the risks of land and sea, but to have a safe business, and settles down in a great business city. Then when he hears of a merchant who is pressed by his creditors and must have money to satisfy them and has none, but has good wares, he gets someone to act for him in buying the wares and offers eight gulden for what is otherwise worth ten. If this offer is not accepted, he gets someone else to offer six or seven, and the poor man begins to be afraid that his wares are depreciating and is glad to take the eight so as to get cash money and not to have to stand too much loss and disgrace. It happens too, that these needy merchants seek out such tyrants and offer their goods for cash with which to pay their debts.

They drive hard bargains and get the goods cheap enough and afterwards sell them at their own prices. These financiers are called "cutthroats," but they pass for very clever people.[31]

What so enrages Luther is, on the one hand, the ruthless competition of the merchants among themselves, but on the other—and this is by far the larger cause—the fact that there are merchants who no longer endure adventures in person and who moreover want to evade any sort of business risk. Luther recognizes exactly the merchant's motives for developing other forms of trade than that of personal adventure: greater security and higher profits. The merchant no longer does battle with highwaymen, footpads, pirates, or natural dangers; instead he carries out the war against his competitor via his agents. He ruins his competitor through financial transactions or forces him to sell his goods under their price after spying out his need or with bluffs. This type of merchant "wishes no longer to subject his goods to the risks of land and sea"; instead, he finances his business and has it carried out by strawmen or employees, and his title of "financier" shows that the connection between commercial capital and usurer's capital had meantime become current.

To be sure, the merchants, especially the sea traders, had long since begun to reduce their risk to the minimum possible. The formation of the guilds or Hansa organizations was part of this attempt, as was the "cashless" traffic, the business of loaning money in the form of the currency transfer we described, that aimed at independence from an individual, more or less unsupervised usurer. The development of "credit associations" began as early as the "twelfth and fourteenth centuries in Venice and Genoa." They "arose from the need for marine commerce and the wholesale trade associated with it to emancipate themselves from the domination of outmoded usury and the monopolization of the money business."[32] At the same time the insurance system began to develop.[33]

Practical measures for making (sea) trade safe went hand in hand with these measures. This took many forms: improvement of the system of communication; improvement and safeguarding of the transport routes (for example by founding branches and establishing settlements of the "nations"); improving shipbuilding and the military equipment of the ships as well as the formation of the *commenda* system, in which one partner invested money or goods, the other undertook to execute the transport (with a share in the business through money or goods, or else without such a share). Profit was then figured and divided according to the share of invested capital (or the agreed-upon share for undertaking the physical risk).[34] Not long afterwards, the partner who undertook the risk in person, who was originally on an equal footing, the *socius* who saw to the transport in the *commenda* system, became the employee, the specialist in transport or shipping hired for this purpose, a mix of trader, captain, and mercenary, the *condottiere* of whom we spoke briefly in the chapter on Machiavelli, or the hired adventurer, etc.

A further safety factor is the acquisition of privileges for the export, transport, and sale of certain goods, which the various trading companies, formed according to the *commenda* system and its historical variations, tried to secure in the form of trade and transport monopolies. In return for certain payments, they placed themselves under the protection of a prince or a city, which granted or sold them land rights, staple rights, and sale rights or even monopolies and in this way tried to eliminate trade rivals with the help of government authorities. The merchant adventurers also behaved according to this principle, for which Luther cannot forgive them (as he cannot forgive setting a rate of profit, which we mentioned in discussing Engels's presentation):

> This trick, I hear, is practiced chiefly and mostly by the English
> merchants in selling English or London cloth. It is said that they have
> a special council for this trade, like a city council, and all the English-
> men who sell English or London cloth must obey this council on
> penalty of a fine. The council decides at what price they are to sell
> their cloth and at what day and hour they are to have it on sale
> and when not. The head of this council is called the "court-master"
> and is regarded as little less than a prince. See what avarice can and
> dare do.[35]

Luther's "court-master" was the Governor of the Courts of the Merchant Adventurers. He was charged with making sure that the "stint" was observed in the settlements of the adventurers and that all other rules and agreements within the company, the fellowship, were respected; otherwise he had to adjudicate any litigations that arose.[36] Luther considers pricesetting, with exclusion (of competition that could lower prices) by the association monopolists, in this case the adventurers, to be an unparalleled sin:

> These people are not worthy to be called men or to live among other
> men, nay they are not worth exhorting or instructing; for their envy
> and greed is so open and shameless that even at the cost of their own
> losses they cause losses to others, so that they may have the whole
> place to themselves. The authorities would do right if they took from
> such people everything they had and drove them out of the country.[37]

This last statement (in connection with Luther's polemics against the large-scale merchants, *because* they turn themselves into kings, that is, because they use their money to reach positions of social power that endanger the feudal system and the position of the nobility) lends credence to Müntzer's reproach that Luther was intentionally silent about the true cause of the general poverty of society, the feudal nobility, in order to flatter them.[38] The reasoning Luther presents is not convincing. While he polemicizes against the Catholic theory of usury, which tolerates financial transactions if they are accompanied by a certain risk ("[that] is pretty and showy"),[39] he attacks trade monopolies in his condemnation of the trading companies or the large-scale merchants, because they lend protection against risk

> so that they remain sure of their profit. All this is against the nature, not only of merchandise, but of all temporal goods, which God wills should be subject to risk and uncertainty. But they have found a way to make sure, certain, and perpetual profit out of insecure, unsafe, temporal goods, though all the world must be sucked dry and all the money sink and swim in their gullet.[40]

It is completely consonant with traditional church logic in economic matters that a theologian with theological arguments should function as an explicit supporter of risk-filled trade and of adventure in commercial capitalism.

Adventure Apprentices and Competition

For the adventurers, entitled since 1490 to bear a coat of arms, parliamentary decrees[41] in the late fifteenth century made it possible to force virtually every English sea trader into their ranks (with the exception of the staplers, whose privilege of exporting the raw material of wool exclusively to the Netherlands, however, did not admit any greater expansion and hence was no threat to the adventurers).[42] Under the leadership of their main organization, the Merchant Adventurers of London, they made extensive use of this right, for two reasons: first, not every trader could pay the requisite initiation fees or fulfill the other requirements for acceptance into the fellowship, so the number of traders was kept small and the total profit of the fellowship large; second, the trade monopoly could be secured and intensified. As Brakel states, "By making it difficult for merchants from other parts of England to trade directly with the Netherlands, the Londoners could buy cloth in England at low prices and could also sell it at high prices, because competition in the 'Marte-Towne' had in part been removed."[43]

Thus the fundamental preconditions were created under which the merchant adventurers were able to become probably the most important political fraction of the bourgeoisie in England in the sixteenth and in part of the seventeenth century as well: the avant-garde of the bourgeoisie. In 1564, only six years after her reign began, Elizabeth I granted them the status of a "body politick" with appropriate privileges,[44] which were reaffirmed in 1586. In 1572 they received the first invitation from the Hanseatic city of Hamburg to settle there; this occasioned angry reactions from other Hanseatic cities, and in 1578 the invitation was withdrawn, under pressure from Lübeck. As of 1611 the adventurers were finally able to settle in Hamburg, where their last office existed until 1805.[45]

In the meantime, they won decisive victories over their greatest opponents. For one thing, the staplers became irrelevant because the raw material for wool was no longer allowed as an export; only finished textile goods could be exported from England,[46] and the adventurers had the monopoly on those goods. For another, the Queen had yielded to pressure from the adventurers and had revoked the trading privileges of the Hanseatic League, which closed its branch in the London Steelyard in 1598.

The adventurers were at the height of their power. Their representatives were called upon by the Crown for important political events: they were present at the receptions of diplomats and princes;[47] nobles became honorary members or even active members of their fellowship;[48] they joined with persons or groups of persons who traveled overseas (to America or the East Indies) and thereby increased the radius of their action (the expansion of trade over the northeast route to Moscow is part of this increase; in 1554-55 the Moscow trading company was formed, and in 1581 the Levantine company).

All these successes of the adventurers, however, signal at the same time their dissolution into other forms of trade or trade organizations. Consideration of the historical data confirms once again, and convincingly, the analyses of the entire process by Marx and Engels. The revolution in the mode of production in the direction of capitalist production, with the resultant free competition, breaks up the cooperative union from within and from without. Already at the beginning of the sixteenth century various adventurers had accumulated sufficient capital funds that they no longer needed to carry out their adventure trade in person:

> A parliamentary act of 1497 instructs us that the traveling merchant who at regularly recurring intervals visited the Flemish fairs with the quantity of textiles allowed by the Fellowship in order to make an honest profit there in the traditional way was typical in the fifteenth century. But from the beginning of the sixteenth century on, commission trade became the dominant way of doing business. The merchant stayed home and directed his commercial enterprises from there.[49]

The traveling merchants disappeared gradually from the practical commercial traffic (a process that took a long time to complete), and a new type of (marine) trader was born: the "apprentice" (at the beginning of the seventeenth century he was actually apprenticed up to seven years, but usually someone else was hiding under the cloak of an "apprentice"). The "apprentice" was at first a young potential merchant (who would have become a merchant according to the ritual of the Fellowship). However, as the merchants disappeared more and more from the practical goods trade, it was increasingly the case that an agent or an employee of the resident merchant used the title "apprentice" as a disguise.

> In the Laws and Ordinances we encounter apprentices who appear as factors or "atturneys.". . . Factors conduct trade on someone else's account, but without giving the name of their principal. . . . But one also often finds the expression "his Masters factor.". . . Atturneys seem to have been confidential clerks who were given a formally written power of attorney to be shown to the governor.[50]

We can clearly read the disintegrating effect of competition from the function of these "apprentices": only someone who could buy his way in or meet all other conditions could become a member of the Fellowship of Adventurers. And the rise to Merchant Adventurers was only formally possible. In reality, only those few rose who also had sufficient capital (usually through inheritance), and their number was constantly declining. There remained the rich "brothers":

> Both in the Laws and Ordinances and in the Records of the Merchant Adventurers of New Castle we find frequent regulations with the purpose of maintaining the initial equality among the brothers and of preventing "that the rich eat out the poor." But obviously these attempts were in vain. It is reported in the year 1548 that the whole wool and textile trade in New Castle was concentrated in the hands of two or three rich brothers.[51]

It is quite clear that a whole series of "brethren" thereby lost the possibility of conducting trade themselves in person or by means of an "apprentice": "While trade was gradually concentrated in the hands of the rich brothers, a group of members arose who could no longer participate in trade on their own account."[52] These so-called untrading brethren shifted over to a different, but still profitable, business. They were unable to conduct trade because they lacked the necessary capital, but as members of the fellowship of adventurers they still had the right, according to the stint of trade, to a certain quota of textiles for export as well as to an apprentice:

> It was forbidden to keep more than one apprentice at one time: but it was permitted for apprentices to transfer from one to another master. Using this regulation, the "untrading brethren" hired apprentices only in order to let them later transfer into the service of rich merchants who needed a larger staff.[53]

It is apparent that this offered an opportunity for all kinds of fictitious transactions in which the textile quotas were directly transferred in a more or less open way.[54] The "untrading brethren" also had smaller investment opportunities in adventures (as a primitive form of share investment). In any case, the large-scale capitalists who were developing of course found all these detours a nuisance.

For the large capitalists gambled everything on circumventing the regulations of the fellowship by more or less honest means. Sir Thomas Gresham (1519-79), the richest adventurer of the nation, is an impressive example of this. He began to serve the Crown early on; he was given the title "royal merchant" by Elizabeth I and was knighted by her in 1559. Gresham, who founded the London Stock Exchange in 1566, supported upholding the fellowship's regulations in public and for representative reasons, but it has been shown that he secretly played the monarch off for his own advantage against his rival adventurers, that is, against his own fellowship.[55] The reason: while the large-scale long-distance merchant was more or less ruthless in using every trick to conquer competition within the fellowship, Gresham used the fellowship against foreign competition because it had privileges that it guarded jealously. With its help the large-scale long-distance merchant, converting the fellowship into an instrument for his own individual interests, struggled against foreign competition (or domestic competition that did not belong to the fellowship), as long as this sort of protection (of the fellowship's trade monopoly) by means of privileges continued to be effective.

Among the foreign, and also the domestic, competitors were the so-called interlopers, marine traders who belonged to no association. Their rise can be explained only by means of the process of centralization of capital into a few hands and the formation of the army of employees, who gradually settled in the trading cities where the adventurers had previously carried out their business in person and had their settlements with their own courts. But now the "apprentices" appeared and formed colonies:

> These colonies consisted primarily of apprentices who spent the largest part of their apprenticeship "on this side of the seas," administered the business of their master here and at the same time learned how to conduct trade. Alongside them arose a group of members who traded from the Netherlands on their own account with their native country or who, as factors, administered the business of brothers remaining in England. Their legal status had to change to reflect the new conditions. For a group of merchants who were abroad only temporarily and who conducted trade according to their own principles, the enjoyment of their native law was a necessity. But this was no longer the case after the transitory crowds were replaced by colonies of people settled for a longer time, who were constantly linked to the natives by daily company, daily business, and marriage, who even began to merge with them.[56]

It is not surprising that this development annoyed the adventurers in England; they adapted to these changes only slowly. If they adapted at all, then only because of business sense, because the question of the "apprentices," including the formation of colonies and their partial independence, was only an expression of the general revolution in the relations of production. From the process we have described we can also deduce the reasons for a further decisive alteration that necessarily helped in destroying the fellowship system, in which the vanishing necessity for legal sovereignty in the "apprentice" colonies joined with the (probably more decisive) growing need for an overarching national system of jurisdiction over the particular, autonomous legal system of the individual colonies. As international commercial traffic intensified, there was a necessary reduction in arbitrary local justice on the part of princes or cities, which obviated any particular legal sovereignty on the part of the trading companies. In other words, the prince or city in question had an increasing interest in no longer frightening off foreign merchants. Moreover, for the same reasons (intensification of trade; exploitation of competition, also in the purchase of goods; strengthening of their own trade or establishment of their own merchant marine) they began to remove the traditional privileges of foreign trade organizations on their own soil wherever possible. If an interloper, for instance, an independent trader, offered his wares more cheaply than a trading company, say the Adventurers, the prince or the city would buy from the interloper (from which was derived the justification of one's own interlopers vis-à-vis foreign companies), and the prince or the city would thus take advantage of the competition between the interlopers and the companies. The interlopers

> did not need to keep to the cumbersome mode of doing business of the Merchant Adventurers; they could instead adopt modern commercial habits, which were beginning to be formed on the Amsterdam Exchange. This process is characteristic of the change in circumstances. No longer was the enjoyment of privileges and membership in the Fellowship of Merchant Adventurers the necessary precondition for Englishmen to participate in trade with the Netherlands. Even without privilege, the merchant was protected against injustice and violence, and many harbors were open to the interlopers. The interlopers' participation in the textile trade could no longer be stopped.[57]

The adventurers reacted in two ways after vain attempts to suppress the interlopers. First, they tried to keep the number of their members as small as possible so that they could distribute the still existing privileges over just a few people. That was, so to speak, the conservative reaction: the merchant adventurers "withdrew in proud consciousness of their superiority as members of the old brotherhood and contented themselves with looking down in a contemptuous, if also somewhat annoyed, fashion on the upstarts, who were doing such good business without privileges and without the stint of trade."[58] Then the progressive reaction to this undesirable competition was to have these competitors work for the adventurers. The adventurers themselves in this case were practicing free entrepreneurship, no longer bound by the fellowship; they were undermining the organization of adventurers still more. As Brakel presents it, the "untrading brethren" (in part to the advantage of the rich adventurers) let

> even the interlopers enjoy the rights of the fellowship by taking them on as nominal apprentices and permitting them to conduct trade on their own account. This abuse seems to have been quite widespread; merchant adventurers allowed interlopers to ship goods in their (the members') names and thereby to profit from the reduced duties charged the members.[59]

Merchant Adventurers and Explorer Adventurers

The development of the Fellowship of Adventurers is characterized by the struggle between the new elements named above and the conservative and conservationist old elements:

> For circumstances as they had developed under the influence of the new way of doing business, the shoe no longer fit. In particular there was a danger that in the General Courts, which still sat on the continent and still counted as the highest organ of the fellowship, not the London wholesalers but the brothers resident in the Netherlands constituted a majority. For not only the fully qualified brothers were able to vote in these courts; the apprentices who were factors or "atturneys" also had that right. It is understandable that the London merchants, who were traditionally used to playing the leading role in the fellowship, did not let this come about without protest. Since they were influential at court too because of their wealth, they often succeeded in making their views prevail.[60]

This observation by Brakel is extremely important because unless we grasp the development described above as a historical process, we will overlook the fact that the adventurers were still if not the leading economic and political power, then one of the leading powers until at least the outbreak of the Revolution of 1642-48; overlooking this in turn prevents us from understanding certain manifestations of the glorification of adventure.[61] This glorification traditionally served to delimit the retailers and the lower strata of the bourgeoisie that were allied with them; that is the side expressed by Thomas Wilson in his 1572 treatise, *A Discourse upon Usury*:

> Touchynge retaylers at home . . . I place them in a lower degree, as not worthy the name of merchaunts. . . . Whereas the merchaunt adventurer is and maye be taken for a lordes fellow in dignitie, aswell for hys hardye adventurynge upon the seas, to carrye out our plentye, as for his royall and noble whole sales, that he makes to dyvers men upon hys retourne, when he bryngeth in our want.[62]

For that reason the merchant adventurer must be "highly chearyshed."

Another source for the developing modern glorification of adventure is the mercantile adventure overseas, the adventure of discovery, with which in a short time the small cooperative adventure of the English marine trader is linked and which necessarily also contributes to the dissolution of the old band of adventurers or of the form of trade corresponding to that band. The anonymous *Libel of English policie* (1436) is a document that makes clear the previous dimensions of action and thought, which in their turn illustrate the explosive force that the discovery of new trade routes to the East Indies or to America had to have with respect to the activities and the world view of the adventurers. The author discusses the importance of trade altogether, specifically the necessity of protecting English sea trade, English shipping, and the coasts of the land. At the end of his survey of the various countries and their commodities trade, the author writes:

> Then here I ende of the commoditiees
> For which neede is well to kepe the seas:
> Este and Weste, South and North they bee.
> And chiefly kepe the sharpe narrow see,
> Betweene Dover and Caleis: and as thus
> That foes passe none without good will of us:
> And they abide our danger in the length,
> What for our costis and Caleis in our strength.[63]

This narrow world naturally becomes disjointed with the great overseas discoveries; that in turn has consequences for the Fellowship of Adventurers. One of the first great explorer adventurers for England is— an Italian, who could have served as a model for the fairy-tale figure of young Fortunatus. Just as Fortunatus left Cyprus for London, in 1477 Giovanni Caboto (1425-98) left Genoa for Bristol, where he remained until the end of his life. As John Cabot he entered the line of ancestors of the great explorers. As early as 1490 he tried to find a new sea trade route to China, and in 1496 he set out to the West, equipped with a charter from the king for a trade monopoly with all countries he might discover. His travels took him among other places from Labrador to Florida. His son Sebastian (born in Venice in 1472, died in London in 1557), with two short interruptions during which the Spanish king called on him as a "pilot," continued his father's voyages of discovery, joining with the adventurers, among others. To be sure, the adventurers sometimes reacted with great hesitation to offers of cooperation with the overseas explorers or adventurers,[64] but in principle this union (in developing dimensions) existed from the very beginning; the overseas explorers were in part adventurers themselves, like the London merchant Robert Thorne, who, ideologizing his undertakings, wrote in 1527:

> I have had and still have no litle mind of this businesse.... I reason, that as some sickenesses are hereditarious, and come from the father to the sonne, so this inclination or desire of this discoverie I inherited of my father, which with another marchant of Bristow named Hugh Eliot, were the discoverers of the New found lands.[65]

His penchant for ideologizing does not, however, prevent him from having realistic insight into other things, as when he determines that Charles V of Spain "putteth in every flote a certaine quantitie of money, of which he enjoyeth of the gaines pound and pounds like as other adventurers doe."[66]

In the same year, 1527, the same Robert Thorne directed an appeal to Henry VIII of England to imitate the Spanish emperor and the King of Portugal: "Experience prooveth that naturally all princes bee desirous to extend and enlarge their dominions and kingdoms."[67] If a prince should not wish to engage in appropriate activities to that end, like all other princes of this age, he continues, the people would certainly take that as evidence that he lacked "noble courage." But Henry VIII has courage, and it would be a pity if he did not participate in this profitable business. However, since Portugal and Spain have already discovered and taken possession of the wide land to the east and the west, what would present itself for England is especially the exploration of foreign lands in the north or the discovery of a northern sea route to the "Tartar" lands and to China. "Your subjects," he cries to Henry VIII, "shall not travell halfe of the way that other doe, which goe round about as aforesayd."[68]

The participation of the Crown in enterprises of this sort was indispensable, because the merchants who undertook the voyages could exploit the discovered lands only if the monarch or prince took possession of them as a conquest before international competition took them away from him and hence from his enthusiastically trading subjects. On the other hand, the participation of other merchants, in this case the merchant adventurers, was necessary so that the capital for such an undertaking could be gathered. The crucial hour for Robert Thorne's plan struck in 1553: Sebastian Cabot received the commission from the Mysterie and Companie of the Marchants adventurers to finance and carry out such an expedition through the Arctic Ocean "for the discoverie of Regions, Dominions, Islands and places unknown," whose governor he was. This commission was almost diametrically opposed to the original activities of the adventurers. In the "Ordinances, instructions, and advertisements" for the journey, which was to claim a substantial sacrifice of human lives, we read that in view of the dangers threatening in the northern sea of ice, all "wavering minds and doubtful heads" should withdraw from this adventure,[69] where "adventure" means both the exploration with its risks and the (risky) business venture. The money was collected by a subsidy campaign, by funds from the adventurers, and in (small) part by royal investment. The northeastern route to Russia was discovered, and two years later the merchant adventurers founded a colony in Moscow, whose history was later written by John Milton.[70] Its first governor was none other than Sebastian Cabot. Among his twenty-four assistants (who did not, of course, leave London) were the largest and richest—stay-at-home, of course—merchants, such as Thomas Gresham and Andrew Judde. In the charter of the company the hope is expressed that the undertaking or the founding of the colony will be a "profitable adventure."[71]

More important for our purpose: the founding of the company of adventurer explorers is greeted by a representative of the king, who, as we mentioned, also took part as an adventurer. "Master Henry Sidney, a noble young Gentleman" declares among other things that the adventurers' capital is, to be sure, necessary, but the glory belongs to the adventurer who carries out the expedition:

> Wee commit a little money to the chaunce and hazard of Fortune: He commits his life (a thing to a man of all things more deare) to the raging Sea, and the uncertainties of many dangers. We shall here live and rest at home quietly with our friends, and acquaintance: but hee in the meane time labouring to keepe the ignorant and unruly Mariners in good order and obedience, with howe many cares shall hee trouble and vexe himselfe? with howe many troubles shall hee breake himselfe? and howe many disquietings shall hee bee forced to sustaine? We shall keepe our owne coastes and countrey: Hee shall seeke strange and unknowen kingdomes. He shall commit his safetie to barbarous and cruell people, and shall hazard his life amongst the monstrous and terrible beastes of the Sea. Wherefore in respect of the greatness of the dangers, and the excellencie of his charge, you are to favour and love the man thus departing from us: and if it fall so happily out that hee returne againe, it is your part and duetie also, liberally to reward him.[72]

This passage is important in several respects: first, the connection among the Crown, merchant adventurers, and explorer or conqueror adventurers is treated as a given; second, the reference to "barbarous and cruell people" justifies their subjugation and exploitation a priori; third, active participation in sea travel, exploration, subjugation, and exploitation is ennobled as manly, courageous, and patriotic. This constitutes, so to speak, the royal blessing for the colonial policy of exploitation and removes any moral scruples that may arise. A new economic and political field of action opens itself for the merchant adventurers. In alliance with absolutist power politics and the policy of conquest, they break through the limitations imposed by caste on their activities in this direction as well and they have the satisfaction of seeing men of their own background elevated into the ranks of the nobility and receiving the very highest state honors on the basis of their business, their deeds, and their wealth. Frobisher, Drake, and Raleigh are only a few of these men, great ones among many others.

The Feudal Noble as Adventurer

We saw in the example of Robert Thorne, but also in the speech by Henry Sidney, that this phase of primitive accumulation was linked with a corresponding ideologization. The name Sidney suggests another source for the ideology of adventure, a thoroughly dubious one for the merchant adventurers, of which they will still make use. It is another Sidney who made a decisive contribution in this area, the noble poet Philip Sidney, born in 1554. After a stay of several years on the continent, he began his poetic production, which was heavily influenced by Spanish and Italian models, by a mixture of pastoral idyll and knightly ideal. His *Arcadia* (first version, 1581; second, 1584) is a prose epic in which pastoral scenes are joined with reports of battles, of shipwreck, and of metamorphoses. The harmonization of the (medieval) knightly ideal with that of the Renaissance courtier or of Arcadia is the more remarkable since Sidney was not an unworldly, withdrawn poet but a statesman who took part in the adventurous life of his time. After he had tried in vain to participate in Drake's voyages of plunder against the Spaniards (Elizabeth I forbade him to take part), he joined the war of liberation in the Netherlands, became governor of Vlissingen, and died in 1586 of a wound he received at the battle of Zütphen.

Sidney's work and his life form an effective unity and are exemplary for a faction of English society that took part in the colonial plundering expeditions for quite other reasons than, say, the merchant adventurers (who were concerned with establishing and developing a worldwide trade network): the feudal upper nobility believed that it had found a playground for its activities of feudal domination. It plunged into the great overseas adventures in order to carry on the old feudal policy of plundering for which there were no more opportunities in England, since the execution of these overseas adventures not only guaranteed a continuation of this policy of plunder on a worldwide scale, but also made a harmonious cooperation with the Crown seem possible: were not non-nobles even elevated into the ranks of nobility on the basis of these overseas adventures? Then too, the competition for the discovery, conquest, and taking possession of distant lands among the various European nations (Spain, Portugal, France, England, the Netherlands) had led to an expansion of warfare to the seas (and into those distant lands). The privateering war against Spain was carried out by the English chiefly on a private level (Frobisher, Hawkins, Cavendish, Drake, for example), although with the implicit or explicit approval by the Crown (Drake owed his knighthood, granted in 1581, to this campaign). It then assumed ever more drastic forms in the phase of open confrontations at the time of the war of liberation in the Netherlands. This is a development that strongly favored the privateering of the time, the capture of ships by private parties; especially in the English Channel, ships of the various nations were threatened by English, but also by Dutch and French, privateers.[73] It is obvious that this was a favorable terrain for freebooters of the feudal aristocracy. Exemplary for this type of pirate were figures like Sir Thomas Cavendish (died 1592) and the Earl of Essex. Cavendish undertook a privateering voyage against Spain in 1586 and took rich plunder, not—as would a merchant adventurer—in order to trade with the plundered capital but to spend the plunder, which he did fairly quickly. In 1591 he went out on another mission. Essex, the favorite of Elizabeth I, behaved similarly; together with Norris and Drake he followed his own policy of piracy, achieved the highest state offices through the favor of the queen (like Drake and Raleigh), but then became involved in plotting a rebellion against the Crown and was executed in 1601.

These few spectacular examples should suffice to indicate the essential effects of the freebooting activity on the part of the feudal upper nobility (but also of the non-noble privateers allied with them). (This activity was removed from any possible criticism at the latest in 1588, after the victory over the Spanish armada with the active cooperation of numerous privateer adventurers, led by Francis Drake.) The first effect is that the alliance with the overseas adventurers was only a transitory, sporadic one, sustained by other class interests than those of the merchant adventurers. George Peckham, for one, bears witness to this in 1583, in his "true report of the late discoveries, and possession taken in the right of the Crowne of England of the Newfound Lands," the extensive report on Humfrey Gilbert's settlements: he divides the adventurers into two categories, the "Noblemen and Gentlemen" on the one hand, to whom he mentions the prospects of conquest, taking possession of the land, fortifications, exploitation of metallurgy and precious stones, and of hunting opportunities, and the "merchants" on the other, to whom he promises good commercial opportunities.[74] In short, he would like to export the feudal conditions of past times to the colonies. The second effect is that the unstable partnership between feudal nobility and overseas adventurers represented a disturbing factor for the systematic development of overseas trade (not to mention the more or less systematic industrial exploitation of the conquered territories); and the third, that the feudal-aristocratic freebooters imported elements of the reactionary knightly ideology of adventure into the bourgeois glorification of adventure, for which among others the poetry of Edmund Spenser is a striking example.

Although of bourgeois origins, Spenser, who for many years maintained a friendship with Philip Sidney, became the poet of the backward-looking, courtly-knightly ideology of adventure. In his epic *The Faery Queen* (1580-99), an unfinished work written in honor of Queen Elizabeth, he tries to reactivate the Arthurian legends as an allegorical glorification of the absolute monarchy (and to this extent, he is progressive). In the center of the glorification are Arthur and the fairy queen, Gloriana (= Elizabeth). His knights, who embody all positive virtues, must of course perpetually undergo adventures of every (medieval) sort (like battles with dragons). *The Faery Queen* impressively represents the attempt of the courtly nobility to articulate a courtly ideology even in the age of rising manufacturing capitalism and of highly developed commercial capitalism or to make such an ideology prevail within the framework of the absolute monarchy. Such an ideology, as a class-specific world view, was a weapon in the battle against the increasingly powerful bourgeoisie. Spenser's epic employs the medieval ideals of knighthood, but not to the exclusion of contemporary influences. The way of life of the adventure-seeking knights is determined by the courtly ideal of the *Governor*, the mirror of the prince by Thomas Elyot (1531), and especially by the *Cortegiano* of Baldassare Castiglione, translated into English in 1561,[75] as well as by the political ideas of Machiavelli. Spenser's work also reflects the more or less spontaneous, external alliance of interests of the two antagonistic classes, the bourgeoisie and the aristocracy, that actually took place in the overseas adventures. In Book 6 of the *Faery Queen*, an allegorical figure (Serena) is cast up on a lonely island, and Spenser provides the following commentary:

> In these wylde deserts, where she now abode,
> There dwelt a saluage nation, which did liue
> Of stealth and spoile, and making nightly rode
> Into their neighbours borders; ne did giue
> Them selues to any trade, as for to driue
> The painfull plough, or cattle for to breed,
> Or by aduentrous marchandize to thriue;
> But on the labours of poore men to feed,
> And serue their owne necessities with others need.[76]

Class Antagonisms and the Magic Word

With the description of the natives on that distant isle, Spenser, in the midst of the courtly-knightly allegory of his fairy-tale epic, *The Faery Queen*, furnishes the justification for colonialist primitive accumulation. The natives do not work, do not even live off "aduentrous marchandize," that is, they conduct no trade, and the irony of the argument is that they allegedly live from thievery and plunder. In short, they are ripe for being made to perform useful work as English slaves and thus becoming "worthy of being human." It is a matter of course that the bourgeois adventurers were pleased with this justification of their own policy of exploitation: their unscrupled subjugation, extermination, enslavement of the natives of distant lands was given its alibi by the Crown's approval of the policy of extermination and enslavement by the overseas adventurers of the feudal nobility (for instance, John Hawkins had received official approval for the slave trade as early as 1564).[77] It did not matter that this involved occasional ideological contradictions; thus at the height of the Spanish-English hostilities, it was possible to polemicize with a clear conscience against the inhuman policy of the Spaniards toward the natives, about which Fray Bartolomé de Las Casas's work *Brevisima relación de la destrucción de las Indias* (*A Briefe Narration of the Destruction of the Indies by the Spaniards*, written 1542, published 1552) had given information.

The magic word in which the interests of the different classes and strata seemed to converge was "adventure." The knightly adventure, the cooperative trade enterprise, the manly deed, the life of employees, of entrepreneurs who no longer went on trade journeys themselves, even the dangerous enterprise and the goods themselves[78]—all went by the same name, adventure. But it would be a mistake to see only this magic key word and to overlook the ideological differences contained in the various ideological systems which seem to be united at this one point: the class antagonisms are only superficially concealed (if at all) in this word. But only by means of these class antagonisms can we explain what has caused bourgeois scholarship so much trouble.[79] The practical (commercial) bourgeoisie drew economic and political advantages from the precarious contact of the classes and their ideologies in adventure and its glorification. Reference to the spontaneous, transitory, seldom long-lasting commercial activity of the nobility in overseas adventures (and here we must distinguish carefully among not only the upper nobility, the petty nobility, and the bourgeoisie elevated into the nobility, but also the nobility who had trade conducted on their behalf), which crops up in the various economic treatises of the epoch,[80] served the bourgeoisie only to emphasize its own dignity and social importance. Trade—the argument runs—is so honorable, the merchant has risen so high, his social usefulness is so apparent, the honor accorded him by the monarch so incontestable, that even all the nobility honors and recognizes trade and hence also the (commercial) bourgeoisie by often conducting trade themselves (and here all the subordinate ideologemes can be made to bear fruit, such as the necessary bravery and the manly running of risks—all this is also worthy of a noble). In truth, however, the bourgeoisie did not place any exaggerated value on the participation of nobles in commerce, and what astonishes a student of Max Weber's like Crohn-Wolfgang, who wrote on the adventurers, is easy to explain: sometime around 1603 the East India Company declared that it would rather give up its planned trips than employ "any gentleman in any place of charge or commandment" of a ship.[81] The merchants had meantime had some experience, or their agents had, with the feudal nobles involved in overseas adventures (plunder and piracy): even Drake did not always get along with this type.[82] Insolent, refractory, lazy, without a plan, greedy for booty, madly plundering, averse to any thought of utility, "never was there a set of men worse adapted for the sober business of establishing a colony, or governing a subject race," as one of their apologists writes centuries later.[83]

Nonetheless, in this age adventure was the magic word that united all men, though with differing motives and for different purposes. In 1617 this apparent unity reached its political climax and its end. James I released Sir Walter Raleigh from the prison in which he had been held since the death of Elizabeth, because Raleigh had presented the court with a plan for a promising voyage to an unknown gold mine abroad. The king gave Raleigh the charter for this voyage and legal sovereignty over the fleet equipped for the voyage:

> Whereas we are credibly informed that there are divers merchants and owners of ships and others well disposed to assist the said Sir Walter Raleigh in this his enterprise, had they sufficient assurance to enjoy their due parts of the profits returned (in respect of the peril of law wherein the said Sir Walter Raleigh now standeth [in prison—M. N.]): And whereas also we are informed that divers other gentlemen, the kinsmen and friends of the said Sir Walter Raleigh, and divers captains and other commanders are also desirous to follow him and to adventure their lives with him in this his journey, so as they might be commanded by no other than himself: Know ye that we, . . . being desirous by all ways and means to work and procure the benefit and good of our loving subjects, and to give our princely furtherance to the said Sir Walter Raleigh his friends and associates herein, to the encouragement of others in the like laudable journeys and enterprises to be hereafter prosecuted and pursued; and especially in advancement and furtherance as well of the conversion of savage people as of the increase of the trade traffic and merchandises used by our subjects of this our kingdom. . .[84]

The only restriction: Raleigh, who like his colleagues and companions-at-arms Frobisher, Drake, and others, had conducted the war of plunder against Spain and others, was prohibited from capturing any Spanish ship or in any other way infringing on Spanish property. For times had changed; the Protestant Elizabeth was dead, and with James I, Catholicism and feudal reaction had returned to England. The Spanish ambassador then also issued a warning about Raleigh, and things came about as they almost had to: Raleigh clashed with the Spaniards in Santo Tomé, was arrested on his return and executed at the urging of the Spanish king in 1618. Among the judges whom James I appointed to formulate the death sentence was one of the greatest apologists for the voyages of discovery: Francis Bacon.

Falstaff; or, The Dismantling of the Knight Adventurer

Externally, the interests of various factions of the fundamentally antagonistic classes coincided in the concept or in the glorification of adventure. But this coincidence partially concealed class antagonisms and divergent interests, while by no means eliminating them. This is the key to the "screaming contradiction"[85]

Robert Weimann notes between the parodistic condemnation of knightly romance and the simultaneous propagation of the ideals of the knightly adventurer, (often) by the (same) bourgeois authors.[86] Their attitude toward adventure manifests the same dialectics characterizing the process of bourgeois appropriation of courtly culture, with a simultaneous refashioning or "refunctioning"[87] of this culture, making it also and primarily a weapon in the struggle against the feudal nobility. This state of affairs explains the interpenetration of the various elements or the ambivalent attitude of the bourgeoisie toward the courtly ideology of adventure, which many members of the (commercial) bourgeoisie used in order to inflate their own significance. Francis Beaumont's *The Knight of the Burning Pestle* (ca. 1613), of which Weimann gives a model interpretation, criticizes this behavior on the part of the commercial bourgeoisie.[88]

Whereas Beaumont's criticism is aimed at the bourgeoisie that bedecked itself with false feathers, a short twenty years before, Shakespeare had mounted an extremely sharp attack against the knightly glorification of exploitation itself. In *King Henry IV* (Part 1, about 1597; Part 2, 1597-98), he portrays the struggle between the absolute monarch and the rebellious feudal nobility. Although Shakespeare's basic sympathy clearly belongs to the monarchy, the enemies of the king are nonetheless presented with respect and understanding. But there is no respect in the fundamental, annihilating criticism of the parasitic feudal nobility, knocking about on adventures. In the person of its depraved representative Falstaff, whose sheer animality alone saves him from being completely unsympathetic, this class is subjected to a regular dismantling of its social existence and of the ideologizing of that existence as knightly adventure. Falstaff belongs to the company of the young prince and heir to the throne Henry, a company of youthful do-nothings whose occupations include drinking, visiting prostitutes, being highwaymen, and dodging creditors. Once in power, Henry will renounce this company and will even arrest its most unrestrained representative Falstaff (who, as Georges Duby found in investigating the medieval *juvenes*, is by no means young). The prince's change in attitude and action is prepared in a most skillful manner throughout both plays: together with his confidant Poins, Henry is already distancing himself from his disorderly companions at the beginning of the action Shakespeare portrays, although he continues for a long time to maintain a distanced, ironic loyalty. But in the battles with the enemies of the monarchy, the estrangement becomes more and more pronounced, so that Henry's final separation from his feudal-knightly retinue after he is crowned comes as a surprise only to his companions.

Up until then, the increasingly sporadic encounters between Henry and Poins and Falstaff and his comrades serve Shakespeare as a means to unmask the useless, parasitic existence of the decadent petty nobility, their bluster and vulgarity. With the help of Poins, Henry constantly sets traps for Falstaff, who stupidly and clumsily stumbles into them. Shakespeare sets this mechanism in motion at the very beginning of the play. Poins suggests to the company around Prince Henry that they ambush some merchants in order to get some money, since they have run out (money by the way—as Shakespeare emphasizes—that actually belonged in the state treasury, so robbing the merchants is also robbing the king and his people):

POINS:

> But, my lads, my lads, to-morrow
> morning, by four o'clock, early at Gadshill!
> There are pilgrims going to Canterbury with
> rich offerings, and traders riding to Lon-
> don with fat purses: I have vizards for you
> all; you have horses for yourselves: Gadshill
> lies to-night in Rochester: I have bespoke sup-
> per to-morrow night in Eastcheap: we may do
> it as secure as sleep. If you will go, I will
> stuff your purses full of crowns; if you will
> not, tarry at home and be hanged.

FALSTAFF:

> Hear ye, Yedward; if I tarry at home
> and go not, I'll hang you for going.

POINS:

> You will, chops?

FALSTAFF:

> Hal, wilt thou make one?

PRINCE:

> Who, I rob? I a thief? Not I, by
> my faith.

FALSTAFF:

> There's neither honesty, manhood,
> nor good fellowship in thee, nor thou cam'st not
> of the blood royal, if thou dar'st not stand
> for ten shillings.[89]

Henry then pretends to go along with the plan in order to lay a trap for Falstaff and two other accomplices whom Poins has prepared in advance. Together with Poins, he intends—in disguise—to take the stolen money from Falstaff in order to unmask Falstaff's cowardice.

POINS:

> Why, we will set forth before or
> after them, and appoint them a place of meet-

ing, wherein it is at our pleasure to fail, and
then will they adventure upon the exploit
themselves; which they shall have no sooner
achieved but, we'll set upon them.

(1.2.189-94)

The two of them set upon Falstaff and his companions, who immediately flee
and abandon the booty of their ambush on unarmed merchants. In order to hide
their cowardice, Falstaff and his companions inflict superficial wounds on
themselves (they scratch their noses with sharp grass to produce nosebleeds and
to get bloodspots on their clothes), and Falstaff even notches his sword to make
it look as if he had been fighting: "if I fought not with fifty of them, I am a bunch
of radish," Falstaff lies to Poins and Henry, "if there were not two or / three
and fifty upon poor old Jack, then am I / no two-legged creature" (2.4.206-8).
But when Henry reveals the true circumstances, exposes Falstaff's cowardice,
and takes him to task, Falstaff answers with crafty, bold folly:

> Why, hear you, my masters:
> was it for me to kill the heir apparent? Should
> I turn upon the true prince? why, thou know-
> est I am as valiant as Hercules; but beware in-
> stinct; the lion will not touch the true prince.
> Instinct is a great matter; I was now a
> coward on instinct. I shall think the better of
> myself and thee during my life; I for a valiant
> lion, and thou for a true prince. But, by the
> Lord, lads, I am glad you have the money.
> Hostess, clap to the doors! Watch to-
> night, pray tomorrow.
>
> (2.4.296-306)

There is no meanness that Shakespeare does not reveal in this sad, comic
figure, no robber-baron baseness, no moral decadence; and his criticism is supported by the bourgeoisie and the monarchy in their common rejection of and
struggle against the parasite caste of the gentry represented by this figure. Falstaff
writes Henry a letter:

POINS:

> [reads] "John Falstaff, knight"—
> Every man must know that, as oft as he has
> occasion to name himself; even like those that
> are kin to the King, for they never prick their
> finger but they say, "There's some of the
> King's blood spilt." "How comes that?" says

he, that takes upon him not to conceive. The
answer is as ready as a borrower's cap, "I am
the King's poor cousin, sir."

PRINCE:

Nay, they will be kin to us, or
they will fetch it from Japhet. But the letter:
[*reads*] "Sir John Falstaff, knight, to the son
of the King nearest his father, Harry Prince
of Wales, greeting."

POINS:

Why, this is a certificate.

PRINCE:

Peace!
[*reads*] "I will imitate the honorable Romans in brevity."

POINS:

He sure means brevity in breath,
short-winded.

PRINCE:

[*reads*]"I commend me to thee,
I commend thee, and I leave thee. Be not too
familiar with Poins; for he misuses thy fa-
vours so much, that he swears thou art to
marry his sister Nell. Repent at idle times
as thou mayest; and so, farewell.
"Thine, by yea and no, which is as much
as to say, as thou usest him, *Jack Falstaff* with my familiars, *John* with my
brothers and sisters, and *Sir John* with
all Europe."[90]

The Merchant Adventurer as Venetian

If Falstaff's unmasking represents a categorical condemnation of the feudal
mode of life of the (robber) barons (and only a partial, implicit condemnation
of the knightly-courtly ideology), then at approximately the same time,[91]
Shakespeare complements this condemnation with an explicit critique of the
courtly-knightly ideology of adventure, while fundamentally affirming bourgeois
adventure, in *The Merchant of Venice*, a play that has been subject to more
misinterpretations than almost any other of Shakespeare's. Let us start out by
mentioning a basic misinterpretation, because it necessarily leads into a no-

man's-land of interpretation or into speculation about the "universally human": the play, many critics claim, takes place in a world other than that of contemporary English reality. The scene of action is Renaissance Venice on the one hand and a fairy-tale locale called Belmont on the other. Of course we do not deny that this play has something of the fairy tale about it, that Belmont is a fairy-like no-place, but as we shall show, it is a utopia in a different sense than Thomas More's. Nonetheless, *The Merchant of Venice* has in common with *Utopia* that it is anchored in the actual social problems of contemporary England: *The Merchant of Venice* is a highly subtle economic-political *pièce à clef* and is moreover the most brilliant artistic portrayal of the dispute between courtly and bourgeois adventuring or the glorification of adventure that has yet been produced (people have rarely distinguished between the two types of adventuring, but have subsumed everything under a vague, modern idea of adventure).

Let us consider what seems to be the most rational of the arguments advanced to prove that the play does not show English society, but rather Renaissance Venice (arguments which often do not progress beyond the banal conclusion that the play must represent Venice since it says so in the title). Shakespeare, writes W. H. Auden, presents in his plays an England whose wealth comes from feudal land ownership and not from "accumulated capital": England, at least in Shakespeare's plays, is economically "self-sufficient," covers its needs itself; "production is for use, not profit."[92] The (large-scale) merchants who appear in Shakespeare's plays must therefore represent another economic system:

> In *The Merchant of Venice* and *Othello* Shakespeare depicts a very different kind of society. Venice does not produce anything itself, either raw materials or manufactured goods. Its existence depends upon the financial profits which can be made by international trade . . . that is to say, on buying cheaply here and selling dearly there, and its wealth lies in its accumulated money capital.[93]

We will not spend time discussing this terminology. The most obvious question is whether Shakespeare meant to present on stage the problems of Rome in his Roman plays or the problems of the fifteenth century in his plays like *Henry IV* or *Henry V*; if so, what a strange "audience of historians" it must have been to enjoy such plays. In general, Shakespearean scholars do not doubt that Shakespeare used historical events or models as examples in order to treat the problems of his time. But doubts still seem permissible in the case of *The Merchant of Venice*, which may well be attributed to the interpreters' ignorance of economic history. It is not only unlikely, it is absurd to imagine that Shakespeare failed to notice what had been under discussion in literary fiction and economic treatises (often by the same authors) from the time of Thomas More at the latest—to say nothing of the fact that he could, in fact had to, experience on a daily basis the revolutionary upheavals in the mode of production. Shakespeare's interpreter Auden, for instance, missed the fact that an "agricultural revolution" had taken place in England, that agriculture had become capitalistic, that manufacturing capitalism had taken an immense upswing, and England's commodities trade was surpassing every previously known measure. The adventurers were everywhere—at the court, on land, at sea, on the continent, in Russia, in Asia, in the New World. In the second half of the sixteenth century, as Robert Weimann summarizes the development, there was

> —according to the judgment of scholars—a "rapid development of manufacturing"..., even an early "industrial revolution." ... Coal production alone increased so much that the deliveries to London rose more than threefold in little over a decade (1580: 11,000 tons; 1591-92: 35,000 tons).... Iron production also increased to an astonishing degree, and the process of production was decisively improved.... Since the production of glass, copper, and tin also rose substantially and the means of transport were much improved, the preconditions were present for that extraordinary boom in building and repair work of Shakespeare's time.... This building activity threatened to overtake what had long been the most important English industry, textile production, in importance for the national economy, as it fostered production and formed markets. It must have stimulated the domestic market as much as the "primitive importing of capital" that resulted from the daring voyages of discovery, mercantile enterprises, and rapacious expeditions overseas. This latter was a violent form of foreign trade that was supported by newly founded joint-stock companies whose stockholders, as in the case of Drake's voyage around the world, were able to pocket a record profit of 4,700 percent.[94]

According to W. H. Auden's view, the only person who must not have noticed any of this was Shakespeare. But what Auden himself obviously overlooked is the fact that Antonio, the royal merchant of Venice, conducts a very *atypical* trade for Venice, *but not for London or England*: his ships travel "From Tripolis, from Mexico, and England, / From Lisbon, Barbary, and India."[95] The interpreters of Shakespeare who were and are so eager to see in Antonio an Italian merchant of the Renaissance[96] have actually failed to note that during the Renaissance no ship traffic was possible to India and America, because neither the route around the Cape of Good Hope nor America had yet been discovered; moreover, Venice had a very small (or no) share in the trade after the discovery of the East Indies shipping route or of America; rather, it was displaced from the center of trade by these discoveries. The sixteenth century was well aware of the loss of importance Venice had suffered. This fact was so current to Shakespeare's contemporaries that they seem to have viewed London or England as the historical successor to Venice,[97] which enables us to give a more rational explanation of why Shakespeare set his play in Venice.

It is obvious that political reasons could also have been decisive in this selection, once one becomes aware of the politically explosive nature of the play. In nearly all ages it has been a piece of literary cunning, in writing the truth about actual economic, political, or philosophical problems, to shift them into other times and other regions.[98] Thus if Shakespeare used an Italian model, a story from Ser Giovanni's *Il Pecorone* (probably written toward the end of the fourteenth century, published in 1558),[99] to rework it as *The Merchant of Venice*, it was not in order to formulate and treat problems of fourteenth- or fifteenth-century Venice, but rather those of the England of his time. Antonio is of course an English merchant adventurer in Venetian garb, an important merchant in a class with Judde or Gresham: he is a stay-at-home "royal merchant."[100]

The Melancholy of the Stay-at-Home Brother

We must bear in mind the development of adventure trade in England in order to arrive at an understanding of the secretive and melancholy Antonio, who has repeatedly caused such astounding difficulties for interpreters.[101] For even where scholars have had no doubt that Antonio is the fictional representative of the English merchant adventurers, they have sometimes reached surprising conclusions. For instance, Jürgen Kuczynski believes that Antonio, "the capitalist, antifeudal merchant," is presented by Shakespeare as a "spendthrift" and does not exhibit the features of the "English merchant."[102] There is an obvious confusion with Bassanio here, because in contrast to him Antonio is actually a "sober merchant who practises economic abstinence" in his own private consumption and his style of life, as W. H. Auden writes.[103] We must also relativize or make more precise Kuczynski's assertion that *The Merchant of Venice* brings into opposition "the old feudal usurer—a figure that plays a special role in the time of the transition to capitalism—in the person of Shylock, and Antonio, the merchant of Venice, who represents the early phase of capitalism."[104] It is true that in Shylock and Antonio are opposed the "two distinct forms of capital" "handed down" by the Middle Ages, as Marx writes in *Capital*: "usurer's capital and merchant's capital,"[105] but Shakespeare's play (1594-97) is by no means at the beginning of the development. Manufacturing capitalism is expanding and commercial capital, as we have seen, has long since run through the development that Engels sketches in discussing the dissolution of cooperative trade. In short, Antonio is one of those stay-at-home "brethren" of the merchant adventurers who do not conduct trade themselves—not for want of capital, but because of their great capital. They have their business conducted for them by employees and agents. Numerous other merchant adventurers are dependent on the stay-at-home brother: first of all, the young adventurer who has no capital, takes out loans, and still goes on ventures in person (in the play, this is Bassanio); second, the "apprentices" or attorneys, who conduct trade for Antonio in the East Indies, in Africa, in the Mediterranean area, and in America (figures like Salanio, Salerio, and Gratiano might well belong to the type of "untrading brethren" who have no capital to conduct trade,[106] but who also do not work as employees; instead they are brokers for labor in supplying "apprentices").

We must see the relationship between Antonio and Bassanio against this background, and it also essentially furnishes the explanation for Antonio's melancholy, as Antonio reveals:

> In sooth, I know not why I am so sad:
> It wearies me; you say it wearies you;
> But how I caught it, found it, or came by it,
> What stuff (tis made of, whereof it is born,
> I am to learn;
> And such a want-wit sadness makes of me
> That I have much ado to know myself.
>
> (1.1.1-7)

His friends suspect that he is sad or troubled because he has invested his capital in various ships that are now sailing all over the world on the unpredictable seas. Antonio rejects this explanation out of hand; he sees his security in the wide distribution of his capital investments, so that does not trouble him:

> Believe me, no. I thank my fortune for it,
> My ventures are not in one bottom trusted,
> Nor to one place; nor is my whole estate
> Upon the fortune of this present year:
> Therefore my merchandise makes me not sad.
>
> (1.1.41-45)

Antonio also rejects the assumption that he could be in love—almost outaged at the imputation. He loans his friend Bassanio three thousand ducats so he can outfit a ship to sail to Belmont, where the rich and beautiful heiress Portia is to be conquered: the candidates for Portia's hand must choose among a golden, a silver, and a lead casket, and whoever chooses the casket containing Portia's portrait may make her his wife. Bassanio is the lucky man.

However, the dramatic complication has already begun in Venice. Since Antonio did not have the liquid assets for which Bassanio asked him, he borrows the three thousand ducats from a moneylender, the Jewish usurer Shylock, who is his enemy. The contract, which we will not discuss in detail, provides that Antonio must repay the money after three months. If he does not manage to do so, Shylock is permitted to cut out a pound of Antonio's flesh. All the participants seem to take this bond as a joke; no one doubts that Antonio will be able to repay the money on time (least of all Antonio himself). But the improbable occurs: all of Antonio's ships sink, the bond falls due, and Shylock demands Antonio's debt before the court—the law is on his side. Antonio is arrested. The court proceedings are imminent. Then the news of his friend's misfortune reaches Bassanio in Belmont, who has meantime won Portia's hand. Portia demands that he return to Venice immediately in order to help his friend.

She herself sets out for Venice without Bassanio's knowledge, together with her confidante Nerissa. Disguised as a lawyer, she appears before the court, confirms the justice of Shylock's claim, but tricks Shylock by granting him the right to take a pound of Antonio's flesh, but without spilling a single drop of blood, since the bond mentioned nothing about blood. If he spills one drop of Antonio's blood, the blood of a Christian, then "thy land and goods / Are, by the laws of Venice, confiscate / Unto the state of Venice" (4.1.310-12). When Shylock recognizes the impossibility of collecting his debt, he tries to secure the money originally offered him by Bassanio instead of the contractual pound of flesh, but Portia as the lawyer blocks this attempt because the agreement had not been so written; moreover the Jew Shylock must be punished for his attempt to "seek the life of any citizen" (4.1.351). He must give half his property to the Venetian state and the other half to the victim of his attempt, Antonio. Antonio renounces his share in favor of Jessica Shylock's daughter and her (Christian) husband Lorenzo.

Jessica had left Shylock when Bassanio set out for Belmont to win Portia's hand and had also gone to Belmont with her lover Lorenzo (equipped with a part of the treasure she had stolen from her father). In Belmont, Portia had installed Jessica and Lorenzo as overseers for the time of her trip to the court proceedings in Venice. After a few contretemps, the various pairs (Portia / Bassanio, Gratiano / Nerissa, Jessica / Lorenzo) are reunited at Belmont, along with Antonio. Everything is resolved in the happiness of the married couples, and even Antonio's ships, which had supposedly been lost, reach harbor and make Antonio richer than ever.

And still, although the play is called *The Merchant of Venice* and although Antonio not only reappears in the midpoint of the play, the court scene, but also, so to speak, helps close the play at the end, Shakespeare criticism has found over and over that Antonio leads a remarkably pale, shadowy existence in the play (which then leads to the unjustified conclusion that not he, but his opponent Shylock, is the center of the play). It is in fact true that all the figures except Antonio are active in some physical way, in person. Their social function and their external appearance merge in this activity, while Antonio's social function, which as we shall show sets the whole play in motion and holds it together, is shifted from Antonio, from his person, to countless others: to junior partners (like Bassanio), to employees like the captains and sailors of his ships. Unlike the miser of the Middle Ages, the usurer, Antonio does not even have cash at his disposal because he has converted everything into commodity capital. Antonio as a person is *nothing*, as personified capital he is the motor of the play, which Shakespeare quite consciously did not name after Shylock, Portia, Venice, Belmont, or whatever else, but called *The Merchant of Venice*. But as personified capital, Antonio is the opposite of the others, including Shylock, in his individual appearance—indifferent, faceless.

Only this perspective allows us to understand the (constantly sought after, "deeper") meaning of the dialogue between Gratiano and Shylock. It has been and still is common to take only the well-known sentences of Antonio from their context here and to interpret them in a psychological, immanent fashion. Gratiano determines that Antonio has changed:

> You look not well, Signior Antonio;
> You have too much respect upon the world:
> They lose it that do buy it with much care.
> Believe me, you are marvellously chang'd.
>
> (1.1.73-76)

So Antonio was not always as he is now, and this alteration (toward melancholy) must be connected with his attempts to "buy" the world "with much care." Antonio's answer has been and still is placed by interpreters somewhere in an assumed world of emotion (as for instance: Antonio is said to have just learned—though there is nothing about this in the text—that Bassanio wants to leave him for a woman, Portia, and therefore Antonio is sad, because— also in keeping with the moral code of his time—he cannot realize his love for Bassanio).[107] Antonio replies:

> I hold the world but as the world, Gratiano;
> A stage where every man must play a part,
> And mine a sad one.
>
> (1.1.77-79)

In contrast to the interpreters of Shakespeare, Gratiano, I believe, understands this answer correctly. He knows that Antonio means the divergence between social function and individual semblance to which Antonio as a capitalist is necessarily subject, and he tries to "console" him by demonstrating that even where social function and individual appearance or activity seem to converge, there is often nothing other than false appearance, deception, and hypocrisy. Why should someone like Antonio, who has none, mourn for such a semblance? Using himself as an example, Gratiano says:

> Let me play the fool!
> With mirth and laughter let old wrinkles come,

And let my liver rather heat with wine
Than my heart cool with mortifying groans.
Why should a man, whose blood is warm within,
Sit like his grandsire cut in alabaster,
Sleep when he wakes, and creep into the jaundice
By being peevish? I tell thee what, Antonio—
I love thee, and it is my love that speaks—
There are a sort of men whose visages
Do cream and mantle like a standing pond,
And do a wilful stillness entertain,
With purpose to be dress'd in an opinion
Of wisdom, gravity, profound conceit,
As who should say, "I am Sir Oracle,
And when I ope my lips, let no dog bark!"
O my Antonio, I do know of those
That therefore only are reputed wise
For saying nothing; when, I am very sure,
If they should speak, would almost damn those ears
Which, hearing them, would call their brothers fools.
I'll tell thee more of this another time;
But fish not with this melancholy bait
For this fool gudgeon, this opinion.

(1.1.79-102)

The Shafts of Antonio

What has seemed to various critics to be a shortcoming in the creation of Antonio, his colorlessness, his facelessness, his lack of individuality, is a particularly brilliant accomplishment of Shakespeare's; it is after all just this quality that allows Antonio's (social) essence to express itself as personified capital. Shakespeare manifests Antonio's essence by representing him in contrast to the other figures, especially to Shylock / Jessica, Bassanio / Portia (but also to Gratiano / Nerissa and even to the fool Launcelot Gobbo / father / Negress) without any private life at all. His house is never shown, as opposed to Shylock's house and Portia's palace; he seems not to have wife and children or any family at all; to the question whether he is in love, he answers "Fie!" If this were not so, if he had family, wife and children, a house, he too would be subject to some kind of emotions, and this would distract from the essential. The *uninteresting* private person Antonio would prevent us from seeing his *social function*, which Shakespeare wants to reveal.

Antonio knows emotion only in three respects: first, with respect to his social activity or his role in society which, as he himself says, fills him with sadness; second, with respect to Bassanio for whom he feels friendship; third, with respect to Shylock whom he hates. If we were to try to explain these three emotional responses by some kind of psychological tendency or cause, as interpreters are fond of doing,[108] we would also be falling victim to the semblance Gratiano warns about: we would only be seeing the exterior, not the interior of the matter, the essential (from which the semblance, the external, or the actualization of the essential in semblance and exterior, cannot be separated in its materialization). Let us consider first his melancholy, which arises from his "lack of semblance," from his individual insignificance, his physical inactivity, from the necessary transfer of his social-material function (of conducting the business of commercial capitalism) to representatives, agents, employees. The only possible alternative that could release him from this melancholy typically never occurs to him: the (actually "romantic," childish or youthful) renunciation of the capital that he has working or earning a profit in circulation, withdrawal into the activity of the independent (very small) entrepreneur, self-reduction to the order of magnitude of a Bassanio. He does not follow a childish (but possible) impulse of that kind; instead he flees into self-pity and sentimentality. The object of his sentimental inclination is Bassanio, which has caused all sorts of speculation among interpreters, including his homosexuality, although (or perhaps because) there is no single concrete indication of it in the play. It is much more likely to suppose that Antonio the merchant adventurer who no longer goes on adventure voyages himself is mourning for his own youth in Bassanio the active adventurer. But let us abandon sentiment for now and turn to its basis.

Bassanio, as we learn from his own lips, has taken loans from Antonio, borrowed money to conduct business that has brought in nothing or too little. In any case, Bassanio has spent too much and is in debt to Antonio. Nevertheless he counts on Antonio lending him money again, and he is not disappointed in his trust. What function does Bassanio have for Antonio? The answer is obvious; it can be found in actual history, it need only be read off: throughout the entire sixteenth century (and in part even later), countless Antonios, rich merchant adventurers who no longer went to sea themselves, invested in overseas adventures, financed overseas adventures to unknown regions in search of gold, silver, new sources of raw materials, new markets for goods and opportunities for trade. These enterprises were by no means always successful, and where possible the merchants invested in them only what capital they could divert from the profit of other businesses without endangering these or their means of support. Antonio behaves no differently (except that he once ignores the rule of caution just mentioned); Bassanio understands it no differently. Bassanio embodies the risk of adventure that the rich merchant who no longer travels himself assumes in financing great adventures and that he loves because of the possible large, sometimes—as in the case of Drake—immense profits.

But what about Bassanio's "true" love for Portia? Antonio also asks Bassanio about this woman, and Bassanio talks—about business. For him, the Portia affair is first of all, and quite simply, an adventurous enterprise with the hope of profit, for which he needs capital investment (from Antonio). Anyone who is surprised by this (and various interpreters have rejected and continue to reject insights of this kind as not worthy of Shakespeare) has not read his Shakespeare attentively enough: in the connection between social prosperity or money (capital) and love, love does not have priority (nor on the other hand is it proper simply to acknowledge the priority of money)—the one is so linked with the other that the two elements cannot be separated. But that is not particularly surprising for a time in which money or capital is the decisive (revolutionary) weapon against feudal oppression, material and spiritual slavery. Only an age in which capital subjugates humanity can find the connection between money and love (or economics and human feelings) suspect (because the ideologues of capital have a great interest in making the connection between economics and human feelings a taboo). In Shakespeare's time, however, the progressive, antifeudal forces completely affirmed the connection between *bourgeois* wealth (in the form of commercial capital, for instance) and love. Just how unconcerned this affirmation was can be seen in *The Taming of the Shrew*. The rich (!) Petruchio comes to Padua and there, through his friend Hortensio, hears about an immensely rich, but difficult, young woman who is eligible for marriage. Hortensio believes that however rich she is, he cannot recommend her to Petruchio; Petruchio responds:

> Signior Hortensio, 'twixt such friends as we
> Few words suffice; and therefore, if thou know
> One rich enough to be Petruchio's wife,
> As wealth is burthen of my wooing dance,
> Be she as foul as was Florentius' love,
> As old as Sibyl, and as curst and shrewd
> As Socrates' Xanthippe, or a worse,
> She moves me not, or not removes, at least,
> Affection's edge in me, were she as rough
> As are the swelling Adriatic seas:
> I come to wive it wealthily in Padua;
> If wealthily, then happily in Padua.[109]

Petruchio is by no means an ugly, unsympathetic old man; he is a handsome, intelligent, determined young man, bursting with life, who owes his vitality not least of all to his wealth, as he says:

> Hortensio, peace! thou know'st not gold's effect:
> Tell me her father's name and 'tis enough;
> For I will board her, though she chide as loud
> As thunder when the clouds in autumn crack.
>
> (1.2.92-95)

Chance (or Shakespeare) dictates that the difficult young woman is also beautiful, so in Petruchio's case love is joined with business, and nothing stands in the way of a comic resolution to the play. In *The Merchant of Venice*, the situation is no different. We are to see in a negative light not money as (commercial) capital but money that hinders or prevents capitalist trade: the accumulated usurer's capital of Shylock. With different premises that is also true in *Timon of Athens*, where Shakespeare contrasts hoarding and prodigality in order to show the horrifying consequences of each, but especially of ruthless hoarding, increasing one's possessions. The speech by Timon quoted in *Capital*[110] shows that Shakespeare was fully aware of the destructive and solvent powers slumbering in money or released by it. This only attests once again to Shakespeare's brilliant sagacity: in *The Merchant of Venice* too, the liberating power of commercial capital is celebrated, but Shakespeare does not overlook its dangers.

For Antonio/Bassanio, money as commercial capital has the function of a weapon with which both oppression by the feudal nobility (Morocco, Arragon, and others) and medieval usurer's capital (Shylock) can be overcome. Bassanio needs Antonio's capital investment in order to equal his competitors in the battle for Portia's hand:

> O my Antonio, had I but the means
> To hold a rival place with one of them,
> I have a mind presages me such thrift
> That I should questionless be fortunate!
>
> (1.1.173-76)

"To hold a rival place with one of them"—? Who are these feared competitors? Without exception they are feudal petty nobles or great feudal lords.

The fact that Bassanio thinks first of adventure trade when Portia is named and only then elevates his thought with talk of love is not only thoroughly "moral," it is thoroughly revolutionary (and anything else would have been an insult to Portia). Bassanio is fighting against feudal enslavement and the slavish mentality, against the morality of feudal masters, and for liberation, for love that would be nothing without this liberation. Love and freedom are seen as one, and the weapon in the struggle for both is the commercial transaction, the commercial adventure, which Bassanio carries out as the representative or junior partner of Antonio. The lack of understanding with which

Shakespeare scholars sometimes diminish Antonio (or Bassanio) where he is great is shown not least by their commentaries on the loan dialogue between Bassanio and Antonio. Asked by Antonio about the "lady" to whom Bassanio wants to travel in order to win her for himself, Bassanio reminds Antonio first of the debts he still owes him and concludes with a correct and daring speech, which the Shakespeare expert Quiller-Couch calls "windy nonsense":[111]

> In my school-days, when I had lost one shaft,
> I shot his fellow of the self-same flight
> The self-same way with more advised watch,
> To find the other forth, and by adventuring both
> I oft found both. I urge this childhood proof,
> Because what follows is pure innocence.
> I owe you much, and, like a wilful youth,
> That which I owe is lost, but if you please
> To shoot another arrow that self way
> Which you did shoot the first, I do not doubt,
> As I will watch the aim, or to find both,
> Or bring your latter hazard back again
> And thankfully rest debtor for the first.
>
> (1.1.140-52)

Just as Raleigh, for instance, proposed that James I finance an adventure expedition to a gold mine in Guayana, Bassanio proposes to Antonio an adventure voyage that should reap high profits. It is not the first undertaking (the first "shaft") in which Antonio will have invested capital, but this undertaking, in Bassanio's opinion, not only will be successful, but also will yield so much profit that it will balance out the losses of the previous undertakings. But the one who is to shoot this new "arrow," this new "shaft," is not Bassanio but Antonio. Thus it is Antonio who must decide on the undertaking, conclude it, and finance it, and it is Bassanio who executes it on Antonio's orders. Another "detail," by the way, reveals that Bassanio considers the undertaking first of all quite soberly as a business transaction and not as a drama of love: what will happen if despite Bassanio's favorable prognosis, the undertaking fails? Bassanio is sober enough to face this possibility. Would his heart then break for unrequited love? These are the concerns of a bourgeois interpreter without good faith, the expression of sentimental moaning "at the discrepancy between bourgeois reality and his no less bourgeois illusions about this reality"![112] Bassanio has only one thought in case of a bad outcome: he will repay Antonio's capital investment. (That means that he assumes a very low risk of loss because in fact he needs money for purposes of representation, for wedding presents, and other small costs. If he does not win Portia, then he will have no further large expenses, and he can repay Antonio's capital.)

That is an undertaking that interests Antonio, because up to now he has financed Bassanio's adventure undertakings from his surplus profits in hope of further profits. If he now refuses to finance him, he is in danger of losing everything he invested previously (Bassanio's story of the two shafts). If he takes another risk, there is the possibility that he will make good the previous losses and in addition make the large profits that Bassanio's undertakings have not yet yielded. Bassanio is confident, his speech is convincing, and Antonio admits:

> You know me well, and herein spend but time
> To wind about my love with circumstance;
> And out of doubt you do me now more wrong
> In making question of my uttermost
> Than if you had made waste of all I have:
> Then do but say to me what I should do,
> That in your knowledge may by me be done.
>
> (1.1.153-59)

At this point the friendship finally comes into its own: with these words with which Antonio expresses his readiness to finance the adventurer Bassanio in his expedition, Antonio has passed the test of friendship posed by the granting of the loan. Quiller-Couch, one of the editors of the edition known as the New Cambridge Shakespeare, completely missed the fact that what he calls "windy nonsense" is a variation of a test of friendship which Shakespeare knew from one of the most significant merchant handbooks of the Renaissance, L. B. Alberti's *Della Famiglia*. Gianozzo Alberti is explaining that he would refuse ever to ask a friend for a loan, as he would refuse to borrow money. Thereupon Adovardo Alberti asks him:

> "Tell me now, Giannozzo, if you had a bow, would you not stretch it often and shoot an arrow in times of peace to see how good it would be in battle against the enemy?" [Gianozzo agrees, and Adovardo continues:] "I want to say that we must do the same with friends. You must try them when things are quiet and peaceful to see what they could do in turbulent times. You must try them in small private matters at home to see how much they would be worth in great public affairs. You must try them to see how ready they are to safeguard your welfare and your honor and how useful in helping and supporting you in misfortune and saving you from adversities."[113]

Shakespeare rearranges things: it is not the borrower who puts the lender to the test (at least with such a large loan and such a risky adventure undertaking), who shoots an arrow off in and through him, but the lender, the capitalist, shoots a shaft (here, one or more in succession). Nevertheless, as in Alberti, here too friendship is realized in granting credit and in trade undertakings. The relations between Bassanio and Antonio are more complicated than the test of friendship in *Della Famiglia*, but they are solid, as solid as Antonio's business. To be sure, it is only after Antonio has been convinced and the time is appropriate that Bassanio can speak privately, personally, about the "lady" Antonio asked about:

> In Belmont is a lady richly left;
> And she is fair and, fairer than that word,
> Of wondrous virtues: sometimes from her eyes
> I did receive fair speechless messages:
> Her name is Portia; nothing undervalu'd
> To Cato's daughter, Brutus' Portia.
> Nor is the wide world ignorant of her worth,
> For the four winds blow in from every coast
> Renowned suitors; and her sunny locks
> Hang on her temples like a golden fleece,
> Which makes her seat of Belmont Colchos' strand,
> And many Jasons come in quest of her.
> O my Antonio, had I but the means
> To hold a rival place with one of them,
> That I should questionless be fortunate!
>
> (1.1.161-76)

The answer Antonio gives confirms once again that Shakespeare sees economics and the heart's emotions as a single entity. Antonio does not ask further about Portia, does not express the wish to meet her, to see Bassanio happy with her (as a married couple). In response to Bassanio's praise of Portia's beauty, he says:

> Thou know'st that all my fortunes are at sea;
> Neither have I money nor commodity
> To raise a present sum: therefore go forth;
> Try what my credit can in Venice do:
> That shall be rack'd, even to the uttermost,
> To furnish thee to Belmont, to fair Portia.
> Go, presently inquire, and so will I,
> Where money is; and I no question make
> So have it of my trust or for my sake.
>
> (1.1.177-85)

There are numerous other examples of this indestructible link between ideas of property or profit and feelings of love—for instance, Portia's first reaction when Bassanio has won her by choosing the correct casket: she would like to be "a thousand times more fair, ten thousand times more rich" (3.2.155). However, to conclude this section another quotation will demonstrate how much Antonio feels himself to be what he in reality is: the financier, the actual bearer of the adventure business. The participants in the expedition want to have a farewell party, but Antonio decides differently. When he meets Gratiano, one of the adventurers going along on the expedition, Antonio calls out:

> Fie, fie, Gratiano! where are all the rest?
> 'Tis nine o'clock; our friends all stay for you.
> No masque to-night: the wind is come about,
> Bassanio presently will go aboard.
> I have sent twenty out to seek for you.
>   (2.6.62-66)

Homo Novus Antonio versus Homo Antiquus Shylock

Scholars have of course not failed to notice that the problem of usury also plays a role in the confrontation between Antonio and Shylock. But I believe they have often started out from a crucial misunderstanding: they have taken Antonio's polemics against Shylock, disguised as religious objections, at face value as a Christian response, and instead of speaking about the actual conflict (or instead of reading the text carefully), they have quoted from the medieval church's discussion of usury or condemnation of usury and subsumed Antonio under this position.[114] Antonio, however, is not the representative of the medieval church or of the churchly prohibition of usury; rather, he represents modern commercial capitalism. In keeping with the general usury debate of his time, as Marx and Engels described it, Antonio polemicizes against medieval usurer's capital and actively supports modern commercial loans. Shakespeare not only condemns the fact that Antonio uses allegedly Christian, religious arguments in his polemics, as we will see, but also makes Antonio, by this condemnation, a thoroughgoing cynic.[115] He is pious only when he is polemicizing against Shylock or against usurer's capital;[116] otherwise he does not give God or the Church a thought. It is impossible to imagine Antonio in prayer.

The mirror image of Antonio, commercial capital personified, is Shylock, usurer's capital personified. Shylock hates Antonio, and Shakespeare makes no bones about the most important reason for his hatred for Shylock says:

> How like a fawning publican he looks!
> I hate him for he is a Christian;
> But more for that in low simplicity

> He lends out money gratis and brings down
> The rate of usance here with us in Venice.
>   (1.3.42-46)

By doing so, Antonio is acting in accordance with the economic ideal of the
time: the age actually demanded a limit on interest, in order to be able to invest money in trade or manufacturing. Whereas Shylock understands his
usurer's credit as consumer credit[117] and polemicizes pointedly against investing
capital in sea trade or in large-scale trade,[118] Antonio uses his money as capital
in commercial transactions. It is against this background that we must interpret the dialogue between Antonio and Shylock when Antonio wants to borrow money for Bassanio's adventure:

ANTONIO:

> Shylock, albeit I neither lend nor borrow
> By taking nor by giving of excess,
> Yet, to supply the ripe wants of my friend,
> I'll break a custom. Is he yet possess'd
> How much you would?

SHYLOCK:

>   Ay, ay, three thousand ducats.

ANTONIO:

> And for three months.

SHYLOCK:

> I had forgot; three months, you told me so.
> Well then, your bond; and let me see; but hear you:
> Methought you said you neither lend nor borrow
> Upon advantage.

ANTONIO:

>   I do never use it.

>   (1.3.62-71)

We must not overlook the essential point of this passage: Antonio does not
give usurious loans. Apart from the fact that he has his own business carried
out by employees with his capital, Antonio makes capital available to other
adventurers like Bassanio, so that they can conduct trade. From the profit they
earn, he receives, as we heard from Bassanio, his share (his investment plus an
appropriate rate of profit). *To this extent* Antonio can correctly claim that he
neither lends nor borrows upon advantage (like medieval or feudal usurers),
the more so as his investments or his loans are to be distinguished from medieval
loans for sea trade, whose rate of interest was about 35 percent.[119] Antonio
makes his money available, as Shylock says, "gratis," which means that he

either lends it at a low rate of interest or provides capital in the form of a share investment and thus takes his interest from the (commercial) profit the enterprise makes, but not from the (basic) property of the borrower. He can even support his practice by calling on Christian virtues like charity, since the Church had always tolerated this form of loan[120] and in the sixteenth century—not least under the influence of Calvin—had shaped a new argument: what is more hardhearted, to lock one's wealth in a chest (as treasure) or to let others use it, who with its help can become active and gain property (Bacon's thoughts move in this same direction)?[121]

Apart from his own direct profit on the trade transactions, Antonio's loans have another purpose: Antonio wants to ruin his competitor Shylock by spoiling his business. In order to understand completely this connection, we must see that Antonio and Shylock are representatives of two different systems: commercial capital versus feudal usurer's capital, or more pointedly, the capitalistic mode of production versus the feudal mode. This alone explains what has baffled so many scholars: why a merchant as powerful as Antonio was not able to find a loan elsewhere (from a brother adventurer, for instance), why other merchants did not come to Antonio's aid when his bond to Shylock was due. Shakespeare presents what he has observed, the historical process of the clash of two economic and political systems. He does, to be sure, create individuals, but these are also symbolic figures who embody the different systems. This alone explains the dimensions of the hatred and the mutual desire to destroy each other on the part of Antonio and Shylock. It is not a question of "normal" competition, but rather of the hostilities between an old and a new system, capitalism and feudalism, bourgeoisie and feudal nobility (along with the corresponding economic system, to which usurer's capital also belongs). These hostilities can only end with the destruction of the enemy. Shylock says, "I will have the heart / of him, if he forfeit; for, were he out of Ven- / ice, I can make what merchandise I will" (3.1.132-34). In reality, of course—and Shakespeare knows this as well as any viewer—there is not just *one* commercial capitalist Antonio. Shylock's speech therefore is meaningful only if Antonio personifies commercial capital in general, which does not prevent Antonio from speaking of other merchants;[122] on the contrary, Shakespeare thereby calls our attention most pointedly to the symbolic function of the figures. As personified commercial capital, Antonio gives his loans with a special impetus. They become a sort of dumping loans to combat usurer's capital:

ANTONIO:

> I oft deliver'd from his forfeitures
> Many that have at times made moan to me;
> Therefore he hates me.
>
> (3.3.22-24)

Shylock has already confirmed that this is actually the case.[123] Antonio is ruining his business, Antonio wants to annihilate him, and Antonio is obviously the stronger, because he succeeds up to the point when he (seemingly) takes too great a risk because he is no longer financing his adventures out of profits he has earned, out of his circulating capital, but takes on foreign capital from the old feudal usury system in his hunt for profits. He drafts the famous bond for Shylock (comprehensible only because it treats of the battle to the death between the two systems, where the modern capitalist system is fully convinced of its victory),[124] and at the first news of Antonio's business misfortunes, Shylock gloats. One of Antonio's friends asks Shylock if it is true that Antonio has had a "loss at sea."

SHYLOCK:

There I have another bad match. A
bankrupt, a prodigal, who dare scarce show his
head on the Rialto; a beggar, that was used to
come so smug upon the mart; let him look to
his bond: he was wont to call me usurer; let
him look to his bond: he was wont to lend
money for a Christian curtsy; let him look to
his bond.

SALARINO:

Why, I am sure, if he forfeit, thou
wilt not take his flesh. What's that good for?

SHYLOCK:

To bait fish withal: if it will feed
nothing else, it will feed my revenge. He
hath disgraced me, and hindered me half a
million; laughed at my losses, mocked at my
gains, scorned my nation, thwarted my bargains, cooled my friends, heated mine enemies;
and what's his reason? I am a Jew.

(3.1.45-60)

Antonio Has the Bloodiest Face

Of all the interpreters of *The Merchant of Venice*, especially with respect to the figure of Antonio, it seems to me that Brecht is the most acute. From Pierpont Mauler's very first appearance in *Die heilige Johanna der Schlachthöfe* (*St. Joan of the Stockyards*) (he enters at the beginning of the play like Antonio, and like Antonio he announces his melancholy), to the games or tricks played around a contract, up to the use of Christianity against the (capitalist) competitors, the analogies are obvious; one cannot fail to note the model *The Mer-*

chant of Venice. Of all the interpreters, Brecht seems to me to have understood most clearly the character of Antonio and to have correctly interpreted it in the figure of Pierpont Mauler, to have appropriated and reworked it into a modern figure of capitalism in the United States in the first half of the twentieth century. Pierpont Mauler has ordered the broker Slift to pretend to be Mauler, so that Joan will not recognize him. But when Joan appears before Mauler, she is not deceived:

> JOAN: [*pointing to Mauler*] You are Mauler.
> MAULER: No, he is.
> JOAN: You are.
> MAULER: How can you tell?
> JOAN: Because you have the bloodiest face.[125]

In *The Merchant of Venice*, Antonio has the bloodiest face. More precisely, as Salanio says, he has two faces: he is two-headed Janus.[126] Still more precisely, like Pierpont Mauler, as personified capital, which has no individual face, Antonio has—and this will occupy us for the moment—a bloody face. Just as Joan recognizes Mauler's face, Shylock recognizes Antonio's. Shylock thereby stumbles on the essence of the matter, reveals the hypocrisy. When Antonio declares to him, with the sentiments of Christian love of neighbor, that he does not lend or borrow "by taking nor by giving of excess," Shylock involves him in a conversation that scholars, I believe, have hardly noticed or have interpreted incorrectly as being primarily concerned with Shylock's financial transactions:

SHYLOCK:

. . . .
Methoughts you said you neither lend nor borrow
Upon advantage.

ANTONIO:

I do never use it.

SHYLOCK:

When Jacob graz'd his uncle Laban's sheep—
This Jacob from our holy Abram was,
(As his wise mother wrought in his behalf)
The third possessor; ay, he was the third,—

ANTONIO:

And what of him? Did he take interest?

SHYLOCK:

No, not take interest; not, as you would say,
Directly int'rest. Mark what Jacob did.

When Laban and himself were compromis'd
That all the eanlings which were streak'd and pied
Should fall as Jacob's hire, the ewes, being rank,
In the end of autumn turned to the rams,
And, when the work of generation was
Between these woolly breeders in the act,
The skilful shepherd pill'd me certain wands,
And, in the doing of the deed of kind,
He stuck them up before the fulsome ewes,
Who then conceiving did in eaning time
Fall parti-colour'd lambs, and those were Jacob's.
This was a way to thrive, and he was blest;
And thrift is blessing, if men steal it not.

ANTONIO:

This was a venture, sir, that Jacob serv'd for;
A thing not in his power to bring to pass,
But sway'd and fashion'd by the hand of Heaven.
Was this inserted to make interest good?
Or is your gold and silver ewes and rams?

SHYLOCK:

I cannot tell; I make it breed as fast.
But note me, signior.

ANTONIO:

Mark you this, Bassanio,
The devil can cite Scripture for his purpose.

(1.3.70-99)

To summarize this passage: Shylock first asks if he has heard correctly that Antonio never lends or borrows money for profit; second, when Antonio affirms that, Shylock tells a story, an example; third, Antonio interrupts him, assuming that Shylock is using the example (of Laban and Jacob) to justify his own usurious transactions. To his question about whether Jacob took interest, Shylock answers, fourth, "No, not take interest; not, as you would say, directly interest," and continues, fifth, with his example. Sixth, Antonio once more rejects a relationship between Shylock's financial transactions and Jacob's profit from his sheep, talks about the venture to which Jacob owed his profit, and justifies this to Shylock because of the risk Jacob has run. As a provocation, he asks Shylock, seventh, whether he means to compare his gold and silver with Jacob's sheep; Shylock, eighth, pointedly breaks off the discussion and wants to turn to Antonio's wish for a loan. The discussion obviously left a thorn in Antonio, so that he, ninth, turns to Bassanio and denounces Shylock as a non-Christian, an anti-Christian, as a devil.

As long as one misunderstands this dialogue as Antonio obviously wants to misunderstand it, the sense of the context cannot be grasped, nor can the meaning of the play, which is to be found in every detail as well as in the totality of the play. Shylock uses the Laban-Jacob legend by no means to explain or to justify his own transactions, but rather to refute Antonio's claim that he never lends or borrows upon advantage. Only in this light can we make sense of the question with which Shylock interrupts the negotiations: Did I hear you correctly, you never lend or borrow upon advantage? When Antonio begins to strengthen this claim, Shylock begins to tell the story, which is comprehensible only if it serves to refute Antonio (Why else should Shylock tell it? in order to justify himself to Antonio?). Antonio understands Shylock immediately, but he wants to distract him. He replaces "advantage" with "interest" and asks, interrupting Shylock, whether Jacob took (usurious or loan) interest. Shylock's answer makes clear how subtly Shakespeare can present the most difficult economic problems. No, Jacob did not take (usurious or loan) interest, at least not in the sense that one usually attributes to "interest": "No, not take interest; not, as you would say, directly interest."

Jacob therefore takes interest *indirectly*. He invests goods or commodity capital (sheep) in an undertaking that is borne jointly by Laban and himself. Jacob runs a risk. Shylock is referring to Antonio, and Antonio understands this quite clearly: he defends and justifies Jacob (which would hardly make sense if Shylock were talking about himself). The text leaves no doubt about the correctness of this interpretation: "This was a venture, sir, that Jacob serv'd for; / A thing not in his power to bring to pass, / But sway'd and fashion'd by the hand of Heaven."[127] This is the justification for (risky) adventure undertakings, the outcome of which is decided by heaven alone. This is Antonio's self-justification to Shylock, the justification of commercial capital to (as Child said, timid and trembling) usurer's capital. But Antonio knows that Shylock has understood that in both cases it is a question of profit, that the profit is merely realized in different ways, and that a moral discussion about the greater right of one or the other form of making a profit cannot result in a decisive advantage, can even perhaps be disadvantageous for commercial capital, because the profit it aims for is infinitely greater than that from usurer's capital. For that reason he answers with a "Christian" polemic, and for that reason Shylock ends the discussion because he sees that it will take them no further; it is a question of annihilating the enemy, of battle (as Antonio correctly says, Shylock should lend him money not as a friend but as an enemy [1.3.133-38]).

Again and again, Shakespearean scholars have disagreed about whether Shakespeare placed Shylock on the stage out of anti-Semitism or not, because in fact the matter is problematic; there had not been any Jewish usurers in England for a long time.[128] The answer to this question is a categorical, certain no. On the contrary, as we shall show, Shakespeare puts Shylock on the stage in part in order to combat racism and religious intolerance. He does not approve of Antonio's slimy, pseudo-Christian polemics. He uses the figure of Shylock to criticize the common manifestations of the feudal system, of the feudal usurer[129] (that means—let us stress this—that he absolutely does not approve of Shylock's social function as a usurer capitalist). On the other hand, he also uses the figure of Shylock (as a victim) to criticize the methods of commercial capitalism: Antonio is conducting colonial trade. As Marx tells us:

> The colonial system ripened trade and navigation as in a hothouse.
> The "companies called Monopolia" (Luther) were powerful levers
> for the concentration of capital. The colonies provided a market for
> the budding manufactures, and a vast increase in accumulation which
> was guaranteed by the mother country's monopoly of the market.
> The treasures captured outside Europe by undisguised looting,
> enslavement and murder flowed back to the mother-country and
> were turned into capital there.[130]

Antonio was also a participant in this looting, enslavement, and murder, and this is the second source of his melancholy, which is first of all that of his creator, Shakespeare. Of course Shakespeare knew what was going on in the colonies or overseas. At this time the polemic against Spanish cruelty to the natives, wherein Las Casas's piece on the destruction of the West Indies has the function of a documentary witness, was creating a furor in England for obvious reasons, but the English were behaving no differently from the Spanish.[131] Marx states: "The treatment of the indigenous population was, of course, at its most frightful in plantation-colonies set up exclusively for the export trade, such as the West Indies, and in rich and well-populated countries, such as Mexico and India, that were given over to plunder."[132]

But Mexico and India are among the places where Antonio is conducting trade, and he conducts it like everyone else, as he must if he hopes to survive the competition—in a bloody way. This is another reason why Shakespeare made Antonio's enemy a Jew: Shakespeare disapproves of the atrocities of colonial exploitation just as he disapproves of religious fanaticism and intolerance (also against Jews).[133] Only the representative of a persecuted, tormented race, humiliated by the pretext of "Christian" arguments, could fling the accusation against Antonio or the representatives of a capitalism that is born "dripping blood and filth from head to toe, from every pore" (Marx) which Shylock raises before the court (and only a Jew could raise it in such a form). When Shylock's opponents in court reproach him with the fact that he cannot hope for mercy in heaven if he insists on redeeming the bond and thus sentencing Antonio to death, he replies:

> What judgment shall I dread, doing no wrong?
> You have among you many a purchas'd slave,

Which, like your asses and your dogs and mules,
You use in abject and in slavish parts,
Because you bought them: shall I say to you,
"Let them be free! Marry them to your heirs!
Why sweat they under burdens? let their beds
Be made as soft as yours and let their palates
Be season'd with such viands"? You will answer,
"The slaves are ours." So do I answer you:
The pound of flesh, which I demand of him,
Is dearly bought; 'tis mine and I will have it.
If you deny me, fie upon your law!
There is no force in the decrees of Venice.

                                        (4.1.89-102)

With his own cruelty, Shylock is holding up a small, modest mirror to the atrocities of the world of commercial capital. With a few exceptions,[134] the many scholars who have discussed Shylock's cruelty have overlooked a crucial detail: Shylock demands his right according to law, and the law, the trading code of Venice (and thus the commercial capitalist law of London), expressly grants him his right. The law is inhuman; the law is valid—none other than Antonio expressly confirms that (like Pierpont Mauler) again and again,[135] and Portia in her role as a lawyer also emphasizes the validity of the law.[136] All Shylock tries to do is to direct this bloody law of the annihilation of the competitor in the bloody trade of slavery and exploitation against what supports it, commercial capitalism; this earns him strange abuse from Gratiano:

O, be thou damn'd, inexorable dog!
And for thy life let justice be accus'd!
Thou almost mak'st me waver in my faith
To hold opinion with Pythagoras,
That souls of animals infuse themselves
Into the trunks of men: thy currish spirit
Govern'd a wolf, who, hang'd for human slaughter,
Even from the gallows did his fell soul fleet,
And, whilst thou lay'st in thy unhallow'd dam
Infus'd itself in thee; for thy desires
Are wolvish, bloody, starv'd, and ravenous.

                                        (4.1.128-38)

Gratiano is mistaken, or he is lying. He acts as if he did not know that the colonial adventure trade is "wolvish, bloody, starv'd, and ravenous" and that Shylock is trying only to defend himself. Still, the old system ("old Shylock")[137]—feudal usurer's capital, that is trying to employ the laws of competition against commercial capital out of which those laws originated (those laws, half a century after Gratiano's speech in *The Merchant of Venice*, will be transformed into the basis of Hobbes's conception of society)—cannot prevail in this battle. Commercial capital and its laws are more powerful. Not only does Antonio not pay his debt to Shylock at the end, not only does he get off unscathed, but Antonio defeats his enemy with the help of Portia, or more precisely, he annihilates Shylock. And here too we see Shakespeare's genius. The harshest physical punishment of Shylock, even the death sentence, would have been a banal conclusion. Shakespeare is concerned with the historical victory of the bourgeoisie, of the capitalist mode of production. Antonio transforms Shylock's accumulated usurer's capital, half of which comes to him according to the court's decree, into commercial capital by bequeathing it to Jessica, Shylock's daughter, and her lover Lorenzo: he puts the treasure into circulation.

International Falstaff

In Shakespeare's basic attitude toward bourgeois adventure, there is a parallel to that of Rabelais: without shutting his eyes to the horror of the capitalist policy of slavery, exploitation, murder, and plunder, while, in fact, condemning this policy most sharply, Shakespeare affirms Antonio's victory and places all his hope in the power of the new economic mode of production, capitalism, to liberate humanity. Although he is sympathetic to the tragic suffering of Shylock as the representative of an oppressed, persecuted race, he has not the least sympathy with Shylock as representative of feudalism, a system that makes human freedom impossible.[138] Driven by a muffled lust for profit, dominated by mean greed, Shylock is arrested in religious delusions. Even the cynical treatment of religious arguments by Antonio is "progress" in comparison, announcing as it does the dissolution of religious hallucinations and hence representing a *preliminary stage* in the move to religious tolerance in Portia's realm. Shylock's form of life and of earning a living entail the ignorance and enslavement of the rest of his world: the servant Launcelot Gobbo is kept like a slave; he is not even given enough to eat; and Jessica, Shylock's daughter, lives in her father's house like a prisoner, subjugated, locked away from the world, treated as less than human.[139] When the youth of Venice expresses its joy at life in a carnival-like masque, Jessica is forced to bolt the windows and doors. Shylock exclaims:

> What, are there masques? Hear you me, Jessica.
> Lock up my doors; and when you hear the drum
> And the vile squeaking of the wry-neck'd fife,
> Clamber not you up to the casements then,
> Nor thrust your head into the public street

> To gaze on Christian fools with varnish'd faces,
> But stop my house's ears, I mean my casements:
> Let not the sound of shallow fopp'ry enter
> My sober house.
>
> (2.5.28-36)

Both Launcelot and Jessica break out of this prison of feudal slavery: the one joins forces with the young adventurer Bassanio, the other flees with the adventurer Lorenzo into a better world, in which the human being is treated as a human being and woman is also treated as a human being. "And now, good sweet, say thy opinion," Lorenzo says to his beautiful Jewess (3.5.76), who had learned only slavish obedience.

But not only in Antonio's victory over Shylock and in Jessica's (and Launcelot's) liberation did Shakespeare hail the *homo novus*, the capitalist. Antonio is a two-headed Janus, and the capitalist mode of production certainly has two faces in the epoch of its conflict with the feudal mode: first, the bloody competitive battle and the still bloodier subjugation of the New World (Shakespeare could not yet have seen the subjugation of the proletariat); and second, the liberation from feudalism, the creation of a brighter, better world— Belmont, Portia's realm. In conquering this realm, Bassanio completes Antonio's economic victory over feudalism with a political victory.

Interpreters of *The Merchant of Venice* have tended to overlook this as well. All Bassanio's rivals in the courtship of Portia are princes or petty nobles who have more or less come down in the world: international variations of Falstaff. And Bassanio defeats them all. First the petty nobility capitulates; it is already so weak that it cannot even submit to a decisive test. The viewer does not even meet its representatives. The petty nobles wooing Portia are only described in a dialogue between Portia and Nerissa, her confidante. Nerissa introduces the individual figures, and Portia provides an ironic commentary.

NERISSA:
> First, there is the Neapolitan prince.

PORTIA:
> Ay, that's a colt indeed, for he doth
> nothing but talk of his horse; and he makes it
> a great appropriation to his own good
> parts, that he can shoe him himself. I am
> much afeard my lady his mother played false
> with a smith.
>
> (1.2.42-48)

Next comes a Palatine count: "He doth nothing but frown;" says Portia, "as who should say, 'if you will not have me, / choose.'. . . I had rather be /

married to a death's-head with a bone in his / mouth than to either of these. God defend me / from these two!" (1.2.50-58). The "young French lord, Monsieur Le Bon" is nothing but a courtly-knightly blowhard, a French Falstaff, and "the young German, the Duke of Saxony's nephew," is a drunkard. Portia likes him "Very vilely in the morning, when he / is sober; and most vilely in the afternoon, / when he is drunk" (1.2.59-93).

Only one of all these useless parasites is judged with politically astute reticence: Falconbridge, the "young baron of England." Portia says, "He is a proper man's picture," but her reason for being able to say nothing more about him is a criticism of the uneducated English nobility, who lack that very skill that belongs to the tools of the commercial bourgeois, as Fortunatus, Pantagruel, and Panurge demonstrate: "You know I say nothing to him, for / he understands not me, nor I him: he hath / neither Latin, French, nor Italian, and you will come into the court and swear that I / have a poor pennyworth in the English"[140] (1.2.72-76). To this is added another criticism of the English nobility: they promote their own trade too little. Portia represents the mercantilist position of contemporary economists, a position the Elizabethan audience would easily understand: "How oddly he is / suited! I think he bought his doublet in Italy, / his round hose in France, his bonnet in Ger- / many, and his behaviour everywhere" (1.2.78-81). It is obvious that this is meant to pillory the English nobility for their general lack of culture (a criticism to which Beaumont will reply a few years later in *The Knight of the Burning Pestle*, simply by reversing the point). Still, the judgment on the English baron is on the whole more positive than that on the other petty feudal nobles; at least the English baron—boldly defending the absolute monarchy (especially in its conflict with the Scottish nobility)—engaged in blows:

NERISSA:
> What think you of the Scottish lord, his neighbour?

PORTIA:
> That he hath a neighbourly char-
> ity in him; for he borrowed a box of the ear
> of the Englishman, and swore he would pay him
> again when he was able: I think the French-
> man became his surety, and sealed under for
> another.

> (1.2.82-89)

All these claimants, however, have already been defeated and have cut their losses. As Nerissa says:

> You need not fear, lady, the having
> any of these lords: they have acquainted me

with their determinations; which is, indeed, to return to their home and to trouble
you with no more suit, unless you may be
won by some other sort than your father's
imposition depending on the caskets.
                                    (1.2.108-15)

The Critique of the Courtly Ideology of Adventure
and Praise of Bourgeois Risk

Every interpretation of the famous episode of the caskets has regarded the fact that the feudal petty nobles do not dare to attempt the test, consider it hopeless from the outset to try to choose the right casket, as a *quantité négligeable*, "something not to be taken into account." But it is far from being a *quantité négligeable*: a historical process is described, a sum is totaled, in the refusal of the feudal petty nobility to enter the competition for Portia. The petty nobility has been defeated. The protagonists of the epoch, the bourgeoisie and the feudal upper nobility, are now facing each other directly. (Understandably, the problem of the absolute monarchy is not addressed; only Antonio's designation as a "royal merchant" allows us to recognize that Shakespeare supports the monarchic form of a civil state in *The Merchant of Venice* as elsewhere.) This confrontation leads also to a debate between the different world views. The elements that seem to converge in the concept of "adventure" are carefully separated and set in opposition by Shakespeare in *The Merchant of Venice*: the courtly-reactionary and the progressive-bourgeois ideologies of adventure.

Since Shakespeare believes (in accordance with the historical data) that the bourgeois ideology of adventure or (more correctly) the bourgeoisie must and will prevail, he is faced with the problem of how to spread this historical truth in a state that is still dominated by the feudal nobility, albeit a nobility that favors the monarchy. In writing the truth, he has recourse to one of his numerous stratagems so admired by Brecht:[141] the representatives of the reactionary upper nobility come from the Spanish-Moorish area, their courtly ideology (of adventure) originates in the mental world of *Amadís* and his followers but also incorporates philosophical ideas that belong to the ideological arsenal of the upper nobility in general, hence also to the English ideology (it should be noted that the *matière espagnole* was extremely popular also in England). Shakespeare thus puts his attack on the upper nobility and the reactionary courtly ideology above reproach; he is, after all, attacking these things in the form of the national enemy Spain (with which England, as we have mentioned, fought a decisive battle in the English Channel in 1588, after years of warlike hostilities; the battle ended with the annihilation of the Spanish armada). Bassanio's only rivals who are nearly his equal in birth are feudal princes, the Prince of Morocco and the Prince of Arragon. They are the first to enter the contest for Portia, which consists of choosing the right one of three caskets, one gold, one silver, and one lead. One of them contains Portia's portrait. Whoever chooses that casket will be her husband, has won her.

The Prince of Morocco is the first to venture a choice, and he does so in the swaggering style of the Spanish knightly romances:

> lead me to the caskets,
> To try my fortune. By this scimitar
> That slew the Sophy and a Persian prince
> That won three fields of Sultan Solyman,
> I would outstare the sternest eyes that look,
> Outbrave the heart most daring on the earth,
> Pluck the young sucking cubs from the she-bear,
> Yea, mock the lion when he roars for prey,
> To win thee, lady.
>
> (2.1.23-31)

On each of the caskets lined up in front of the prince is an inscription to guide the suitor, and Morocco reads:

> The first, of gold, who this inscription bears,
> "Who chooseth me shall gain what many men desire;"
> The second, silver, which this promise carries,
> "Who chooseth me shall get as much as he deserves;"
> This third, dull lead, with warning all as blunt,
> "Who chooseth me must give and hazard all he hath."
>
> (2.7.4-9)

Each of the three suitors (Morocco, Arragon, Bassanio) explains in detail what sways him to choose one casket and not the others. First the Prince of Morocco speaks:

> Some god direct my judgment! Let me see;
> I will survey th' inscriptions back again.
> What says this leaden casket?
> Who chooseth me must give and hazard all he hath.
> Must give: for what? For lead? Hazard for lead?
> This casket threatens. Men that hazard all
> Do it in hope of fair advantages;
> A golden mind stoops not to shows of dross.
> I'll then nor give nor hazard aught for lead.
>
> (2.7.13-21)

Morocco's considerations hover between two negations. He does not want to hazard anything for lead because lead seems to him as inappropriate as a frame for Portia's portrait as the motivation the inscription gives for choosing lead: desire for profit, or more precisely, active work for the sake of profit. The representative of the great nobility holds the view that to him must be given, that only *largesse*, spending, squandering is appropriate for him (an official ideology still openly represented in the eighteenth century by Montesquieu). Nor does Morocco want silver, because while he believes that he deserves Portia on the basis of his birth, his rank, and his education, he tries at the same time to combine the courtly casuistry of love with his arrogance about his social rank: Portia deserves still greater honor than he himself, for everyone should honor her according to her value and her beauty. Morocco chooses the golden casket and opens it:

> O hell! What have we here?
> A carrion Death within whose empty eye
> There is a written scroll! I'll read the writing.
>> "All that glisters is not gold;
>> Often have you heard that told.
>> Many a man his life hath sold
>> But my outside to behold.
>> Gilded tombs do worms infold.
>> Had you been as wise as bold,
>> Young in limbs, in judgement old,
>> Your answer had not been inscroll'd.
>> Fare you well; your suit is cold."
>
> (2.7.62-73)

The Prince of Arragon has the same opinion of the lead casket as Morocco, but he scorns the gold one as well, because he does not want "what many men desire":

> What many men desire! that many may be meant
> By the fool multitude, that choose by show,
> Not learning more than the fond eye doth teach;
> Which pries not to th' interior, but, like the martlet,
> Builds in the weather on the outward wall,
> Even in the force and road of casualty.
> I will not choose what many men desire,
> Because I will not jump with common spirits
> And rank me with the barbarous multitudes.
> Why, then to thee, thou silver treasure-house;

Tell me once more what title thou dost bear:
"Who chooseth me shall get as much as he deserves":
And well said too; for who shall go about
To cozen fortune and be honourable
Without the stamp of merit? Let none presume
To wear an undeserved dignity.
. . . .
. . . . Well, but to my choice:
"Who chooseth me shall get as much as he deserves."
I will assume desert. Give me a key for this,
And instantly unlock my fortunes here.

(2.9.25-52)

Arragon's arguments correspond completely to the feudal-princely world view: desert cannot be won; it originates in nobility by birth, is thus innate in the ruling class. But Arragon's choice is also, or course, wrong:

What's here? The portrait of a blinking idiot,
Presenting me a schedule! I will read it.
How much unlike art thou to Portia!
How much unlike my hopes and my deservings!
"Who chooseth me shall have as much as he deserves."
Did I deserve no more than a fool's head?
Is that my prize? are my deserts no better?

(2.9.54-60)

The winner in the contest for Portia is Bassanio—with historical necessity, which is reflected in the dramaturgical logic: Bassanio is Portia's last suitor, is the representative of the victorious bourgeoisie. Before Bassanio proceeds to choose a casket, Portia has music play while a chorus tells Bassanio which casket he should choose. This chorus is one of the keys to understanding the play:

[ONE VOICE—M. N.]:

Tell me where is fancy bred,
Or in the heart or in the head?
How begot, how nourished?

ALL:

Reply, reply.

[ONE VOICE—M. N.]:

It is engender'd in the eyes,
With gazing fed; and fancy dies
In the cradle where it lies.

Let us all ring fancy's knell:
I'll begin it,—Ding, dong, bell.

ALL:

Ding, dong, bell.

(3.2.63-72)

Shakespeare has constructed this text to admit two opposite readings, which exactly corresponds to Portia's intentions in having it sung. If Bassanio chooses wrong, it is mourning music; if he chooses correctly, it is a chorus of jubilation. The key word for the understanding of the lines is "fancy," which on the one hand means taste, fashion, and desire, but on the other can mean imagination, intuition, fantasy, and (creative) thought. The song has a positive or a negative sense depending on which meaning one attributes to "fancy." We shall expound only the positive meaning, the one that guides Bassanio correctly; it lies in the direction of fancy as imagination. A paraphrase of the song would be:

Tell me where imagination is bred,
In sensory perception (the heart, the emotions) or in
    reason (the head)?
How is it engendered? How is it maintained?

Reply, reply.

It is engendered by sensory perception (in the eyes),
But if it is maintained only by the eyes,
Then it dies in its cradle.

Shakespeare's song represents a poetic version of the bourgeois (revolutionary) philosophy of the time, empirical sensualism: the philosophical quintessence of Francis Bacon's system, disguised as poetry. The first edition of Bacon's *Essays* was published in 1597 (around the time of the final version of *The Merchant of Venice*), but as we learn from the dedication to his brother, numerous drafts had already circulated earlier in élite circles[142] (and it is unlikely that Shakespeare, who was closely connected to court life, should have failed to see them). In the first of these ten essays, Bacon asserts that studies are useful not in themselves but for the domination of nature: "They perfect *Nature*, and are perfected by experience. Craftie men continue them, simple men admire them, wise men vse them: For they teach not their own vse, but that is a wisdome without them: and aboue them wonne by observation."[143] Shakespeare's poem about fancy is a polemic against contemplation and a priori thinking,[144] against scholasticism and inactivity, against the idea of the immutability of the world that is represented by Morocco and Arragon. It is the affirmation of sensory perception (in contrast to Arragon), but this sensory perception leads to nothing (dies) unless it is nourished by an active attitude toward nature, by practical activity and experience (in contrast to Morocco's condemnation of praxis). The merchant adventurer Bassanio, who is also a "scholar, and a / soldier" (1.2.124-25) is thus a typical contemporary explorer (in the *Novum Organum* Bacon repeatedly points out the significance of the voyages of discovery for the natural sciences, for modern scientific thinking). Bassanio, in his adventure voyage to Belmont, his risky wooing of Portia, his choice of casket, is living out the philosophical credo of the (revolutionary) bourgeoisie. He chooses the lead casket with the inscription that could be the motto of adventure trade: "'Who chooseth me must give and hazard all he hath'": in a concrete sense, he must give his share of capital or his abilities, his labor. He gives an indirect / direct answer to the chorus:

> So may the outward shows be least themselves:
> The world is still deceiv'd with ornament.
> In law, what plea so tainted and corrupt
> But, being season'd with a gracious voice,
> Obscures the show of evil? In religion,
> What damned error, but some sober brow
> Will bless it and approve it with a text,
> Hiding the grossness with fair ornament?
> There is no vice so simple but assumes
> Some mark of virtue on his outward parts;
> How many cowards, whose hearts are all as false
> As stairs of sand, wear yet upon their chins
> The beards of Hercules and frowning Mars;
> Who, inward search'd, have livers white as milk;
> And these assume but valour's excrement
> To render them redoubted! Look on beauty,
> And you shall see 'tis purchased by the weight;
> Which therein works a miracle in nature,
> Making them lightest that wear most of it:
> So are those crisped snaky golden locks,
> Which make such wanton gambols with the wind
> Upon supposed fairness, often known
> To be the dowry of a second head,
> The skull that bred them in the sepulchre.
> Thus ornament is but the guiled shore
> To a most dangerous sea; the beauteous scarf
> Veiling an Indian beauty; in a word,
> The seeming truth which cunning times put on
> To entrap the wisest. Therefore, thou gaudy gold,

Hard food for Midas, I will none of thee;
Nor none of thee, thou pale and common drudge
'Tween man and man; but thou, thou meagre lead,
Which rather threat'nest than dost promise aught,
Thy plainness moves me more than eloquence;
And here choose I. Joy be the consequence!

(3.2.73-107)

Belmont; or, Fortuna Vanquished

Freud criticized Bassanio's speech in front of the caskets; he thought it too modest: "What he finds to say in glorification of lead as against gold and silver is little and has a forced ring."[145] To be sure, Freud also believed he had found the key (always the same key!) to understanding the choice of caskets. The caskets, he wrote, are "symbols of what is essential in woman, and therefore of a woman herself—like coffers, boxes, cases, baskets, and so on"[146]—in short, the essential part of woman is the vagina, and that means that the essential part of Portia, Jessica, Nerissa is also the vagina and that world history is reduced to the few variations on the antagonism between the vagina and the penis (Bassanio, Gratiano, Lorenzo). But that is not yet the climax of Freud's interpretation, which Shakespeare scholars still consider a groundbreaking, brilliant accomplishment:[147] the essential part of Bassanio—which in an inversion of the essential part of Portia or of woman in general can also only be that certain universal in general—manifests itself in a special way. To present this, Freud adopts the interpretation of Eduard Stucken:

> The identity of Portia's three suitors is clear from their choice: the Prince of Morocco chooses the golden casket—he is the sun; the Prince of Arragon chooses the silver casket—he is the moon; Bassanio chooses the leaden casket—he is the star youth.[148]

Shakespeare did not, in fact, hide his mythological allusions, but the mythological gods alone know what sense it could have made to tell an Elizabethan audience that a Prince of Morocco was the sun, a Prince of Arragon the moon, and Bassanio the "star youth." Since ancient times gold has been a metaphor for delusion and (deceptive) appearance, silver for the (moonlit) night and death—that is neither particularly new nor exciting. But in *The Merchant of Venice*, gold and silver can have no other meaning than the one Shakespeare gives them. Bassanio scorns gold because it represents the false appearance (feudal-princely magnificence) and because it is "hard food for Midas." King Midas of Phrygia had prayed to Dionysos that everything he touched would turn to gold. As a consequence, he could neither drink nor eat, since everything became gold in his mouth. If Morocco's striving for gold and Arragon's for silver have a meaning in Shakespeare's play, it is first of all that of constituting the correlate to Shylock's usurer's capital in the feudal-noble accumulation of treasure: heaped up in huge amounts, gold, silver, wealth, lose their meaning as the source of useful property.[149] Bassanio, on the other hand, is interested in money only as capital to invest in goods or in trade ventures. For that reason he chooses lead, and with lead, adventure.

At this point, mythology comes into its own—not as it is understood by psychoanalysis, but as Shakespeare's time used it. Gold does in fact also symbolize the sun (Helios, Sol, Apollo) and silver the moon (Luna), and Shakespearean scholarship has long since determined that astrology plays a significant role in *The Merchant of Venice*.[150] But scholars seem not to have been concerned about the meaning of lead. Let us recall Salanio, who put Antonio in conjunction with two-headed Janus. Janus, god of the beginning and of the end (as Antonio is the protagonist of the beginning and the end of this play), was the first king of Italy, according to a Roman legend. Originally from Greece, he came to Italy with a fleet, and toward the end of his reign took a coregent who was also to be his heir: Saturn. Saturn's rule was known to antiquity, the Middle Ages, and the Renaissance—hence also to Shakespeare—as the *Golden Age*. Saturn, who educated humanity and instituted the rule of law, was the god of—lead.

Various interpreters have in fact mentioned Portia's realm, Belmont, in connection with the Golden Age, but usually this is a more or less informal way of speaking about a land where peace and happiness reign and which is a dream of a happy, lost past.[151] But this is meaningless. For does Antonio the commercial capitalist, does Bassanio the adventurer, does the bourgeoisie engage in a material and ideological struggle with the petty and great feudal nobility, with usurer's capital and the entire feudal mode of production or the entire feudal system, and annihilate it, only in order to dream of a better past? If Shakespeare affirms Antonio's victory, if he welcomes the defeat of the feudal nobility, if he lets Bassanio win Portia, then it is because he is convinced that the new (revolutionary) forces are preparing humanity's way to freedom through all the injustice (caused by them also), through all the exploitation, through all the blood. Belmont is not the dream of a *past Golden Age*; Belmont is the *confidence* in a *Golden Age to come*, at which bold human beings who assume the risk of battle will arrive. Bassanio will arrive as Hercules, as Portia designates him, but he is a new Hercules, the embodiment of courage, of Titan-like self-confidence proclaimed by Philip Sidney's friend Giordano Bruno in his *De gli eroici furori* (Of the Heroic Passions), published in 1585 and dedicated to Sidney: Bassanio will arrive as Hercules the merchant adventurer.

Belmont is the realm of Fortuna, and Portia is secularized Fortuna, so completely formed as an individual character that modern Shakespeare scholars seem to have missed it entirely.[152] Nonetheless, it is only from this perspective that the figure and function of Portia become intelligible.[153] For what sense would it make to give a symbolic, dramatic portrayal of the historical struggle between usurer's capital and commercial capital on the one hand, between feudal nobility and the bourgeoisie on the other, if the historical prize for the victorious class, for the victorious mode of production, was only a woman chosen at random (however beautiful, young, and rich)? Would the petty nobility of all Europe assemble in a contest for such a woman, and then not even be able to enter the contest? Would the feudal great nobility (after Morocco's arrival) stream in from all over the world for this contest and then engage in battle with the bourgeoisie and lose, for the sake of such a (randomly chosen) woman? Only if one sees Fortuna in Portia does this huge struggle make sense, because this struggle between the classes is about economic and political power, about fate, about the future, about Fortuna. While the petty nobility is already so exhausted that it cannot even participate in the battle for the future, for fate, fate overtakes the feudal great nobility in the struggle against the bourgeoisie, which wins the future, triumphs over fate: subjugates Fortuna.

And this is the decisive turn for the discussion of Fortuna in the sixteenth century; I believe that *The Merchant of Venice* signals the end of the Renaissance view of Fortuna. Here it is no longer a question of the fate of an individual, of *the* individual, who has to defend himself against the power of the stars, of Fortuna; it is not even simply the attempt of the individual to prevail against Fortuna, to vanquish her:[154] this individual battle against Fortuna is subsumed in the battle between *classes* that Shakespeare presents! One can analyze the play in its smallest details and still find no other antagonism than that among petty nobility, feudal great nobility, and bourgeoisie, between feudal exploitation or usurer's capital and commercial capital. And the decisive point: the victory in the struggle for Fortuna falls to one class, not because Fortuna is fickle, but because only this class can conquer her by its activity and its courage and daring, since the other classes are no longer in a position to do so.

But let us proceed systematically. First, theorists of the Middle Ages and Renaissance agree that Fortuna's home (according to a portrayal by Alanus ab Insulis, ca. 1118-ca. 1203, that was generally adopted) is a (more or less) accessible mountain (described in Fregoso's treatise *Dialogo di Fortuna*, 1531, as "a beautiful place on top of a mountain, where Fortuna distributes her gifts").[155] As Howard R. Patch demonstrates, using a passage from *Troilus and Cressida* (1600-01; 3.3), Shakespeare was thoroughly familiar with this tradition. Portia lives in Belmont = beautiful mountain. Second, Fortuna's palace is constantly filled with music.[156] In Portia's palace, music plays as Bassanio is selecting the casket, and when Portia returns from Venice, musicians emerge from the palace:

> Come, ho! and wake Diana with a hymn!
> With sweetest touches pierce your mistress' ear,
> And draw her home with music.
>
> (5.1.66-68)

This reading even provides an explanation for another episode: the scene between Jessica and Lorenzo in which Lorenzo explains to her the significance of music. Lorenzo has brought Jessica to Fortuna's palace, to Belmont, to the realm of actively won freedom, in which—as in the Golden Age—peace and harmony reign. Lorenzo presents Jessica with the example of wild beasts made "modest" by music:

> therefore the poet
> Did feign that Orpheus drew trees, stones, and floods;
> Since nought so stockish, hard, and full of rage,
> But music for the time doth change his nature.
> The man that hath no music in himself,
> Nor is not mov'd with concord of sweet sounds,
> Is fit for treasons, strategems, and spoils;
> The motions of his spirit are dull as night,
> And his affections dark as Erebus:
> Let no such man be trusted. Mark the music.
>
> (5.1.79-88)

Third, Fortuna's palace has a lovely garden.[157] The harmonious final scene, characterized by music and play of lights, which brings the play to a happy end (5.1), takes place in Portia's beautiful palace garden. Fourth, there is a "celestial atmosphere"[158] in Fortuna's residence. Lorenzo calls to Jessica:

> Sit, Jessica. Look how the floor of heaven
> Is thick inlaid with patens of bright gold.
> There's not the smallest orb which thou behold'st
> But in his motion like an angel sings,
> Still quiring to the young-ey'd cherubins.[159]
>
> (5.1.58-62)

And when Portia returns from Venice, the following happens, pointedly, because Portia places emphasis on it (5.1): a comparison between day and night, between the moon and the sun (according to the astrological views of the Renaissance, Fortuna is the distance between the sun and the moon).[160] And Portia's comments on the moon can all have only one purpose: to evoke Fortuna, to make the audience think about Fortuna (and it must be remembered that such ideas were quite current at that time). The changeableness of Fortuna, as Patch writes, "leads inevitably to a comparison with the moon,"[161] since the moon also changes every day. When on her return from Venice by night Portia sees a candle glowing from within the palace, she says to Nerissa, "So doth the greater glory dim the less"; Nerissa responds with a comment to the effect that they would be unable to see the candle if the moon were shining.[162] This scene, like the whole night / morning concluding scene, is unintelligible unless it is seen in connection with the myth of Fortuna.

PORTIA:

> So doth the greater glory dim the less.
> A substitute shines brightly as a king
> Until a king be by; and then his state
> Empties itself, as doth an inland brook
> Into the main of waters. Music! hark!
>
> (5.1.93-97)

But there are still more links between Fortuna and Portia. What do we really learn explicitly about Portia? Only a few indications that do not amount to much. Portia, the mistress of Belmont, is the "living daughter" of "a dead father" (1.2.26-27)—like Fortuna. Fortuna was the only one of all the divinities of antiquity, as Patch writes, who survived the change of religion at the rise of Christianity.[163] All the others, even her father Jupiter disappeared, but Fortuna appears again and again throughout the whole Middle Ages and the Renaissance, as the executrix of the divine (Christian) will. Therefore it is by no means a contradiction when Portia, who by the way constantly speaks in mythological similes, evokes God and God's mercy before the court. Her "dead father" provided in his last "will" that she allow the suit only of a man who selects correctly among the three caskets. She complains to Nerissa:

> Is it not hard,
> Nerissa, that I cannot choose one nor refuse none?

whereupon Nerissa answers:

> Your father was ever virtuous, and
> holy men at their death have good inspira-
> tions: therefore, the lottery, that he hath de-
> vised in these three chests of gold, silver, and
> lead, whereof who chooses his meaning
> chooses you, will, no doubt, never be
> chosen by any rightly, but one who shall
> rightly love.
>
> (1.2.28-37)

Shakespearean scholarship has correctly pointed out that the model for this choice of the caskets is found in the medieval Latin collection of legends, fairy tales, and novellas called the *Gesta Romanorum*, which was written in England in the middle of the thirteenth century and which served as a kind of folk-book until into the sixteenth century. But it seems to me more important in this context that Nerissa speaks of a "lottery." The idea of lottery (and chance) and Fortuna was very common in the Middle Ages and Renaissance.[164] Nerissa's speech only makes sense if one introduces Fortuna. In fact, Fortuna can be sure that she will not be chosen rightly by anyone who does not rightly love, or in other words, that the one who chooses her also loves her. On the other hand, Portia's dependence on the choice of the casket fits perfectly with the view of the late Renaissance that only the courageous, active man can conquer Fortuna or be loved by her.

Fortuna gives and takes.[165] Portia gives and takes: she gives herself and her wealth to Bassanio, after he has conquered her, has earned her, in the selection of a casket. But she thereby takes everything from Antonio at the same time because Bassanio's adventure allowed Antonio to become Shylock's victim, annihilated him. Now, through Bassanio, Portia returns manyfold the money Antonio lent him. But at the same time, she knows that this will not help, that Shylock will insist on redeeming the bond, and she hurries to Venice in order, in a changed form, to take everything from Shylock, who had risen high with her help, and to cast him down. She raises Antonio up again: he receives half of Shylock's fortune from Portia, and from Portia he also receives—his ships back. The movement to which Shakespeare has given dramatic shape is that of the wheel of fortune: Fortuna loves to test people, for instance through imprisonment,[166] and in the course of their testing, it becomes clear what true friendship is.[167] Antonio frees Bassanio from prison, and Bassanio declares before the court that he is prepared to give up everything including Portia, if he can thereby save Antonio (here again he shows courage, renounces Fortuna, which she cannot hold against him, but which must instead increase her respect for him).

In connection with the court scene we must mention another aspect that has given Shakespeare interpreters much trouble.[168] Apart from her "dead father," Portia has only one other relative: a "cousin" in Padua, who is a doctor of laws. The cousin provides not only the legal arguments Portia uses before the court, but also the—disguise. Before she sets out for Venice, she sends her servant Balthasar to this cousin with a letter and tells him:

> And, look, what notes and garments he doth give thee,
> Bring them, I pray thee, with imagin'd speed
> Unto the traject, to the common ferry
> Which trades to Venice.

(3.4.51-54)

It is quite strange that a doctor of laws should also be a master of disguise: if we look in the handbooks of the time for a relative of Fortuna who would know how to perform such tricks and who moreover was versed in law, we come across—Mercury. In a remarkable portrayal in the *Emblemata* of Alciati, which Shakespeare of course knew, like every poet of his time, we find Fortuna shown with one foot on a globe, with the other (to emphasize her instability) on the sea, and next to her sits Mercury, who is rarely shown seated in pictorial presentation.[169] He embodies (commercial) law and jurisprudence. Mercury (Hermes in Greek), however, as Shakespeare's contemporaries well knew, is linked with the image of the ram he carried on his shoulders. The lead ram of a flock is called a bellwether, or in French, *bélier*. Portia's "cousin," the doctor of laws from Padua who knows about law and about disguises, is called Bellario. Bellario not only provides Portia with the disguise that is so effective that even Bassanio does not recognize her before the court, but also gives Portia a letter to the duke, recommending to the Venetian court that it admit the "young doctor" (Portia) despite her tender age: "I beseech you, let his lack of years be no impediment to let him lack a reverend estimation, for I never knew so young / a body with so old a head" (4.1.163-64). "Her face seemed young, but she was ripe in years," writes Trissino in his epic, *L'Italia liberata dai Goti* (Italy Liberated from the Goths, 1547ff.), about a variant of Fortuna.[170] If Portia is Fortuna, Bellario's sentence quoted above yields a deeper meaning.

Portia / Fortuna does not, however, actually need Mercury's aid to appear before the court and to be allowed to plead: Fortuna as judge or as legal scholar before the court was not unknown to Shakespeare's contemporaries (quite apart from the fact that in mythological tradition as the daughter of Jupiter she was also the daughter of the law and that human thought and judgment were her relatives).[171] In England between 1583 and 1586, Giordano Bruno wrote his *Spaccio della bestia trionfante* (The Expulsion of the Triumphant Beast), a work, like *De gli eroici furori*, dedicated to Philip Sidney. The aging mythological gods hold court in this satirical piece; blind Fortuna also appears and demands a place among the judging gods. But although they acknowledge Fortuna's acuteness,[172] she receives permission only to wander around in heaven. The gods refuse to include Fortuna in their council because of what Giordano Bruno distrusts in his portrayal of her: her absolute lack of concern for the person affected by her decisions, which would border on cynicism if it were not a case of the blind Fortuna. She is a goddess hostile to everyone (and here she clearly bears traces of the Italian Renaissance tradition), the representative of a largely pessimistic attitude toward fate, or of one without perspective, of blind Fortuna. Shakespeare's Portia / Fortuna is a philanthrope and as such appears before the court and rules; this could easily be a response to

Giordano Bruno's critique of blind Fortuna. The (commercial) bourgeoisie does not fear Fortuna, it conquers her.

In any case, if Portia is Fortuna, then one of the questions she poses before the court gains another dimension: "Which is the merchant here, and which the Jew?" (4.1.174). Gustav Landauer believes that Portia actually has no doubt which is Antonio and which Shylock, but that she asks only to emphasize through the ugly, foreign name Shylock for the audience (and the court) that it is a question of a vile wretch and a Jew[173] (although everyone is already aware of that), but the actual reason could lie elsewhere. Portia/Fortuna does not recognize Antonio, whom she wants to save, because for her he is—as faceless as for the public (and for scholars). Antonio should really have been out of Fortuna's favor because in principle he no longer risks anything, dares anything— does not conquer Fortuna. As we saw, he told us at the beginning of the play that he has no risks and no fears in his business because he has invested his capital in such a way that if, say, one ship is lost, that still constitutes no threat to his wealth. And nevertheless, Antonio did risk something, but his risk is invisible, is realized apart from his person in a thing, in a loan he takes out from his mortal enemy in the form of a commercially unviable usurer's loan, and is finally realized in a material, visible way in Bassanio's adventure. Only through Bassanio's activity does Portia/Fortuna take notice of Antonio: *Shakespeare uses Bassanio to justify the modern capitalist.* Bassanio reveals to Portia/Fortuna that he was able to carry out his enterprise only thanks to a capital investment by Antonio and that Antonio raised this capital through a loan from the usurer:

> for, indeed,
> I have engaged myself to a dear friend,
> Engag'd my friend to his mere enemy,
> To feed my means.
>
> (3.2.263-66)

Portia/Fortuna (and with her the audience) recognizes that Antonio has undertaken a risk with Bassanio's adventure, and she immediately offers Bassanio any amount of money so that he can free his friend from debt. But at the same time she knows, as we have mentioned, that Bassanio cannot do this, that she alone can do this. Nonetheless she sends Bassanio to Venice (she tests Bassanio's friendship) and charges him with bringing Antonio to Belmont (now, after his risk is revealed). When Lorenzo praises her for having such a "true conceit" for true friendship and generously being willing to bear the "absence of your lord" for the sake of this friendship, she answers as Fortuna must answer:

> I never did repent for doing good,
> Nor shall not now: for in companions
> That do converse and waste the time together,
> Whose souls do bear an equal yoke of love,
> There must be needs a like proportion
> Of lineaments, of manners and of spirit;
> Which makes me think that this Antonio,
> Being the bosom lover of my lord,
> Must needs be like my lord. If it be so,
> How little is the cost I have bestowed
> In purchasing the semblance of my soul
> From out of the state of hellish misery!
> This comes too near the praising of myself.
>
> (3.4.10-22)

Here, too, each detail is intelligible if one sees that Fortuna is speaking: just as Bassanio won her on the basis of his readiness to run risks, his sober eye, and the practical test he passed, so she as Fortuna favors him as she favors everyone like him. That includes Antonio, although he has become faceless. Before the court she has meantime gained information, before the court she gives the wheel a mighty spin and from one second to the next plunges the gloating Shylock into the abyss, lifts Antonio up again. But not—and this is again evidence of Shakespeare's genius—because divine will (alone) wants it so, but rather because Antonio has earned it with his venture via Bassanio, with his "shaft." It is a fairy-tale conclusion, certainly, but from a historical perspective it is absolutely no fairy tale: commercial capital triumphs over feudal usurer's capital, is presented by Fortuna with the fortune of usurer's capital, and transforms it into commercial capital—and even the lost ships are suddenly restored. And anyone who has doubted that Portia embodies Fortuna must have been convinced by the end of the play. Antonio, together with Bassanio and Gratiano, comes to Belmont, where Portia and Nerissa have arrived shortly before.

PORTIA:

> Antonio, you are welcome;
> And I have better news in store for you
> Than you expect: unseal this letter soon;
> There you shall find three of your argosies
> Are richly come to harbour suddenly.
> You shall not know by what strange accident
> I chanced on this letter.
>
> (5.1.273-79)

Once more and finally, it is Portia who brings wealth in this play, and she announces it with a letter in such a way that any alert viewer (of the time) must notice at least at this point that he is seeing Fortuna: the letter is not opened, but she knows what is in it. How she chanced on this letter, she does not want to say. If Portia were not Fortuna, this scene would be "unbelievable" indeed and the conclusion of the play as "absurd" as the editor of the Cambridge critical edition believes it, because he has failed to grasp the logic of the play.[174]

The Beautiful Jew and the Fool

We could adduce much other proof or evidence that Portia embodies Fortuna: from the fact that Portia knows before it is opened which casket contains her portrait (1.2.102-5); she would like to set a wineglass on one of the other two in order to mislead the drunken Saxon suitor), to Jessica's statement (3.5.87-88) that "the poor rude world / Hath not her fellow," to the statement that Portia is Bassanio's venture—and venture and Fortuna have been possible synonyms in English literature since the time of Chaucer.[175] But none of that is as important as the fact that while Portia does embody Fortuna, she is also Portia at the same time, not only Bassanio's adventure, not only Fortuna, not only a beautiful, intelligent woman, but also Bassanio's beloved: a human being. Shakespeare's unique accomplishment lies among other things in completely demythologizing the myth of Fortuna, in completely secularizing it: it is human beings who rule fate, who remove the old, unfree social conditions through calculation and science, through experiment and rational, courageous activity, who build a future world, free, bright, and joyous. *The Merchant of Venice* is the play of the revolutionary bourgeoisie; it is the most subtle, because the most critical, affirmation of bourgeois adventure and simultaneous negation of the feudal system and the corresponding courtly-knightly ideology of adventure. Shakespeare, in affirming bourgeois adventure (despite its crimes, which he recognizes and condemns), directs his gaze at a future in which humanity will live happily—liberated, emancipated, in full equality, free of all religious or racial delusions.

To conclude, let us examine only one aspect of this vision of the future: the struggle against religious intolerance and racism. Shakespeare scholars have long fought, and are still fighting, over whether Shakespeare was an anti-Semite because he supplies Shylock with such murderous hatred. Against the background of a careful reading, this discussion is quite incomprehensible. Shakespeare pointedly bans racial prejudice and religious zeal from Belmont, the future realm of freedom, and that means that he condemns them as elements of the realm of the old (medieval, feudal) world. Things could not be more obvious than Shakespeare makes them: the Prince of Morocco is a Moor, and since he is obviously used to racial prejudice and insults, he asks Portia not to reject him because of the color of his skin. Portia answers him quite clearly that the color of his skin is not an issue for her (an answer she gives both as Fortuna and as an enlightened, educated human being):

> In terms of choice I am not solely led
> By nice direction of a maiden's eyes;
> Besides, the lottery of my destiny
> Bars me the right of voluntary choosing:
> But if my father had not scanted me
> And hedg'd me by his wit, to yield myself
> His wife who wins me by that means I told you,
> Yourself, renowned prince, then stood as fair
> As any comer I have look'd on yet
> For my affection.
>
> (2.1.13-22)

It is not the color of his skin that defeats Morocco in the competition. Launcelot Gobbo, the fool, impregnates a Moor and—intends to marry her (in Belmont). He explains with his usual puns: "It is much that the Moor should be / more than reason; but if she be less than / an honest woman, she is indeed more than / I took her for" (3.5.43-46). No one takes offense at Launcelot's relationship with a Moor.

In Belmont, Lorenzo will finally marry his beautiful Jew, who is respected by all: by Gratiano, who sees her and calls her "a gentle and no Jew" (2.6.51); by Launcelot, who loves and teases her; by Portia, who leaves her, with Lorenzo, in charge of her property. There is no one in the whole play who condemns Jessica because she is a Jew, and apart from Shylock himself, the only ones to condemn her for her flight from her father's house and the theft of his jewels and ducats are—Shakespeare's interpreters! Even as clever a critic as Heine calls Jessica's theft— although with his usual irony—one of "the most infamous domestic thefts," for which the punishment would be "fifteen years in the penitentiary, according to Prussian law."[176] But one of the editors of the New Cambridge Shakespeare edition, Sir Arthur Quiller-Couch, does his best to outdo Shylock, with no irony whatsoever (and it should be noted here that Shylock curses Jessica and loves her at the same time, which we cannot say about Quiller-Couch): "Jessica is bad and disloyal, unfilial, a thief; frivolous, greedy, without any more conscience than a cat and without even a cat's redeeming love of home. Quite without heart, on worse than an animal instinct, pilfering to be carnal."[177] An anti-Semite could not evince more contempt for a human being than this humanistic philologist who believes he must excuse Shakespeare for his creation of Shylock because Shakespeare's age had a very different attitude from "our modern tolerance" on the Jewish question.[178]

To be sure. In order to show that miserliness is not Jewish, is not biological, is not the mark of a race, to show how hypocritical Antonio's pseudo-Christian arguments are, Shakespeare put the beautiful Jessica on stage and brought her to Belmont, where she is loved and respected by everyone. Her father's hoarded, useless, life-denying money kept her in his house in a state of humiliating slavery and ignorance. The appropriation of the jewels and the money was her right, her right of self-defense, the means to freedom, to emancipation, a natural right (Harpagon's son in Molière's *Avare* acts in a similar way, for Harpagon enslaves his children just as Shylock does). But the bonds that torment her in Shylock's house are by no means specifically Jewish; miserliness, the source of this bondage, oppression, enslavement, and ignorance, is not Jewish, but is the expression and form of a particular economic way of earning a living that is part of medieval feudalism. Shakespeare makes very clear that Jessica is completely Jewish, of Jewish mother and father (3.5.11-20), and it is obvious that Shakespeare has a reason for emphasizing this: Jessica has not one single quality decried as "Jewish"—she does not hoard money, does not hate Christians (just as the enlightened Christians do not hate her). On the contrary, Jessica spends money, brings it into circulation,[179] and together with Lorenzo she will use her father's capital, which Portia/Fortuna and Antonio passed to her, to build at Belmont in order to live there as a free human being among free human beings. The forces that make possible this emancipation inhere in the new economic mode of production. Antonio's friend Lorenzo loves Jessica and helps her in her flight; Antonio's, Bassanio's, and Portia's friends give Jessica protection, and they do so unconditionally.

Only one figure seems not to share this general joy and sympathy: the servant Launcelot (but as we know from his earlier declarations of sympathy with Jessica, he does not mean it). He says to Jessica in Belmont that she is damned as a Jew and nothing and no one can save her from this damnation. When Lorenzo joins them, Jessica complains (in jest) about Launcelot, and Lorenzo (also in jest) scolds the foolish servant, who answers him with a series of puns. As he leaves the stage, Lorenzo comments:

> O dear discretion, how his words are suited!
> The fool hath planted in his memory
> An army of good words; and I do know
> A many fools, that stand in better place,
> Garnish'd like him, that for a tricksy word
> Defy the matter.
>
> (3.5.70-76)

That is to say, Shakespeare pointedly puts the Christian, anti-Jewish thesis of damnation in the mouth of a fool, but through Lorenzo he says that there are, unfortunately, many highly placed men who would say the same foolishness in all seriousness. Shakespeare was doubtless thinking less about criticizing his interpreters than about the ideologues of the feudal Middle Ages: his fool is, after all, called—Launcelot!

Chapter 8
From the Glorification of Adventure to the Thesis of *Bellum Omnium Contra Omnes*

The Counterrevolutionary Denunciation of Bourgeois Adventure

The praise of the long-distance merchant that was merely sketched out in Christopher Marlowe's *Famous Tragedy of the Rich Jew of Malta* (ca. 1588) reached its high point in *The Merchant of Venice.* The surrounding or succeeding wave of more or less significant glorifications of the merchant in narrative and dramatic literature brought two myths to the forefront: that of the poor merchant who comes into wealth (whether he moves from being a small adventurer to being a large one, or from being a grocer to becoming a great adventurer) and that of the rise of the merchant into the ranks of the nobility or to equality with the nobility. Thomas Deloney distinguishes himself particularly here, with his "use of motifs from the knightly romance and the lives of saints to glorify the bourgeois artisans and merchantry."[1] The so-called Whittington legend[2] and Thomas Heywood's play *The Four Prentices of London,* ca. 1600, tend in the same direction. In the play, four sons of an earl become merchants, praise the profession of their choice and equate it with noble service, and unite it with the knightly ideal by setting out for the Holy Land on a crusade, as merchants and knights.[3]

The reaction against this was, of course, not long in coming. As court politics became more reactionary after Elizabeth's death and with the ascension of James I, the reaction against merchant adventurers also grew (James, however, had *The Merchant of Venice* performed in 1605).[4] Political reaction and repression were intensified by an economic crisis of considerable dimensions for which the merchant adventurers were held responsible, with their monopoly on raw textiles (typically, the adventurers denied this accusation and named the inter-lopers as scapegoats).[5] In any case, the hostility toward the merchant adventurers grew apace. It had fertile soil in James I's reactionary policies, for the king him-self was distrustful and contemptuous of the merchants. Jürgen Kuczynski quotes the king as saying "in one of his fits of feudalism":

> The Merchants thinke the whole common-weale ordeined for making them vp; and accounting it their lawfull gaine and trade, to enrich themselues vpon the losse of all the rest of the people, they transport from vs things necessarie; bringing backe sometimes vnnecessary things, and at other times nothing at all.[6]

The confrontation between the feudal-absolutist reactionaries and the bour-geoisie came to a head primarily in the fights between the king and the merchant adventurers; the adventurers' rivals (like William Cockayne)[7] doubtless added fuel to the fire. The adventurers reacted in a typical way: they issued special decrees (especially from 1608 on)[8] to increase their already considerable ex-clusivity. When they then refused to pay certain duties to the king, open conflict erupted. It climaxed in 1614, with the removal of their privileges and the estab-lishment of a new trading company under government supervision: the King's Merchant Adventurers of the New Trade of London.[9]

The absolutist reactionaries found one ideological expression of their opposi-tion to the adventurers in Francis Beaumont's play *The Knight of the Burning Pestle*.[10] Compared with *The Merchant of Venice,* this is, to be sure, a relatively flat polemic. The affirmation of bourgeois adventure, of the merchant adven-turer, is free of all reminiscences of knightly adventure in Shakespeare (only antiquity is great enough for the bourgeois adventurer to identify with, as when Bassanio and his companions identify themselves with Jason and the Argonauts). Indeed, the glorification of bourgeois adventure is even directed polemically against the petty and great feudal nobility and against their courtly-knightly world view. The only use made of the courtly-knightly romance of adventure apart from the nobility is to name the fool: calling him Launcelot is of course an ironic criticism of the courtly ideal of humanity. Beaumont now wants to reverse the point and impute to the (commercial) bourgeoisie an unsuccessful imitation of courtly society in its adoption of the ideology of knightly adven-ture. The means Beaumont employs are, however—apart from a few matters of stage technique—insufficient; in their purposeless exaggeration, which tends to travesty, they reveal the dishonesty of the criticism.

A troupe of actors wants to perform a play called *The London Merchant,* but after the first few sentences of the prologue, the play is interrupted by a member of the audience. He introduces himself as Freeman, member of the "noble citty," a grocer by occupation, who rejects this newfangled stuff and wants to know why the actors do not perform one of the well-known stories: the Whittington legend, the history of Queen Eleonore, "or the life and death of sir Thomas Gresham? with the building of the Royall Exchange?"[11] And he would like to see something honoring the "Commons of the City." When asked what he would think of a play about the "life and death of fat Drake,"[12] he answers: "I do not like that, but I will have a Citizen, and hee shall be of my own trade." His wife, who has meantime joined in the conversation between the grocer and the actors, proposes that Rafe, the grocer's assistant, be given a part in this suggested play. The actors agree, and Rafe and two apprentices, Tim as a squire and George as a dwarf, come on stage. As the "Knight of the Burning Pestle," Rafe intervenes in the action of the "real" play, and the grocer and his wife support him or criticize him with loud shouts and commentaries.

A London merchant with the telling name of Venturewell appears on stage and fires his "apprentice" Jasper (who is the typical adventurer's pseudo-apprentice, in charge of all Venturewell's domestic and foreign business)[13] because Jasper loves Venturewell's daughter Luce (they belong to different classes). Venturewell wants to marry her to his rich friend Humphrey. Of course Luce opposes this plan. She flees with Jasper into a forest, where they meet Rafe, who as the "Knight of the Burning Pestle" is beaten by Jasper; in the end Jasper wins Luce, Rafe turns back into the grocer's employee. The play is basically without literary interest.

What interests us here is something else: it is the author's implicit and explicit polemic against the poorly imitated, displaced, courtly-knightly idea of adventure he imputes to the commercial bourgeoisie and against the commercial bourgeoisie itself. Venturewell, the stay-at-home adventurer, is a grotesque, despotic figure; his friend Humphrey is a coward who says of himself, "I am of gentle bloud and gentle seeme."[14] Jasper is the son of a drunkard and a half-mad woman; the grocer and his wife are clumsy and uneducated; and Rafe is a naïve bumpkin. Typically, the adventurer Venturewell and the figures connected to him never think about adventure, but instead about profit and rich marriage (Luce and Jasper think about private love), and it is assumed that the sedentary grocer, his wife, his employee, and his apprentices are all mad about (knightly, fairy-tale) adventures. While Shakespeare's support of bourgeois adventure is combined with a clear condemnation of the courtly ideology of adventure, Beaumont presents the bourgeoisie as the alleged adherents of this ideology, which is accompanied by a distancing from their own class, with delusions of grandeur, with stupidity. Rafe, for instance, after receiving the role of the "Knight of the Burning Pestle," says he has never heard of a "grocer-errant." If he is to play the role of a knight, he wants to play it correctly, and that requires a squire and a dwarf, according to the books on knighthood.[15] His speech is larded with quotations from *Amadís* and *Palmerin of England* (a successor to *Amadís,* written in Portugal around the middle of the sixteenth century). When Rafe, together with squire Tim and dwarf George, meets the other (bourgeois) figures in the play, he gets beaten in a very unknightly way. Beaumont in every respect denies and makes ludicrous any connection between bourgeoisie and (courtly-knightly) adventure: according to him, the bourgeoisie has no claim to an adventurous life and the corresponding ideals (or the corresponding world view). His *Knight of the Burning Pestle* is the aggressive complement to the *Declaration of the Demeanor and Carriage of Sir Walter Raleigh, Knight* of 1618, which declares that Raleigh succeeded in finding "many brave captains and other knights and gentlemen of great blood and worth to hazard and adventure their lives and the whole or a great part of their estates and fortune in this his voyage,"[16] his expedition to Guyana.

Reaction in Vain; or, New Dimensions of Adventure

In *The Knight of the Burning Pestle,* Beaumont seems to want to stamp the experience of adventures and their glorification as an exclusive right of the feudal nobility. Meanwhile, the bourgeoisie was actually experiencing practical adventures (and was by no means as simple and stupid as Beaumont presented it). The bourgeoisie already possessed economic power; it was shortly to win political power. An imitation of the courtly-knightly style of life and of the knightly ideology of adventure by the bourgeoisie would in fact have been ridiculous; it is difficult even to imagine. But Beaumont thereby proves what he certainly did not intend to prove: the rising, revolutionary class, the bourgeoisie, has no more use for knightly adventure and its glorification. Beaumont only confirms indirectly what Shakespeare had already presented: the knightly ideology of adventure was no longer useful.

That is of course true for the nobility as well. In the world of expanding manufacturing capitalism, a knight adventurer, even a noble one, could only have been a comic figure (or, at most, a sad one like Don Quijote). The political reaction of the feudal-absolutist monarchy in England was condemned to fail from the very outset. The mode of production had changed to a capitalist mode, and a return to the old-fashioned feudal mode was naturally impossible. That is also reflected (as a detail in the overall context) in the further development of the Adventurer Company. In 1617 the royal society was dissolved as a complete failure and the adventurers were restored to their old rights, which were renewed in 1634. Nonetheless, they begin to lose interest for us because they become increasingly irrelevant in the whole context of the capitalist development in England.[17] In 1688, the year of the Glorious Revolution, the privilege of monopoly on textile export was removed because it had become as obsolete as the corporate organization or as what was left of it: the adventurers led only a shadow existence in the eighteenth century. In 1805 they closed their last office in Hamburg.[18]

Their significance for the formation of the modern bourgeois ideology of adventure, however, is considerable, as we hope to have shown. Ideologizing the activity of adventure began at a relatively early date, and the emphasis on the ethical qualities that were put to the test in the adventure (such as bravery and a willingness to take risks) was always combined with the emphasis on its utility for (private) trade and for the state (discoveries, conquests, enlargement of national wealth, and production of trade connections).[19] In his comedy *The Two Gentlemen of Verona* (1590-94), Shakespeare praises adventure from a different perspective, in which the ideas of youth, activity, trade, and navigation common since antiquity are linked with modern adventure and exploration. The play begins with a dialogue between Valentine and Proteus, the two friends from Verona. Proteus is in love with Julia, and Valentine makes fun of him, advising him not to be enslaved by love but to follow his, Valentine's, example:

VALENTINE:

> Cease to persuade, my loving Proteus:
> Home-keeping youth have ever homely wits.
> Were't not affection chains thy tender days
> To the sweet glances of thy honour'd love,
> I rather would entreat thy company
> To see the wonders of the world abroad,
> Than, living dully sluggardized at home,
> Wear out thy youth with shapeless idleness.[20]

A little later, however, Proteus must also leave Verona and keep Valentine company in Milan—at the command of his father, who sees travel as a pedagogical necessity. Here too, the ancient topos is joined with observed modern practice. Panthino, the servant of Proteus' father Antonio, relates a conversation with Antonio's brother about Proteus in which the former "wonder'd that your lordship would suffer him to spend his youth at home":

PATHINO:

> While other men, of slender reputation,
> Put forth their sons to seek preferment out:
> Some to the wars, to try their fortune there;
> Some to discover islands far away;
> Some to the studious exercises,
> He said that Proteus your son was meet;
> And did request me to importune you
> To let him spend his time no more at home,
> Which would be great impeachment to his age,
> In having known no travel in his youth.

ANTONIO:

> Nor need'st thou much importune me to that
> Whereon this month I have been hammering.
> I have consider'd well his loss of time,

And how he cannot be a perfect man,
Not being tried and tutor'd in the world:
Experience is by industry achieved,
And perfected by the swift course of time.
                                        (1.3.6-23)

Leaving the narrow world of home, traveling in one's youth, is discussed from two different perspectives: that of the young man who sees travel as the opposite of his useless idleness and as a change from his everyday reality at home, and that of the adult (with pedagogical interest). It is, to be sure, two persons who represent the perspective of the adult, but their views coincide, so we can treat their opinions as one. First, travel is obviously not only the privilege of well-situated circles, but is also a proof of social standing. Second, travel serves a useful purpose. (Shakespeare gives us a precise gradation of types of travel. Going to war to seek one's fortune must have been the most conventional form of travel and is therefore mentioned at the beginning of the climax. The second type of travel is the modern voyage of adventure and exploration; the high point of travel is study at a foreign university.) Third, travel is a privilege of youth; in age, one no longer travels and cannot make up what might have been missed in youth. Fourth, only through travel does one become a complete man.[21]

Let us bear in mind that Shakespeare has presented us with an overarching context that subsumes a whole complex of different activities under the key word "travel." From the activity of the soldier to that of the adventurer / explorer to that of the scholar, the idea dominating this whole complex is that travel or exploration serves the active, practical gaining of knowledge,[22] an idea fundamental to the philosophical system of Francis Bacon. This is one of the typical, explicable, necessary contradictions of the state of the class struggle in the early seventeenth century in England: James I, with whom the reaction of the feudal-absolutistic monarchy against the bourgeoisie began in a massive way in 1603, knighted the most important representative of the bourgeois-revolutionary worldview in 1603 and made him a royal counselor; in 1619 James even appointed this man Lord Chancellor. The man was Francis Bacon, the "real founder of *English materialism* and all *modern experimental* science," as Marx says of him.

For him natural science was true science and *physics* based on perception was the most excellent part of natural science. . . . According to his teaching the *senses* are infallible and are the *source* of all knowledge. Science is *experimental* and consists in applying a *rational method* to the data provided by the senses. Induction, analysis, comparison, observation and experiment are the principal requisites of rational method. The first and most important of the inherent qualities of *matter* is *motion,* not only *mechanical* and *mathematical* movement, but still more *impulse, vital life-spirit, tension,* or, to use Jacob Böhme's expression, the *throes [Qual]* of matter.[23]

Marx's characterization of Bacon, which describes his essential position, corresponds to Bacon's affirmation of movement toward what is (still) unknown, distant lands, information about what has yet to be reached empirically, his affirmation of the discovery of new worlds in the microcosm and the macrocosm. The frontispiece of Bacon's *Instauratio Magna* (The Great Revewal, 1620) shows two ships. One is about to sail through the Pillars of Hercules; the other has already sailed through and is slowly disappearing on the horizon. According to the view of antiquity and the Middle Ages, the Pillars of Hercules symbolize the Straits of Gibraltar, and these in turn indicate the end of the known Old World. For Bacon, they signal the narrowness of this Old World and the limitations of traditional science.[24] The two ships, on the other hand, represent both ship travel in a concrete sense and, in an abstract sense, the curiosity of the human being, his appropriation of nature, science. The *impulse, vital life-spirit, tension, motion* of which Marx speaks dominate human thought. As Bacon says: "The human understanding is unquiet; it cannot stop or rest, and still presses onward, but in vain. Therefore it is that we cannot perceive of any end or limit to the world; but always of necessity it occurs to us that there is something beyond."[25] The boundaries of human knowledge and information, which have advanced steadily in the dialectics between the unquiet human understanding and the practical activity of exploration, prove the narrowness of the earlier world, of previous knowledge, of previous science and hence necessarily also prove that the human being, empirically and through reflection, must constantly overstep the boundaries of the known and accepted. For that reason, we must approach a priori thinking, which is based on little or no experience, with skepticism; this is true especially of the thought of antiquity:

> For at that period there was but a narrow and meagre knowledge of either time or place; which is the worst thing that can be, especially for those who rest all on experience. For [the ancients—M. N.] had no history, worthy to be called history, that went back a thousand years; but only fables and rumors of antiquity. And of the regions and districts of the world they knew but a small portion; giving indiscriminately the name of Scythians to all in the North, of Celts to all in the West; knowing nothing of Africa beyond the higher side of Aethiopia, of Asia beyond the Ganges; much less were they acquainted with the provinces of the New World, even by hearsay or any well-founded rumor; nay, a multitude of climates and zones, wherein innumerable nations breathe and live, were pronounced by them to be uninhabitable.... In our times on the other hand both many parts of the New World and the limits on every side of the Old World are

known, and our stock of experience has increased to an infinite
amount.[26]

Let us mention only in passing that the polemic against the ignorance of the
ancients also embraces the Middle Ages and the courtly glorification of fairy-
tale and knightly adventures (*Amadís de Gaula* is mentioned by name).[27] Bacon
takes for granted the fact that the knowledge of his time has grown immensely
in comparison with that of antiquity; the ancients are the youths, his contemporaries on the other hand come later and are the older with respect to the
development of humanity (which anticipates the famous battle between the ancients and the moderns in France toward the end of the seventeenth century).
Those who come later have been able to gather experience not yet available to
the youths:

> Nor must it go for nothing that by the distant voyages and travels
> which have become frequent in our times, many things in name have
> been laid open and discovered which may let in new light upon
> philosophy. And surely it would be disgraceful if, while the regions of
> the material globe,—that is, of the earth, of the sea, of the stars,—
> have been in our times laid widely open and revealed, the intellectual
> globe should remain shut up within the narrow limits of old
> discoveries.[28]

Over and over, Bacon stresses the importance of the discovery of the New World
for revolutionizing thought and science:

> Again, it is well to observe the force and virtue and consequences of
> discoveries; and these are to be seen nowhere more conspicuously than
> in those three which were unknown to the ancients, and of which the
> origin, though recent, is obscure and inglorious; namely, printing,
> gunpowder, and the magnet. For these three have changed the whole
> face and state of things throughout the world; the first in literature,
> the second in warfare, the third in navigation.[29]

Bacon is not merely drawing an analogy between physical and intellectual
discoveries: he sees that they also share a method. In both physical and intellectual investigation, the method to be used is that of (experimental) induction:

> As the common logic, which governs by the syllogism, extends not
> only to natural but to all sciences; so does mine also, which proceeds
> by induction, embrace everything. For I form a history and tables of
> discovery for anger, fear, shame, and the like; for matters political;
> and again for the mental operations of memory, composition and
> division, judgment and the rest; not less than for heat and cold, or
> light, or vegetation, or the like.[30]

It is against the background of Bacon's scientific credo that we must see his lifelong efforts to describe the human psyche: his psychological studies do actually look like tables of position and description (see especially his table of spiritual qualities in *De Dignitate et Augmentis Scientiarum* [On the Dignity and the Advancement of the Sciences], 1623, arranged antithetically according to pro and con).[31] From this positioning and description, conclusions are then derived according to the principle of *causality* (psychological data) and *effect* (social behavior), just as if the observed human qualities were physical truths. This procedure is important for our discussion in several ways. To name the positive aspect most important for the historical situation: the reasons for human actions are freed of any religious, metaphysical context and hence of the unalterable predestination of human action by divine will or social (medieval-feudal) hierarchies and structures, and are shifted into the acting individual, into his *nature*. In the last analysis, it is his nature that rules and guides the individual and gives the impetus to his actions: "Nature is often hidden; sometimes overcome; seldom extinguished," as Bacon writes in the *Essays*.[32] He therefore places great weight on the education that is necessary to make the individual useful to society. Society itself plays a crucial role here as an educator: "Certainly the great multiplication of virtues upon human nature resteth upon societies well ordained and disciplined."[33]

The demystification of the human being by the scientific or putatively scientific view of his nature or his psyche and the explanation of his actions through this view represent a large step toward liberating the human being from his "minority." To be sure, this idea of locating the individual in terms of natural science, derived from actual human behavior, already contains elements that contribute to turning this intellectual weapon in the struggle to free humanity into an ideological system of oppression. The reasons are obvious: Bacon's scientific conviction that human actions can be derived from a methodical observation of human nature or the psyche is a revolutionary idea directed against medieval, religious thinking, but this idea is objectively false. It represents an impermissible transfer of empirical, inductive methods of natural science to an "imagined" object: what Bacon calls human nature or the psyche is merely his own conception of human nature or the psyche (and hence that of the bourgeois faction whose ideologue Bacon is), a conception compiled from clichés adopted from antiquity, from modern authors like Montaigne, and from Bacon's own experience. This procedure of deriving human behavior or human practice from the nature or psyche of the human being, which is the result of speculation (of whatever description), must necessarily lead to an explanation or justification of social relations in general. Bacon already shows a tendency toward what becomes systematic in Hobbes: the justification of social relations by an imputed biological law, a procedure which, together with that of explaining social relations and forms of behavior by psychological (sometimes in combination with biological) factors, still constitutes the basis for the ideological justification and glorification of the capitalist system—and that means the exploitation and oppression of the proletariat. In this process, the psychologistic and biologistic variants of the ideology of adventure play a decisive role.

Bacon, as we have said, displays this tendency already; the biological or psychologistic explanation for individual behavior is transferred to human society at large: "As the laws of society are to customs and practices, so is nature to habit in the individual."[34] This identification of social laws and individual nature can also be reversed, which necessarily leads to conclusions about the theories of domestic and foreign policy:

> No body can be healthful without exercise, neither natural body nor politic, and certainly to a kingdom or estate, a just and honourable war is the true exercise. A civil war indeed is like the heat of a fever, but a foreign war is like the heat of exercise, and serveth to keep the body in health, for in a slothful peace both courages will effeminate and manners corrupt. But howsoever it be for happiness, without all question, for greatness it maketh, to be still for the most part in arms.[35]

If the direction of his remarks still seems indefinite here, it soon becomes clear what concrete ideas Bacon is pursuing, among others, with this thesis about the necessary (martial) exercise of the "body politic":

> Plantations [i.e., colonies—R. C.] are amongst ancient, primitive, and heroical works. When the world was young it begat more children; but now it is old it begets fewer, for I may justly account new plantations to be the children of former kingdoms. I like a plantation in a pure soil; that is, where people are not displanted to the end to plant in others. For else it is rather an extirpation than a plantation. Planting of countries is like planting of woods, for you must make account to leese almost twenty years profit, and expect your recompense in the end. For the principal thing that hath been the destruction of most plantations hath been the base and hasty drawing of profit in the first years. It is true, speedy profit is not to be neglected.[36]

That such ideas were thoroughly in the interests of the bourgeoisie is revealed by the nature of the thing described: "The people wherewith you plant ought to be gardeners, ploughmen, labourers, smiths, carpenters, joiners, fishermen, fowlers, with some few apothecaries, surgeons, cooks, and bakers."[37] But Bacon admits a little later that those who really profit are the merchants: "Let there be freedom from custom till the plantation be of strength, and not only freedom from custom, but freedom to carry their commodities where they may make their best of them."[38] It is a foregone conclusion that Bacon's demand is in harmony with contemporary apologists for free trade (like Misselden, Mun, and others).

The development that will lead to an equation of freedom in general with free trade (especially in the eighteenth century) begins at this time. But in Bacon we can see that at least an (important) fraction of the bourgeoisie seems to be ready to reach an accommodation with existing social relations; although Bacon liquidates the intellectual substance (the *ordo* based on religion), he believes he can still save or maintain the form, the political constitution. Politically, Bacon is wholly the representative of the absolute monarchy, whose major enemies he sees in the high clergy and the upper nobility,[39] while he considers the gentry to be harmless. To him too, the thought of the gentry seems to evoke the figure of Falstaff: "They may sometimes discourse high, but that doth little hurt."[40]

But more important for us than his views of the clergy and the nobility are his views on the last two members of the "body politic" he mentions. First, he sees the bourgeoisie (the merchant class) as the most important class of society (it holds the economic power); second, he sees the "commons" as not (yet) presenting a threat to the existing social relations:

> For their merchantts, they are *vena porta* [the large vein which conveys blood to the liver], and if they flourish not, a kingdom may have good limbs, but will have empty veins, and nourish little. Taxes and imposts upon them do seldom good to the king's revenue, for that that he wins in the hunddred he leeseth in the shire, the particular rates being increased, but the total bulk of trading rather decreased. For their commons, there is little danger from them, except it be where they have great and potent heads, or where you meddle with the point of religion or their customs or means of life.[41]

Mechanics versus Adventure?
On Borkenau's Attempt to Revise Marx with Max Weber

Bacon even gives biologistic-psychologistic expression—or a justification aimed at perpetuating the status of employees—to the fact that in (commercial) capitalism the functions of personified capital and of the agent who carries out the capitalist enterprise, who realizes it in a practical sense, are separated (that is, that the capitalist no longer carries out his business personally, no longer undertakes adventures). In his essay on boldness, we read that boldness

> is ill in counsel, good in execution; so that the right use of bold persons is that they never command in chief, but be seconds and under the direction of others. For in counsel it is good to see dangers, and in execution not to see them, except they be very great.[42]

Here we already see glimmers of later "myths," such as the myth of the "cowardly, philistine" (small) entrepreneur (a "myth" that will be launched and propagated by large capital but also by the radical petty bourgeoisie) and the "myth"of the power of the manager to change society. These are, to be sure, only the first seeds of the later ideological blend. In any case, entrepreneurship, courage, making war, and governing have become for Bacon completely questions of individual *nature*, of natural tendencies,[43] and that means that those who are enslaved, exploited, in poverty, are so for biologistic or psychologistic reasons—their situation can be justified by *nature*. Bacon did not, to be sure, develop this into a system. Rather, even with respect to his concept of society, we can subscribe to what Marx writes in *The Holy Family*: "In *Bacon,* its first creator, materialism contained latent and still in a naive way the germs of all-round development. Matter smiled at man with poetical sensuous brightness. The aphoristic doctrine itself, on the other hand, was full of the inconsistencies of theology."[44]

We must point out these inconsistencies and contradictions clearly in order to counter misreadings like that of Borkenau. In a polemical reaction to Marx's statement that the real founder of *English materialism* and all *modern experimental* science was *Bacon,*[45] Borkenau writes:

> Bacon is not the founder of modern thought; rather, he stands at the extreme end of the destruction of the medieval world view. His concept of nature is absolutely consistent in expressing the decay of the concept of an intentional world order. At this point the European spirit could have sunk into a senseless collection of observations of qualities, which would probably soon have become conventionally fixed, if the interconnection of ideas were a matter of their self-development. For there is nothing in Bacon's system of categories that pushes beyond this point of inertia.[46]

Borkenau derives the justification for his position from the fact that Bacon did not question the system of the absolute monarchy,[47] only half-heartedly laid the foundations of the natural sciences through experimentation, and did not shore them up adequately with theory (through systematization).[48]

The implied polemic against Marx (whom Borkenau knows, but does not quote in his discussion of Bacon) forces Borkenau to polemicize against Bacon. The result represents a rather strange positioning of Bacon, (even) for the (bourgeois) history of philosophy: on the one hand, Bacon represents the medieval "worldview" (although in the age of its "destruction"); on the other, his "doctrine of forms" is a "final simplification of the world view of the Renaissance."[49] On the one hand, he does not yet represent "the mechanical conception of natural law," but on the other, he has "paved the way for it."[50] But his students, especially Hobbes and Descartes, "adopted from him just that revolutionary denial of the old world views, the demand that all science be checked against experience, the battle-cry that all science be constructed anew starting with the simplest and most everyday elements."[51]

The reason for Borkenau's confused polemic against Bacon (and by implication Marx) lies in his attempt to lend "Marxist," "materialist" support to Max Weber's theory of the origin of modern European capitalism in the Protestant spirit. Partly in agreement with Sombart's theses (but also with Nietzsche's and especially Burckhardt's), partly in a simple falsification of Marxist positions, Weber developed a theory of the origin of modern capitalism around the turn of the nineteenth to the twentieth century; we will sketch here one important aspect of that theory. Like many bourgeois ideologues who elevate particular modes of thought within capitalist society to "the spirit of capitalism" or—still more absurd—who try to derive capitalism or its origin from this or that mode of thought, Max Weber consciously or unconsciously ignored what Marx, Engels, and Lenin[52] stressed again and again: the dialectics of the manifestation of capitalist production (the anarchy of production together with the hierarchical subordination of the proletarian and commercial wage-laborers who see to the physical production or who participate in it). For everything that seems like order, that is determined by order, or that effects order in the manifestations of capitalist production, Weber makes something else responsible: the "modern" "capitalist spirit"; or Protestantism or Calvinism, which is supposed to have produced that spirit and hence all of modern capitalism. A key passage that immediately reveals Weber's fundamental methodological error is his reply to Felix Rachfahl's criticism of his views. Rachfahl observes that the behavior of modern capitalists can hardly be subsumed under the catchword of "worldly asceticism" that Weber declares an essential characteristic. He asks Weber what other capitalist types exist apart from this "ascetic." Weber's answer is as arrogant as it is speculative and revealing:

> To give a short answer to at least *one* question with which R. has been pestering me in the most helpless way: namely the question as to *which* figures in the total picture of modern capitalism can and should *not* be understood on the basis of worldly asceticism, let me note: the adventurers of the capitalist development. . . . Their importance for the history of economics is known to be extremely significant in (but not only in) the history of early caplitalism—still, in a certain sense and with a grain of salt, one can almost equate the development of the increasing domination of capitalism over all economic life with *the development from occasional economic profit to an economic system;* and the genesis of the capitalist "spirit". . . with the development *from the romantic view of economic adventure to the rational economic methodology of life.*[53]

Apart from the patent absurdity of assuming that the merchant adventurer lived on "occasional economic profit" or that the commercial capitalist was a victim of "the romantic view of economic adventure": if we abstract from the historical relations of production, we can of course engage in unlimited intellectual-"historical" speculations about the genesis of these relations of production. For example, if we overlook the manifestations of capitalist production analyzed by Marx and Engels, with their external social anarchy and their internal hierarchical subordination, we can use "the rational economic methodology of life" to create edifying fictions and conflate the banal praxis of living of the religiously tinged personifications of capital (the Calvinist capitalists) with the capitalist production they direct, or to "explain" capitalists and production by means of the ascetic spirit of belief.[54]

As Weber himself already expressed in condensed form in his reply to Rachfahl, his conception of modern capitalism reaches its peak in the idea of a "sober," rational, calculating, "ascetic" capitalism, which is the successor to the unbridled, rapacious, wild, "romantic" "adventure capitalism" (of the Middle Ages). But since even Weber could apparently not overlook the fact that there are legions of completely "unascetic" capitalists even today and especially today—which is by the way fully irrelevant for political economy—he keeps a back door open with saving formulations, such as the adventurer as the type of (but not only of) early capitalism. At the same time Weber categorically states that the "capitalist spirit" has reigned at all times and in all places: the drive for profit is inherent in the human being. (With this rhetorical trick, real history has already been dissolved into spirit.) Consequently, a special event must occur for the "capitalist spirit" (that as a drive for profit must naturally also have been inherent in the medieval adventurer) suddenly to produce what Weber then "explains" with his own construct: "modern capitalism." Weber sees this event as Protestantism in general, as Calvinsim in particular, with its "worldly asceticism" mentioned above—a thesis with which Borkenau fully agrees, despite all his pretended or actual reservations.[55] But Borkenau does try to "improve" Weber. Where Weber says that the "spirit of capitalism" preceded "modern capitalism," Borkenau supplements this thesis by asking how the formation of this wonderful "capitalist spirit" came about, since, as he correctly determines, nothing comes from nothing.

It is apparent that Weber's intellectual-historical explanation of capitalism is untouched by Borkenau's question. Borkenau tries to provide a "materialist" prop for this false thesis of Weber's (and the thesis is demonstrably false, as the material presented here shows; if that is not enough, a critical analysis of ideology will also prove it). He believes he has found this prop in the development of technology:

> One of the most important insights in all of M. Weber's investigations is that the basic stock of manufacturing entrepreneurs, who first systematically introduced capitalist methods into the process of production, does not come from the financial and commercial bourgeoisie

but from the rising artisans. Between the two strata, adventurous money capital and sober manufacturing capital, there is a bitter struggle.[56]

If Borkenau means the increasing subjugation first of the production of use-values to trade, then the rise of the production of goods and the resultant subjugation of trade ot manufacturing or industrial production, as analyzed by Marx, then his adjectives "adventurous," "sober," and "bitter" are so psychologically colored that one can no longer recognize the historical process in them. Moreover, the process took place largely without leaving any kind of trace in the economic treatises of the time; it was mostly unseen by the protagonists (which is not surprising, since manufacturing was dependent on flourishing trade and trade on flourishing industry). In any case, Weber's undertaking and Borkenau's in his wake come down to a simplification and coarsening of dialectical and historical materialism, despite their virtues (among which is Borkenau's attempt to prove the link between technological development and modern scientific thought). Marx speaks of three fundamentally different kinds of origin of capitalist production and hence of the capitalist: first, the merchant becomes an industrialist directly (for instance, through importing a luxury industry including raw materials and wage laborers); second, the merchant makes the small master dependent on him, buys from the producer of the goods without changing the mode of production; third, the industrialist becomes a merchant[57] (which Marx called the "revolutionary path"). The process of forming the capitalist mode of production takes place, however, as Marz and Engels stressed again and again, over a long stretch of time,[58] develops differently from region to region; stagnates here, is driven forward there; takes place with all three paths of development coexisting (with the third path developing quanititatively and qualitatively more). That epoch is characterized by this very coexistence or crossing of these paths (for example, a producer who became a merchant could, as merchant or competitor, make other producers dependent on him), with the increasing importance of manufacturing capital. Not only does the old feudal mode of production coexist in this epoch with the capitalist mode, but the three different processes of development (or modes of production) of capitalist production also coexist. However, *as capitalist production* these modes were always subject to the immanent laws Marx analyzed, even when their manifestations were historical, local, and individual variants.

Instead of analyzing the historical development of the capitalist mode of production, Weber and Borkenau deduce their conclusions from particular, albeit important, manifestations of the capitalist mode of production (the hierarchichal internal organization for Weber, the technological development for Borkenau). They then generalize their findings and declare them the essence of modern capitalism or of the "bourgeois worldview." One victim of the one-sided perspective Weber and

Borkenau employ is that "most complete anarchy" established and described over and over by Marx, Engels, and Lenin: the anarchy that prevails among the capitalists who encounter each other "as owners of goods" (Engels), and which is as integral to the capitalist mode of production as the internal hierarchical order and the subjugation of the working class. Borkenau is thus forced to contradict himself constantly in his attempt to shore up Weber's periodization of European history into (medieval) adventure capitalism and modern, rational capitalism determined by "worldly asceticism." In this attempt, Borkenau derives the "mechanistic philosophy" of the seventeenth century (that of Hobbes and Descartes above all), as a correlate to Protestant asceticism, from the "rational technology"[59] of artisans' production within manufacturing. It must be disturbing to him, first, that significant developments in mechanics demonstrably took place before the historical watershed he chooses, from the sixteenth to the seventeenth centuries;[60] second, he must be disturbed by the presence of manufacturing or industrial production *before* the seventeenth century and of corresponding mechanical innovation,[61] although neither the one nor the other is in doubt;[62] third, the role of commercial capital in the formation of modern capitalism or its world view must disturb him;[63] and fourth, all the ideologemes or ideologies that are derived from circulation and the competitive battle of the time after 1600 must disturb him—and quite a bit.

Solomon's House

Only with the knowledge of the constraints arising from this idealistic construct can we understand and explain the contradictions of Borkenau's polemic against Bacon and hence against Marx, which finally bogs down in a pointless paradox:

> It is precisely the close connection of Bacon with the most highly
> developed forms of industrial praxis, book printing, warfare, navigation,
> that denied him access to the simple, basic forms of modern technology
> that developed completely apart from the Renaissance discoveries and
> that became the basis of the mechanistic world view. The connection with
> the industrial praxis of his time and his class kept Bacon in the bonds of
> the Renaissance view of nature.[64]

It is correct that Bacon's work reflects the internal contradictions of the economic and political development in the transition from the predominance of commercial capital to the definitive predominance of industrial capital; this can be seen most clearly in his utopian novel *New Atlantis* (1623). Its beginning is the classic emergency at sea: a ship, one of whose crew members is the narrator, sets sail from Peru toward China, is blown off course in a storm, arrives in unexplored regions, and finally lands on an island to which no one has access but whose inhabitants are well informed about the rest of the world. There was a similar construct in *Utopia,* in which More tried to account for the inhabitants' information about the rest of the world by the device of travelers who come to Utopia with information. Bacon uses a different fictional trick. About three thousand years ago, the inhabitants of the island relate, there was a much more intensive world trade than at present:

> At that time this land was known and frequented by the ships and vessels of all the nations before named. And (as it cometh to pass) they had many times men of other countries, but were no sailors, that came with them, as Persians, Chaldeans, Arabians; so as almost all nations of might and fame resorted hither.... And for our own ships, they went sundry voyages, as well to your Straits which you call the Pillars of Hercules, as to other parts in the Atlantic and Mediterrean Seas; as to Paguin (which is the same with Cambaline) and Quinzy upon the Oriental Seas, as far as to the borders of the East Tartary.[65]

Later, as the inhabitants explain, this commerce died out. The fictional reasons Bacon gives for this are irrelevant for us, except for one: the decline of nautical technology.[66] What interests us is the connection between commercial and manufacturing capitalism that Bacon establishes in his literary fiction: nineteen hundred years ago, a King Solamona ruled the island and founded an "order or society," the "House of Solomon." This is a sort of institute with huge chambers, some of them subterranean, in which experiments are carried out relating to the appropriation of nature for the use of humanity. The house also contains a gallery with the statues of the most famous inventers and explorers (among them Columbus). "We also have engine-houses, where are prepared engines and instruments for all sorts of motions," says one of the "Fathers of the House of Solomon." "There we imitate and practise to make swifter motions than any you have, either out of your muskets or any engine that you have," he tells his European visitor. Moreover, the islanders try

> to make [motions] and to multiply them more easily and with small force by wheels and other means, and to make them stronger and more violent than yours are....We have ships and boats for going under water....We have divers curious clocks and other like motions of return and some perpetual motions.[67]

Given the mechanistic, ahistorical, and hence undialectical periodization of history that Borkenau adopts from Weber, it is predictable that he refuses to see that Bacon's *New Atlantis* reflects the dialectical connection between commercial and manufacturing capitalism—albeit in a more or less unprecise, contradictory, fairy-tale-like, and in any case unmethodical way. He considers the novel "insignificant"[68] up to the chapter on the "House of Solomon," just as he, in contradistinction to Marx, grants Bacon only minor importance.

The War of All against All

Only Hobbes meets the criteria that the Borkenau has obviously established for the ("ideal type of") ideologue or philosopher of emerging industrial capitalism (which once more shows the artificiality of his construct): "The materialism of *Hobbes* is the only consistent mechanistic materialism in the entire seventeenth century.[69] Borkenau's demotion of Bacon in favor of Hobbes is diametrically opposed to Marx's view; Marx, true to his dialectical method, sees in Hobbes's writings the unity of the contradictions, the further development, both positive and negative, of Bacon's thought. The most important aspect on the minus side is that the openness to "all-round development" of Bacon's view of materialism, the affirmation of matter in its "poetical sensuous brightness" that "smiled at man," has given way in Hobbes to an "anti-human" rigor.

> In its further development materialism became *one-sided*. Hobbes was the one who *systematized Bacon's* materialism. Sensuousness lost its bloom and became the abstract sensuousness of the *geometrician*. *Physical* motion was sacrificed to the *mechanical* or *mathematical, geometry* was proclaimed the principal science. Materialism became *hostile* to *humanity*. In order to overcome the *anti-human incorporeal* spirit in its own field, materialism itself was obliged to mortify its flesh and become an *ascetic*. It appeared as a *being of reason,* but it also developed the implacable logic of reason.[70]

The importance of these observations, which owe much to Renouvier,[71] becomes clear where Hobbes submits the most inappropriate object to his geometric, mechanistic, and mathematical approach: the human psyche. In discussing this, let us recall the movement that runs through geometric-mathematical thinking from Bacon to Hobbes. Geometric and mathematical laws are derived from observation of material nature, from experimental physics; these are then in turn applied to human *nature* or to the explanation of the *nature* of the human being, the explanation of human behavior. Thus it is assumed that the *nature* of the human being, which includes both physical and psychological nature, is dependent on physical-mechanistic impulses and hence can also be explained by geometric-mathematical means: "Every human passion is a mechanistic movement that is ending or beginning," as Marx characterizes this view.

We still do not have a science of the human psyche that can lay claim to absolute validity (the explanation of human behavior by historical and dialectical materialism cannot follow from the biological nature or the psyche of the human being, but only from his social being, as Marx defines it, from the "ensemble of social relations").[72] Hence it is clear how Hobbes directed bourgeois thinking down the wrong path. The openness of Bacon's materialism was also openness to overcoming its errors. But Hobbes systematizes, among other things, just that element that in Bacon emerged easily and largely unsystematically from a conglomerate of ancient practical wisdom, Montaigne's self-observations, and Hobbes's own experience: the image of the human being. In other words, in Hobbes, even the view of human nature is largely a priori, speculative, and idealist, although increasingly influenced by the discoveries of experimental science and of biology and medicine (for instance, Harvey's discovery of the function of blood circulation in 1623).

On the other side, Hobbes's concept of the human being, radically oriented toward quantification, that is, toward measurability as in the natural sciences, contributed substantially to overcoming theistic, irrational ideas. The dialectics of this a priori conception of the human being and radical demystification characterizes the development of the modern theory of natural law by the bourgeoisie and its representative, Hobbes. As Winfried Schröder writes:

> For *Hobbes* there was neither an absolute nor a relative natural law. He believed—as one can see from his political writings *De cive* (1642) and *Leviathan* (1651)—that the human instinct for self-preservation, in a state in which everything belonged to everyone and in which there was no power to guarantee the observance of any possible contracts about peaceful coexistence, that is, in a state of nature, must necessarily lead to a war of all against all. For Hobbes, this by no means ideal state of nature is, however, but the beginning of a development that leads to a peaceful coexistence of human beings in a state constituted on the principles of human reason. The same instinct for self-preservation and the human ability to think cause the human being to attempt to overcome the state of nature and to enter into a contract by which power is transferred to a ruler whose task is to see to harmony and peace. In keeping with these views, *Hobbes* distinguishes between *natural right,* by which he understands the freedom of every individual to use his powers as he sees fit to ensure his safety and to do everything his reason dictates to best reach this goal, and *natural law,* which obliges him to renounce his right to everything and to support the maintenance of peaceful relations in human society.[73]

Thus, as Schröder correctly writes, the creation of human social life, the social cooperation of all forces, is delegated to the practical activity of the "reasonable citizen"; and this also fundamentally breaks the back of the old feudal social order, penetrated by the religious idea of *ordo:*

> If *Hobbes* demands legal protection for private property and grants absolute sovereignty to the political power established by contract, that does not mean that he is legitimizing the feudal absolute monarchy. He never failed to see the errors of the monarchies of his time.

> The progress of *Hobbes's* theory of the natural rights society and state
> in the history of ideas is well known. Modern political philosophy
> finds its first systematic form in *Hobbes*.[74]

That is incontestably true. Unfortunately, it is also true that this primacy of human reason, which becomes the directive force for the reasonable constitution of society under Hobbes's natural law, was held in low esteem by his epigones (especially in the nineteenth and twentieth centuries). For them (and hence also for their ideology of adventure) Hobbes's idea of *natural right* alone, the speculative, a priori aspect of his concept of nature or of natural right, was and is (to the extent that they are familiar with their source) of crucial importance. The postulated state of nature as the war of all against all, isolated from its context in Hobbes's system, serves later generations of bourgeois ideologues until the present as a perpetual (biologistic) justification for capitalism, exploitation, war, the cult of the Great Man, and for adventuring[75]—which is not entirely inappropriate. For in fact, this thesis of the state of nature, the war of all against all, is nothing other than the generalized description of what Hobbes observed in contemporary society, the competitive battle of capitalism, as Marx describes it in *Capital*:

> Division of labour within the workshop implies the undisputed authority
> of the capitalist over men, who are merely the members of a total mech-
> anism which belongs to him. The division of labour within society
> brings into contact independent producers of commodities, who ac-
> knowledge no authority other than that of competition, of the coercion ex-
> erted by the pressure of their reciprocal interests, just as in the animal
> kingdom the "war of all against all" more or less preserves the condi-
> tions of existence of every species.[76]

This war of all against all, which can only be conducted at the expense of or thanks to the production of those who are exploited and oppressed in the "division of labour within the workshop," is the very element in which the "freedom" of the bourgeoisie, the victorious class in seventeenth-century England (and in all capitalist systems thereafter) is realized:

> The same bourgeois consciousness which celebrates the division of
> labour in the workshop, the lifelong annexation of the worker to a par-
> tial operation, and his complete subjection to capital, as an organization
> of labour that increases its productive power, denounces with equal
> vigour every conscious attempt to control and regulate the process of
> production socially, as an inroad upon such sacred things as the rights
> of property, freedom and the self-determining "genius" of the in-
> dividual capitalist.[77]

The decisive ideas of Hobbes, who of course was not clearly aware of the economic context underlying his views of human nature and the constitution of society, confirm Marx's observations:

> So that in the nature of man we find three principal causes of quarrel: first, competition; secondly, diffidence; thirdly, glory. The first makes men invade for gain, the second for safety, and the third for reputation.... Hereby it is manifest that, during the time men live without a common power to keep them all in awe, they are in that condition which is called war, and such a war as is of every man against every man. For WAR consists not in battle only, or in the act of fighting, but in a tract of time wherein the will to contend by battle is sufficiently known; and therefore the notion of *time* is to be considered in the nature of war as it is in the nature of weather. For as the nature of foul weather lies not in a shower or two of rain but in an inclination thereto of many days together, so the nature of war consists not in actual fighting but in the known disposition thereto during all the time there is no assurance to the contrary. All other time is PEACE.[78]

Peace is thus an unnatural, artificial state of society; the natural state is war, both the war of all against all and the war of each individual: concepts like "just" or "unjust" are inappropriate here. Since it is a question of a state of *nature,* the refusal of a combatant to engage in war would be tantamount to self-sacrifice, to suicide: war must therefore be fought by each person, or by every person, for reasons of self-preservation. "And by consequence, such augmentation of dominion over men being necessary to a man's conservation, it ought to be allowed him,"[79] Hobbes writes:

> To this war of every man against every man, this also is consequent: that nothing can be unjust. The notions of right and wrong, justice and injustice, have there no place. Where there is no common power, there is no law; where no law, no injustice. Force and fraud are in war the two cardinal virtues. Justice and injustice are none of the faculties neither of the body nor mind. If they were, they might be in a man that were alone in the world, as well as his senses and passions. They are qualities that relate to men in society, not in solitude.[80]

Man becomes man in society, however, through another form of the instinct of self-preservation—through fear: "The passions that incline men to peace are fear of death, desire of such things as are necessary to commodious living, and a hope by their industry to obtain them."[81] The coexistence of human beings in society is directed by reason according to these fears and desires. The human being enters into a contract with his enemy according to which individual freedom may be realized only within certain set norms, certain definite boundaries:

The RIGHT OF NATURE . . . is the liberty each man has to use his own power, as he will himself, for the preservation of his own nature—that is to say, of his own life—and consequently of doing anything which, in his own judgment and reason, he shall conceive to be the aptest means thereto. By LIBERTY is understood, according to the proper signification of the word, the absence of external impediments. . . . A LAW OF NATURE . . . is a precept or general rule, found out by reason, by which a man is forbidden to do that which is destructive of his life.[82]

The Adventurer Has the Right to Exploit

Hobbes's ideas were trivialized by the bourgeois ideologues of the nineteenth and twentieth centuries and linked with an equally trivialized Heraclitus (battle or war is the "father of all things"), and especially with the ideas of social Darwinism and elements of the philosophy of Schopenhauer, Burckhardt, Nietzsche, and others, in order not only to justify the wars of imperialism, but also to justify the civil wars against the working class in individual nations and internationally. An element of these ideas, on which many variants of the ideology of adventure are based, is the concept of thievery as the original form of earning a living; we have already encountered this concept in the anti-Marxist variations of Sombart and Weber. Interestingly, in Hobbes it is connected with the mention of Mercury, the ancient god of trade. Homer, Hobbes writes, summarized Mercury's heroic deeds as follows:

"Being born in the morning, he had invented music at noon and, before night, stolen away the cattle of Apollo from his herdsmen." Also among men, till there were constituted great commonwealths, it was thought no dishonor to be a pirate or a highway thief but rather a lawful trade, not only among the Greeks but also among all other nations, as is manifest by the histories of ancient times.[83]

As we saw in Sombart, the thesis that thievery was the first human trade in history, based on a natural rights argument, served bourgeois ideologues as an ideologeme to justify the brutal competitive battle among the international monopolies or nations, especially in the age of imperialism, the age of the "exploitation of an ever greater number of small or weak nations by very few rich or powerful nations," an age in which capitalism was in a "parasitic, decaying" state[84] (right up to the present). According to this view, the unscrupulous capitalist who annihilates his competition and commits mass murder is merely the "modern" variant of the "primitive" capitalist setting out to rob and plunder. Of course, only the seeds of all this are present in Hobbes, but important elements that will nourish the modern bourgeois ideology of adventure as an ideology of oppression and exploitation are already in evidence.

The first edition of Hobbes's *Leviathan* was published in 1651. The bourgeoisie had accomplished its revolution in England: two years before, Charles I was beheaded. Two years after the appearance of *Leviathan,* Cromwell became Lord Protector of England, Scotland, and Ireland, and the poets, John Milton in the vanguard, celebrated their bourgeois hero,[85] sometimes striking notes that seem to anticipate the later glorification of the imperialist adventurer leader. In 1650 Andrew Marvell, for instance, wrote "Horatian Ode upon Cromwell's Return from Ireland." Cromwell had made the rebelling Irish see reason, and Marvell celebrates the victor using remarkable terminology, with youth and the drive to adventurous, warlike activity in the foreground:

> The forward youth that would appeare,
> Must now forsake his Muses deare,
> Nor in the shadows sing
> His numbers languishing:
> 'Tis time to leave the books in dust,
> And oyle th'unusèd armour's rust;
> Removing from the wall
> The corselett of the hall.
> So restlesse Cromwell could not cease
> In the inglorious arts of peace,
> But through adventurous warre
> Urgèd his active starre;
> And, like the three-forked lightning, first
> Breaking the clouds where it was nurst,
> Did thorough his own Side
> His fiery way divide.[86]

The image is completed by a comparison with Caesar and Hannibal:

> As Caesar, he, ere long, to Gaul,
> To Italy an Hannibal,
> And to all States not free,
> Shall clymatérick be.[87]

And still, for all the triumphing, Marvell does not forget that the revolution in England had also inscribed on its banner the liberation from feudal bonds. After gaining economic power, the English bourgeoisie also seized political power, a state which could not last long in that form (also and especially because of the contradictions within the bourgeoisie). In 1660 the republic was dismantled. Under Charles II (1660-85), but especially under James II (1685-88), there was a pronounced political reaction which, however, was doomed by historical events: the bourgeoisie did not cease to augment its economic power, and when the political reaction began to be an impediment to the bourgeoisie, it looked around for new political solutions. In "Britannia and Raleigh" the good Marvell therefore presents Raleigh as a national hero: Britannia enters into a dialogue with Raleigh, whom she rouses in the realm of the dead. She complains about the cowardly—James I (a complaint naturally aimed at contemporary absolutist reaction). James I, when he stopped Raleigh's breath, also stopped Britannia's. Now Britannia is calling upon Raleigh to show him the condition of England under Charles II or James II; she uses the French model to flog the ideological orientation of the reactionary English court:

> A colony of French possess the Court;
> Pimps, priests, buffoons, in privy-chamber sport.
> Such slimy monsters ne'er approacht a throne,
> Since Pharaoh's days, nor so defil'd a crown.
> In sacred ear tyrannick arts they croak,
> Pervert his mind, and good intentions choake,
> Tell him of golden Indies, fairy lands,
> Leviathan, and absolute commands.[88]

Britannia challenges Raleigh to remind England's youth of the great past, that is, the bourgeois revolutionary epoch:

> my Raleigh, teach our noble youth
> To love sobriety, and holy truth;
> Watch and preside over their tender age,
> Lest Court-corruption should their souls engage;
> Teach them how arts, and arms, in thy young days,
> Employ'd our youth—not taverns, stews, and plays;
> . . . .
> Make 'em admire the Talbots, Sydneys, Veres,
> Drake, Cavendish, Blake; men void of slavish fears,
> True sons of glory, pillars of the State,
> On whose fam'd deeds all tongues and writers wait.[89]

Only when England proves herself worthy of her dead heroes will Britannia return and bring blessings to the land: "So shall my England, in a holy war, / In triumph lead chain'd tyrants from afar" (332, lines 187-88).

Britannia's or Marvell's wish comes true in 1688: the bourgeoisie, both Whigs and Tories, expelled James II, but after learning from the experience with the republic and with their own partially bourgeois nobility (in that the nobles engaged in capitalist activity), the bourgeoisie placed no particular stress on the renaissance of the revolutionary past that Marvell calls for. The bourgeoisie assumed power, as Engels says, "by making [the nobility] more and more bourgeois, and incorporating it as their own ornamental head.''[90] The bourgeoisie brought William of Orange in to succeed the exiled James II in 1688 and called this event the "Glorious Revolution.'' The real glory of this revolution for the bourgeoisie, which guaranteed its own privileges in 1689 with the *Declaration of Rights,* was that the form of the bourgeois monarchy it had created secured the economic and political power of the bourgeoisie against the forces of the people, whose dangerousness was at least suspected (as Bacon testifies in his *Essays*).

The Bank of England was founded in 1694,[91] and in 1702 the decisive step toward a British colonial empire was taken with the founding of the East India Company:

> The true commencement of the East India Company cannot be dated from a more remote epoch than the year 1702, when the different societies, claiming the monopoly of the East India trade, united together in one single Company. . . . It was under the ascendancy of that Dutch Prince when the Whigs became the farmers of the revenues of the British Empire, when the Bank of England sprang into life, when the protective system was firmly established in England, and the balance of power in Europe was definitively settled, that the existence of an East India Company was recognized by Parliament. That era of apparent liberty was in reality the era of monopolies not created by Royal grants, as in the times of Elizabeth and Charles I, but authorized and nationalized by the sanction of Parliament . . . the old landed aristocracy having been defeated, and the bourgeoisie not being able to take its place except under the banner of moneyocracy, or the "haute finance.'' The East India Company excluded the common people from the commerce with India, at the same time that the House of Commons excluded them from Parliamentary representation. In this as well as in other instances, we find the first decisive victory of the bourgeoisie over feudal aristocracy coinciding with the most pronounced reaction against the people.[92]

For the bourgeoisie as the ruling class, the modern ideology of adventure offered the most diverse possibilities for justifying not only its "reaction against the people'' but also its colonial and war policy. What had functioned against feudal absolutism in an emancipatory way, as secularization, demystification, and affirmation of the real human being in his useful activity, has the reverse ideological function with respect to the proletariat or the preproletariat: the social state of alleged war of all against all is justified by the "natural right'' of the stronger over the weaker. Success belongs to those who have the tendency to it, who are born to it; and those whose misfortune it is to be a loser, to be subordinate, to be exploited, are also born to that. This is a position that is adumbrated in Hobbes and which, together with the ideas on the social dangers of Christian virtues developed by

Pierre Bayle (especially in his *Continuation des Pensées diverses sur la comète* [Continuation of Various Thoughts about the Comet], 1704), is systematized in *The Fable of the Bees: or Private Vices, Publick Benefits* (1706-28) by Bernard de Mandeville (1670-1733).

According to Mandeville, human beings are born masters or slaves; to rule, one needs an innate instinct,[93] and the virtues necessary for ruling as well as for the practice of adventure, such as joy in discovery or courage, arise from vices like cruelty,[94] greed,[95] hunger, and the sex drive.[96] All those natural qualities of the human being that are vices become socially necessary virtues, according to Mandeville, in the interaction of human beings, that is, in society[97] or in the struggle of competition.[98] People lacking these natural vices are condemned to form the dregs of society; not much time should be wasted on them, since as the dregs, they are forced to perform physical labor. Mandeville writes,

> It is manifest, that, in a free nation, where slaves are not allowed of, the surest wealth consists in a multitude of laborious poor; for besides that they are never failing nursery of fleets and armies, without them there could be no enjoyment, and no product of any country could be valuable. To make the society happy and people easier under the meanest circumstances, it is requisite that great numbers of them should be ignorant as well as poor.[99]

For the mass of the population, not only for the poor but for all noncapitalists, adventure was already out of reach with the political victory of the bourgeoisie; as Marx had observed in talking about the East India Company, "the common people" were excluded from commerce (as well as from establishing manufactures). That means that adventure could no longer exist for them except in the negative sense of adventure as a fate one suffers, as trouble, punishment, injustice, as dealt with in an increasing number of novels (not least in those with a criminal theme).[100] Nonetheless, we should note that the bourgeoisie and its ideologues, or capital and its apologists, pursued a double strategy from the beginning, the first elements of which are already adumbrated in Bacon. While the poor in Mandeville's sense, those in the population engaged in physical labor, the (pre)proletariat, are shown that adventure is a privilege reserved to people who are (necessarily) superior to them by virtue of their innate nature, another tactic is applied with the employees or agents of capital. It cannot be hidden from these people that the capitalist himself is hardly still active or courageous, since they themselves are employed to perform the activities that the capitalist no longer carries out in person. For them, the myth of (disinterested) boldness is propagated (as already sketched unprogrammatically in Bacon's *Essays*). This is the myth of the active, courageous (commercial) person whom one cannot lock up in an office but who still needs guidance from an uncourageous, cautious person (the capitalist). The capitalists have to make decisions and direct actions because they are born to it; they are born office animals who are more to be pitied than envied because they are not active "out there," like the "real man." The praxis of adventure was first the activity of real employees and then increasingly decays into a suggestive adventure myth for employees, which has the function of distracting and appeasing them. For this function of distraction and appeasement, the ideology of adventure invents ever more subtle forms that are based primarily on the 'originally unthinkable) propagation of the idea of the disinterested adventure for the sake of adventure.

The newly created injustice (enslavement and exploitation, which came to European attention first in the fate of the natives of subject lands overseas) is justified in two different ways. First (the orthodox method), the natives must allegedly be educated to Christianity or freed from their animal-like minority (which presupposes a process of education that is realized especially well through physical labor). Second (the modern argument), the subjugation of foreign peoples comes about thanks to the biological superiority of the victor, the conqueror, the exploiter.

Notes

Notes

All translations are my own, unless otherwise indicated—R.C.

Preface. Adventure in a Chance-Determined World

1. Michael Nerlich, "Plädoyer für Lázaro: Bermerkungen zu einer 'Gattung,'" *Romanische Forschungen* (1968): 354-94.

2. Michael Nerlich, *Kunst, Politik, und Schefmerei: Die Rückkehr des Künstlers und des Intellektuellen in die Gesellschaft des zwanzigsten Jahrhunderts, dargestellt an Werken von Charles de Coster, Romain Rolland, André Gide, Heinrich, und Thomas Mann,* (Frankfurt/Main and Bonn, 1969).

3. Werner Krauss died before publication of the present book, but he was so committed to the subject that he dedicated his last study to my book: "Reise als 'adventure' und als Funktion," *Lendemains* 5 (1977): 4-8.

4. See especially Marianne Kesting, *Romanische Forschungen* (1979): 408-13, and Edward Reichel, *Kritikon Litterarum* nos. 1-4 (1980): 11-16.

5. See especially Ulrich Schulz-Buschhaus, *Zeitschrift für französische Sprache und Literatur* 91, no. 1 (1981): 45-50, but see also Frank Benseler, "Ein großer aufklärerischer Wurf," *DVZ* 9 November 1978, p. 29; Martin Fontius, *Weimarer Beiträge* no. 2 (1979): 152-56; Horst Heintze, *Deutsche Literaturzeitung* 99, no. 12 (1978): 839-41, and Heinz Thoma, "Ideologem oder Ermunterung zum Handeln? Zu zwei Arbeiten über das Abenteuer in Literatur und Gesellschaft," *Romanistische Zeitschrift für Literaturgeschichte* no. 4 (1980): 475-84. For particular aspects see also G. Barthel, *Dixhuitième Siècle* no. 11 (1979): 491; Karl-Heinz Bender, *Zeitschrift für Romanische Philologie* 98, nos. 1-2 (1982): 168-72; Barbara Könneker, *Daphnis* no. 8 (1979): 408-13; Karl-Heinz Magister, *Shakespeare-Jahrbuch* (Weimar) no. 115 (1979): 181-82; Ernstpeter Ruhe, *Bulletin*

Bibliographique de la Société Internationale Arthurienne 31 (1979): 44; Taino, *Studi Francesi* (Turin) 24 (1980): 196-97.

6. A summary of the intermediate stage of my research can be read in Michael Nerlich, *On the Unknown History of Our Modernity,* Center for Humanistic Studies, University of Minnesota, Occasional Paper No. 3 (Minneapolis, 1986); and Michael Nerlich, "Pensar la aventura: Reflexiones sobre un asunto filosóficamente desacreditado," *Revista de Occidente,* no. 38-39 (1984): 191-214.

7. As early as 1977, I insisted that the term "ideology" was a makeshift (*Kritik der Abenteuer-Ideologie,* 1:18) to denote a quite complex system of adventurous qualities (thought, feeling, practice, glorification, and so on). Today I would prefer the term "adventure-mentality."

8. Nerlich, *On the Unknown History of Our Modernity,* 21-22.

9. Herbert Hörz, *Zufall—Eine philosophische Untersuchung* (Berlin, 1980), 85.

10. Hörz, *Zufall,* 83-84.

11. Isabelle Stengers and Ilya Prigogine, *La Nouvelle Alliance* (Paris, 1979); in English translation as, *Order out of Chaos: Man's New Dialogue with Nature* (Toronto, New York, London and Sydney, 1984).

12. Stengers and Prigogine, *Order out of Chaos,* 312-13.

Chapter 1. The Adventure of the *Chevalier*

1. "Tout ce qu'Homère nous raconte des dangers de la navigation d'Ulysse: des Circés, des Lestrigons, des Cyclopes, des Sirènes, de Charybde et de Scylla, étoient des fables répandues dans le Monde et établies par des navigateurs qui, faisant le commerce d'économie, voulaient dégoûter les autres peuples de le faire après eux." [Everything Homer tells us about the dangers of Ulysses's voyages, about Circe, Lestrigon, the Cyclops, the sirens, Scylla and Charbydis, all were fables spread about in the world and vouched for by sailors who, beginning commercial trade, wanted to discourage others from following in their steps.] (Montesquieu, "Dossier de L'esprit des loies," in *Oeuvres complètes,* ed. Roger Caillois, Bibliothèque de la Pléiade [Paris, 1949-51], 2:1087)

2. Mikhail Bakhtin, "Forms of Time and of the Chronotope in the Novel: Notes toward a Historical Poetics," in Bakhtin, *The Dialogic Imagination. Four Essays,* ed. Michael Holquist, trans. Caryl Emerson and Michael Holquist, University of Texas Press Slavic Series 1 (Austin, 1981), 84-258. See also Otto Weinrich, who writes about the *Aithiopika* of Heliodorus: "In these events, in their scenes and their actors, there is a further unifying tendency in a deeper sense, a teleological, meaningful law governing the action. Over the whole human sphere with the most varied portrayal of social levels, the power of the gods reigns." ("Zum Verständnis des Werkes," in Heliodorus, *Aithiopika: Die Abenteuer der schönen Chariklea* [Hamburg], 1962, 219-59, 245)

3. To be sure, Mikhail Bakhtin mentions three different kinds of novel, but the third type he names does not exist in classical antiquity, so that only two types are relevant for that period. See Bakhtin, "Forms of Time," 130: "By this third type we have in mind a *biographical novel,* although antiquity did not produce the kind of novel that we (in our terminology) would call a 'novel,' that is, a large fiction influenced by biographical models."

4. Ibid., 86ff.

5. Ibid., 111ff., esp. 122. (Of course, Bakhtin's description of types is more extensive and more subtle.)

6. Ibid., 115f.

7. Ibid., 105. Unchangeability is the only thing that is not true of the second type. In these two types of (Latin) novel, the time in which the protagonists endure the events leaves traces in the individuals. However, that does not change the fact that they undergo their adventures against their will. "It is not the time of a Greek romance, a time that leaves no traces. On the contrary, it leaves a deep and irradicable mark on the man himself as well as on his entire life. It is, nevertheless, decidedly

adventure-time: a time of exceptional and unusual events, events determined by chance, which, moreover, manifest themselves in fortuitous encounters (temporal junctures) and fortuitous nonencounters (temporal disjunctions)." (116)

8. Gustav Ehrismann, "Die Grundlagen des ritterlichen Tugendsystems," in *Ritterliches Tugendsystem*, ed. Gunther Eifler (Darmstadt, 1970), 1-92, 50f.

9. Elena Eberwein, "Die Aventure in den altfranzösischen Lais," in *Zur Deutung mittelalterlicher Existenz*, Kölner Romanistische Arbeiten 7 (Bonn and Cologne, 1933), 27-53, 29.

10. See Erich Köhler, *Ideal und Wirklichkeit in der höfischen Epik: Studien zur Form der frühen Artus- und Gralsdichtung*, 2, expanded ed. (Tübingen, 1970), 78. In the meantime, this work has appeared in French translation with an unaltered text but with an important new foreword by Jacques Le Goff, as *L'aventure chevaleresque: Idéal et réalité dans le roman courtois. Etudes sur la forme des plus anciens poèmes d'Arthur et du Graal* (Paris, 1974).

11. See Reto R. Bezzola, *Liebe und Abenteuer im höfischen Roman* (Hamburg, 1961); Erich Köhler, "Quelques observations d'ordre historico-sociologique sur les rapports entre la chanson de geste et le roman courtois," in *Chanson de geste und höfischer Roman*, ed. Pierre le Gentil et al., Studia Romanica 4 (Heidelberg, 1963), 21-30, 26-27.

12. This is a thesis of Elena Eberwein's ("Die Aventure," 30) with which Erich Köhler (*Ideal und Wirklichkeit*, 66) agrees. But it seems to me that the following objection must be made to Eberwein's methodology. When she asserts that *aventura* also has the meaning of *eventus*, "luck," "fate," and that "the constant reference to an incomprehensible, foreign, otherworldly power that can ambush the life of the individual" is also supposed to have been present in *aventura*, she is only apparently exercising philological rigor. Actually these are unprovable speculations (see especially the faulty reasoning on p. 32, where what was previously assumed is now treated as a fact).

13. Yvain, the Knight of the Lion, hero of *Le chevalier au lion* (ca. 1180) by Chrestien de Troyes.

14. Köhler, *Ideal und Wirklichkeit*, 69-70. See also in this context the discussion about Köhler's work in *Chanson de geste und höfischer Roman*, 31-36, 33-34.

15. Cited in Köhler, *Ideal und Wirklichkeit,* 18.

16. Ibid., 32. See also 71.

17. See ibid., 37ff.

18. See in this context Carl Erdmann, *Die Entstehung des Kreuzzugsgedankens* (reprint Darmstadt, 1955). Among more recent works, Georges Duby's is especially important: "The Origins of Knighthood" and "The Transformation of the Aristocracy," both in Duby, *The Chivalrous Society*, trans. Cynthia Postan (Berkeley and Los Angeles, 1977), 158-70, 162ff., and 178-85, 180ff.

19. Köhler, *Ideal und Wirklichkeit*, 71. See also Erich Auerbach, *Mimesis: The Portrayal of Reality in Western Literature*, trans. Willard R. Trask (Princeton, 1974), 133ff.

20. Köhler, *Ideal und Wirklichkeit,* 70.

21. Ibid., 71.

22. See Duby, "The Origins of Knighthood."

23. Georges Duby, "Youth in Aristocratic Society," in *The Chivalrous Society,* 112-22, 116-17.

24. Ibid., 117.

25. Ibid.

26. Ibid., 117-18.

27. See Duby, "The Origins of Knighthood," 165ff.

28. Duby, "Youth in Aristocratic Society," 112-13.

29. Ibid., 119.

30. Ernst Pitz, professor of medieval history at the Technical University, West Berlin, gave me valuable suggestions for the following discussion.

31. See Jacques Le Goff, *Das Hochmittelalter* (Frankfurt / Main, 1965), 55ff.

32. Arno Borst, "Das Rittertum im Hochmittelalter: Idee und Wirklichkeit," *Saeculum* 10 (1959): 213-31, 216. On this period, see also Georges Duby, *The Early Growth of the European Economy:*

Warriors and Peasants from the Seventh to the Twelfth Century, trans. Howard B. Clarke (Ithaca, N.Y., 1974). In my opinion, with the exception of Duby, almost all studies of knighthood in the early Middle Ages err in treating it as a homogenous group that underwent or helped to produce historical change as a closed group. This seems mistaken; the knighthood of the early Middle Ages seems to me already as fragmented as that of later times.

33. See especially Duby, *The Early Growth of the European Economy*; but see also Borst, "Das Rittertum im Hochmittelalter," 217.

34. Borst, "Das Rittertum im Hochmittelalter," 217.

35. Ibid., 221.

36. Ibid., 220.

37. See Duby, "Youth in Aristocratic Society," 120-21.

38. See Le Goff, *Das Hochmittelalter*, 246ff; 240ff.

39. See ibid., 155ff. For an understanding of the broader context, see especially Marc Bloch, *Feudal Society*, trans. L. A. Manyon (Chicago, 1961), 2:352ff.

40. See Arno Borst, "Krieg," in Borst, *Lebensformen im Mittelalter* (Frankfurt / Main and West Berlin, 1973), 433-36.

41. See Duby, "The Transformation of the Aristocracy," 178-79.

42. See ibid., 182: "At this period, indeed, the theme giving expression to this sentiment in literature was a common one. It was the theme of the *vilain* upstart. . . . The person appearing in the romances and tales of about the year 1200 is a base-born man, badly educated, who has enriched himself and raised himself to economic equality with the knights; he is a man who has taken the knight's place, become a lord, usurped the noble's position, his house, his lands, and who apes his manners in a way that is both uncouth and unattractive. He is a grotesque and disreputable personage, but a very real one. The bad prince who tolerates such an intruder and encourages a non-noble to rise in the social scale, by admitting such a person into his counsel or army, also behaves in a scandalous way."

43. Köhler, *Ideal und Wirklichkeit*, 77.

44. See ibid., 83. See also the relevant remarks by Karl-Heinz Bender on the varying literary protrayal of the function of the court in the *chanson de geste* and in the courtly romance in *König und Vasall: Untersuchungen zur Chanson de Geste des XII. Jahrhunderts*, Studiea Romanica 8 (Heidelberg, 1967), 116-17.

45. Köhler, *Ideal und Wirklichkeit*, 71.

46. See Hans Robert Jauss, "Chanson de geste und roman courtois," in *Chanson de geste und höfischer Roman*, 61-77, and the following discussion, 78-83, 78-79.

47. Auerbach, "The Knight Sets Forth," in *Mimesis*, 123-42, 127.

48. Ibid., 130-31.

49. Ibid., 131.

50. Ibid., 130.

51. Ibid., 136.

52. Borst, "Das Rittertum im Hochmittelalter," 230.

53. See ibid., 231. See also Johan Huizinga, *The Waning of the Middle Ages* (Garden City, N.Y., 1954), 83-84; and Jacques Heers, *Fêtes, jeux, et joutes dans les sociétés d'occident à la fin du Moyen Age* (Montreal and Paris, 1971).

54. On Guibert de Nogent, see among others Heinz Köller and Bernhard Töpfer, *Frankreich: Ein historischer Abriss* (Berlin, 1969), 1:66ff., 58f.

55. Le Goff, *Das Hochmittelalter*, 136.

56. Ibid., 137.

57. Ibid., 145.

58. Köller and Töpfer, *Frankreich*, 1:60.

59. Le Goff, *Das Hochmittelalter*, 143.

60. Geoffroy de Villehardouin, *La conquête de Constantinople*, ed. Edmond Faral (Paris, 1961), 1:34 and passim.

61. Ibid., 1:60.

62. Ibid., 1:36.

63. Ibid., 1:46.

64. Ibid., 1:60.

65. Ibid., 1:110-12.

66. See Köller and Töpfer, *Frankreich*, 1:86ff.

67. Friedrich Engels, "Über den Verfall des Feudalismus und das Aufkommen der Bourgeoisie," in Karl Marx and Friedrich Engels, *Werke* (Berlin, 1956-1971), 21:392-401, 398.

68. Köller and Töpfer, *Frankreich*, 1:96. See also Frederick Engels, "Infantry," in Karl Marx and Frederick Engels, *Collected Works* (New York, 1982), 18:340-63, 348ff.

69. Köller and Töpfer, *Frankreich*, 1:159.

70. Ibid., 1:185-86. See also Frederick Engels, "Army," in Marx and Engels, *Collected Works*, 18:85-126, 106ff.

71. See Köller and Töpfer, *Frankreich*, 1:186.

72. Quoted from the chapter in *Textes d'études (Ancien et moyen français)*, ed. Robert Léon Wagner (Lille and Geneva, 1949), 186-87.

73. François Rabelais, *Gargantua*, in *Gargantua and Pantagruel*, trans. Sir Thomas Urquhart and Peter Motteux, Great Books of the Western World 24 (Chicago, London, Toronto, 1952), 32.

74. Engels, "Infantry," 18:354.

75. Marguerite de Navarre agrees that the *advanturiers* were bad, but not quite as bad as the priests. As a character says in her *Hemptaméron*, ed. Félix Frank (Paris, 1879), 2:141: "J'ay veu le temps que en nostre pays il n'y avoit maison où il n'y eust chambre dédiée pour les beaux-pères; mais maintenant ilz sont tant congneuz, qu'on les craint plus qua advanturiers." [I remember the time in our country when every house had a room set aside for priests; but now they have become so rowdy that they are more feared than adventurers.]

76. Examples from Edmond Huguet, *Dictionnaire de la langue française du Seizième Siècle* (Paris, 1925-67), 1:82-83.

77. Examples from Jacob Le Duchat, quoted from the introduction in *Dictionnaire étymologique de la language françoyse par M. Ménage* (Paris, 1750), 1:107.

Chapter 2. The Adventure of the *Hidalgo*

1. See Martín de Riquer, "Introducció," in Joannot Martorell, *Tirant lo Blanc* (Barcelona, 1947), 152-57.

2. For one of the few treatments, see the relevant chapter in Hans-Jörg Neuschäfer's excellent book, *Der Sinn der Parodie im Don Quijote* (Heidelberg, 1963), 23-33.

3. Pierre Vilar, *Histoire de l'Espagne*, 3 ed. (Paris, 1955), 18.

4. In this context see especially William J. Entwistle, *The Arthurian Legend in the Literature of the Spanish Peninsula* (London, Toronto, and New York, 1925).

5. See Ramón Menéndez Pidal, "Poésia e historia en el Mio Cid," in *De primitiva lírica española y antigua épica* (Madrid, 1951), 11-33.

6. See especially Claudio Sanchez-Albornoz, *España un enigma histórica* (Buenos Aires, 1962).

7. It is almost a matter of course that this principle was not upheld in reality. As early as 1354 the Arcipreste de Hita, in the "Exemplo de la propriedad qu'el dinera ha" of the *Libro de Buen Amor*, complains about the buying of *hidalgo* titles: "Take any stupid man or ignorant peasant,

/ Money turns him into a hidalgo and a wise man." (Clásicos castellanos edition [Madrid, 1951-54], 1:182)

8. Alfonso el Sabio, *Las Siete Partidas* (Madrid, 1972), 213.

9. Don Juan Manuel, *Libro del Caballero y del Escudero*, Biblioteca de Autores Españoles (Madrid, 1860), 51:234-57.

10. Ramón Llull, *Libre del Orde de Cavallería*, in *Obras doctrinales del illuminat Doctor Mestre Ramón Llull*, ed. A. M. Alcover, M. Obrador i Beumánar (Palma de Mallorca, 1906), 1:201-47, 214.

11. Ibid., 1:217-18. Don Juan Manuel names the lay classes more specifically, in the order "merchants, officials, and peasants" (*Libro del Caballero*, 1:236).

12. Llull, *Libro del Cavallería*, 1:234.

13. Ibid., 1:214-15.

14. Ibid., 1:218-19.

15. Ibid., 1:244. On the idea of knighthood in Llull, see Miguel Sanchis Guarner, "L'ideal cavalleresc definit per Ramón Llull," *Estudios Catalans* 2 (1958): 37-62. On the relationship between the ideas of Ramón Llull and those of Alfonso the Wise see Sánchez-Albornoz, *España un enigma histórica*, 1:267-636.

16. See Vilar, *Histoire de l'Espagne*, 24-25.

17. See Jaime Vicens Vives, *An Economic History of Spain* (Princeton, 1969), 339ff.

18. Richard Konetzke, "Zur Geschichte des spanischen Hidalgos," *Spanische Forschungen der Görresgesellschaft* 19 (1962): 147-60, 152.

19. See Werner Krauss, "Wege der spanischen Frührenaissancelyrik," in *Gesammelte Aufsätze zur Literatur- und Sprachwissenschaft* (Frankfurt / Main, 1949), 113-51, 121.

20. "Repúblico, el hombre que trata del bien común. . . ." The quotation is from Sebastian de Covarrubias, *Tesoro de la Lengua Castellana o Española*, ed. Martín de Riquer (Barcelona, 1943), 906.

21. Miguel de Cervantes, *Don Quijote*, ed. Francisco Rodriguez Marín, Clásicos castellanos (Madrid, 1911), 1:161-62. For an interpretation of this passage, which has presented problems for critics (see *Don Quijote*, ed. Marín, footnote to 162-64), see also Riquer, "Introducció," in Martorell, *Tirant lo Blanc*, 189-90. For a historical context see also Riquer, *Cavalleria fra realtà e letteratura nel Quattrocento* (Paris, 1970).

22. *Tirant lo Blanc*, 8. On *Tirant lo Blanc* see Dámaso Alonso,"'Tirant-lo-Blanc,' Novela Moderna," in *Primavera temprana de la literatura Europea* (Madrid, 1961), 203-53.

23. Riquer, "Introducció," in *Tirant lo Blanc*, 132.

24. But Riquer claims ("Introducció," in *Tirant lo Blanc*, 85) "que aquesta novella presenti múltiples i diversos aspectes que en certa manera li donen un carácter variat i poc constant" [that this romance presents many and varied aspects that tend to give it a varying, inconstant character].

25. Neuschäfer, *Der Sinn der Parodie im Don Quijote*, 29-30.

26. See Konetzke, "Zur Geschichte des spanischen Hidalgos," 156-58.

27. This is certainly the reason for the limited popularity of the book—and not, as Felicidad Buendia claims, in *Libros de caballerías españoles* (Madrid, 1954), 1060, the "obscenity" of certain passages, which did not harm the popularity of other "obscene" books.

28. See Richard Konetzke, "Forschungsprobleme zur Geschichte der wirtschaftlichen Betätigung des Adels in Spanien," in *Homaje a Don Ramón Carande* (Madrid, 1963), 1:135-51, 145-57.

29. Konetzke, "Zur Geschichte des spanischen Hidalgos," 154.

30. See "Hidalgo" in the *Enciclopedia Universal Ilustrada*, Espasa, 27: 1377-1380, 1380a.

31. See Krauss, "Wege der spanischen Frührenaissancelyrik," 126-27.

32. Fray Antonio de Guevara, *Menosprecio de Corte y Alabanza de Aldea*, Clásicos castellanos (Madrid, 1928), 100-101.

33. See Wolfgang Lepenies, *Melancholie und Gesellschaft* (Frankfurt / Main, 1969).

34. Guevara, *Menosprecio de Corte*, 107.

35. Ibid., 108-9.

36. Ibid., 112-13.

37. Ibid., 114.

38. Ibid., 117. This quotation alone would be enough to contradict the conservative Spanish opinion stated again and again that there were no poor *hidalgos*.

39. See Vicens Vives, *Economic History of Spain*, 174.

40. Ibid., 316.

41. Ibid. See in this context especially Sānchez-Albornoz, *España un enigma histórica*, 2:500-514.

42. Vicens Vives, *Economic History of Spain*, 317.

43. On the Spanish knightly romance, see Henry Thomas, *Novelas de caballerías españolas y portuguesas: Despertar de la novela caballeresca en la peninsular ibérica y expansión e influencia en el extranjero* (Madrid, 1952).

44. This is true if one ignores a predecessor like *El Libro del Cavallero Zifar* (The book of Caballero Cifar, 1299-1304), which would require a special investigation. In any case, it is an isolated example, was not particularly successful, and—significantly—did not become popular until a printing of 1512.

45. Hans-Jörg Neuschäfer, "Amadís," in *Lexikon der Weltliteratur 2, Hauptwerke der Weltliteratur in Charakteristiken und Kurzinterpretationen*, ed. Gero von Wilpert (Stuttgart, 1968), 34.

Chapter 3. The Counterrevolutionary Ideology of Knightly Adventure

1. Karl Marx and Frederick Engels, *Collected Works* (London, 1978), 10:397-482, 403-4.

2. Ibid., 10:404.

3. Arnold Hauser, in *The Social History of Art* (New York, n.d.), is much too indiscriminating when he writes about the chivalric romance of the sixteenth century and its precursors that they are "essentially a symptom of the incipient predominance of authoritarian forms of government, of the degeneration of middle-class democracy and the gradual assimilation of Western culture to the standards of the courts. Chivalrous ideals and conceptions of virtue are the sublimated form in which the new aristocracy, rising from the lower classes, and the princes, tending toward absolutism, disguise their ideology." (2:144)

Not only does he lump together the Emperor Maximilian, Ignatius Loyola, the Italian petty princes, and the absolute monarchs, but he ignores the fact that the absolutist monarchy could not assume the knightly ideology of adventure as its own until the knights and the feudal nobility that had opposed absolutism had been conquered, and even then its assumption was only partial. It is another matter altogether that the court had earlier taken on elements of the knightly ideology of adventure in order to play the various forces off against each other; but the court did not use this ideology against the bourgeoisie until it no longer needed that class to gain predominance. For Spain, see the recent study of Maxime Chevalier, "El público de las novelas," in *Lectura y lectores en la España del Siglo de Oro* (Madrid, 1976), 65-103.

4. Frederick Engels, *The Origin of the Family, Private Property, and the State* (New York, 1972), 160.

5. Frederick Engels, "The Peasant War in Germany," 10:412.

6. Ibid., 10:411.

7. Werner Krauss, *Gesammelte Aufsätze zur Literatur und Sprachwissenschaft* (Frankfurt / Main, 1949), 152-76.

8. For a survey of the reception and criticism of the Spanish chivalric romance, see the (unfortunately rather undifferentiated) work by Henry Thomas, *Las novelas de caballerías españolas y portuguesas: Despertar de la novela caballeresca en la peninsular ibérica y expansión e influencia en el extranjero* (Madrid, 1952), 137ff.

9. Krauss, *Gesammelte Aufsätze*, 153.

10. Engels, "The Peasant War in Germany," 10:404.

11. See Thomas, *Las novelas de caballerías*, 129.

12. See Krauss, *Gesammelte Aufsätze*, 158ff.; Thomas, *Las novelas de caballerías*, 129.

13. Thomas, *Las novelas de caballerías*, 136.

14. Ibid.

15. See Engels, "The Peasant War in Germany," section 4 on the revolt of the nobles, 10:441-45. See also the correspondence between Marx and Engels and Lasalle in Karl Marx and Friedrich Engels, *Über Kunst und Literatur* (Berlin, 1967), 1:166-217.

16. See Baldassare Castiglione, *Il libro del Corteggiani, in Opera de Baldassare Castiglione, Giovanni della Casa, Benvenuto Cellini*, ed. Carlo Cordié, Storia e testi 27 (Milan and Naples, 1960), 265.

17. It is quite interesting that Castiglione (*Il libro del Corteggiani*, 59) registers the word "to adventure" / *avventurare* as a neologism, which of course leads to some suggestive conclusions.

18. See Frank Pierce, *La poesia épica del siglo de oro*, 2 ed. (Madrid, 1968); Michael Nerlich, *Untersuchungen zur Theorie des klassizistischen Epos in Spanien (1700-1850)* (Paris and Geneva, 1964).

19. See Jaime Vicens Vives, *An Economic History of Spain* (Princeton, 1969), 316ff.; and José Antonio Maravall, *Estado moderno y mentalidad social* (Madrid, 1972), 2:185-92.

20. See in this context Michael Nerlich, *Kunst, Politik, und Schelmerei: Die Rückkehr des Künstlers und des Intellektuellen in die Gesellschaft des zwanzigsten Jahrhunderts, dargestellt an Werken von Charles de Coster, Romain Rolland, André Gide, Heinrich Mann, und Thomas Mann* (Frankfurt / Main and Bonn, 1969), 9ff.

21. Kurt von Fritz, "Tragische Schuld und poetische Gerechtigkeit in der griechischen Tragödie," in *Antike und moderne Tragödie* (West Berlin, 1962), 1-112.

22. On the one hand, see the introduction to *La vida de Lazarillo de Tormes / La vie de Lazarillo de Tormes*, trans. Alfred Morel-Fatio (Paris, 1968), 11-60. On the other hand, see Michael Nerlich, "Plädoyer für Lázaro: Bemerkungen zu einer 'Gattung,'" *Romanische Forschung* 80 (1968): 354-94.

23. La *vida de Lazarillo de Tormes*, 33, 68.

24. Ibid., 92-93 (Clásicos castellanos edition: 88).

25. Ibid., 170-71 (Clásicos castellanos edition: 243).

26. Ibid., 33.

27. Enrique Tierno Galván relates the novel to the uprisings of the *comuneros*, the representatives of the city burghers, against Charles V—a thoroughly plausible thesis, in *Es el "Lazarillo" un libro comunero?* Boletín informativo del Deminario de Derecho Público de la Universidad de Salamanca 89 (Salamanca, 1956), 217-20.

28. *La vida de Lazarillo de Tormes*, 16-17.

29. Carlos García, *La desordenada codicia de los bienes ajenos: Antigüedad y nobleza de los ladrones*, ed. Fernando Guitiérrez (Madrid, 1959). In an ironic comparison between himself and the upper classes, the agent asks the thief: "Isn't it fortunate to find ready-made clothes that fit in the midst of the worst desolation and need, without having to pay for the material, the tailor, or the wages? Is there any greater nobility in this world than being a knight without income and regarding everyone else's property as your own, so that you can dispose of it as you will, with no more cost to you than the taking of it?"

30. On the question of Don Quijote's melancholy, see among others Hans Jörg Neuschäfer, *Der Sinn der Parodie im Don Quijote* (Heidelberg, 1963), 81ff.; and H. Weinrich, *Das Ingenium Don Quijotes: Ein Beitrag zur literarischen Charakterkunde*, Forschungen zur Romanischen Philologie 1 (Münster, 1956), 47-62. Neither author, however, investigates the social function of the melancholy in *Don Quijote* (Weinrich merely assembles quotations from treatises on melancholy).

31. Werner Krauss, *Miguel de Cervantes: Leben und Werk* (Neuwied and West Berlin, 1966), 155. See also Werner Krauss, "Cervantes und der spanische Weg der Novelle," in *Studien und Aufsätze* (Berlin, 1959), 93-138.

32. Cervantes, *Don Quijote*, ed. Francisco Rodriguez Marín, Clásicos castellanos (Madrid, 1911), 8:327.

33. Hans-Jörg Neuschäfer writes: "For the first time a romance of chivalry ends with the disillusionment of the hero. For the first time he neither pursued the path of adventure to its end nor did he win his lady" (*Der Sinn der Parodie im Don Quijote*, 98). But Neuschäfer is wide of the mark because he overlooks the fact that *Don Quijote* was from the outset not a romance of chivalry but the novel of a pseudo-knight with his pseudo-squire (or of an imaginary knight with a peasant as squire). The reader is perfectly aware of this, and the novel, which for that reason cannot be a romance of chivalry, lives from this irony or from the complicity between author and reader in this *engaño* which is understood from the beginning.

34. Karl Borinski, *Baltasar Gracián und die Hoflitteratur in Deutschland* (Halle / Saale, 1894), 126.

35. Baltasar Gracián, *El Criticón* (Madrid, 1957), 39.

36. Ibid., 35. A basilisk is a fantastic evil monster.

37. Ibid., 52.

38. Ibid., 191-201. In this context see Werner Krauss, *Graciáns Lebenslehre* (Frankfurt / Main, 1947), 74ff.

39. See Krauss, *Graciáns Lebenslehre*, 108ff.

40. Gracián, *El Criticón*, 39.

41. The other side of Gracián's use of the concept *vulgo*-: he applies it to the other classes as well, since it functions as a category of thought which he uses primarily to criticize intellectual and moral corruption (see Krauss, *Graciáns Lebenslehre*, 96).

42. See Krauss, *Graciáns Lebenslehre*, 94.

43. Gracián, *El Criticón*, 185.

44. Ibid., 34, 312f.

45. Ibid., 386.

46. Ibid., 54. See Krauss, *Graciáns Lebenslehre*, 156.

47. Gracián, *El Criticón*, 384.

48. Ibid., 213.

49. Ibid., 216.

50. Ibid., 386.

51. Ibid., 410.

52. Ibid., 157-58.

53. Ibid., 383. See Krauss, *Graciáns Lebenslehre*, 89.

54. Gracián, *El Criticón*, 416.

55. Ibid., 417.

56. Ibid., 174.

57. See Krauss, *Graciáns Lebenslehre*, 138ff.

58. Ibid., 160.

59. Ibid., 121.

60. Ibid., 94.

61. Baltasar Gracián, *El Héroe*, in *El Héroe, El Discreto*, 6 ed., Colleción Austral. 49 (Madrid, 1958), 9-44, 44.

62. See Krauss, *Graciáns Lebenslehre*, 159-60; Borinski, *Baltasar Gracián*, 18, 109ff.

Chapter 4. The Adventurous Prince

1. See among others Erich Auerbach, "Frate Alberto," in Auerbach, *Mimesis: The Portrayal of Reality in Western Literature,* trans. Willard R. Trask (Princeton, 1974), 203-31.

2. Hans-Jörg Neuschäfer, *Boccaccio und der Beginn der Novelle: Strukturen der Kurzerzählung auf der Schwelle zwischen Mittelalter und Neuzeit* (Munich, 1969), 70.

3. Friedrich Engels, "Über den Verfall des Feudalismus und das Aufkommen der Bourgeoisie," in Karl Marx and Friedrich Engels, *Werke* (Berlin, 1962), 21:392-401, 396-97.

4. Yves Renouard, *Les hommes d'affaires italiens du moyen âge* (Paris, 1968), 237.

5. Michael Seidlmayer, *Geschichte Italiens: Vom Zusammenbruch des Römischen Reiches bis zum Ersten Weltkrieg* (Stuttgart, 1962), 239-40.

6. Niccolò Machiavelli, *The Prince*, trans. Leo Paul S. de Alvarez (Irving, Texas, 1980), 67.

7. Ibid., 75.

8. Ibid., 72.

9. Ibid.

10. That there are limits to this will become clear when we discuss the example: law = human being / force = animal.

11. This tendency is illustrated on p. 57 of *The Prince*, where we read: "For in every city these two different humors are to be found. Thus it is that the people desire not to be commanded or oppressed by the great, and the great desire to command and to oppress the people."

12. Hans Freyer, introduction, in Machiavelli, *Der Fürst*, trans. Ernst Merian-Genast (Stuttgart, 1961), 25.

13. Machiavelli, *The Prince*, 94.

14. Ibid., 147.

15. Ibid., 89.

16. Ibid., 107.

Chapter 5. The Business of the Adventurer

1. Not until the sixteenth century do we encounter examples of "Tristan l'adventurier" (see Robert Mandrou, *De la culture populaire aux 17e et 18e siècles* [Paris, 1975], 148), but here it is already the "successors" who use the term, and they do so sparingly.

2. Elena Eberwein, *Zur Deutung mittelalterlicher Existenz*, Kölner Romanistische Arbeiten 7 (Bonn and Cologne, 1933), 52.

3. Ibid., 29, 31, 49.

4. Frédéric Godefroy, *Dictionnaire de l'ancienne langue française et de tous ses dialectes du IXe au XVe siècle* (Paris, 1880), 1:516a-b.

5. See for instance Georges Duby in "Youth in Aristocratic Society," in Duby, *The Chivalrous Society*, trans. Cynthia Postan (Berkeley and Los Angeles, 1977), 113, who quotes from *l'Histoire de Guillaume le Maréchal:* "... ains s'esmovit en mainte terre / Por pris e aventure quere / Mais souvent s'en revenait riche..." ["then he roamed in many lands / To search for wealth and adventure / More often he came back rich"—H. Meleh].

6. *Les deux rédactions en vers du Moniage Guillaume: Chanson de Geste du XIIe siècle*, ed. Wilhelm Cloetta (Paris, 1906; reprint, 1968), 1: lines 1025-1120.

7. Ibid., 1: lines 3392-99.

8. Ernst Robert Curtius, "Über die altfranzösische Epik," *Zeitschrift für Romanische Philologie* 64 (1944): 233-320, 319.

9. See Jacques Le Goff, *Marchands et banquiers au Moyen Age* (Paris, 1969), 111-12.

10. See among others Shlomo Dov Goitein, "Artisans en Méditerranée orientale au haut moyen âge," *Annales* (1964): 847-68; and Robert S. Lopez and Irving W. Raymond, *Medieval Trade in the Mediterranean World* (New York, 1955).

11. Jacques Le Goff, *Das Hochmittelalter* (Frankfurt / Main, 1965), 145.

12. See Armando Sapori, *Le marchand italien au Moyen Age: Conférences et bibliographie*, introduction by Lucien Fèbvre (Paris, 1952), 49ff.

13. Italo Siciliano, *Les chansons de geste et l'épopée: Mythes—histoires—poèmes*, Bibliotheca di Studi francesi (Torino, 1968), 1ff.

14. On this process, see among others Henri Sée, *Französische Wirtschaftsgeschichte* (Jena, 1930), 1:57ff.

15. See among others François Hincker, "Contribution à la discussion sur la transition du féodalisme au capitalisme: la monarchie absolue française," in *Sur le féodalisme* (Paris, 1971), 61-66.

16. See Emile Coornaert, *Les corporations en France avant 1789*, 2 ed. (Paris, 1968), 44.

17. See among others Marc Bloch, *Feudal Society*, trans. L. A. Manyon (Chicago, 1961), 2:354-55.

18. See Coornaert, *Les corporations en France*, 56-57; 59.

19. Ibid., 66.

20. Pierre Vilar, "La transition du féodalisme au capitalisme," in *Sur le féodalisme*, 35-48, 38.

21. Coornaert, *Les corporations en France*, 267-68.

22. Quoted in Eleonora Mary Carus-Wilson, *Medieval Merchant Venturers: Collected Studies*, 2 ed. (London, 1967), xvi.

23. Quoted in Dietrich Walter Jöns, *Das "Sinnen-Bild": Studien zur allegorischen Bildlichkeit bei Andreas Gryphius* (Stuttgart, 1966), 195.

24. Quoted in Marianne Skowronnek, "Fortuna and Frau Welt: Zwei allegorische Doppelgängerinnen des Mittelalters," dissertation (West Berlin, 1964), 75.

25. Both quotations are from Hans Kurath and Sherman M. Kuhn, *Middle English Dictionary* (Ann Arbor, 1956 ff.), 1:547.

26. See *Middle English Dictionary*, 1:547: "No guod he hep pet et god ne he hit him y -yeve, no guodes of kende, ase uayrhede. . . ne guodes of auenture, ase richesses."

27. Quoted in Carus-Wilson, *Medieval Merchant Venturers*, xvi.

28. On the whole trade / church complex, see Le Goff, *Marchands et banquiers*, 70-98.

29. On the following, see especially Raymond S. de Roover, *L'évolution de la lettre de change, XIVe-XVIIIe siècle* (Paris, 1953). On the relationship church / moneychanging, see for instance p. 19: "Tant que les règles canoniques contre le prêt à intérêt étaient en rigueur, il était illicite d'escompter des effets de commerce, mais l'Eglise ne condamnait pas les opérations de change." [As long as canonical law prohibited moneylending for interest, it was illegal to cash commercial bills, but the Church did not prohibit moneychanging transactions.]

30. Ibid., 25.

31. See ibid., 20.

32. See Karl Marx, *Capital* (New York, 1981) 3:732: "In the Middle Ages, there was no generally prevailing interest rate in any country. The Church prohibited all interest dealings from the start. Laws and courts gave little security for loans. All the higher was the interest rate in particular cases. The low monetary circulation and the need to make most payments in cash compelled people to borrow money, and all the more so, the more undeveloped the system of bills of exchange. There was great variation in both the rate of interest and the concept of usury. In Charlemagne's time,

it was considered usurious to take 100 per cent interest. At Lindau am Bodensee in 1344, some local burghers took 216-2/3 per cent. In Zurich the town council fixed 34-1/3 per cent as the legal interest. In Italy, 40 per cent had to be paid on occasion, though from the twelfth century to the fourteenth the rate did not usually exceed 20 per cent.''

33. See Roover, *L'évolution de la lettre de change*, 20.

34. See F. A. Brockhaus, *Conversations-Lexikon. Allgemeine deutsche Real-Encyklopädie*, 12 ed. (1875-79), 7:688: "In shipping, a *high adventure contract* is a contract according to which a loan is granted for an overseas expedition that cannot be recalled in case of shipwreck. Interest on such a loan is naturally high because it includes a premium for risk-taking; but the lender can insure the advanced capital. . . . *High adventure trade* is trade by a merchant who, because of a lack of means, borrows capital and buys goods which he ships abroad to sell himself to overseas consumers. The entrepreneur is called the *aventurier*. Of course, he can still set his prices low, because his goods are not burdened with the costs of many middlemen. High adventure trade is limited to countries where large-scale trade has advantages over small-scale trade . . . recently it has declined sharply in importance.''

35. See Bruno Kuske, "Die Begriffe Angst und Abenteuer in der deutschen Wirtschaft des Mittelalters: Ein Beitrag zur Geschichte des Unternehmertums," *Zeitschrift für handelswissenschaftliche Forschung*, N.F. 1 (1949): 547-50.

36. Ibid., 548.

37. Quoted from Erich Maschke, "Das Berufsbewusstsein des mittelalterlichen Fernkaufmanns," in *Beiträge zum Berufsbewusstsein des mittelalterlichen Menschen*, Miscellanea Mediaevalia 3 (West Berlin, 1964), 306-35, 318. See also Eduard Brinckmeier, *Glossarium diplomaticum*, 2 ed. (Gotha, 1856; reprint, 1967), 1, under *aventure*.

38. Brinckmeier, *Glossarium diplomaticum*, 1.

39. Werner Welzig, "Der Wandel des Abenteurertums," in *Pikarische Welt: Schriften zum europäischen Schelmenroman*, ed. H. Heidenreich (Darmstadt, 1969), 438-54, 440.

40. Kuske, "Die Begriffe Angst und Abenteuer," 549.

41. Maschke, "Das Berufsbewusstsein des mittelalterlichen Fernkaufmanns," 318.

42. See Carus-Wilson, *Medieval Merchant Venturers*, xxxi.

43. Quoted in Kurath and Kuhn, *Middle English Dictionary*, 1:547.

44. Carus-Wilson, *Medieval Merchant Venturers*, xxix.

45. Ibid., xxix-xxx.

46. Ibid., xxx.

47. Ibid, 151.

48. Ibid.

49. Ibid., 152.

50. Ibid.

51. Ibid.

52. See ibid., 158ff.

53. Ibid., 165.

54. Ibid., 166.

55. Ibid. On the entire development during the time of Elizabeth I, see George Unwin, "The Merchant Adventurers' Company in the Reign of Elizabeth," in Unwin, *Studies in Economic History* (London, 1927).

56. On bourgeois acquisition of (courtly) manners, see Norbert Elias, *The Civilizing Process: The History of Manners*, trans. Edmund Jephcott (New York, 1978). The work is methodologically suspect but full of material.

57. As Johan Huizinga writes in *The Waning of the Middle Ages* (New York, 1954), 46-47: "This same cult of forms [that flourished at the court of princes], however, spread downwards from the nobility to the middle classes, where they lingered on, after having become obsolete in

higher circles." This view is, of course, one-sided and idealistic. The bourgeoisie struggled to acquire noble culture in order to "re-function" it to use it against the oppressor class; the role of acquisition and refunctioning of culture in class warfare has been overlooked.

58. See *The Cambridge Economic History of Europe* (Cambridge, 1952), vols. 1-3.

59. See the articles "Knighthood" and "Chivalry" in *Encyclopedia Britannica*, 1963, 13:430-36. See also Bloch, *Feudal Society*, 2:330ff.

60. See in this context Wolfgang Iser, "Mittelenglische Literatur und romanische Tradition," in *Grundriss der romanischen Literaturen des Mittelalters*, ed. Hans Robert Jauss and Erich Köhler (Heidelberg, 1972), 304-32, 311-17.

61. Geoffroy Chaucer, *The Works of Geoffroy Chaucer*, ed. F. N. Robinson, 2 ed. (London, 1957), 18: line 72.

62. Ibid., 17: lines 20ff.

63. See among others Ingeborg Spriewald, *Vom "Eulenspiegel" zum "Simplicissimus": Zur Genesis des Realismus in den Anfängen der deutschen Prosaerzählung*, Reihe Literatur und Gesellschaft (Berlin, 1974), 23ff.

64. Guillaume de Lorris and Jean de Meun, *Le Roman de la Rose*, ed. Ernest Langlois (Paris, 1914-24), 4:235-40.

65. Mikhail Bakhtin, "Epic and Novel: Toward a Methodology for the Study of the Novel," in *The Dialogic Imagination: Four Essays*, ed. Michael Holquist, trans. Caryl Emerson and Michael Holquist (Austin, 1981), 3-40, 6.

66. See among others Spriewald, *Vom "Eulenspiegel" zum "Simplicissimus,"* 91ff.

67. Sapori, *Le marchand italien au Moyen Age*, xlvi-xlvii.

68. See the attempt at structuring these data in Le Goff, *Marchands et banquiers*, 42-69.

69. Ibid., 81.

70. Ibid., 79-80.

71. German literary scholarship assigns an earlier date to the writing of this novel, but I disagree (on the dating by German literary scholars, see among others Marjatta Wis, "Nochmals zum 'Fortunatus': Quellen und Datierungsprobleme," *Neuphilologische Mitteilungen* 66 (1965): 199-209; Renate Wiemann, *Die Erzählstruktur im Volksbuch Fortunatus* (Hildesheim and New York, 1970), 1-3. On my own dating of the work, see the following text as well as note 118 below.

72. Leon Battista Alberti, *The Albertis of Florence: Leon Battista Alberti's Della Famiglia*, trans. Guido A. Guarino (Lewisburg, 1971), 177.

73. See among others Aby Warburg, "Francesco Sassetis letztwillige Verfügung," in *Gesammelte Schriften*, Bibliothek Warburg 1 (Berlin and Leipzig, reprint 1969), 127-58; Alfred Doren, *Fortuna im Mittelalter und in der Renaissance*, Bibliothek Warburg 2 / 1 (Berlin and Leipzig, 1924), 71-144, 100; Ernst Cassirer, *Individuum und Kosmos in der Philosophie der Renaissance*, Bibliothek Warburg, ed. Fritz Saxl (Berlin and Leipzig, 1927), 77ff.

74. See Marsilio Ficino's Platonic advice to the Florentine merchant Francesco Sassetti at the end of the fifteenth century: "It is good to fight Fortuna with the weapons of caution, patience, and high mindedness, it is better to withdraw and flee such a battle in which only the very few are victorious and these few only with great stress of spirit and extreme difficulty; the best is to make peace and an armistice with her, adapting our will to hers, and willingly to go where she points, so that she does not pull us there by force. We will be able to accomplish all of this if strength, wisdom, and will are united in us." (Warburg, "Rucellai letztwillige Verfügung," 148)

75. Alfred Doren, *Italienische Wirtschaftsgeschichte,* vol. 1 *of Handbuch der Wirtschaftsgeschichte*, ed. Georg Brodnitz (Jena, 1934), 658.

76. See in this context Cassirer, *Individuum und Kosmos*, 81.

77. For instance with Pontanus, see Doren, *Fortuna*, 124; Warburg, "Francesco Sassetis letztwillige Verfügung," 148ff.

78. Doren, *Italienische Wirtschaftsgeschichte*, 479.

79. See Robert Mandrou, *De la culture populaire aux 17e et 18e siècles*, 57ff., 201.

80. Karl Marx and Friedrich Engels, *Manifesto of the Communist Party*, in Marx and Engels, *Basic Writings on Politics and Philosophy* (Garden City, N.Y., 1959), 10.

81. Ibid., 9. On the role of money (and usury) in *Fortunatus*, see especially Dieter Kartschoke, "Weisheit oder Reichtum? Zum Volksbuch von Fortunatus und seinen Söhnen," in *Literatur im Feudalismus*, ed. Dieter Richter (Stuttgart, 1975), 213-59, 224ff., 236. The discussion by Walter Raitz, *Zur Soziogenese des bürgerlichen Romans: Eine literatursoziologische Analyse des "Fortunatus"* (Düsseldorf, 1973), 98, is a questionable summary of partial aspects of Marx's analysis of money; one would do better to read Marx. There is little or no relationship between Raitz's discussion and *Fortunatus*.

82. See *Fortunatus*, ed. Hans Günter, in *Neudrucke deutscher Literaturwerke* 240-41 (Halle / Saale, 1914), 135: "[Andolosia] sends for the adventurers from whom he had bought the treasure and pays them all in cash."

83. Ibid., 215.

84. Ibid., 20.

85. Ibid., 53.

86. Ibid.

87. See on the other hand, Raitz, *Zur Soziogenese des bürgerlichen Romans*, 101, who largely disputes the importance of trade (not to mention shipping) for *Fortunatus*.

88. *Fortunatus*, 6.

89. Ibid.

90. Ibid., 17.

91. Ibid., 19.

92. Ibid., 18.

93. Karl Marx, *Grundrisse: Foundations of the Critique of Political Economy*, trans. Martin Nicolaus (New York, 1973), 163.

94. Ibid., 233.

95. Ibid.

96. *Fortunatus*, 35.

97. The independently traveling merchant is a retail merchant, a small merchant, as opposed to a wholesale or long-distance merchant (this distinction begins to be found as early as the thirteenth century). The problem for the anonymous author of *Fortunatus* is: How can one accumulate enough capital to become a wholesaler, or what are the laws that effect this change?

98. The difference between Fortunatus and his father does not lie in Fortunatus's "physicality," as Raitz (*Zur Soziogenese des bürgerlichen Romans*, 56f.) maintains, but rather in the different class-struggle situation between the rising bourgeoisie and the petty nobility and knights; between the rising urban bourgeoisie and the petty nobility on the one hand and the great nobility on the other (that is, in the change in favor of the bourgeoisie). For quite apart from the fact that we learn nothing about his father's appearance (who is to say that he did not possess the same "physicality"?), the little that we learn about his activity inclines us to contradict Raitz, because Fortunatus's father also goes to tournaments, and so forth. In contrast to Fortunatus, however, his father could not afford to do that, because while the father had only accumulated or spent his treasure, Fortunatus in the meantime turns his treasure (money) into capital. He learned this lesson from the pimp! Therefore it is mere psychological speculation when Raitz writes: "For Fortunatus . . . physicality is unique and the sole constituent of his individuality. Since he is not embedded in the other guarantees of feudal existence, property, birth, and clan spirit, this is his only possibility to make his existence secure [but what about the moneybag?—M. N.] in a feudal system. For that reason, physical integrity is inalienable for him (56-57). Raitz is here adding a new speculative "explanation" for capitalism (whereby he is enriching the horde of existing speculative theses à la Sombart): the birth of capitalism out of the "physical integrity" of the capitalist!

99. See Marx, *Grundrisse*, 221.

100. *Fortunatus*, 64.

101. Ibid., 71.

102. Ibid., 72; see also 64.

103. Kartschoke, "Weisheit oder Reichtum?" 215.

104. Karl Marx, *Capital* (New York, 1977), 1:254-55.

105. *Fortunatus*, 76.

106. Walter Raitz disagrees. He obviously considers the fairy tale to be of first importance and the actual historical context to be derivative: "Fortunatus disguises his departure as a trading voyage and comes to Alexandria as a rich Cyprian merchant." (*Zur Soziogenese des bürgerlichen Romans*, 77)

107. *Fortunatus*, 78.

108. Ibid., 81.

109. Ibid., 84.

110. Ibid.

111. See Hans Mottek, *Wirtschaftsgeschichte Deutschlands: Ein Grundriss*, 5 ed. (Berlin, 1971), 1:248.

112. See *Fortunatus*, 80.

113. See Mottek, *Wirtschaftsgeschichte Deutschlands*, 1:247ff.

114. *Fortunatus*, 93.

115. Ibid., 128.

116. The anonymous author was certainly aware of the policy of the Spanish kings regarding tribute or tolls, which was to have far-reaching consequences for the Spanish monarchy (see Jaime Vicens Vives, *An Economic History of Spain* [Princeton, 1969], 311-12).

117. *Fortunatus*, 143.

118. In the special case of this novel, another historical event might well play a background role. In 1495 the Catholic Majesties Ferdinand and Isabella married their daughter Juana to the son of Maximilian I, Philip Duke of Burgundy, an event that was to influence the history of Germany and of Europe. Maximilian, as a debtor of the Fugger banking family in Augsburg, was very closely linked to the city in which the novel doubtless originated and appeared. The marriage of Agrippina and the King of Cyprus could be the literary echo of this event, as the whole piece was a political manifesto. That this is by no means pure speculation becomes apparent when we look at historical events. In 1498 the sea-trade route to India was discovered; Alexandria thus lost its "little wishing cap," which also affected the interests of Venice. In the novel, King Soldan demands his "wishing cap" back and threatens war if he does not get it: in 1498-1500 the Turks were perhaps 60 miles from Venice and were actually threatening to expand the war (see Ruggiero Romano and Alberto Tenenti, *Die Grundlegung der modernen Welt: Spätmittelalter, Renaissance, Reformation* [Frankfurt / Main, 1967], 291). In 1505, however, Jacob Fugger was already shipping East Indian wares around the Cape of Good Hope. In the same year the House of Fugger extended Emperor Maximilian a credit of seventy thousand gold gulden, for which Jacob was elevated to the nobility three years later. In 1504 Juana became queen of Spain. In 1506 Maximilian's son and Juana's husband died, making Maximilian's grandson Charles heir to the throne of Spain. In 1509 *Fortunatus* appeared in Augsburg. It is well known that the city was much involved in the above events through the Fuggers. Just as Andolosia deals almost as an equal with the King of Cyprus and the King of England and much surpasses them in wealth (and wisdom), the House of Fugger deals with the House of Hapsburg as its creditor, as the famous letter of 1523 from Jacob Fugger to Charles V, son of Juana and Philip of Burgundy, shows: "It is also known and quite clear that Your Imperial Majesty would not have attained the Roman crown without me, as I can prove by the documents of commissions from Your Imperial Majesty." (quoted in Romano and Tenenti, 320)

119. Friedrich Engels, *Dialectics of Nature* (Moscow, 1954), 29-30.

Chapter 6. The Times That Bred Giants

1. Karl Marx, *Capital* (New York, 1981), 3:1038.
2. Ibid.
3. Simon van Brakel, "Die Entwicklung und Organisation der Merchant Adventurers," *Vierteljahresschrift für Sozial- und Wirtschaftsgeschichte* 5 (1907): 401-32, 402.
4. Frederick Engels, "Supplement and Addendum to Volume 3 of *Capital*," 1038-39.
5. See William Ezra Lingelbach, *The Merchant Adventurers of England: Their Laws and Ordinances with Other Documents* (Philadelphia, 1902), 67f.; Brakel, "Merchant Adventurers," 508; Hermann Felix Crohn-Wolfgang, "Der englische Ubersee kaufmann im Zeitalter der Entdeckungen," *Zeitschrift für die gesamte Staatswissenschaft* 76 (1921): 397-426, 397.
6. See Lingelbach, *The Merchant Adventurers of England*, 174-75.
7. See ibid., 189-94; see also Brakel, "Merchant Adventurers," 414. This regulation was designed to keep adventurers from coming under foreign jurisdiction.
8. See among others Crohn-Wolfgang, "Der englische Überseekaufmann," 414f.
9. Engels, "Supplement and Addendum to Volume 3 of *Capital*," 1039-40.
10. Brakel, "Merchant Adventurers," 403.
11. See *Management Encyclopedia* (Frankfurt / Main, 1975), 8:2845ff.
12. V. I. Lenin, "The Victory of the Cadets and the Tasks of the Workers' Party," in *Collected Works* (Moscow, 1962), 10:199-276, 260: "Mr. Blank's arguments on this subject deserve the closest attention of Social-Democrats, for they provide an example of how Marx is misrepresented by quotations from Marx. Just as Brentano, Sombart, Bernstein and Co. substituted Brentanoism for Marxism by employing Marxian terminology, by quoting some of Marx's statements and by assuming a Marxist disguise."
13. Werner Sombart, *Der Bourgeois: Zur Geistesgeschichte des modernen Wirtschaftsmenschen,* 3 ed. (Munich and Leipzig, 1923), 281. The English version of this work, *The Quintessence of Capitalism: A Study of the History and Psychology of the Modern Business Man*, trans. and ed. M. Epstein (New York, 1915), translates the term *Blutsgläubigen* not quite correctly as "latent tendencies" (220).
14. Sombart knew Marx too well not to know that he was distorting him (see the praise he received from Engels in 1895 for his review of the third volume of *Capital*, in Marx and Engels, *Werke* [Berlin, 1956-71], 39:415, 427-39). In order to construct his theorems, therefore, he deliberately falsifies Marx. See for instance: "Despite these instances, however, the ranks of the middlemen or 'clothiers' were recruited for the most part from among traders; so much so that this tendency must be regarded as having been the general rule. The process has not escaped the observation of historians, Marx among them, who, reducing it to a simple formula, speaks of a gradual application of commercial capital to the work of production." *The Quintessence of Capitalism*, 95) See on the other hand, Marx, *Capital*, 3:440ff.
15. Sombart, *The Quintessence of Capitalism*, 209.
16. Ibid., 67.
17. Ibid., 337.
18. Ibid., 171.
19. Ibid., 69.
20. One should note in addition that the concept "adventure" at first meant any risky economic undertaking (including mining ventures; see Bruno Kuske, "Die Begriffe Angst und Abenteuer in der deutschen Wirtschaft des Mittelalters," *Zeitschrift für handelswissenschaftliche Forschung*, NF 1 [1949]: 548, 550). This was the case until into the sixteenth century. We saw in *Fortunatus*, for instance, that moneychanging and usury also was called "adventure" and moneychangers were designated as "adventurers."

21. Dühring, quoted by Friedrich Engels, *Anti-Dühring: Herr Eugen Dühring's Revolution in Science*, 2 ed. (Moscow, 1959), 223.

22. Engels, *Anti-Dühring*, 223-24. Karl Marx, in *Grundrisse: Foundations of the Critique of Political Economy*, trans. Martin Nicolaus (New York, 1973), had already noted: "It is a received opinion that in certain periods people lived from pillage alone. But, for pillage to be possible, there must be something to be pillaged, hence production. And the mode of pillage is itself in turn determined by the mode of production. A stock-jobbing nation, for example, cannot be pillaged in the same manner as a nation of cow-herds." (98)

To be sure, rapine and violence play an extremely important role in history (see Marx, *Capital* [New York, 1977], 1:874: "In actual history, it is a notorious fact that conquest, enslavement, robbery, murder, in short force, play the greatest part." See also *Capital*, 1:876ff., 914ff.), but as the expression of forms of political domination, they are dependent on the economic preconditions and are derived from these. To make them the precondition of economic conditions is—to use a favorite term of Marx's—all the more tasteless when as in Sombart the violent forms of past means of production, of feudalism (see in this context Engels, "Über den Verfall des Feudalismus und das Aufkommen der Bourgeoisie," in Marx and Engels, *Werke* [Berlin, 1956-1971], 21:392-401), are styled the cause of new forms of production, of capitalism, or are seen as the source of the "capitalist spirit."

23. Marx, *Capital*, 3:448.

24. Ibid., 3:447.

25. Ibid., 3:445.

26. Ibid.

27. Ibid.

28. Ibid., 1:266-67.

29. Ibid., 3:448.

30. Engels, "Supplement and Addendum to Volume 3 of *Capital*," 1040.

31. Marx, *Capital*, 3:450.

32. Engels, "Supplement and Addendum to Volume 3 of *Capital*," 1040-41.

33. See Marx, "So-called Primitive Accumulation," *Capital*, 1:873-940.

34. Ibid., 1:874-75.

35. Ibid., 1:876.

36. Marx, *Capital*, 3:448.

37. Ibid., 3:449-50.

38. Ibid., 3:450.

39. We must of course remember that this development also did not arise from nothing. See in this context Engels, "Über den Verfall des Feudalismus und das Aufkommen der Bourgeoisie," 21:393: "A certain amount of world trade had developed; the Italians navigated the Mediterranean and the Atlantic coast up to Flanders, the Hanseatic league still dominated the North Sea and the Baltic, with emerging competition from the Dutch and the English. Between the northern and southern centers of sea trade, a land connection was maintained; the routes over which this connection took place ran through Germany."

40. Marx, *Capital*, 3:450-51.

41. Karl Marx, *A Contribution to the Critique of Political Economy* (New York, 1970), 157.

42. Even the most conservative historian must concede just how fitting this observations of Engels is in the case of the very first overseas expedition, Columbus's voyage of discovery: "Apart from the mandate of discovery, the project of 1492 was a contractual trade agreement between the Spanish majesties and the Genovese Columbus. Isabella and Fernando, as rulers of Castile, brought to the undertaking the license for ocean voyages in a westerly direction and the cost of equipping the fleet, a sum of about 5,000 gold ducats of that time. Columbus, as leader of the ex-

pedition, contributed his plan and his nautical ability, and used the loans he had taken out to subsidize the costs of the voyage. On this basis the share of the profits of the contractual partners were set down in the Capitulations of Santa Fe. Columbus was to receive for each voyage one tenth of all wares and products of every kind acquired, after deducting the costs involved in their gain, and was given a one-eighth share of the costs and profits of every fleet equipped for trade with the discovered lands. As 'Admiral of the Ocean' he was entitled to adjudicate all disputes arising from trade in his jurisdiction. The other participants in Columbus's voyage, sailors, craftsmen, and doctors, received set wages, and as employees were not permitted to engage in trade themselves. Thus there was a privileged trade company, which could be called 'The Catholic Majesties and Columbus,' in which from the very beginning the private participant was in a dependent and subordinate position with respect to the power of the state." (Richard Konetzke, *Entdecker und Eroberer Amerikas* [Frankfurt / Main and Hamburg, 1963], 12-13)

43. Engels, "Supplement and Addendum to Volume 3 of *Capital*," 1041.

44. Marx, *Capital*, 3:273ff.

45. Ibid., 3:332ff.

46. Ibid., 1:582.

47. Ibid., 1:929.

48. Ibid., 3:448-49.

49. Ibid., 1:915.

50. Engels, "Über den Verfall des Feudalismus und das Aufkommen der Bourgeoisie," 21:393-94.

51. Marx, *Capital*, 3:729.

52. See in this context, ibid., 3:729. On the fact that usury continued under capitalism, see ibid., 3:735f.

53. See ibid., 3:732.

54. Ibid., 3:730.

55. Ibid.

56. On Luther, see especially Karl Marx, *Theories of Surplus-Value* (Moscow, 1971), 3:527ff.

57. Marx, *Capital* 3:731-32.

58. See for instance Martin Luther, "On Trading and Usury," in *Works of Martin Luther* (Philadelphia, 1931), 4:12-69, 65ff.

59. "Luther is *superior* to Proudhon. The difference between *lending and selling* does not confuse him, for he perceives that usury exists equally in both. The most striking feature of his polemic is that he makes his main point of attack the fact that *interest is an innate element of capital*." (Marx, *Theories of Surplus-Value*, 3:528)

60. See Marx, *Capital*, 3:431ff.

61. Ibid., 1:914-15.

62. On the relationship between usury and the credit industry in the sixteenth century, see Richard Henry Tawney, "The Financing of Capitalist Industry," in *Introduction to Thomas Wilson, A Discourse upon Usury,*" ed. Richard Henry Tawney (1925; reprint New York, n. d.), 43-60.

63. See Tawney, "The Financing of Capitalist Industry," 31ff.

64. Ibid., 60ff. See also Marx, *Capital*, 3:611-12.

65. Marx, *Capital*, 3:612.

66. Ibid., 3:612. See among other passages, Marx, *Theories of Surplus-Value*, 3:532: "At the outset capitalist production has to fight against usury to the extent that the usurer himself does not become a producer. With the establishment of capitalist production the domination of the usurer over surplus labour, a domination which depends on the continued existence of the old mode of production, ceases. The industrial capitalist collects surplus-value directly in the form of profit; he has also already seized part of the means of production and he appropriates part of the annual

accumulation directly. From this moment, and especially as soon as industrial and commerical wealth develops, the usurer—that is, the lender at interest—is a person who is differentiated from the industrial capitalist only as the result of the division of labour, but is subordinated to industrial capital.''

67. Marx, *Theories of Surplus-Value*, 3:527. See also 3:468ff.

68. Ibid., 3:534. See also Marx, *Capital*, 3:735: "The credit system develops as a reaction against usury. But this should not be misconstrued, nor by any means taken in the sense of the ancient writers, the Fathers of the Church, Luther or the early socialists. It means neither more nor less than the subordination of interest-bearing capital to the conditions and requirements of the capitalist mode of production.''

69. Marx, *Capital*, 3:505.

70. Banks sometimes offer small loans or certain investment opportunities to predominantly young customers, using a jargon the advertisers think is "youthful," but which is a vehicle for the perpetual ancient ideologemes of the ideology of adventure. (This connection will have to be examined more closely later.)

71. Marx, *Capital*, 3:735.

72. Marx, *Theories of Surplus-Value*, 3:469.

73. Thomas Wilson, *A Discourse upon Usury By Way of Dialogue and Orations, for the Better Variety and More Delight of all Those That Shall Read this Treatise (1572)*, ed. Richard Henry Tawney (1925; reprint New York, n. d.), 236. On Wilson's concept of usury, see Ernst Schulin, *Handelsstaat England: Das politische Interesse der Nation am Aussenhandel vom 16. bis ins frühe 18. Jahrhundert* (Wiesbaden, 1969), 62-64.

74. Wilson, *A Discourse upon Usury*, 155.

75. Ibid., 351f.

76. Ibid., 238 and passim.

77. See ibid., 246-47.

78. See ibid., 300.

79. See ibid., 249.

80. Ibid., 248.

81. Ibid., 249.

82. Ibid., 350.

83. Ibid., 210-22.

84. Ibid., 171.

85. Francis Bacon, "Of Usury," in *Essays, Advancement of Learning, New Atlantis, and Other Pieces*, ed. Richard Foster Jones (New York, 1937), 118.

86. Ibid., 119-20.

87. Ibid., 120-21.

88. Ibid., 121. On Bacon's concept of usury, see Schulin, *Handelsstaat England*, 63f.

89. Bacon, "Of Usury," 123. When observations of this nature are immediately decorated with quotations from Latin authors, that should not lead us to confuse cause and effect; nothing would have been further from an author like Bacon than to subject reality to nonempirical, a priori knowledge or even to the trappings of education.

90. Thomas Mun, *England's Treasure by Forraign Trade. Or the Ballance of our Forraign Trade is the Rule of our Treasure* (London, 1664; reprint Oxford, 1967), 58-59.

91. All quotations from Marx, *Capital*, 3:738. See also Marx, *Theories of Surplus-Value*, 3:527ff. On Child see Schulin, *Handelsstaat England*, 233-53. For a thorough discussion of economics in this period, see also Jürgen Kuczynski, "Wie eine Wissenschaft entsteht," in *Studien zu einer Geschichte der Gesellschaftswissenschaften* (Berlin, 1975), 1:104-72.

92. Luther, *Works of Martin Luther*, 4:33. See also Marx, *Capital*, 3:448-49.

93. Luther, *Works*, 4:34-35.

94. Ibid., 4:35.

95. Ibid.

96. Ibid., 4:33.

97. See among others Charles Lee Lewis, *Books of the Sea: An Introduction to Nautical Literature* (Annapolis, 1943), 3. On Utopia, see Karl Kautsky, *Thomas More und seine Utopie* (Berlin, 1947); and A. C. Morton, *Die englische Utopia* (Berlin, 1958), 42-75.

98. For a fundamental definition of utopia, see especially Werner Krauss, *Reise nach Utopia: Französische Utopien aus drei Jahrhunderten* (Berlin, 1964); and Arnhelm Neusüss, *Utopie: Begriff und Phänomen des Utopischen*, 2 ed. (Neuwied and West Berlin, 1972).

99. See Winfried Schröder, "Utopie," in *Philosophisches Wörterbuch*, ed. Georg Klaus and Manfred Buhr, 10 ed. (Leipzig, 1974), 2:1249ff.; as well as Schröder, "Socialismus und Kommunismus, utopischer," in *Philosophisches Wörterbuch*, 2:1131.

100. Schröder, "Utopie," 2:1249.

101. Sir Thomas More, *Utopia*, trans. Robert Adams (New York, 1975), 14. On this passage, see Marx, *Capital*, 1:880. For general information on this period, see Richard Henry Tawney, *The Agrarian Problem in the Sixteenth Century* (London, 1912; reprint New York, n.d.), 155ff.

102. More, *Utopia*, 49.

103. Ibid., 40ff.

104. Ibid., 35.

105. See among others Engels, *Anti-Dühring*, 376.

106. More, *Utopia*, 48ff.

107. Ibid., 64.

108. Ibid., 7.

109. Ibid., 64.

110. Ibid.

111. See H. Mottek, *Wirtschaftsgeschichte Deutschlands*, 5 ed. (Berlin, 1971), 1:218; Josef Kulischer, *Allgemeine Wirtschaftsgeschichte des Mittelalters und der Neuzeit* (Munich and Berlin, 1928; 4 ed., Munich and Vienna, 1971), 218: "The total value of English export trade around the middle of the sixteenth century hardly surpassed a million pounds, and most exporting at this time still fell to foreign merchants; 42 percent of exported cloth, 54 percent of skins went through the hands of the Hanseatic League, which also imported almost the entire supply of wax used in England."

112. Eleanora Mary Carus-Wilson, *Medieval Merchant Venturers: Collected Studies,* 2 ed. (London, 1967), 169.

113. More, *Utopia*, 89.

114. Ibid., 50 and 78.

115. Ibid., 26-27.

116. Ibid., 39.

117. François Rabelais, *Gargantua and Pantagruel*, trans. Sir Thomas Urquhart and Peter Motteux, Great Books of the Western World 24 (Chicago, London, and Toronto, 1952), 131.

118. More, *Utopia*, 40.

119. Rabelais, *Gargantua*, 65. On the Abbey of Thémèle, see Erich Köhler, "Die Abtei Thélème und die Einheit des Rabelaisschen Werks," *Germanisch-Romanische Monatsschrift* 9 (1959): 105-18.

120. Rabelais, *Pantagruel*, 133.

121. Ibid.

122. Ibid., 136.

123. Ibid., 137.

124. Ibid.

125. See Erich Maschke, in *Beiträge zum Berufsbewusstsein des mittelalterlichen Menschen*, Miscellanea Mediaevalis 3 (West Berlin, 1959), 308: "The efforts the long-distance merchants made for profit were on principle without limits, since the possibilities of making fortunes were limitless."

126. Doubtless, Mikhail Bakhtin is right when he sees Rabelais's number games as a means of undermining the medieval symbolism and mysticism of numbers (*Rabelais and His World*, trans. Helene Iswolsky [Cambridge, Mass. and London, 1968], 437ff.). Still, I believe that is only one side of the game, which is not excluded by nor does it exclude the other, at least as serious, side. Because the number as shown in the text contributes to expressing or characterizing the huge changes of that era in its understanding of time, space, and society, the number itself is an element of realism in art (and thus opposed to antique and medieval number mysticism).

127. Rabelais, *Pantagruel*, 127. It is highly unlikely that Rabelais, who knew his Lancelot and all the other knights of the grail, should not have intended a reference to the grail when he mentioned the "divine bottle."

128. Ibid., 131.

129. See Abel Lefranc, *Les navigations de Pantagruel* (Paris, 1905).

130. Rabelais, *Pantagruel*, 241.

131. Ibid., 222.

132. See Heinz Köller and Bernhard Töpfer, *Frankreich: Ein historischer Abriss* (Berlin, 1969), 1:215.

133. Erich Auerbach, *Mimesis: The Representation of Reality in Western Literature*, trans. Willard R. Trask (Princeton, 1974), 277.

134. On this subject, see Arnold Hauser, *The Social History of Art* (New York, n.d.), 2:4ff.

135. Auerbach, *Mimesis*, 277.

136. Rabelais, *Pantagruel*, 81.

137. Ibid., 82.

138. Ibid., 83.

139. See among others Ludwig Schrader, *Panurge und Hermes: Zum Ursprung eines Charakters bei Rabelais* (Bonn, 1958).

140. See Jean Plattard's notes in François Rabelais, *Pantagruel*, ed. Plattard (Paris, 1959), 191.

141. See Rabelais, *Pantagruel*, 245ff.

Chapter 7. The Merchant Adventurer Leaves the Ship

1. Friedrich Engels, *Dialectics of Nature* (Moscow, 1954), 30-31.

2. Friedrich Engels, *Anti-Dühring: Herr Eugen Dühring's Revolution in Science*, 2 ed. (Moscow, 1959), 375.

3. Karl Marx, *Capital* (New York, 1981), 3:453-54.

4. Ibid., 3:452.

5. Ibid., 1:488.

6. Here we must be careful to distinguish between the (commercial) capitalist who, on the basis of the development of capitalist means of production and according to its immanent laws, personally moves beyond the process of material production and circulation or is set free by that process, and the bourgeois (whether merchant or usurer) who from the Middle Ages on, after earning a fortune and perhaps performing some services at court, retired as a (feudal) landowner or imitated the nobility and lived from the income from renting his land. *The Albertis of Florence: Leon Battista Alberti's Della Famiglia* (Lewisburg, 1971), for instance, illustrates that the two phenomena can merge in periods of transition. Alberti unites a strong, enthusiastic desire to own land (196ff.) with the concept of agricultural capitalism on the one hand (240ff.) and with the establishment of (silk or wool) manufacture (204) and the resultant (and welcomed) "liberation" of the capital-

ist (or his change in function to an authority for control or supervision) on the other hand (204). Our interest in this context, however, centers on the type of the capitalist "liberated" by the immanent laws of capitalist production, capital personified.

7. See Marx, *Capital*, 1:740f.

8. Ibid., 1:254. See also ibid., 2:196-97.

9. Ibid., 1:739; "What is true for the individual capitalist, is true also for the capitalist class." (Ibid., 2:197)

10. Ibid., 1:740.

11. Ibid., 1:741.

12. Ibid., 1:667. See also especially ibid., 3:365-66.

13. Ibid., 1:635.

14. Ibid., 1:448-49.

15. Ibid., 1:449.

16. Ibid., 1:449-50. After the capitalist has personally assumed the function of controller or supervisor, in the course of the development of capitalist production he increasingly passes that function on to paid supervisors: "Just as at first the capitalist is relieved from actual labour as soon as his capital has reached that minimum amount with which capitalist production, properly speaking, first begins, so now he hands over the work of direct and constant supervision of the individual workers and groups of workers to a special kind of wage-labourer. An industrial army of workers under the command of a capitalist requires, like a real army, officers (managers) and N.C.O.s (foremen, overseers), who command during the labour process in the name of capital. The work of supervision becomes their established and exclusive function." (Ibid., 1:450)

17. "The proletariat created by the breaking-up of the bands of feudal retainers and by the forcible expropriation of the people from the soil, this free and rightless proletariat could not possibly be absorbed by the nascent manufactures as fast as it was thrown upon the world. On the other hand, these men, suddenly dragged from their accustomed mode of life, could not immediately adapt themselves to the discipline of their new condition. They were turned in massive quantities into beggars, robbers and vagabonds, partly from inclination, in most cases under the force of circumstances. Hence at the end of the fifteenth and during the whole of the sixteenth centuries, a bloody legislation against vagabondage was enforced throughout Western Europe. The fathers of the present working class were chastised for their enforced transformation into vagabonds and paupers. Legislation treated them as 'voluntary' criminals, and assumed that it was entirely within their powers to go on working under the old conditions which in fact no longer existed." (Ibid., 1:896)

18. Engels, *Anti-Dühring*, 377. How the virtues that are forced upon the proletariat in its hierarchical subordination can then become revolutionary virtues will be investigated later.

19. Ibid., 376.

20. See in this context Marx, *Capital*, 3:414-15.

21. Engels, "Supplement and Addendum to Volume 3 of *Capital*," 1021.

22. See Bruno Kuske, "Die Begriffe Angst und Abenteuer in der deutschen Wirtschaft des Mittelalters," *Zeitschrift für handelswissenschaftliche Forschung* N.F. 1 (1949): 550.

23. Engels, *Anti-Dühring*, 145.

24. Ibid., 145-46.

25. Ibid., 146.

26. Karl Marx, *Grundrisse: Foundations of the Critique of Political Economy*, trans. Martin Nicolaus (New York, 1973), 162. See also Marx, *Capital*, 1:733ff.

27. *Fortunatus*, ed. Hans Günter, in *Neudrucke deutscher Literaturwerke* 240-41 (Halle / Saale, 1914), 61-62. See also p. 3, where we are told that Fortunatus is distinguished by

a combination of language ability and talent in trade, and p. 42, where the language abilities of a figure named Lüpoldus are emphasized—they are part of the reason Fortunatus employs him as an adviser.

28. See Alfred Doren, *Italienische Wirtschaftsgeschichte*, vol. 1 of *Handbuch der Wirtschaftsgeschichte*, ed. Georg Brodnitz (Jena, 1934), 480-81. On the merchant handbooks, see among others Jacques Le Goff, *Marchands et banquiers au Moyen Age* (Paris, 1969), 99-124.

29. Francis Bacon, *The Works of Francis Bacon*, ed. James Spedding et al. (London, 1857-74), 1:210.

30. See in this context the conclusion of John Aikin from the year 1795, quoted by Marx in *Capital*, 1:741-42, in which this development is described.

31. Martin Luther, "On Trading and Usury," in *Works of Martin Luther* (Philadelphia, 1931), 4:29-30.

32. Marx, *Capital*, 3:588.

33. See L. A. Boiteux, *La "Fortune de mer": Le besoin de sécurité et les débuts de l'assurance maritime*, Ecole pratique des Hautes Etudes, Paris Ve section, Centre de recherches historiques, Publications Série Ports, routes trafic, 24 (Paris, 1968).

34. See Armando Sapori, *Le marchand italien au Moyen Age* (Paris, 1953), xxxff. See also the documents in Robert S. Lopez and Irving W. Raymond, *Medieval Trade in the Mediterranean World* (New York, 1955), 174ff.

35. Luther, "On Trading and Usury," 4:30.

36. See Simon van Brakel, "Die Entwicklung und Organisation der Merchant Adventurers," *Vierteljahresschrift für Sozial- und Wirtschaftsgeschichte* 5 (1907): 401-32, 414f.

37. Luther, "On Trading and Usury," 4:28-29.

38. See Günther Rudolph, "Thomas Müntzers sozialökonomische Konzeption und das Traditionsbewusstsein der sozialistischen Arbeiterbewegung," *Deutsche Zeitschrift für Philosophie* 4 (1975): 558-69, 567-68.

39. Luther, "Treatise on Usury," 4:46.

40. Luther, "On Trading and Usury," 4:34.

41. See Brakel, "Merchant Adventurers," 410, 413.

42. See ibid., 413. On the whole process see Eleonora Mary Carus-Wilson, *Medieval Merchant Venturers: Collected Studies*, 2 ed. (London, 1967).

43. Brakel, "Merchant Adventurers," 411.

44. See William Ezra Lingelbach, *The Merchant Adventurers of England: Their Laws and Ordinances with Other Documents* (Philadelphia, 1902), xxxi.

45. See ibid., xxxix; on the history, see ibid., xxix.

46. It is noteworthy that under pressure from the adventurers a group of staplers from Newcastle even joined them (see Brakel, "Merchant Adventurers," 415-16).

47. See Hermann Felix Crohn-Wolfgang, "Der englische Überseekaufmann im Zeitalter der Entdeckungen," *Zeitschrift für die gesamte Staatswissenschaft* 76 (1921): 397-426, 422.

48. Ibid., 411ff.

49. Brakel, "Merchant Adventurers," 418.

50. Ibid., 424.

51. Ibid., 422.

52. Ibid.

53. Ibid., 423.

54. See Crohn-Wolfgang, "Der englische Überseekaufmann," 410-11.

55. Ibid., 424. On the other hand, see Brakel, "Merchant Adventurers," 425.

56. Brakel, "Merchant Adventurers," 419.

57. Ibid., 420.

58. Ibid., 421.

59. Ibid., 423.

60. Ibid., 424.

61. Crohn-Wolfgang's essay "Der englische Überseekaufmann" is a model of misinterpretation. He starts out from Max Weber's position and draws completely false conclusions about the self-awareness of the adventurer burgher (especially as concerns his confrontations with the nobility). For instance, he mentions (400) a "tendency to form guilds" emerging from the "personal qualification" (caste consciousness) of the burgher or the merchant at the time of Elizabeth I—as if there had been no guilds in the Middle Ages. The tendency during Elizabeth's reign was the dissolve those guilds!

62. Thomas Wilson, *A Discourse upon Usury By Way of Dialogue and Orations, for the Better Variety and More Delight of all Those That Shall Read this Treatise* (1572), ed. Richard Henry Tawney (1925; reprint New York, n.d.), 203.

63. Richard Hakluyt, *The Principal Navigations Voyages Traffiques & Discoveries of the English Nation* (New York, 1965), 2:114-47, 137.

64. See Crohn-Wolfgang, "Der englische Überseekaufmann," 423-24.

65. Hakluyt, *Principal Navigations*, 2:178.

66. Ibid., 2:166.

67. Ibid., 2:159.

68. Ibid., 2:163.

69. Ibid., 2:204.

70. John Milton, *A Brief History of Moscovia*, in *The Works of John Milton* (New York, 1931-38), 18:327-83, 363-82.

71. Hakluyt, *Principal Navigations*, 2:305.

72. Ibid., 2:243.

73. This led Werner Sombart to the usual speculations about the birth of the "capitalist spirit" from this privateering (Sombart, *The Quintessence of Capitalism: A Study in the History and Pyschology of the Modern Business Man,* trans and ed. M. Epstein [New York, 1915,] 63ff.).

74. Hakluyt, *Principal Navigations*, 7:89-131, 113ff.

75. On the English translation, the *Courtier* by Sir Thomas Hobby, see Robert Weimann, *Drama und Wirklichkeit in der Shakespearezeit: Ein Beitrag zur Entwicklungsgeschichte des elisabethanischen Theaters* (Halle, 1958), 110ff. The following quotation from Weimann, 112, makes clear that the courtly glorification of adventure was opposed to the bourgeoisie: "You know in great matters and adventures in warres the true provocation is glory: and who so for lucres sake. . . taketh it in hand. . . deserveth not the name of a gentleman, but is a most vile merchaunt."

76. In *The Works of Edmund Spenser*, ed. Edwin Greenlaw et al. (Baltimore, 1932-45), 1:97.

77. See Walter Raleigh, "The English Voyages of the Sixteenth Century," in Hakluyt, *Principal Navigations*, 12:1-120, 48f.

78. See *Oxford English Dictionary* (Oxford, 1933; new ed. 1961), 1:136a; 12:113a, s. v. *venture* (one example is taken from Shakespeare's *Henry IV*: "There's a whole Marchant's venture of Burdeux-Stuffe in him.").

79. See Crohn-Wolfgang, "Der englische Überseekaufmann," 416. On the other hand, see the discussion on the fundamental ideological (class) antagonism in Weimann, *Drama und Wirklichkeit in der Shakespearezeit*, 106-39.

80. See among others Crohn-Wolfgang, "Der englische Überseekaufmann," 412ff.

81. Quoted in ibid., 416. On trade activity among the nobility see Ernst Schulin, *Handelsstaat England: Das politische Interesse der Nation am Aussenhandel vom 16. bis ins frühe 18. Jahrhundert* (Wiesbaden, 1969), 58f.

82. See Raleigh, "The English Voyages," 12:55.

83. Ibid., 12:68.

84. Quoted from Bacon, "Declaration concerning Sir Walter Raleigh," in *Works*, 13:384-413, 387-88.

85. See the discussion in Weimann, *Drama und Wirklichkeit in der Shakespearezeit*, 200ff.

86. It is well known that even thoroughly competent bourgeois economic historians fall victim to rapt speculation when they come to speak about the capitalist, the *homo novus* of the early capitalist era. They normally take an immediate leap into explaining capitalism by means of the "capitalist spirit" and the like. One example of this can be found in Doren, *Italienische Wirtschaftsgeschichte*, 654-56, where we can identify the methodological errors with precision.

First error: Neither the position of the capitalist in the capitalistic process of production nor that process itself is used in the analysis of the capitalist individual. To be sure, Doren is somewhat skeptical about the concept of the "capitalist spirit," especially in its Sombartian version, but in the end he simply replaces this concept with a list of the capitalist's mental qualities: "The image of the commercial and monetary economy of early capitalism would be incomplete, however, without a consideration of the *new type of man* that this new system created and who then undertook to mold it in his own image. This new type is the *capitalist entrepreneur,* whom we encounter, certainly not yet completely mature but present in his essential features, as one of the first figures gradually to outgrow the religious and social constraints of the individual in the Middle Ages. I think the decisive thing about him is not that he represents the capitalist spirit, the 'will to earn,' in the sense of the Fuggers' famous slogan, . . . but that he represents a type of human being who, although in the depths of his soul he still has many roots in the solid medieval belief in God and the saints, recognizes the goal for his *earthly* life in the *conquest* and *taming of the world and of human beings through his own strength, through virtù*. This goal is no longer seen as being in the service of God, of the Savior, of courtly love, of the grail, of warriorlike daredeviltry for the joy of battle and victory, but is understood in the sense of fruitful utilization and harnessing of his own material capital, and soon also of the capital that others put at his disposal, by unbridled engagement of his own seemingly boundless initiative and ability in enterprise, and finally by the employment and utilization of workers, insofar as they offered themselves to him, in order make ends meet, at terms favorable to him."

Second error: The abstraction from historical reality or from the actual process of production and from the actual means of production leads to arbitrariness in treating the superstructure, in order to "explain" by means of the superstructure what the abstraction from actual historical process or the process of production and the displacement of "history" into speculation about the mind of the capitalist individual have distorted, veiled, and made unrecognizable. In this case (and this is what makes Doren so interesting for the present work, because he reveals in an exemplary way the falsity of using the intellectual historical explanation of the development of capitalism out of the capitalist's tendency toward adventure; for this reason he is quoted extensively), the bourgeois scholar uses a constructed ideology of adventure, demonstrably drawn from the most heterogeneous sources and impossible to harmonize with historical reality. See, for instance, how Doren shies away from the historical merchant adventurer and turns instead to a merchant adventurer "in the broadest sense," who never existed but who is now brought forth as a witness. In doing this Doren never asks who produced this ideology of adventure or its individual elements, who used it at what time for what purpose, whether class antagonisms are even perhaps manifest in it—not even whether any capitalist ever used this product (created in the twentieth century): "It is the 'merchant adventurer'—the word taken in its broadest sense, not in the narrow sense of the English merchants—who was born at that time, at least in the Christian world; the freebooter, for whom this world to its farthest known limits serves for him to know it and—chiefly in an economic sense—subjugate it; and who finally—Columbus!—bursts its limits and expands them. He incorporates feudal knightly elements into his ranks and takes over from them the martial virtues of knighthood, love of adventure, a desire for faraway places."

At the end of the sixteenth century we encounter false appearance in the glorification of adventure (completely recognized by its contemporaries as such), and we recognize it as the self-contradictory result of ideological, materially based class antagonisms, a result splintering into its individual components and investigate its historically variable causes and functions. This same false appearance serves as the basis for the bourgeois historian of economics, Doren, to write economic history!

87. In my opinion, Lenin's concept of the "assimilated, refashioned" appropriation ("On Proletarian Culture," in V. I. Lenin, *Collected Works* [Moscow, 1966], 31:317) is better than the Brecht-Eissler term, "refunctioning," although both terms doubtless mean the same, since Lenin's concept brings out the fact that the object necessarily changes in the assimilation and is therefore no longer the same; Brecht's, on the other hand, allows one to think of the object as remaining the same. It does not change, but instead is only employed in unchanged form for another purpose. But that is not the way in which the process of assimilation of the culture of one class by another works.

88. See Weimann, *Drama und Wirklichkeit in der Shakespearezeit*, 183ff. On other portrayals of burghers in the role of adventuring knights, see 200ff.

89. William Shakespeare, *The First Part of Henry The Fourth*, in Shakespeare, *Twenty-three Plays and the Sonnets*, ed. Thomas Mark Parrott (New York, 1938), 1.2.137-58. All quotations from this play are from this edition; I give act, scene, and lines in the text.—R. C.

90. William Shakespeare, *The Second Part of Henry the Fourth*, in ibid., 2.2.118-46.

91. See John Dover Wilson, "The Copy for the Merchant of Venice, 1600," in William Shakespeare, *The Merchant of Venice*, ed. Arthur Quiller-Couch (Oxford, 1926), 91-119. The time of writing must lie between about 1594 and 1598.

92. W. H. Auden, "Brothers and Others," in *Shakespeare's Comedies: An Anthology of Modern Criticism*, ed. Laurence Lerner (London, 1967), 138-54, 138.

93. Ibid., 139.

94. Robert Weimann, *Shakespeare und die Tradition des Volkstheaters: Soziologie, Dramaturgie, Gestaltung* (Berlin, 1967), 270.

95. William Shakespeare, *The Merchant of Venice*, in Shakespeare, *Twenty-three Plays and the Sonnets*, ed. Parrott, 3.2.271-72.

96. See especially Crohn-Wolfgang, "Der englische Überseekaufmann," 426. He even ventures the following formulations: "How insignificant must have been the social position of the English merchant and the role which he played in the life of the nation can best be seen from the circumstance that Shakespeare, who like no other poet before or since gave a complete picture of his nation and all its social classes, never, not even among the extras, allows an English merchant to appear. Antonio is a Venetian nobleman, a Renaissance figure in appearance, life-style, and manner, and no English burgher could have served as a model for the poet, even unconsciously." Not even Sir Thomas Gresham? and others of that significance? Why not? But whatever the case, the typically Renaissance features of Antonio's "appearance" and "life style" do not reveal themselves in the reading. Antonio's life style is not presented (except for his commerce with the Jews), and his appearance is so pallid that no particulars can be detailed.

97. See the commentary by S. B. Liljegren in his edition of James Harrington, *Oceana: Skrifter utgivna av Vetenskaps-Societeten* (Lund-Heidelberg, 1924), 228-29.

98. "The Englishman Thomas More described in his *Utopia* a country in which just conditions prevailed—it was quite a different land from the one he lived in, but it was similar, except for the conditions." (Bert Brecht, "Fünf Schwierigkeiten beim Schreiben der Wahrheit," in *Gesammelte Werke* [Frankfurt / Main, 1967], 18:232)

99. See "Introduction" to *Merchant*, ed. Quiller-Couch, vi.

100. Let us just mention that Shakespeare himself emphasizes this. Salerio says (1.1.38) that he would be as "sad" as Antonio if he had ships at sea like Antonio and thought about the dangers

they— like the "Wealthy Andrew"—were running. The commentary to the Quiller-Couch edition of *Merchant* (123) notes that a ship of this name was seized by the Duke of Essex in 1596, but in July 1597 it suffered heavy storm damage; the courtroom scene is modeled after the highest English court of the time (159); a ship of Antonio's sinks near the Goodwins in the English Channel.

101. In his *Shakespeare*, 2 ed. (Leipzig, 1850), 2:65f., Georg Gottfried Gervinus writes that Antonio is suffering from the "disease of the rich, who have not been shaken or tested by anything and have never experienced the pressures of the world. He is spleenish, he is melancholy; a sadness has seized him whose source no one knows." Levin L. Schücking, on the other hand, in *Die Charakterprobleme bei Shakespeare: Eine Einführung in das Verständnis des Dramatikers* (Leipzig, 1919), 170-71, sees the reason for Antonio's melancholy in the fact that Shakespeare was using an unknown model and adopted from it the melancholy without its explanation. However, most scholars tend to take the relationship between Antonio and Bassanio as the basis for explaining Antonio's melancholy. Interpretations of this sort range from the contention that Shakespeare wanted to expand the friendship / love discussion by one more variant (commentary to Quiller-Couch edition of *Merchant*, 122-23) to more or less open allegations of Antonio's homosexuality (see for instance Auden, "Brothers and Others," 149f.).

102. Jürgen Kuczinsky, "Shakespeare: Dramatiker des Bürgertums in der Zeit des Übergangs vom Feudalismus zum Kapitalismus," in *Studien über Schöne Literatur und Politische Ökonomie* (Berlin, 1954), 7-16, 10-11.

103. Auden, "Brothers and Others," 152.

104. Kuczinsky, "Shakespeare," 10.

105. Marx, *Capital*, 1:914. See in this context the Soviet Shakespeare scholar Alexander Anikst, "Der Kaufmann von Venedig," in *Shakespeare Jahrbuch* (Weimar, 1966), 209-66, 214-15. Anikst relates Shakespeare's play to the sentences quoted from Marx and concludes correctly: "One can only be astonished at the clarity of vision with which the great dramatist saw the social situation."

106. Although we must assume that Shakespeare meant the sum of three thousand ducats only symbolically, we must also assume that it was symbolically high, for a huge sum was necessary to equip a large ship. Quiller-Couch ("Introduction" to *Merchant*, xxiii) is too naive in asserting that Antonio's friends do not really care about him, otherwise they would have let him have the three thousand ducats to pay his debt to Shylock.

107. See Auden, "Brothers and Others," 148-50.

108. It would still make more sense to revert to the traditional intellectual-historical "explanation" that Antonio's melancholy was a variation on a popular literary topos of the Renaissance (on melancholy see among others Erwin Panofsky and Fritz Saxl, *Melancholie*, 2 ed. [New York, 1961]). Of course Shakespeare was familiar with these topoi and used them, but he used them operatively, that is, for a purpose, to say something, to portray something. Understanding this specific use seems to me the true task of the reader / interpreter.

109. William Shakespeare, *The Taming of the Shrew*, in *The Complete Works of William Shakespeare*, ed. William Aldis Wright (Garden City, 1936), 1.2.64-75. All quotations from this play are from this edition.

110. Marx, *Capital*, 1:230.

111. "Introduction" to *Merchant*, ed. Quiller-Couch, xxiv.

112. Engels on Karl Grün's interpretation of an (adventure) proverb of Goethe, in "German Socialism in Prose and Verse," in Marx and Engels, *Collected Works* (New York, 1976), 6:49-73, 261.

113. Alberti, *Della Famiglia*, 252.

114. See Auden, "Brothers and Others," 143ff. E. C. Pettet has greater expertise in the matter, but draws more problematic conclusions in "*The Merchant of Venice* and the Problem of Usury," in *Essays and Studies* (n.p., 1945), 31:19-33.

115. That such an interpretation is also hinted at by other figures of the play is made clear in

the dialogue between Salanio and Salerio. Salanio reports that Antonio has met with a business disaster. "SALANIO:. . . But is it true, without any / slips of prolixity or crossing the plain highway / of talk, that the good Antonio, the honest An- / tonio,—O that I had a title good enough to / keep his name company!— / SALERIO: Come, the full stop. / SALANIO: Ha! what sayest thou? Why, the / end is, he hath lost a / ship." (3.1.12-20) It is hard not to take Solanio's speech as ironic.

116. Note the passage where Antonio suddenly demands that Shylock lend him money not as a friend but as an enemy (1,3). The medieval Church viewed usury as permissible between strangers or enemies, as Shakespeare could have known for instance from Thomas Wilson's *A Discourse upon Usury*, 222, 237, 255-57, 283.

117. Shylock says about Launcelot Gobbo when the latter moves into Bassanio's service: "Therefore I part with him; and part with him / To one that I would have him help to waste / His borrow'd purse." (2.5.49-51)

118. Shylock calls Antonio a "good man" and adds: ". . . my meaning / in saying he is a good man is to have you un- / derstand me, that he is sufficient. Yet his / means are in supposition: he hath an argosy / bound to Tripolis, another to the Indies; I / understand, moreover, upon the Rialto, he hath a third at Mexico, a fourth for Eng- / land, and other ventures he hath, squandered / abroad. But ships are but boards, sailors but / men; there be land-rats and water-rats, land- / thieves and water-thieves, I mean pirates, and / then there is the peril of waters, winds, / and rocks." (1.3.15-26)

119. See Max Weber, *Wirtschaftsgeschichte*, 3 ed. (West Berlin, 1958), 183.

120. See Marx, *Capital*, 3:748.

121. See Francis Bacon, "Of Usury," in *Essays, The Advancement of Learning, New Atlantis, and Other Pieces*, ed. Richard Foster Jones (New York, 1937), 118ff.

122. Antonio, for example, says: "I am a tainted wether of the flock, / Meetest for death: the weakest kind of fruit / Drops earliest to the ground, and so let me." (4.1.114-16) These other merchants, however, are not highlighted, are not named or described in their activity.

123. On this issue see Anikst, "Der Kaufmann von Venegic," 111-12, and Pettet, "*Merchant* and the Problem of Usury," 19ff.

124. Bassanio hesitates and demands that Antonio not sign the bond with this provision, but Antonio is completely sure of himself: "Within these two months, that's a month before / This bond expires, I do expect return / Of thrice three times the value of this bond." (1.3.158-60)

125. *Die heilige Johanna der Schlachthöfe*, in Brecht, *Gesammelte Werke*, 2:685.

126. When Antonio explains that he is not sad because of love, Salanio responds: "Not in love neither? Then let us say you are sad, / Because you are not merry; and 'twere as easy / For you to laugh and leap and say you are merry, / Because you are not sad. Now, by two-headed Janus, / Nature hath fram'd strange fellows in her time." (1.1.47-51)

127. Harold C. Goddard, *The Meaning of Shakespeare* (Chicago and London, 1951), 90-91, correctly states that the terms "directly" and "venture" must have a special significance in this dialogue between Shylock and Antonio. But he misses this significance by identifying the activities of Shylock and Antonio and then by submitting Antonio's arguments to a psychological analysis. Analyzing Antonio's unconscious, Goddard concludes that if Antonio does not understand Shylock's arguments concerning usury, that is because "Antonio was created for nobler things." (91) That may be true. But who created Antonio? Would it not be better to analyze Shakespeare's consciousness instead of Antonio's unconscious?

128. See Gustav Landauer, *Shakespeare, Dargestellt in Vorträgen*, ed. Martin Buber (Frankfurt/Main, 1920), 1:51f., and Pettet, "*Merchant* and the Problem of Usury," 21, 25.

129. The fact that in Shakespeare's time there were no Jews or no Jewish usurers remaining in England is hardly the discovery of modern Shakespeare research. Rather, it played a role in the contemporary discussion of usury. In Thomas Wilson's *A Discourse upon Usury*, for instance,

we read about Jewish usurers before they were driven out of England: "These Iewes are gone. Would God the Christyans remayninge and our country men at this time dyd not use theire fashyons." (378) This is clearly the context in which the *Merchant of Venice*, or the use of a Jew as a criticism of English usurers of the age, is to be understood.

130. Marx, *Capital*, 1:918.

131. Although they are always ready with polemics against the Spanish, even when they are essentially referring to themselves (see Francis Bacon, "Advertisement Touching an Holy Warre" [1622], in *Works*, 7:1-36, 20-22).

132. Marx, *Capital*, 1:917.

133. See Shylock's famous speech (3.1.60-76): "I am a Jew. Hath / not a Jew eyes? hath not a Jew hands, organs, / dimensions, senses, affections, passions?"

134. John Palmer, "Shylock," in *Shakespeare's Comedies*, ed. Lerner, 127-37, 135, was correct about this matter: "Shylock, carrying his hatred to extremes, exposes the injustice and ferocity of the social institutions from which it springs. He appeals to the twin laws of retribution and property on which the society in which he lives is based."

135. Antonio comments, when Salanio says that the Doge would not permit Shylock to take his pound of flesh: "The Duke cannot deny the course of law: / For the commodity that strangers have / With us in Venice, if it be denied, / Will much impeach the justice of the state; / Since that the trade and profit of the city / Consisteth of all nations." (3.3.26-31) See also Shylock's first speech before the court, 4.1.35-62.

136. "...there is no power in Venice / Can alter a decree established: / 'Twill be recorded for a precedent, / And many an error by the same example / Will rush into the state. It cannot be." (4.1.18-22)

137. Gustav Landauer, in *Shakespeare*, noted the oddness of designating Shylock as "old Shylock" in contrast to the names of the others (1:51), but concludes that this "old" serves the duke's purpose before the court of contrasting that ugly name with the harmonious name of Antonio. This becomes problematic, however, because Shylock earlier (2.5.2) calls himself "old Shylock."

138. Landauer's cardinal mistake in interpretation is his failure to distinguish between these two aspects. He sees Shylock as the "representative of a downtrodden, oppressed class" (*Shakespeare*, 1:66). Nor is Shylock a representative of the "underworld" (1:66); he represents medieval usurer's capital and in this function the feudal Middle Ages (along with petty nobility, princes, and so forth), and that is harmful multiplicity enough.

139. The connection between the feudal usury system or feudalism altogether and the enforced ignorance and sequestration of (young) women is one of Molière's main themes. This sequestration might be due to the exigencies of feudal land ownership and its attendant life style: only the first-born son could inherit, and daughters were preferably shunted off into nunneries.

140. Interestingly, according to reliable handbooks like Jacques Savary des Bruslon's *Dictionnaire de Commerce*, English was not considered a commercial language even well into the eighteenth century.

141. In Brecht, "Fünf Schwierigkeiten beim Schreiben der Wahrheit." On the class situation of the nobility in that era see also Lawrence Stone, *The Crisis of the Aristocracy 1558-1640* (Oxford, 1965).

142. See Bacon, *Works*, 12:289.

143. Ibid., 12:291.

144. See in this context the arguments against *contemplatio* in Francis Bacon, *De Dignitate et Augmentis scientiarum*, in *Works*, 1:698.

145. Sigmund Freud, "The Theme of the Three Caskets," in *The Standard Edition of the Complete Psychological Works of Sigmund Freud*, ed. and trans. James Strachey (London, 1958), 12 (1911-13): 291-301, 291.

146. Ibid., 12:292.

147. Freud, "Portia's Verbal Slip," in *Shakespeare's Comedies*, ed. Lerner, 123-24.

148. Freud, "The Theme of the Three Caskets," 12:291-92.

149. It is by no means unlikely that Shakespeare associated gold and silver with the idea of the pope and the (Spanish) emperor: "an image of pope and emperor as the two 'great lights' that God set in the firmament, according to the figural interpretation of Genesis 1:3-19, current in the Middle Ages—the 'larger'—the sun, which sheds its own light, the pope—and a 'smaller'—the moon, which receives its light from the sun." (Karl Maurer, "Dante als politischer Dichter," *Poetica* 2 [1975]: 158-88, 167-68) In this context, see Portia's reflections on light in 5.1.89-97.

150. See among others the notes on the starry firmament and the music of the spheres in *Merchant*, ed. Quiller-Couch, 167ff.

151. See "Introduction" to *Merchant*, ed. Quiller-Couch, xxx: "One would like to believe that against Venice with its moral emptiness, Shakespeare consciously and deliberately opposed Belmont (the Hill Beautiful) as the residence of that better part of the Renaissance, its 'humanities,' its adoration of beauty, its wistful dreams of a golden age."

152. Even where Gervinus determines that Portia is the character who holds all the strings, dominates all the other characters, and is essentially the complementary figure to Antonio, he does not draw the conclusion to which Shakespeare was clearly pointing (*Shakespeare*, 2 ed. [Leipzig, 1850], 2:67ff.).

153. Shakespeare unequivocally indicates the connotation when Portia is mentioned for the first time (1.1.165-66): "Her name is Portia," Bassanio explains to Antonio and adds: "nothing undervalued / To Cato's daughter, Brutus' Portia." Shakespeare refers explicitly to M. Porcius Cato. The name of the *porcia gens* "was derived by the Romans from *porcus*, a pig, and was compared with *Ovinius, Caprilius*, and *Taurus* . . . (Plut. *Public.* 11; Varr. *de R. R.* ii, 1). (*A Dictionary of Greek and Roman Biography and Mythology*, ed. William Smith [reprint New York, 1967], 3:498) We know that in the emblemata of the sixteenth century, a pig is frequently associated with Fortuna, as is the quest for the "golden fleece": ". . . her sunny locks / Hang on her temples like a golden fleece; / Which makes her seat of Belmont Colchos' strand, / And many Jasons come in quest of her." (*Merchant*, 1.1.169-72) To make it more evident still, Bassanio claims that if he had the means to compete he would "questionless be fortunate." But there exists still another surprising aspect. In 1928, W. Landsdown Goldsworthy, in a study whose speculative character does not interest us here, drew attention to the fact that the 1546 edition of Alciati's *Emblemata* introduced an "entirely new Emblem" bearing the Motto, *In dies meliora*, and illustrated by a curious Device of a Boar's head upon a dish." (*Shake-Speare's Heraldic Emblems; Their Origin and Meaning* [London, 1928], 21) This emblem was replaced in Christopher Plantin's 1577 edition of the *Emblemata* by a more elaborated one which continued to bear the motto *In dies meliora (In better days):* "The earlier Device of a Boar's head upon a dish is replaced in the later by several of Bacon's wellknown Emblems, there being a Boar with a Motto, *Ulterius*, the equivalent of *Plus Ultra*, placed above it, and twin Pillars with the Motto, *Plus Ultra*." (22)

154. See among others Alfred Doren, *Fortuna im Mittelalter und in der Renaissance*, Vorträge der Bibliothek Warburg 2/1 (Berlin and Leipzig, 1924), 71-144, 101ff., 116f., 124ff.

155. See Howard R. Patch, *The Goddess Fortuna in Mediaeval Literature* (New York, 1967; reprint of 1927 edition), 132ff.

156. Ibid., 140.

157. Ibid., 136ff.

158. Ibid., 146. Compare Francis Bacon, "Fortune is like the Milky Way; a knot of impenetrable virtues without names" (*De Dignitate*, in *Works*, 1:693).

159. On Fortune and the stars see also Patch, *Goddess Fortuna*, 76ff.

160. See Tommaso Campanella, "La Città del Sole," in *Opere di Giordano Bruno e di*

Tommaso Campanella, ed. Augusto Guzzo and Romano Amerio (Milan and Naples, 1956), 1098, note 2.

161. Patch, *Goddess Fortuna*, 50.

162. Portia and Nerissa appear on the stage, which is darkened to represent night. Portia remarks: "That light we see is burning in my hall. / How far that little candle throws his beams! / So shines a good deed in a naughty world." Nerissa replies: "When the moon shone, we did not see the candle." At this point Portia comments about the larger and smaller lights, sun / moon, king / substitute. (5.1.89-97)

163. See Patch, *Goddess Fortuna*, 3; Doren, *Fortuna*, 95.

164. See Patch, *Goddess Fortuna*, 80-81. On the wheel of fortune in Shakespeare, see Doren, *Fortuna*, 139.

165. See Patch, *Goddess Fortuna*, 63; Doren, *Fortuna*, 95.

166. See Patch, *Goddess Fortuna*, 67.

167. Ibid., 74.

168. See a note by Quiller-Couch, ed., in *Merchant*, 162: "The whole Bellario business is left very obscure.... It seems possible ... that the old play had a Bellario scene of some kind."

169. On Fortune with her sphere and Mercury with the *sedes quadrata*, see Doren, *Fortuna*, 136f.

170. Quoted in Patch, *Goddess Fortuna*, 136.

171. See ibid., 48-49.

172. Giordano Bruno, "Spaccio della bestia trionfante," in *Opere di Giordano Bruni e di Tommaso Campanella*, 529-30. On the *Spaccio* see Ernst Cassirer, *Individuum und Cosmos in der Philosophie der Renaissance* (1927; reprint Darmstadt, 1974), 78f.

173. See Gustav Landauer, *Shakespeare*, 1:51.

174. "Introduction" to *Merchant*, ed. Quiller-Couch, xxxi.

175. See Patch, *Goddess Fortuna*, 39f.

176. Heinrich Heine, "Shakespeares Frauen und Mädchen," in *Werke und Briefe,* ed. Hans Kaufmann (Berlin, 1961-64), 5:545.

177. "Introduction" to *Merchant*, ed. Quiller-Couch, xx.

178. Ibid., xiii-xiv.

179. Auden, "Brothers and Others," 153, sees this differently. Jessica embodies the opposite sin to her father's: prodigality instead of avarice. But what is that supposed to mean? Why does Jessica come to Belmont? Shakespeare was no mystery-play writer. John Palmer ("Shylock," 134) has another thesis: he thinks that Shakespeare needed Jessica to make Shylock's behavior before the court understandable.

Chapter 8. From the Glorification of Adventure to the Thesis of *Bellum Omnium contra Omnes*

1. See Annemarie Pietzker, *Der Kaufmann in der elisabethanischen Literatur* (Quakenbrück i. Hann., 1931; diss. Freiburg / Breisgau), 30. This useful work, like many other bourgeois investigations, suffers from its basic Sombartian (anti-Marxian) position, which does not permit an actual historical perspective. Pietzker takes as her point of departure a "bipartite division of English merchantry," with the (aristocratic) large-scale merchant or large entrepreneur on the one hand, the "bourgeois small-scale merchant" on the other. Such a perspective, shaped by biological and intellectual-historical categories, necessarily misses the fact that as the guild system declined and the transition was accomplished from quota profits to "equalization of the rate of profit" by competition, large-scale merchants emerged from the mass of merchants and new groups began to con-

duct trade on the basis of the altered relations of production—and that regardless of all the differentiations among individuals and groups, their interdependencies must also be taken into account. On this view, there have been large-scale merchants and "bourgeois" small-scale merchants since Adam and Eve, because their existence is predetermined by the spirit that Pietzker draws from Sombart's *Quintessence of Capitalism*. She writes: "This bipartite division of Elizabethan merchantry is so characteristic and so essential for its literary portrayal that I would like to examine it more closely. It becomes clear when we look at the individual components that grew together to form the capitalist spirit: the spirit of enterprise and the bourgeois spirit. While in the course of their further development, these two streams are united in the type of the bourgeois trader, they are distinct at their beginnings. At this moment we still have on the one hand the bold, outreaching merchant lord, the gentleman adventurer, who conducts England's trade with the most distant lands, who, in order to protect his ships, which ply all the seas, must unite in himself a warrior's courage, a mariner's knowledge, and a merchant's skill." (9)

2. See Pietzker, *Kaufmann*, 36ff.

3. See ibid., 44f.

4. See *The Merchant of Venice*, ed. Arthur Quiller-Couch (London, 1926), 178.

5. See Ernst Klein, *Die englischen Wirtschaftstheoretiker des 17. Jahrhunderts* (Darmstadt, 1973), 23.

6. "Basilikon Doron," in *The Political Works of James I,* ed. Charles H. McIlwain (New York, 1965), 26.

7. See Klein, *Englische Wirtschaftstheoretiker*, 26f.

8. See Eli F. Heckscher, *Der Merkantilismus* (Jena, 1932), 1:356. See also the appropriate laws and ordinances in William Ezra Lingelbach, *The Merchant Adventurers of England. Their Laws and Ordinances with Other Documents* (Philadelphia, 1902), 174ff.

9. See Lingelbach, *The Merchant Adventurers of England*, xxxii.

10. Pietzker, in *Kaufmann*, 16-17, abstracts from the economic and political development of the epoch and attributes the positive or negative presentation of the merchant or the adventurer more or less to the subjective feeling of the individual author. Thus she interprets the reactionary play by John Webster, *The Dewil's Law-Case* (1623), in which a merchant is shown as a bloodsucking, murdering monster, as indirect positive evidence about the merchant / adventurer. The criterion for such an interpretation is the image of the Renaissance admiration for the great, even the criminal, individual that is found in Burckhardt, Nietzsche, and Sombart.

11. Francis Beaumont, *The Knight of the Burning Pestle*, in *The Dramatic Works in the Beaumont and Fletcher Canon*, ed. F. Bowers (Cambridge, 1966), 1:11, Induction, scene 2, lines 19–20.

12. Ibid., 1:12, Induction. 2.27–28.

13. Ibid., 1:14, act 1, scene 1, lines 1–9.

14. Ibid., 1:17, 1.1.81.

15. Ibid., 1:22-23, 1.1.251–52.

16. Francis Bacon, *Works,* ed. James Spedding et al. (London, 1857-74), 12:392.

17. But see the praise of adventurers still being written in 1640, in Ernst Schulin, *Handelsstaat England: Das politische Interesse der Nation am Aussenhandel vom 16. bis ins frühe 18. Jahrhundert* (Wiesbaden, 1969), 120.

18. On English sea trade after 1688 see Schulin, *Handelsstaat England*, 230ff.

19. In 1616, at the high point of the campaign against adventurers, Nicholas Breton in *The Good and the Badde* writes the following polemic in favor of adventurers: "A worthy merchant is the heir of adventure, whose hopes hang much upon the wind: . . . he is a discoverer of countries, and a finder out of commodities . . . : he is the life of traffic and the maintainer of trade, the sailor's master, and the soldier's friend: . . . he fears no Scylla, and sails close by Charybdis. . . . In sum, he is the pillar of a city, the enricher of a country, the furnisher of a court, and the worthy

servant of a king." (in *Archaica: A Reprint of Scarce Old English Prose Tracts*, ed. Sir. E. Brydges [London, 1815], 1:20)

20. William Shakespeare, *Two Gentlemen of Verona*, in *The Complete Works of William Shakespeare*, ed. William Aldis Wright (Garden City, 1936), 1.1.1-8. All quotations from this play are from this edition.

21. On travel as a means of education see Francis Bacon, *Essays, Advancement of Learning, New Atlantis, and Other Pieces*, ed. Richard Foster Jones (New York, 1937), 51ff.

22. Robert Weimann's excellent interpretation of *The Tempest* was published after the present work was completed ("Shakespeares 'Sturm' und die Kunst der Weltaneignung," *Sinn und Form* 28 / 1 [1976]: 210-18). The title (Shakespeare's *Tempest* and the Art of Appropriating the World) indicates that this interpretation agrees with those global or partial interpretations of Shakespeare discussed here. Weimann points out the historical context in which the *Tempest* was written (1610-11)—the time of the disintegration of the Tudor Compromise with the death of Elizabeth I—and writes: "Once the true course of the world had been recognized, on this side of the old order and beyond the new, as an instance not of morality but of temporality, then its poetic and political exploration was elevated to a 'self-generated' task of history. The closed world of that time was broken open, temporally and spatially, by historical consciousness and by geographic exploration. As the navigable globe of the natural world became the object of spatial discovery, the experienced course of the social world became the object of historical reflection. But once the historical and physical world was recognized in its self-determination, then the question as to its social and natural appropriation by human beings had inevitably to arise." (212)

There was "little room there" "for a glance into the future," Weimann continues; "only *A Winter's Tale* and especially *The Tempest* open up new dimensions and imaginative possibilities." Here I must disagree with Weimann; *The Merchant of Venice* already does this, and confirms the correctness of Weimann's observations: the more Shakespeare's "plot" "encodes the real world in a fantastic, even mythological way, the more deeply does Shakespeare reveal the actual problems and dangers in the appropriation of the historical reality of which one was conscious in a new way and of the geographical reality which had been discovered in a new way. In this sense *The Tempest* is a contemporary play, and in the full sense of the word a political play." From the perspective of *The Merchant of Venice*, this conclusion, too, can only be affirmed. Perhaps a new reading of Shakespeare's late plays, including the comedies, is in order.

23. Karl Marx and Frederick Engels, *The Holy Family; or, Critique of Critical Critique* (Moscow, 1956), 172.

24. On this theme in Bacon, see Hans Blumenberg, *Die Legitimität der Neuzeit* (Frankfurt / Main, 1966), 355; and especially Bernhard Fabian, "Der Naturwissenschaftler als Originalgenie," in *Europäische Aufklärung: Herbert Dieckmann zum 60. Geburtstag*, ed. Hugo Friedrich and Fritz Schalk (Munich, 1967), 47-68. On Bacon generally see among others Jürgen Kuczynski, "Francis Bacon— Philosoph der Industriewissenschaft," in *Studien über Schöne Literatur und Politische Ökonomie* (Berlin, 1954), 21ff.

25. Bacon, *Novum Organum*, in *Works*, 8:81. That is, with every advance, there is still something farther on that draws him forward again.

26. Ibid., 8:104.

27. Ibid., 8:121.

28. Ibid., 8:117. On the problem of the Ancients and the Moderns in Bacon, see among others Hans Baron, "The Querelle des Anciens et des Modernes as a Problem for Renaissance Scholarship," *Journal of the History of Ideas* 20 (1959): 3-22.

29. Bacon, *Novum Organum*, 8:162.

30. Ibid., 8:159.

31. Bacon, *De Dignatate et Augmentis Scientiarum*, in *Works*, 1:413-844, 689ff.

32. Bacon, *Essays*, 112.

33. Ibid., 116.

34. Bacon, *De Dignitate*, 1:692.

35. Bacon, *Essays*, 90-91.

36. Ibid., 98.

37. Ibid.

38. Ibid., 100.

39. Ibid., 57ff.

40. Ibid., 58.

41. Ibid.

42. Ibid., 34-35.

43. The first beginnings of an (experimental) scientific psychology can already be seen in Juan Huarte de San Juan, *Examen de ingenios para las ciencias*, 1575. (See this work, by the way, for its discussion of the effects of reading courtly romances.)

44. Marx and Engels, *The Holy Family*, 172.

45. Ibid.

46. Franz Borkenau, *Der Übergang vom feudalen zum bürgerlichen Weltbild* (Paris, 1934; reprint of the text and appendix published in Henryk Grossmann, *Die gesellschaftlichen Grundlagen der mechanistischen Philosophie und die Manufaktur*, Junius-Drucke [n.p., n.d.]), 95.

47. See Borkenau, *Übergang*, 90f.

48. See ibid., 91ff.

49. Ibid., 94.

50. Ibid.

51. Ibid., 95.

52. See among others "A Characterization of Economic Romanticism," in V. I. Lenin, *Collected Works* (Moscow, 1960), 2:129-266, and "The Taylor System—Man's Enslavement by the Machine," in Lenin, *Collected Works* (Moscow, 1960), 20:152-54, and passim.

53. "Antikritisches Schlusswort zum 'Geist des Kapitalismus,' " first published in *Archiv* 30, here from Max Weber, *Die protestantische Ethik*, ed. Johannes Winckelmann, 2 ed. (Tübingen, 1969), 2:283-345, 322-23.

54. Of course, it cannot be denied that ideological reactions of all kinds (especially political, but also religious) have influenced the historical development of capitalism in the most various ways. But the ideological phenomena that sustained those reactions were based on the historically demonstrable relations of production, on whose development they otherwise had only a secondary effect and whose economic laws they were obviously not able to suspend. But all this has been treated sufficiently (only bourgeois science, as bourgeois, refuses to take cognizance of it). In the context of the present work, it would be more interesting to draw up a systematic list of the effects of the various religious or theological ideas on the development of the ideology of adventure (for instance, the affirmation of large-scale or foreign trade by Calvin), a task that, however, would swell the present investigation boundlessly.

55. Borkenau, *Übergang*, 158ff.

56. Ibid., 158.

57. See in this context *Ideology of Adventure*, chapter 7, the section "The Threefold Birth of the Capitalist."

58. See in this context Henryk Grossmann's critique of Borkenau in "Die gesellschaftlichen Grundlagen der mechanistischen Philosopie und die Manufaktur," *Zeitschrift für Sozialforschung* 4/2 (Paris, 1935): 161-231, 178ff.

59. Borkenau, *Übergang*, 90.

60. In this context see Grossmann's critique, "Die gesellschaftlichen Grundlagen," 166ff.

61. Ibid., 192ff.

62. See John Desmond Bernal, *Die Wissenschaft in der Geschichte* (Berlin, 1967).

63. See Grossmann's critique, "Die gesellschaftlichen Grundlagen," 179ff. Leo Kofler's critique of Borkenau gets no further than Grossman's, even lags behind it, because Kofler—instead of proceeding from an analysis of the capitalist means of production and their genesis, or of the capitalist, for which Marx provided not only a differentiated typology but also a scale of priorities—attributes to Marx "a vacillating position on this question." (*Zur Geschichte der bürgerlichen Gesellschaft. Versuch einer verstehenden Deutung der Neuzeit*, 4 ed. [Neuwied and West Berlin, 1971], 290) He claims that Marx once asserted that the merchant is the ancestor of the modern capitalist, but that according to evidence that an informant of Kofler's assembled from *Capital*, "Marx also more or less granted the opposite." The insight that Marx "granted" the one thing and the other in varying degrees of importance, according to quality and quantity, but unambiguously believed that the *modern* industrial capitalist originated in the producer and not in the trader, is apparently inaccessible to nondialectical thinking.

64. Borkenau, *Übergang*, 90.

65. Bacon, *Essays*, 462-63.

66. Ibid., 465-66.

67. Ibid., 487-88.

68. Borkenau, *Übergang*, 89.

69. Ibid., 474.

70. Marx and Engels, *The Holy Family*, 173.

71. See Olivier-René Bloch, "Marx, Renouvier et l'histoire du matérialisme," *La Pensée* (February 1977): 3-42.

72. See Lucien Sève, *Marxisme et théorie de la personnalité*, 2 ed. (Paris, 1972), and "Postface de la 3e édition de *Marxisme et théorie de la personnalité*" (Paris, 1974).

73. Winfried Schröder, "Naturrecht," in *Philosophisches Wörterbuch*, ed. Georg Klaus and Manfred Buhr, 10 ed. (Leipzig, 1974), 2:840-48, 843-44.

74. Ibid., 2:844.

75. See Alexander Wernecke, *Biologismus und ideologischer Klassenkampf* (Berlin, 1976).

76. Karl Marx, *Capital* (New York, 1977), 1:476-77.

77. Ibid., 1:477.

78. Thomas Hobbes, *Leviathan Parts I and II* (New York, 1958), 106-7.

79. Ibid., 106.

80. Ibid., 108.

81. Ibid., 109.

82. Ibid.; see also 143ff., 262.

83. Ibid., 83. On Hobbes and English trade, see Schulin, *Handelsstaat England*, 154ff.

84. V. I. Lenin, "Imperialism, the Highest Stage of Capitalism, A Popular Outline," in *Collected Works* (Moscow, 1964), 22:185-299, 278.

85. See John Milton, "The Reason of Church-government urg'd against Prelaty," in *Works* (New York, 1931-1938), 3:179-279, 237.

86. "An Horatian Ode upon Cromwell's Return from Ireland," in *The Complete Works of Andrew Marvell*, ed. Alexander B. Grosart (n.p., 1872; reprint New York, 1966), 1:161, lines 1-15.

87. Ibid., 1:165, lines 101-4.

88. 1:326, "Britannia and Raleigh," in *Complete Works of Marvell*, lines 25-32.

89. Ibid., 1:330-32, lines 161-66 and 173-76. John Dryden's "Annus Mirabilis" of 1667 shows that the reactionary fraction of the bourgeoisie was able to use England's shipping and trade or its history in the opposite sense of Marvell, in order to glorify the absolutist reaction of Charles II.

90. Friedrich Engels, *Anti-Dühring: Herr Eugen Dühring's Revolution in Science*, 2 ed. (Moscow, 1959), 226.

91. See Marx's comments on the Bank of England throughout vol. 3 of *Capital*.

92. Karl Marx, "The East India Company—Its History and Results," in Marx and Engels, *Collected Works* (New York, 1979), 12:148-49.

93. Bernard de Mandeville, *The Fable of the Bees, or, Private Vices, Publick Benefits*, ed. F. B. Kaye (Oxford, 1924; reprint Oxford, 1957, 1966), 2:223f.

94. Ibid., 1:195-96.

95. Ibid., 1:250.

96. Ibid., 1:204ff.

97. Ibid., 2:223.

98. Ibid., 1:61ff.

99. Ibid., 1:287-88. On Mandeville see Marx, *Capital*, 1:764ff.

100. See in this context Frank Wadleigh Chandler, *The Literature of Roguery* (1907; reprint New York, 1958).

Theory and History of Literature

Michael Nerlich is professor of literary criticism and romance philology at the Technical University of West Berlin and chief editor of the scientific quarterly *Lendemains, Etudes comparées sur la France*. He has written books on epic theory in Spain, Hebraic thought in Fray Luis de León, and political engagement in the German and French artistic "picaresque" novel of the twentieth century.

Currently self-employed, **Ruth Crowley** has been an assistant professor of German at the University of California, Irvine, and assistant professor of comparative literature at Queens College, CUNY. She was assistant editor of *German Quarterly*, in 1980-81. Crowley received her Ph.D. in German Studies from Stanford University in 1975.

Wlad Godzich is professor of comparative literature and French studies at the Université de Montréal as well as professor of comparative literature and director of the Center for Humanistic Studies at the University of Minnesota. He serves, with Jochen Schulte-Sasse, as editor of the series Theory and History of Literature.